PATTON'S FORWARD OBSERVERS

PATTON'S FORWARD OBSERVERS

History of the 7th Field Artillery Observation Battalion

XX Corps, Third Army

By John K. Rieth

BRANDYLANE PUBLISHERS, INC.

Richmond, Virginia

Copyright 2004 by John Kurt Rieth All rights reserved.
No portion of this book may be reprinted without the written permission of the publisher.
Printed in the United States.

ISBN 1-883911-62-1

Library of Congress Control Number: 2004095327

Brandylane Publishers, Inc.
Richmond, Virginia
www.brandylanepublishers.com

*Patton's Forward Observers is dedicated to all the soldiers who served
with the United States Army's premier counterbattery organization
during the Second World War, the 7th Field Artillery Observation Battalion.*

TABLE OF CONTENTS

Introduction	xii
1: Stateside: The Forging of the 7th Field Artillery Observation Battalion	1
2: England: The Battalion joins XX Corps and Readies for War	19
3: Normandy: The Breakout into France	30
4: The 7th Field Artillery Observation Battalion at War	43
5: Northern France: August 1944	57
6: Metz I: Meeting Europe's Strongest Citadel	69
7: Metz II: The Attack on Fort Driant	81
8: Metz III: The Objective Taken	89
9: To the Saar and the Ardennes	123
10: The Saar Moselle Triangle: Against the Westwall	135
11: Breaking the Siegfried Line	146
12: A Disaster at Lampaden	154
13: To the Rhine	163
14: Final Victory: Into the German Heartland	172
15: Occupation Duty and Homeward Bound	186
Afterword	195
Awards, Roster	207
Endnotes	218
Bibliography	223

LIST OF ILLUSTRATIONS

Photographs
William Jessel, Fort Bragg 1941
Camp Shelby
Lt. Col. James Schwartz
Destroyer Escort USS Donnell
Headquarters Staff
Battery A Mess Sgt Wandzioch
The Battery A Cooks
7th FAOB Medical Detachment
Tech Sgt. Kurt Rieth (2 photos)
Battery A Men
Lt. Don Slessman
Lt. Marlin Yoder
Battery A Officers
Senior Brass Visit XX Corps, Metz
James Rutledge and Arthur Sutliff
The Road to Metz, Fall, 1944
Flash Observers
John French
B Battery Flash Survey Squad
B Battery Men relaxing
7th FAOB Crossing the Danube
German Prisoners of War
7th FAOB Troops in German uniforms
B Battery Marching on Parade
Medic Amos Robinson
Mondsee Austria
Ed Piatrowski at Chiemsee
Headquarters Battery, 7th FAOB
Battery A, 7th FAOB
Battery B, 7th FAOB
Home
Group Picture 2003

Maps
The Allied Breakout from Normandy
Advance to Metz
Fort Driant
The Saar Moselle Triangle
The Orscholz Switch
Lampaden
To the Rhine
The Final Push into German

Illustrations:
7th FAOB Christmas Card, December, 1944

ACKNOWLEDGMENTS

Patton's Forward Observers would not have been possible without a lot of assistance of family, friends, and some superb publishing professionals. My wife Joanna and children, Andrea and David, were extremely patient and always supportive in the many hours it took to put this project together. I have to thank my mother, Marian Rieth, who was a major source of inspiration in getting this story told. For encouragement, editing and guidance, I was blessed to have the support of these remarkable individuals: Captain (USN, Ret.) George E. Thibault, a distinguished naval officer and seasoned military history editor; Colonel (USAF, Ret.) David Eberly, a true American hero who was the senior most Allied POW in the Gulf War; Ed Ruggero, a former infantry officer comrade and highly successful author/motivational speaker; General James T. Hill, U.S. Army, who gave me a lifetime's worth of leadership education in the 18 months he was my battalion commander in the 25th Infantry Division; Mr. Floyd Paseman, a long-standing friend and mentor; and to my publisher, Robert Pruett, whose craft, vision, and courage makes Brandylane such a unique and excellent publishing house. Finally, I owe a huge debt of gratitude to those veterans of the 7th Field Artillery Observation Battalion who contributed their stories, counsel, and most importantly — service to nation.

INTRODUCTION

This is the story of a unique United States Army unit that served in the Second World War—the 7th Field Artillery Observation Battalion (FAOB). By tracing the formation, training, and combat experience of this battalion, we get a fascinating glimpse of a premier American fighting unit at its best. The 7th FAOB played an important role in every significant action in which the Third Army's famed XX "Ghost" Corps participated. From the time they landed in Normandy in July 1944, up through the war's end at Hitler's birthplace on the German-Austrian border, the 7th FAOB was engaged in combat operations without respite.

This is not the first written history of the 7th FAOB. At the conclusion of the Second World War, the battalion published a fine twenty-eight-page pamphlet on its history entitled *From Bragg to Braunau*. It is in the spirit of that official history that this book is intended. As well as presenting the battalion's operational activities, *From Bragg to Braunau* also captured some of the everyday experiences of the battalion's soldiers. However, this brief account was written shortly after the war ended, rendering it impossible to place into context the impact of greater events. With sixty years having passed and thousands of volumes written on the most studied war in history, we can now look at the accomplishments of the 7th FAOB with a fresh perspective.

At the 2001 reunion of the 7th FAOB Association, I was asked to write a history of the unit. I was honored to do so, but with the understanding that this story should be told in the words of the veterans themselves. I beseeched the association members to give me some of their most prominent wartime accounts, and as a group they certainly came through.

My connection to the 7th FAOB is through my father, Kurt A. Rieth, a veteran of the battalion. Like many World War II veterans, my father never really had much to say about his wartime experiences. By the time of his death in 1985, all I really knew was that he was a communications sergeant who served in a field artillery observation unit in General George Patton's Third Army. While there were a few stories that he shared, I was left with a woefully incomplete understanding of his service. I suspect that this is probably the case with most of the descendants of our nation's World War II veterans. I intend this book as a means to help bridge that gap for those with special interest in this unit as well as in World War II history as a whole.

In 1996, I was introduced to the 7th FAOB Association through the efforts of founding member, Bill Rogge. During the years that immediately followed World War II, the veterans of the 7th FAOB did hold a few reunions. By the late 1940s, the men gradually moved on building their post-war careers, and the unit reunions fell by the wayside. With a few exceptions, most of the men entirely lost track of each other as time passed. In the late 1980s, Bill and several other former members of the 7th FAOB launched a nation-wide search to renew interest in getting together. Over one hundred men were found and contacted. Beginning in 1990, annual reunions were held each fall, where both long-time friendships were reconnected and new friendships were established. Generations of families were introduced as these reunions became an increasingly important part in the association members' lives. No individual was more active in the association than Bill Rogge, and he worked ceaselessly to track down former battalion members throughout the country. In an effort to find my father, Bill was put in touch with me, and that contact began my association with the group. Sadly, Bill passed away just a few weeks short of the 1999 reunion, when I was greatly looking forward to finally meeting him in person. This book would not have been possible without his involvement and dedication in continuing the legacy of the 7th Field Artillery Observation Battalion.

It was coincidental that my correspondence with Bill Rogge began just as I was trying to get more information on my father's wartime experiences. At the time I first heard from Bill, I was an army officer assigned in Germany. In my spare time, I wanted to use the opportunity of being posted in Europe to study my father's unit history. As well as sending me a copy of *From Bragg to Braunau*, Bill put me in contact with a host of association members, many who sent me their recollections of my father as well as their own experiences of the war. Around this time I also received another boon of information when my mother discovered the entire collection of my father's wartime letters written to his parents. Now, knowing something about the battalion's service and relation to Third Army and XX Corps, I was able to study in detail those battles and operations that they participated in. I also toured some of the more prominent battlefields in the battalion's journey through France and Germany, further adding to my understanding of their experience.

When asked by the association to write their history, it seemed to me somewhat presumptuous to be the one to tell the story, as they had lived the experiences I could only read about and listen to. With this in mind, I canvassed the 7th FAOB Association and asked the men to send me their recollections of the war. I have done my best to let their accounts tell the story of the unit, while I intersperse a historical context of what greater Third Army and XX Corps operations were occurring at the time.

Three of my primary sources are based on information that was recorded at the time of the war. I use these most frequently, and they warrant some additional explanation.

While I did not want to over-represent my father's service in the unit, I found the entire collection of his wartime letters to be an invaluable resource. He wrote virtually every three days or so throughout the entire course of the war. The details of my father's letters were of greatest use when describing his pre-deployment training and the period after hostilities ended (when the battalion was on occupation duty in Austria and Germany). From the time the battalion was deployed to England and up through the war's end, all letters were strictly censored for security reasons. As a result, the bulk of his letters from April 1944 through May 1945 were more focused on matters of innocuous correspondence and such things as requests for food packages. Still, even snippets from a good number of these letters reveal some interesting glimpses of the lifestyle of a common soldier in the 7th FAOB in a combat environment. In addition, I found that the continuity of the letters captured the transition of a typical twenty-year-old draftee into a seasoned combat veteran.

Another primary resource came from Lt. Donald Slessman, who first served with B Battery and eventually commanded A Battery. (By pure coincidence, my father served as Lieutenant Slessman's radio operator and German translator from October 1944 through the end of the war.) Lieutenant Slessman graciously allowed me to use the text from a highly detailed letter that he wrote his wife in June 1945 after censorship restrictions were relaxed. This letter gives a rich overview of the combat operations of the battalion from a commander's perspective. In bits and pieces, I used the letter almost in its entirety.

The final important first-hand source came from Edward A. Marinello's book *On the Way: General Patton's Eyes and Ears on the Enemy*. Published in 1998, it is based from a diary of Marinello's wartime service as an observer with the 286th Field Artillery Observation Battalion. This Third Army (XII Corps) battalion was a sister unit to the 7th FAOB. Both battalions trained together at Camp Shelby, Mississippi, and both shared many common experiences throughout the war. Marinello provides a unique and graphic optic of the wartime daily grind and the dangers of being a forward observer assigned to a Third Army field artillery observation battalion.

In my quest for additional personal accounts from battalion veterans, some of the men were more prolific than others. I included every story that I could. In the end, I like to think that the aggregate collection of all accounts represents the experience of the common GI assigned to a field artillery observation battalion.

The story of the 7th Field Artillery Observation Battalion is completely interwoven with the Third Army and XX Corps history. As will be explained in some detail, the 7th FAOB covered vast stretches of territory as they sought to find and silence German artillery firing at XX Corps units. Whatever XX Corps' primary focus was on any given day, so was that of the 7th FAOB. Many pages of this book are seemingly focused on greater XX Corps operations without direct reference to the battalion. The reader is asked to view these events with the presumption that elements of the 7th FAOB were there through virtually every step of Third Army's invasion of Europe.

Of all the personalities that have emerged from the study of World War II, none have achieved the legendary status of the 7th FAOB's army-level commander, General George S. Patton Jr. In his classic speech given to the Third Army just prior to D-Day–an event at which a number of the 7th FAOB leaders were present–Patton concluded with these comments:

"There is one great thing you men will be able to say when you go home. You may all thank God for it. Thank God that, at least thirty years from now, when you are sitting around the fireside with your grandson on your knee and he asks you what you did in the great World War II, you won't have to say, "I shoveled shit in Louisiana."[1]

Indeed, the soldiers of the 7th Field Artillery Observation Battalion did more than their share to claim their part in American's greatest generation. This is their story.

Night in a Fox Hole

A bright full moon beams down on me
Diamond like stars twinkle and smile at me
Your beautiful soft warm body is nestled close to my side
I press my face into your sweet smelling hair
The scent permeates my whole being
Of such things love has been described for centuries
Oh to hold you forever speaking of my undying love
Your soft breath on my neck almost lulls me to sleep
Suddenly my whole body is tense
My ears strain to filter sounds assailing them
My eyes stab into the darkness
Seeking one who would take my life
Cradled against my side not your warm body
But the weight of my gun
It's cold barrel pressed to my cheek
Instead of the full moon the brilliant flash of
Enemy artillery exploding in the sky
Tearing at the earth around me
The ever present chatter of our machine guns
The instant bursts of enemy fire
I wonder will I ever hold my love again
Lord take me into Your arms protect me
That I may once more see morning

Charles J. Wright Jr.,
7th Field Artillery Battery, 1943-1945

CHAPTER 1

Stateside: the Forging of the 7th Field Artillery Observation Battalion

The origin of the 7th Field Artillery Observation Battalion actually predates America's entry into World War II. By the time that Europe went to war in 1939, America's isolationist policies of the 1920s and '30s left its armed forces ill-prepared for global conflict. Assuming that World War I would be the end of war on a big scale, the government demobilized to the extent that the U.S. Army became the world's seventeenth-ranked military power. For two decades the army was manned at less than 200,000 men, and received scant funding for training and equipment. The army discarded many hard-earned valuable lessons of the First World War, and put aside armor and aviation development to retain the culture and traditions of the horse cavalry. As Europe headed for global conflict in the late 1930s, the U.S. Army was better configured to fight Third World armies—or even 1916-era Mexican bandits, for that matter—than it was to counter the growing Axis threat. However, as badly prepared as the American military was at the start of World War II, it would have been far worse off had it not undergone a dramatic growth beginning eighteen months prior to the attack at Pearl Harbor.

The German blitz through France in 1940 would finally wake America. The stunningly quick fall of France gave President Franklin Roosevelt the mandate to launch a crash course to greatly build up the size and capability of the armed services. Congressional appropriations between May and October 1940 reflected this determination, and the army received more than eight billion dollars for its needs during the succeeding year—a sum greater than its total operating budgets during the previous 20 years! During the last six months of 1940, the active army more than doubled in strength, and by mid-1941, it numbered nearly 1.5 million officers and men.[2] It was during this period of great military expansion that the 7th Field Artillery Observation Battalion was born.

Perhaps the greatest compliment regarding the ability of the United States to transform its obsolete pre-war army into the most powerful army in the world came from one of its most competent foes, German Field Marshal Erwin Rommel. Rommel once remarked, "What was really amazing was the speed with which the Americans adapted themselves to modern warfare. They were assisted by their tremendous practical and material sense and by their lack of all understanding for tradition and useless theories. Starting from scratch an army has been created in the very minimum of time, which in equipment, armament, and organization of all arms surpasses anything the world has ever seen."[3] It was the professionalism of the pre-war army that served as the cornerstone for its tremendous growth, and units such as the 7th Field Artillery Observation Battalion were part of its core foundation.

The 7th FAOB was activated at Fort Bragg, North Carolina on June 1, 1941. Under the initial command of Major Edward J. McGaw, the battalion transformed from an ad hoc collection of transfers and recruits to a fully operational unit. At full strength, the battalion consisted of about 500 enlisted men and 30 officers. Its battlefield mission was clear in purpose as it was in its complexity and danger: to identify the location of enemy cannon by tracking incoming fire and to direct American artillery back in response. The battalion's motto succinctly summed up their mission—"WE SEEK."

By all accounts of those early days of the battalion, Major McGraw stands out as a strict taskmaster who set very high standards for his new battalion. Given the difficulties he faced, he needed to be tough. The challenges of creating a new unit in the summer of 1941, particularly one as specialized as a field artillery observation battalion, were immense. Although new equipment was rolling off the line at unprecedented rates, getting it to the newly established field units challenged an overtaxed logistical infrastructure. Manning the battalion with reasonably experienced officers and non-commissioned officers (NCOs) was also difficult. Like every other new army unit created around that time, the battalion's leadership was largely manned by reassigning officers and sergeants from other pre-existing units. Major McGaw had to push and pull to get the best men possible to form a cadre capable of leading and training a deluge of recent draftees. The leadership of the battalion staff and batteries had to be quickly selected and formed into teams. Tremendous amounts of equipment, vehicles, and weapons had to be issued, maintained, and accounted for. Newly built barracks were signed for, readied, and moved into. Mess halls needed to be established, chains of command formed, and a thousand other tasks had to be performed relating to creating and sustaining an organization of over 500 soldiers. Above all, the unit had to be trained to a high level of performance, both in individual skills and as a collective organization.

Many of the initial troops that made up the 7th FAOB's roster were men who were drafted in late 1940 and early 1941. One of these soldiers was Stephen Wandzioch, who would later become the mess sergeant for A Battery. Drafted into the army from Buffalo, New York, in April 1941, Wandzioch recalls that his entire initial uniform and equipment issue was made up of World War I surplus supplies. Transported to North Carolina, unaccustomed northerners like Wandzioch suffered terribly from the sweltering southern heat and exposure to new viruses. Not long after his arrival at Fort Bragg, Wandzioch came down with spinal meningitis and nearly died when he lapsed into a two-week coma. When he finally came around he was offered a medical discharge but refused it, citing that he was afraid that people back home would think that his family "paid the army off" to get him released. Wandzioch stoically told the doctor he would do his full term of service. (Wandzioch did at least get a thirty-day furlough to recover from his illness, which left him with a permanent hearing loss.)

Another original member of the battalion was Amos Robinson, who would eventually be assigned to the medical detachment in B Battery. A native of Gastonia, North Carolina, Amos was drafted into the army in April 1941 and reported to the 7th FAOB just as it was becoming activated at Fort Bragg. In those early months, Robinson first served in the wire and survey sections, and later became a truck driver for the medical detachments. This last job piqued his interest in the medical field, and he eventually was trained and qualified and served as a combat medic.

Robinson recalled with amusement the blending of soldiers from different geographic regions. In one instance he was driving a truck full of Headquarters Battery men off base when they passed a field of cotton. Some of the northern boys were so excited at their first sight of a cotton field that they insisted on stopping to pick some to send to the folks back home. Also commenting on regional differences, Wandzioch recalled the first time he was served grits, and how he broke up the mess hall by joking, "My god, they're even serving us moth balls for food!" Amos Robinson was struck by the large number of men who entered the army without having ever driven a vehicle and was surprised at the time and effort that had to be invested in providing basic driving lessons.

Much of the training was focused on building basic soldier skills. Some rules were sacrosanct: always be alert on guard duty, never lose sight of your weapon, and never store anything inside of your gas mask pouch other than the mask itself. Amos Robinson remembers once directing a skit in a training session that highlighted this latter requirement. As the rest of the battery watched, Robinson and a few others played the role of a patrol taking a break under a tree. Robinson writes: "We all laid down, with some using their gas mask covers as pillows, and others casually casting them aside. After a little while, I came awake and yelled 'Gas, Gas, Gas!' Everybody jumped up and scrambled for their mask covers. As we frantically pried them open, out poured apples, oranges, candy bars, and books—everything but masks. The men all pantomimed gasping for breath but it was too late, we all 'died.' I was given praise from the battery commander for a job well done."

At Fort Bragg, the battalion designed its distinctive unit insignia. The shield of the coat of arms shows a bomb burst emitting four crosswise lightning flashes, all within the shape of a compass rose. The color of the shield is red to represent artillery; the bomb burst symbolizes sound ranging; the lightning flash represents flash ranging, and the compass represents coordination for the successful operation of the battalion. Beneath the shield is the 7th's motto, WE SEEK. The insignia was approved by the Department of the Army on the last day of peace - December 6, 1941.[4]

As early as October 1941, the battalion was sufficiently ready to participate in a major field exercise. The 7th's first operational test was two months of arduous training in the Carolina maneuvers. This was a period of tremendous transition for the army. Even as late as 1940, there remained old-time generals who still thought horse cavalry would have a major role in the next war. The Nazi's conquest of France and latest Blitzkrieg into the Soviet Union had finally proven the need for the American Army to have a much more mobile and armored-based combat force to meet the modern threat. Throughout 1941, large-scale army maneuvers that involved up to 500,000 soldiers at a time were conducted in Tennessee, Louisiana, and the Carolinas. The field exercises were intended to train the two-fold increase in new recruits, test command and control procedures, and to create a new doctrine for armored warfare. The Carolina maneuvers that the 7th FAOB would participate in would be significant as they were a test of the mobility of armor against the numerical superiority of conventional light forces equipped with the latest in anti-armor guns.[5] As well as solidifying the role of tanks in the coming war, the Carolina maneuvers also brought forth into further national prominence the brilliant and colorful commander of the 2nd Armored Division, Major General George Patton.

Shortly after returning from this exercise, Amos Robinson was at the motor pool working on a truck at 10:00 A.M. when he received the news that Pearl Harbor was attacked. On December 7, 1941, seven months after the 7th FAOB was activated, America was at war. The onset of war instilled a new sense of urgency in the already frantic pace of getting the unit to a combat footing.

Another soldier who was assigned to the 7th FAOB around this time was Robert Geiges, who would later become the Headquarters Battery Supply Sergeant. Drafted in July 1941, Geiges was sent to Cooks and Bakers School at Fort Bragg after someone learned of his civilian experience as a short order cook. Geiges immediately found there was a lot to learn about being an army cook, and one of the many challenges was to learn how to use a coal stove and keep an even, steady heat. He joined the battalion at Fort Bragg in November 1941 and was assigned to the headquarters mess section. He remembers the emphasis on cleanliness and a quote from a seasoned mess sergeant at the time: "Everyone is going to eat a pound of dirt before they die, but there is no reason to have to eat it all at once!" Geiges also learned the hard way that age-old army adage about never volunteering. Aghast at the amount of excess food that was thrown way, Geiges complained to the mess sergeant about the waste. In return for his interest on conservation, Geiges was assigned the task of making leftovers for the men. Still, Geiges remarked that the men actually seemed to enjoy the increased diet of leftovers, as it was something of a reminder of home cooking. Geiges also was impressed at the can-do spirit of the cooks, who always found a way to adapt to ever-present challenges and shortages (such as occasions when they substituted ice cream in recipes when they were short of milk).

By January 1942, the battalion's manning was complete enough to transfer from Fort Bragg to Camp Blanding in northern Florida. Geiges recalls the motor march from Fort Bragg. The mess trucks were configured so that it was possible to cook even while driving. Preparing food in the back of a bumpy and swaying 2 ½ ton truck traveling at 40 mph was no easy task, but still the cooks were able to serve meals within ten minutes after halting for chow breaks. Once in Florida, Geiges was surprised at how cold northern Florida could be in the wintertime, and remembers how the men would be bundled up in overcoats as they fell out after morning reveille.

At Camp Blanding, the battalion became part of the 74th Field Artillery Brigade, a unit comprised of firing artillery battalions as well as command and control elements, with the 7th FAOB rounding out its counterbattery direction capability. In contrast to the nice new barracks of Fort Bragg, the men now had to live in tents. The 7th FAOB's stay at Camp Blanding was short, but filled with intensive unit-level field training exercises. The battalion's experience at Camp Blanding was remembered largely by six miserable weeks living in sand, swamps, and rain. In March 1942, the battalion cleaned its gear, inspected it time and again, and packed up via motor march to Camp Shelby, near Hattiesburg, Mississippi.

In the course of the movement, rumors ran fast as to what would be the final destination. It was widely assumed that that the battalion would only be at Camp Shelby for a short time and then embark from New Orleans for overseas service. Like most army rumors, these proved false. The weeks at Camp Shelby turned into months, and their stay at this sprawling Mississippi training base would last two years.

Shortly after the battalion arrived at Camp Shelby, Major McGaw was transferred to Washington, D.C. The battalion's official history characterizes Major McGaw's demanding leadership style as one that often chaffed against "old-time" regulars, those veteran soldiers who had long since had their share of by-the-book command. That said, this very discipline is what gave the 7th FAOB the toughness and tactical competence that ensured its future wartime success. Major McGaw did well in his subsequent army career and was eventually promoted to brigadier general with command of the 63rd Divisional Artillery.

Major McGaw was briefly replaced in command by Major Archer F. Fruend. Shortly thereafter, Fruend was promoted and transferred. (Fruend eventually became the commanding officer of the 285th Field Artillery Observation Battalion. This unit was fated to have one of its batteries wiped out in the infamous Malmedy Massacre during the Battle of the Bulge in December 1944.) Command of the 7th fell to then Major, and later Lieutenant Colonel, James P. Schwartz. Only several months earlier, Schwartz had been a first lieutenant and served as the battalion's first motor officer. The rapid command changes were reflective of the battalion's overall contributions to the army's dramatic buildup to full mobilization. Although still in its infancy, the 7th FAOB was one of the few artillery observation commands in the pre-war army. While this constant cycling of officers and NCOs was disruptive to the battalion's own operations, it added great value to the army by sending forward a collection of experienced personnel to create new units.

Despite this turnover, the battalion was starting to gain traction in building a core cadre that would lead it through the war. A number of men who were there at the battalion's 1941 activation, stout soldiers such as Emeric Ujczo, Paul Asman, Amos Robinson, Stephen Wandzioch and Ed Piatkowski, were still in the ranks when the unit entered combat in August 1944. This thread of continuity was critical in ensuring that the constant stream of new replacements was grounded by seasoned leadership—men who knew their jobs and could train the steady influx of new recruits.

While Major McGaw can be given credit for successful standup of the 7th FAOB, it would be Lieutenant Colonel Schwartz who saw it through the rest of the war. In the American Army in World War II, it was generally unusual for a battalion level unit to retain the same commander for a three-year period. This stability, combined with Lieutenant Colonel Schwartz's demanding yet competent leadership, would later be a significant factor in the 7th's effectiveness on the battlefield. Like Major McGaw before him, Schwartz was a strict officer who demanded a great deal from his men. While his harsh style of leadership made him unpopular with many of the officers and men he commanded, there was no doubt that he knew his business. In unit reunions sixty years later, his former soldiers generally remember him with respect.

The 7th FAOB was very much Lieutenant Colonel Schwartz's battalion, and he deserves much credit for its accomplishments.

The men who served in the battalion were more or less a cross section of the rest of the army. If anything, the technical nature of their work required a higher level of intelligence for many of the specialties, and a majority of the soldiers assigned to the 7th tested highly on entrance level mental aptitude exams. In geographical terms, about 40 percent came from the Northeast, 25 percent from the Southeast, 25 percent from the Midwest, and 10 percent from the West. New York and Ohio were the two states with the greatest representation.

Looking back from today, America in the early 1940s was a much more insulated world, with many of the recruits having never previously traveled far from their hometowns. Family units were closer then, and the impending unknown of the war often made departures from home difficult. Some men had completed high school while others didn't, many had some work experience and a relatively few were college graduates. A good number of them left wives and children behind. While the average age group for soldiers was between twenty and twenty-three, at least one soldier, medic Clarence Brennan, was a relatively ancient forty years old by the time he shipped overseas.

One common thread among soldiers of that day was that they grew up as depression-era children. Many came from very poor families where a twelfth-grade education was considered a luxury. Quite a few had responsibilities at home that belied their young ages. One of these men was Jim Royals, who became a heavy machine gunner for B Battery. Growing up on a small farm in south Georgia, Royals had to leave school at a very early age in order to take care of his ailing parents and five siblings. After trade school he got a job in the Brunswick Shipyards, where, at age nineteen, he married a fifteen-year-old girl named Ruby. Four months later, Ruby got pregnant and Jim got drafted. Reporting to basic training at Fort Bragg, Royals needed to stretch his meager pay of fifty dollars a month a long way to care for himself and his new family.

America was involved in a war that the nation had not sought, but once attacked, the country was committed to victory. The average soldier simply wanted to do his duty to defeat the enemy so he could return home as quickly as possible.

The typical 7th FAOB enlisted soldier was a draftee who came to the unit after going through basic training. In World War II, about 60 percent of American soldiers were conscripts. Once receiving their selective service announcements, those drafted had a period of several weeks' notice before having to report to a regional induction center. At the induction center, the prospective recruits would be given a physical exam and, if passed, would be sworn into service. In the days that followed, they would be issued uniforms, receive lectures on military courtesy, and be subjected to a series of aptitude exams, vaccinations, and a host of other requirements expected of a military bureaucracy. Once fully processed, the new recruits would be assigned to occupational specialties and sent by rail to a basic training posts.

Basic training was, and still remains, a process to turn the average young American into a combat soldier. It exists to break down individuality, instill a sense of teamwork, and build common skills that every good soldier in every army must possess: discipline, physical fitness, marksmanship, and basic fieldcraft.

Twenty-year-old Kurt Rieth, who would join the battalion's A Battery as a radio operator in December 1944, entered his seventeen-week basic training program at Fort Bragg's Field Artillery Replacement Training Center in mid-August 1943.

Rieth was a unique draftee only in that he was a native-level German speaker. His own father, Albert G. Rieth, saw horrific combat as a German Army conscript in the opening days of the First World War. After the war Albert and his family emigrated to Providence, Rhode Island where he took up a career as a toolmaker in the jewelry industry. Kurt Rieth wanted nothing more than to follow his father's career when his draft notice arrived in June 1943. An only son, he was heading into a war where he would have to fight against virtually all of his blood relatives. His parents knew the terrors of modern world war from first-hand experience and were tremendously worried about his welfare.

Rieth's basic training unit was comprised of soldiers who would be communications specialists in field artillery units. In a composite sampling of letters home to his parents, he had this to say about his initial army training experiences, which were similar to that of most of the soldiers who eventually were assigned to the 7th:

> August 15, 1943 [Week 1]: All the men we have talked to who are almost finished with this course tell us how lucky we are. In the field we will not have to do any shooting of cannons, all our work will consist of radio and telegraph communications. We will also have to learn to drive trucks. I learned last night that in order to get into this outfit we had to have IQs of 115 points, for Officers Training you only have to have 110 points. By the way, you wanted me to tell you honestly how I like the army. Well, I would much rather be home, but as long as I am in something I think I will like, I am going to make the best of it and try to get as much out of it as possible. I miss you both very much, but don't worry about me being homesick from morning until night, they keep you far too busy for anything like that.
>
> September 2, 1943 [Week 3]: Yesterday afternoon, we had four hours of truck driving. They told us we were going to the driving range, and I expected nice straight, smooth roads. What a difference, however, as the driving range proved to be sort of an obstacle course for trucks that twists through the woods. When we got back, one truck had a broken spring and several had crushed fenders. I was driving a 1 ½ ton truck with about eight or nine fellows sitting in back. I hit one bump so hard most of their helmets bounced off their heads and out of the truck. The truck behind them had to stop and collect them. They're still kidding me about it.
>
> October 14, 1943 [Week 5]: I'm very tired tonight because last night we had guard duty again. I got just about three and a half hours sleep and we had a very tough day today. I was on guard from 10:00 P.M. to 12:00 P.M., and then again from 4:00 A.M. to 6:30 A.M. Then I rushed over to the mess hall, had breakfast, cleaned up for inspection, and went to the first class at 8:00 A.M. The first class was two hours of machine gun instruction, then one hour of physical training and another hour of gas-mask practice. After lunch we had an hour of code practice, two hours of radio procedures and then another hour of code practice. Our last class was at 5:00 P.M., and we had fifteen minutes to put on clean uniforms and get ready for inspection again. You can see that they still keep us pretty busy. The beds aren't bad at all, but after a day around here you could sleep on a flat board without minding it.
>
> October 24, 1943 [Week 6]: "We had a battery party last Friday night and had a swell time. Last payday we took up a collection for the party and we had about two hundred dollars. The party took place at the mess hall. The mess sergeant really put out a good meal. We had steak, french fried potatoes, peas, rolls, salads, pickles, olives, etc., and apple and blueberry pie. After that, each platoon in the battery put on some sort of entertainment and they also had a small band. All of the officers were there and some of the boys gave imitations of them. Every rule and regulation was thrown aside. After the entertainment we had ice cream and candy, cigars and cigarettes. Some of the sergeants washed all the dishes and cleaned up the kitchen.
>
> By the way, I never told you about the organization of the field artillery [as described for a basic training battalion]. There are four platoons or barracks, in each battery, with each platoon consisting of about fifty men. Each platoon is headed by a sergeant who has a few

corporals to help him with the work. The battery itself is headed by the battery commander, who is either a first lieutenant or captain. Each battery has its own mess hall and cooks. Perhaps this will give you a better idea of what I am talking about when I write about my life here.

November 5, 1943 [Week 10]: I'm busy again tonight cleaning my equipment for tomorrow's inspection. We lay it all out on the bed, everything just a certain way. When the time comes for it to be inspected, we stand at attention by our beds and a flock of lieutenants, captains, and majors come through the barracks, inspecting each and every item. Having so much as a bar of soap with the label upside down means an afternoon of detail in the kitchen or a week's restriction. You can imagine what a relief it is when noon comes around and we are free for the weekend.

Well, I've been in the field artillery for three months now and I haven't even seen a cannon fired. About the only thing we do now is practice establishing radio nets, and learning all the procedures used in sending and receiving messages over radio. You can't just say anything you want when sending a message. There are special phrases, abbreviations and commands for everything. We have plenty of things to memorize.

November 28, 1943 [Week 15—midpoint of two week-long field exercise]: We moved again last night and are in a new area. This time we had to march to the new camp, the distance being about six miles. They set a very fast pace however, and we had to do a lot of running. Whenever we move at night it is always done without any lights. You can imagine how confusing it is to find a place to sleep in the pitch dark and still stay with your platoon. Of course when we pitch tents they must be at least twenty yards apart, otherwise it would be too good of a target for the enemy. We have plenty to do in the evenings. Classes are scheduled for every night till 10:00 P.M. and a few nights till midnight. There are no lights allowed after dark, not even cigarettes.

December 9, 1943 [Week 17] Well, I was on kitchen patrol today and about 11:00 this morning the sergeant came in and told me I was on shipping orders. I had to turn in some of my equipment and will have to be ready to leave at any time. The whole platoon is on shipping orders now except for a few men. There will probably be only a few men sent to the same camps however. Just remember, if you shouldn't hear from me for a few days it means I am on my way.

December 14, 1943: [Week18] Well folks, I'm leaving Fort Bragg tomorrow at noon. I still have no idea where I'm going, but I'll find out soon enough. I have everything packed and ready to go. There is really not much more for me to write on this subject and you will just have to wait until you hear from me. There are plenty of rumors, of course, as to where we are going, and according to them, everywhere from Maine to California. I just hope it won't be farther away from home than I am now.

I had it pretty soft today, spending most of the time just lying around the barracks. The only trouble was that every now and then they would call up from the orderly room and ask for a number of men to do some work. The idea then is to look as if you were very busy or else make yourself sort of scarce. Some of our ambitious fellows even went so far as to hide underneath the beds.

Although no recruit would probably ever recall enjoying their basic training, all but the most cynical could come out with a sense of accomplishment and a distinct degree of pride. Mentally and physically, they had been pushed to do things that they previously had no idea they could do. They had new levels of self-confidence and could now lay claim to having become a soldier in the United States Army.

The composition of the battalion's officers was also representative of a typical World War II outfit. Some were pre-war reservists and a good number, like Lieutenant Marlin Yoder, were graduates of college Reserve Officer Training Corps programs. Lt. Warren Sockwell was a graduate of Alabama's Auburn University (Class of 1943). Sockwell, like all his other classmates in Auburn's chemical engineer program, were sent to Officers Candidate School and then branched as field artillery officers. After taking the Basic Field Artillery Officers Course at Fort Sill, Oklahoma, Sockwell stayed on for the three-month sound and flash course. Sockwell recalls that the counterbattery training program was excellent, and that one of his survey instructors, a lieutenant colonel, was one of the best teachers that he ever experienced. Upon graduation, Sockwell had the choice of assignment to any one of the army's (then) seven field artillery battalions. Sockwell selected the 7th FAOB, as its posting at Camp Shelby was the closest to his Alabama home. (This rationale to get near home turned out to be a bust for Sockwell. As soon as he reported to the unit in the spring of 1944, Sockwell was sent with some other officers to Fort Rucker, Alabama, to observe field artillery firing exercises. He caught pneumonia and was hospitalized for a month. By the time he was released for duty, the battalion was preparing to deploy overseas. He never did get that trip home.)

Other officers were inductees who had scored well on entrance exams and were selected for the Officer Candidate School. There was at least one officer, First Lieutenant Fearn Field, who was a graduate of the United States Military Academy at West Point (Class of 1943). First Lieutenant Don Slessman was another graduate of a military school, in this case, the Virginia Military Institute (Class of 1939). Lieutenant Slessman was branched as a standard field artillery officer, and initially served in training cadre assignments at Fort Bragg through 1943. Expecting a highly sought after firing-battery command, Lieutenant Slessman was instead diverted to the artillery school at Fort Sill, where he was trained in advanced observation skills. He joined the 7th FAOB at Camp Shelby in early 1944, and was made chief of B Battery's flash platoon.

Most of the men destined for the 7th FAOB were unaware of their onward assignments until they actually arrived at the unit. Kurt Rieth describes his transition from basic training to arrival with the 7th FAOB at Camp Shelby two days before Christmas, 1943. His trip from Fort Bragg became an eight-day ordeal, with a two and a half day delay because of a train wreck, a sixty-hour ride to Camp Polk, Louisiana where he had a forty-eight-hour transition point stay, and final arrival at Camp Shelby on December 23. He wrote home of his introduction with the 7th FAOB on Christmas Day:

> I am writing this letter Christmas morning. I hope you have a nice day today and don't feel too badly about my not being with you. I miss being home very much, but I suppose there are lots of families worse off than us. They are fixing up a swell dinner at the mess hall and I may go to Hattiesburg this afternoon. I sent a telegram last night with my address. I couldn't wish you a "Merry Christmas" in it because they won't send any greetings in telegrams this year…This outfit I am in now is a Field Artillery Observation Battalion. They have absolutely nothing to do with firing guns but have equipment to pick up sound waves sent out by enemy guns when they shoot. This equipment can figure out where the enemy guns are located, and our artillery shoots back at them…There are only three boys from our old platoon at Fort Bragg here. There is a good chance for getting into radio work here, because there may be some vacancies in that section soon. This is lucky because usually only about five or six men from the whole platoon trained as radio operators ever actually get that job.

It was not uncommon for new men to arrive at Camp Shelby and find that the battalion was out training in field exercises. Such was the case when Jim Royals reported from basic training at Fort Bragg in 1943. Jim had the chance to briefly visit with his parents and pregnant teenage wife between the end of basic training and his travel to Mississippi. Jim describes his arrival to the 7th:

> As I returned to Fort Bragg, I was surprised to learn the buddies that I had gone through basic training with had been shipped out to Camp Shelby, Mississippi. Myself, along with a few others who had been on sick call or gone for some other reason were also shipped to Camp Shelby as well. Once there, we were notified we had been assigned to the 7th Field Artillery Observation Battalion. The 7th was in Louisiana on maneuvers, so we were put on fatigue details and worked our butts off; KP, trash pickup and we even helped build a tennis court. After a few weeks, the 7th FAOB returned and I was assigned to B Battery where I was then put in the machine gun section. That was after I had become an expert on the M-1 Carbine, and was very proficient on the .45 cal. automatic pistol and the .30 cal. Enfield Rifle. I was trained on the .30 cal. water-cooled machine gun and the .50 cal. Air-cooled heavy machine gun.

The 7th FAOB was organized into a Headquarters Battery, A Battery, and B Battery. Headquarters Battery was responsible for all battalion level command, control, administrative, and logistical support. Lieutenant Colonel Schwartz's staff consisted of the following sections: S-1 (personnel), S-2 (intelligence), S-3 (operations), S-4 (logistics). In addition, there were separate platoons and other sections for such functions as communications, maintenance, and supplies. As well as supporting and controlling the two line batteries, the headquarters company was responsible to the corps-level artillery commander to receive the battalion's overall taskings and orders.

The A and B Batteries were parallel outfits that conducted the primary mission of the battalion—locating active enemy artillery and directing the fire of American cannons back upon them. Each battery had a headquarters element that had a communications platoon, as well as sound and flash platoons. While the functions of these platoons will be described in detail later, sound observers determined the source of a cannon by assessing the noise of its firing, flash observers watching for the light of it's blast. The 7th FAOB Headquarters Battery would assign each of the line batteries a certain sector of area to provide counterbattery cover.

The training cycle at Camp Shelby was endless, with the NCOs teaching men individual soldier skills; the sections, platoons, and batteries training on collective tasks; and the entire battalion participating in more of the massive army-wide training maneuvers. These complex field exercises covered terrain that expanded over several states. During its twenty-four-month stay at Camp Shelby, the 7th FAOB participated in five of these army-level maneuvers that would last for months at a time and involve training throughout vast stretches of territory that would include Louisiana, Mississippi, and Texas. Robert Geiges remembered the maneuvers for the hazardous long night drives operating in "blackout drive." When daylight broke, he would be amazed at some of the dangerous roads and bridges they had been speeding across the preceding nights while in virtual blackness.

Camp Shelby was a sprawling installation that was initially brought into service during World War One and later used to train the Mississippi National Guard during the 1920s and '30s. Mobilized for national service in 1941, Camp Shelby saw a tremendous buildup during the first years of the war, and overnight became Mississippi's second largest city. The base contained over 400,000 acres with more than 100 miles of hard surfaced highways. In the early days at Camp Shelby, men of the 7th FAOB first had to live in tents, but later were able to move into huts. To complement the endless rows of barracks, the army did its best to add some creature comforts and built six service clubs, eight movie theaters, bowling alleys, and more than sixty post exchanges. To help assuage the worried parents back home, the army produced glossy pamphlets of the post for the men to send back home. The Camp Shelby "propaganda" no doubt made the base seem far more attractive then it was in real life.

Kurt Rieth described some observations on life at Camp Shelby in at letter home on January 8, 1944: The huts we live in are of two sizes. The larger type that I live in has about twelve men in it and the smaller ones are big enough for six men. Yes, we have to leave the huts when we go to the latrine, but it is only about sixty feet from the hut and you can dash to it in a few seconds. The shower room is in the latrine and is quite large. I wonder what you would do, Mom, if you saw me take a shower and then put on my overcoat and run out into the open to the hut.

...We did have a pretty big inspection this morning. I was a bad boy because I managed to have some dirt on my canteen cover. Now I will have to spend about two hours tomorrow morning cleaning pistols and rifles. I won't be alone on this, however, there is a whole list of us, including a few sergeants. I believe I'll go to the service club tonight, they have a big library there.

For off duty time, those too infrequent Saturday nights and Sundays when there was no guard duty, field exercises, inspections, or remedial punishment for some minor infractions, the men could get passes to nearby Hattiesburg. A small southern town, Hattiesburg was so swamped with military personnel that going there hardly seemed like getting away from base. That said, some of the men, such as Jim Royals were able to establish a close relationship with local families. (In an interesting footnote, Royals lost touch with his local family friends shortly after the war. However, after attending the 7th FAOB's sixtieth reunion in Huntsville, Alabama in October 2001, Royals happened to be driving by the area, and on a whim, tried to re-contact one of the family members. By pure luck, he was able to find one of them, which led to a happy reunion of a friendship that survived a half-century long gap.)

For a far more interesting getaway, New Orleans beckoned, a few hours drive farther south. New Orleans obviously offered a young soldier a much greater variety of attractions than did sleepy Hattiesburg, but also was considerably more difficult to reach. To be able to get to New Orleans on weekend passes, the men needed to quickly get off base, as the buses and trains destined there quickly sold out.

On a more routine basis, the soldiers spent their off duty time playing sports, hanging out in their unit's dayrooms, and watching movies. Films of that era included *Phantom of the Opera*, Ginger Roger's *Tender Comrades* (somewhat marred by excessive war bond propaganda), *The Uninvited* with Ruth Hussy and Ray Milland, *Up in Arms* with Danny Kaye, and, much to the troops' amusement, *See Here Private Hargrove*.

Mail has always been a critical morale issue for soldiers, and the men spent many hours writing home and eagerly waiting for mail in return. The mail system worked relatively efficiently, and it was common for letters to reach home within a two to three day period. Telephone calls back home were rare, if not out of the question, and special events such as birthday greetings and furlough travel coordination were handled by Western Union telegraphs, a process where a message could be delivered in the space of hours.

It's hard to overstate the importance of mail for the GIs. In one notable instance, medic Roy Barber told his buddy Amos Robinson about Wilma, his girlfriend's sister in Missouri. Amos began writing to Wilma in 1943 and they continued to correspond throughout the war. On returning to North Carolina after his 1945 discharge, Amos bee-lined to Missouri to meet Wilma face-to-face. The couple became engaged after only two visits. As it turned out, Roy Barber also married his girlfriend, Oma, and the two 7th FAOB vets eventually became brothers-in-law as well as lifelong friends.

For some of the more musically inclined men (including Barber and Robinson), participation in the battalion's chorus became a major part of their Camp Shelby experience. Organized by Chaplain Guiliand, the sixteen-man chorus sang at the Sunday morning and midweek services, as well as making numerous guest visits to neighboring churches in Hattiesburg.

The most prized recreational objective for any soldier was a furlough back home. Furloughs, which consisted of two weeks leave plus two travel days, were generally authorized to men after having completed their first six months of active duty. The men had to arrange and pay for their own train transportation home, a task sometimes made difficult by the tremendous demands the war put on America's rail system. Both for family members and the soldiers, these furloughs were extremely valued celebrations, and sadly, for several of the 7th men, would be the last occasions that they would ever see their loved ones again.

The process of cycling men out of the battalion to fill up newly created units continued. In February 1944, fully half the men in the battalion were transferred to other units. This dynamic required the assimilation of a steady stream of new replacements to get the battalion back to a war-ready footing. To bring the new men up to speed, the battalion organized an intensive three-week program to train them on the unique mission and equipment of a field artillery observation battalion. One week after his arrival to the battalion, Kurt Rieth wrote this of the replacement orientation program: "We started classes today to get a sort of basic training in the work this outfit does. There is quite a bit of mathematics involved and everything I learned in high school will come in handy. This basic course will last about three weeks."

The officers constantly had their work cut out for them. In addition to running their respective sections, platoons, and batteries during the day, they also had to become proficient in their own professional skills and battlefield responsibilities. The officers were expected to spend their evenings studying the tactics, manuals, and regulations in order to internalize knowledge that would become critical in leading their men into combat. Lieutenant Colonel Schwartz was tough on his officers, and for the most part, they tried to steer clear of him when they could.

Some men were able to transfer their job specialties. Cook Robert Geiges had to have a medical operation done in New Orleans, and was put on restricted duty upon his return to the unit. Working for the battalion S-4, Geiges was temporarily assigned to run the small battalion post exchange (PX). Compared to the life of the cook, Geiges enjoyed working supply duty and was able to get the S-4 to bring him on as the new Headquarters Battery Supply Sergeant. Geiges still recalls the gung-ho attitude of the men in the supply section. Although the odd hours of their duties excused them from regular physical training, the supply men would run the obstacle course on their own when time permitted.

When possible, the army tried to use a soldier's civilian experience to some practical use. Such was the case with Ed Shock, who joined the Headquarters Battery back in August 1942. Growing up on a farm, Ed had learned woodworking skills and was thus assigned as a battery carpenter. Having a skilled carpenter on hand was an invaluable asset to the battery first sergeant, and Ed was employed in such tasks as making building repairs, building furniture, and a myriad of light construction tasks associated with any army battalion-sized element. When not building things, Shock drove the supply truck for battery supply sergeant Geiges.

The battalion's training program was rigorous, and Kurt Rieth described some typical training days in a sampling from letters in January 1944.

> Well, we might have had it easy when we first came here but they are making up for it now. We got up at 5:45 this morning and then had an hour of drill in marching and a half-hour of calisthenics. Then we went over to the motor park, cleaned some trucks and then at 10:00 we left for the close combat range. On this range you walk through dense woods with your rifle, and targets operated by wires jump up around you for about two seconds and you have to shoot at them. You never know where they will pop up and you don't even have time to put the gun to your shoulder, you simply fire from the hip. To make it more interesting, most of the course is through a swamp and you wade through water up to your knees. After this we came back to the camp and practiced throwing dummy hand grenades. The last item on the program was a two-hour hike from 4:00 to 6:00. Then we finished supper and had to scrub and dust the

hut. We finished this at 9:00 and now I will just have time to write this letter and read a little. Tomorrow we will also have training until nine or ten in the evening.

. . .Last Thursday night we went over the infiltration course in the dark. This is the course where they fire machine gun bullets a few inches over your body as you crawl along the ground. Every few feet there are strands of barbed wire you have to lift and push yourself under. It's really some feeling when you see the tracer bullets whizzing over your head. The main object, of course, is to keep as close to the ground as possible, which no one has to tell you to do.

...Today I went on my first twenty-five-mile hike and I hope my last. We started at 7:00 this morning and got back at 3:10 in the afternoon. Every man that went on the hike is limping around as if he had just got over a broken leg. I didn't think it would be so tough but I know now it's the most strenuous thing I ever did in my life. It seems as if those last few miles will never end. There is no sense in falling out unless you have to because they will make you try it every Saturday until you make it.

After his first several weeks in the battalion, Jim Royals convoyed out to a field exercise in Leesville, Louisiana. Royals has these memories of this period. "There, we learned how to walk for miles, did battle drills, and dug foxholes. After the maneuvers were over, we got a short furlough home. I was able to see Ruby and pat the stomach where little Donnie was a'waiting his time to come into the world." On his return to the battalion, some elements received special training specific to their varied missions. Royals describes some specialized gunnery training his machine gun section received:

In September 1943, the machine gun section was sent out west to take a course in anti-aircraft firing with the .50 cal. machine gun. Using towed targets and radio controlled planes, we were attached to the 442nd Combat Battalion and sent to Indianola, Texas. The 442nd was made up of Japanese-Americans and later on in Europe became one of the most highly decorated outfits in the U.S. Army. I was proud to have been attached to them for a while. On Sunday morning, November 7, 1943, while lazing around in a four-man tent, I was awakened and told I was a father of a bouncing baby son and that the mother was OK. I was proud and so much wanted to see my son and his mom, but we had another month of special training before I would be able to get a short pass back to Georgia.

As a result of the enormous wartime buildup, the army's Quartermaster Corps was forever playing catch-up to meet basic soldier needs, such as cold weather clothing and field laundry services. Most units were blessed to have soldiers with the wherewithal to take care of themselves and their buddies when the army supply system failed to do it for them. One such soldier was A Battery's Donald Paschal. At thirty years old, Paschal was considerably more mature than most of his comrades and had the knack and ambition to get things accomplished in spite of the army's bureaucracy. When the men froze at night during maneuvers, it was Paschal who came to the rescue. For five dollars he would sew together a GI's issue of two army blankets into a sheet of canvas (and virtually invent the concept of a sleeping bag long before most men had even envisioned one). When the men had no access to field showers, Paschal produced an old tub and charged men twenty-five cents per bath. With food scarce, many units would supplement their rations by purchasing fried chicken dinners from local farmers. One evening, Don took advantage of this opportunity when he went to a farmhouse and picked up a large order of chicken for his section, despite the fact it that had previously been placed by some other unit!

In time, as the men became more familiar with the unit, its function, and their comrades, they began to get into a routine. Kurt Rieth in March 1944:

> You know that I am actually beginning to enjoy myself in the afternoons. Every afternoon we go to our radio section room and learn about adjusting the sets, practice code, or do almost anything we please. There are also a few books in the section room and sometimes I just sit down and read . . . Yesterday we were inspected and the radio section was complimented very highly. We set up a practice net with sets that send Morse code and the inspecting officer said it was the fastest net he had ever heard in the field artillery.

Still, there was the ever-present drudgery of routine inspection after inspection. Rieth continued: "This morning we had an inspection of all our equipment, everything the army ever issued us. This time we had to put our beds outside the huts, place some of the equipment in the beds, and the rest on our shelter-half that we spread out on the ground. A pretty strong wind started blowing. The dust and dirt blew all over everything. On top of that the soot from the kitchen chimney also settled on everything. It was quite a mess."

Marksmanship was an important part of the training program and the men spent many hours on the dusty firing ranges. On one occasion, Robert Geiges found himself on the rifle range next to Battalion Commander Schwartz. To his horror, Geiges realized that he was accidentally shooting at Schwartz's target (an easy error to make given the long line of targets before them). An officer standing behind him realized the mistake at the same time. As Geiges had just scored a bulls-eye for Schwartz, the officer wisely counseled Geiges to "keep his mouth shut."

While fine-tuning individual soldier skills was important, the bottom line remained the battalion's capability to find enemy cannon. The army's field artillery battalions of the 1940s were an outgrowth of the first attempts to locate artillery using flash and sound ranging techniques during World War I. The application of these skills became an art form, requiring expert precision in geometry, trigonometry, land navigation, acoustics, and spit-on-the-fingers estimation of the distance between flashes and bangs. Precise training in counterbattery work was virtually impossible, as it would require being on the receiving end of actual artillery attack. To simulate battlefield conditions for sound ranging, the men used their equipment to measure TNT bursts and pre-set artillery shells. When they finally did arrive in combat, it became apparent that the actual detection of distant guns was much more difficult than training could ever simulate.[6]

The tempo of training gave the men hearty appetites, and for the most part, the camp food wasn't bad. The mess sergeants did their best in a difficult job and always provided the hungry young men with plenty of chow when they were in garrison.

Stephen Wandzioch became a cook rather by default. Because he had pre-war experience as a baker, Wandzioch was initially assigned to be a cook with A Battery when he first arrived in the battalion in July 1941. At that time, the battery already had a full complement of six cooks, and he was instead assigned as a truck driver. While at Camp Blanding, in Florida, the regular complement of A Battery cooks got into some sort of trouble in Jacksonville, and couldn't make it back to camp for the next day's meals. Desperate for a solution, First Sergeant Larry Banes woke up Wandzioch at three in the morning and ordered him to make breakfast for the battery. After managing to do so in a decent fashion, Wandzioch then had to make lunch, then after nine straight hours in the kitchen, dinner as well. From that day on, Wandzioch remained a cook, rising up in ranks as a second and first cook, and finally as the A Battery mess sergeant.

While in the field, and when time and refrigeration allowed to set up mess operations, the cooks would prepare hot A-rations for breakfast and dinner. Typical A-Ration meals consisted of mass-produced fares such as scrambled eggs, chipped beef on bread (also known as "SOS"), and chili-macaroni. Combat conditions and mobility requirements often rendered hot meal service impossible. In these occasions the

GI's would have to rely on the less desirable, man-portable C- and K-rations. The C-ration included ten different meat compounds (the most notorious being the ubiquitous Spam), stews, spaghetti, vegetables, and dehydrated eggs and potatoes. K-rations comprised ingenious compounds that were at least nourishing. The main trouble with army food was that it was monotonous, and the men welcomed any type of food from back home.[7] To further break up the routine, the GIs could get snacks at the PX or when on pass, take in a meal at a local Hattiesburg diner (where a steak dinner with all the trimmings could be had for a dollar).

It was fortunate for the men that meals out on the town were cheap (by today's comparison), for they certainly were not paid much. Up through 1943, privates only received $20.00 per month (not much more than the $13.00 pay that Civil War soldiers received). In 1944, the monthly pay increased to $50.00. For a typical unmarried private, $18.75 was deducted for a $25.00 savings bond, and $6.50 for life insurance. When payday came around, the men were left with about $25.00 to get them through the month. One can only imagine how difficult it was for those men married and with children to support.

Perhaps in spite of the sense of uncertainty ahead, some of the soldiers, like Walter Damiano, felt compelled to get married to their sweethearts before the inevitable deployment came. In February 1944, Damiano was returning to Camp Shelby by bus after enjoying a weekend pass in Jackson, spent with his girlfriend, Rubye. An officer boarded the bus and recognized Damiano as an old childhood friend. Damiano recalled the officer by his nickname, "Bananas." Damiano was further taken by surprise when he saw the crucifix on the collar of his uniform and realized that "Bananas" was now a priest. The chaplain was en route to his new assignment at Camp Shelby and asked Damiano for directions to the chapel. Damiano describes what happened next:

> As we are riding on the bus, a fantastic thought came to me. What if I asked him to officiate my marriage to Rubye. "Father," I said (I couldn't believe I was calling him father instead of "Bananas") "I think it would be great if you would marry Rubye and me." He said he would be glad to. We made the arrangements for the wedding to take place in two weeks in the chapel at Camp Shelby. Rubye, incidentally, was not aware at all of what was taking place.
>
> Well it so happens that two of my buddies came back from their furlough with a used car they had just bought. (The car reminded me of the legendary "Bonnie and Clyde" car made famous by the outlaws.) They offered to drive Rubye and me to the chapel. After the wedding took place, the priest said he just received some cookies from his mother and we could have them as our wedding cake.
>
> Rubye and I often think back to that beautiful little wedding; the ride to the chapel in the "Bonnie and Clyde" limo, the cookies as our wedding cake, and most of all, that my childhood friend "Bananas" was the priest who married us.

During the Camp Shelby years, the perpetual rotation of men in and out of the unit continued as many of the more experienced men were sent on to help form other forward artillery observation battalions. One such unit that was formed was the sister 286th FAOB, which stood up at Fort Bragg and was sent to Camp Shelby in the spring of 1944. One of the 286th soldiers was Edward A. Marinello. Throughout the war, Marinello kept detailed notes of his experiences, and went on to write a book in 1998 titled *On the Way: General Patton's Eyes and Ears on the Enemy*. The 286th ended up deploying to France about a month after the 7th FAOB went into combat. Assigned to XII Corps of Third Army, the 286th was often located parallel to the 7th FAOB, and at times, one of their batteries was placed under 7th FAOB control. As such, Marinello's experience as a sound platoon member was virtually identical to those of the men of the 7th FAOB, and it is appropriate that his excellent book is frequently referenced in this history of the 7th.

For the men of the 7th, the daily grind and tedium of endless training exercises and austere garrison life made the Camp Shelby experience seem to go on forever. While they marched, trained, cleaned, and were inspected, they also observed the progress of the war intently. Much of the early news wasn't good. In the Pacific, the destruction of the fleet at Pearl Harbor was followed by the loss of Wake Island, Guam, and the Japanese capture of 15,000 American soldiers in the Philippines in May 1942. Naval victories at Coral Sea and Midway finally stopped the spread of the Japanese conquests, but bringing the war directly to Imperial Japan would be a long and bloody process. Eventually, gains in McArthur's island-hopping campaign in places like Guadalcanal, Tarawa, and Guam moved things forward, but at a slow and costly pace.

In Europe, the war raged from the heart of Russia down through the Mediterranean Sea and into Africa. From 1941 to 1942, German forces almost annihilated the Soviet Army as panzer columns reached as far as Leningrad, Moscow, Stalingrad, and down to the Black Sea. Although the Germans began to suffer terrible losses by early 1943, whether or not the Soviets could hold out for the duration of the war was anybody's guess. U-boats patrolled the entire Atlantic Ocean as Hitler attempted to strangle Great Britain. In November 1942, a 100,000-man Allied force landed in Northern Africa to help the British defeat Rommel's Afrika Corps. The Americans suffered a sharp defeat at the hands of Rommel at Kasserine Pass in Tunisia, but learned valuable lessons in the process. With Northern Africa in Allied hands in May 1943, the next objective was breaking through what Winston Churchill coined "Hitler's soft underbelly" via the Mediterranean Sea. While Sicily quickly fell to Patton's American and Field Marshall Sir Bernard Montgomery's British troops, the invasion of Italy was far more difficult than expected. The "soft underbelly" of Europe proved to be anything but, and it was clear that it would take a full-scaled Allied invasion of France to finally win the war. In the course of three years, the Americans and the British had built up an enormous invasion force in England for this purpose. For all of the resources in firepower and material, the outcome still depended on the ability and courage of young American fighting men to storm through heavily fortified France to bring the war to a conclusive end.

While the training continued at Camp Shelby, close friends from home, comrades from basic training, and men transferred out of the 7th FAOB to form new units were already deployed, fighting, and in many instances, dying. Watching two years of global warfare from the sidelines, the men of the 7th waited impatiently, instinctively knowing that their time in combat would someday come, but having no idea as to where and when.

One of the first 7th FAOB alumni to see fighting was Arnold Price. Price was one of the original 7th FAOB men who was with the unit during its activation and for much of its Camp Shelby service. Along with Private Wulf, Price was transferred from the 7th FAOB and sent to Fort Ord, California. After only two weeks at Fort Ord, it was then on to combat operations in the Pacific Theater. There, Price served with a field artillery observation battalion's communication section in such places as Brisbayne, Goodenough Island, Aitape, Finchaven (New Guinea), and Saidor.

Many historians characterize the battles in the Pacific Islands as perhaps the worst in the entire war. Fueled by propaganda, the clash of two vastly different cultures resulted in a uniquely intense degree of hatred between the combatants. Prisoners were rarely taken and many of the bitter island battles were fought to the last man. The relentless jungle conditions, insects, malaria, and constant exposure made life miserable. Death could come when it was least expected. As relayed to his daughter, Julie, Price remembered the time in Finchaven, New Guinea when he and a group of several hundred men were watching a movie on the beach, on a set-up screen. The movie was *Checkers* starring Jane Withers. A Japanese plane came out of nowhere and dropped a bomb on the beach. "We heard him pull out," Price recalled. "Four people on the front row died, but the screen was still standing." Terrified at the suddenness of attack, the men scattered in all directions. When asked if the men gathered afterward to talk about the attack, Price replied, "No, we just went back to our pup tents."

Actual combat was still in the future for the 7th FAOB, but the battalion first had to get through Camp Shelby intact. Throughout the years at Shelby, Lieutenant Colonel Schwartz continued to lead the battalion with a heavy hand and insisted on the strictest levels of discipline. Invariably, this resulted in complaints and resentment among the ranks. While the American soldier, by reputation, is known for a fair degree of grousing, concerns on the effect of Schwartz's leadership style on the battalion's morale came to the attention of senior leaders in the spring of 1944. A special inspector general (IG) evaluation was conducted and the entire battalion underwent an exhaustive operational assessment. Despite their complaints about the commander, the men performed superbly. The IG concluded that whatever command environment Lieutenant Colonel Schwartz had created, it was obvious the battalion was combat ready. Schwartz remained in command and soon the battalion became preoccupied in preparing for movement.

Inevitably, the men eventually knew that their time would come to go overseas. Like most typical army movements, the date of the actual departure came with a series of fits and starts. Rumors of deployment abounded throughout the long stay at Camp Shelby, but most of them proved false. The first indications that a legitimate final movement order was imminent came about in mid-March 1944. Kurt Rieth described the notification to his parents on March 16:

Well folks, I'm afraid I will have to write something now that isn't exactly good news. The indications are that after the outfit moves to another camp, the next movement will be overseas. I also realize that it's no use telling you not to worry, but I assure you that once we are across we will only continue training for at least six months, since almost 50 percent of the outfit are new men. The whole business may be a false alarm, so do as I do and simply don't think about it.

Preparations for the deployment began in full swing. By the time the men were initially assigned to the battalion, the army had pretty much stripped them of any civilian clothing or private property. Additional scrubs of personal items were made, and the men sent back all remaining belongings (lighters, watches, etc.) that were not part of government issue. Field training was halted, and equipment was cleaned and recleaned, inspected and reinspected. Vehicles were loaded in carefully prepared packing plans and made ready for movement by rail. With all their equipment cleaned and packed, the men were occupied with classes, lectures, and training films.

Beginning March 24, the men were restricted to base. To let some steam loose, there were occasional "beer calls," as described by Kurt Rieth on March 26: "Last night the battery had a beer party in the back of the mess hall. They had about forty cases of beer and everyone was feeling pretty good. The officers were there and one captain had so much he finally wound up flat on the ground. They whisked him away pretty fast." A few days later, it was announced that the departure was being delayed, and the men again were granted passes up through April 7.

On March 31, Lieutenant Colonel Schwartz held a battalion-level inspection where he personally checked the equipment outlay of every soldier. (Before the battalion commander inspected any of the privates, they were first pre-inspected by their corporals, sergeants, lieutenants, and captains.) Schwartz's exhaustive inspection of the 500-man battalion lasted the better part of six hours, with the men standing at either attention or parade rest throughout. Kurt Rieth: "What a day we had today. We had an inspection this afternoon of all our equipment packed just the way it will be when we leave Shelby. After everything was strapped on we could hardly move. On top of all this stuff on our backs we had to carry our duffel bag filled with everything we owned. We marched, or I should I say staggered, all the way over to the drill field and then laid every item of equipment out on the ground on our blankets to be inspected. Then the commander of the battalion, Lieutenant Colonel Schwartz, inspected the whole battalion of about 500 men himself. We stood out there beside our display for just about six hours until he finished inspecting every man. The names we called him weren't exactly nice. He thinks nothing can be done right unless he does it himself." Although Lieutenant Colonel Schwartz rated some additional ire from his troops that day, that degree of command-level attention to detail is what instills soldiers with the natural instinct to stay alert and be thorough in all they do. The high degree of discipline and situational awareness established within the 7th FAOB no doubt accounted for its high degree of future battlefield effectiveness.

In the days just before departure, young Ruby Royals, along with her infant boy, made an arduous trip (in the wake of a bus strike) to Camp Shelby in hopes of seeing her husband Jim. Captain Keith Chandler, the B Battery Commander, allowed Royals to go into town and see her for couple of hours. Royals: "After a visit that lasted just a few hours Captain Chandler arranged for the military police to bring me back to base. I thanked him for the opportunity to go off base. Ruby and Donnie returned back to Georgia and I did not see them until after the war ended and I was discharged."

By April 6, the men were again locked down on base, and allowed to write home one last time before departure. The actual deployment date from Camp Shelby came to be on Easter Sunday, 1944. After two long years in training there, some joked that the 7th FAOB almost seemed like a permanent station complement. Although the battalion's time at Camp Shelby was often difficult and full of drudgery, this prolonged stay played an important role in the history of the battalion. Those two years of hard training allowed the 7th to mature and train to a level of competency that was far and above most other American Army units in World War II.

The 286th FAOB would leave Camp Shelby three months after the 7th FAOB's departure. Marinello described the reaction of his battalion to the news of their impending deployment, as well as his less-than-fond remembrance of Camp Shelby:

The first hint that we were going overseas came from the battalion commander, Lieutenant Colonel Kuhlman. The timing could not have been more welcomed, at least for those anxious for action. The unit had been stationed, not by popular choice, at Camp Shelby, Mississippi for several months just then. Camp Shelby was referred to as "the hellhole of the South." The day of the message was hot and muggy, not the regular kind, but the Mississippi kind. Even men banking on the war to end before they could be sent into action were willing to leave that day, from that place."[8]

On April 9, 1944, in a movement marked with great secrecy, the 7th FAOB uploaded on trains and moved north to New York. The men were not briefed of their destination, and for the first time, their outbound mail was censored by officers. Shortly after leaving Mississippi, the ride became eventful when the locomotive threw a rod and gouged out a half mile of track. Fortunately, none of the cars was derailed, and after a period of time, a new locomotive was attached and the movement continued. The train ride was a long one, and on April 11, the battalion finally reached Camp Shanks, New York, a large troop pre-shipping staging area thirty miles up the Hudson River from New York City.

Arriving at Camp Shanks, the men experienced more of the army's classic "hurry up and wait." They ended up having thirteen days before shipment, and much of the time was spent in redundant administrative processing. The 7th FAOB history records this time as: "a busy one, punctuated with numerous clothing inspections (every man was checked at least three times to see that he had an extra pair of shoe laces), physical inspections ('if you can walk and breathe, you're qualified for overseas service'), and lifeboat drills ('now when you get aboard that troopship, there's only two things we're afraid of—that's fire and panic')."

While not being inspected, poked, probed and briefed, the men were allowed some time to take buses and explore New York City. Rieth on April 16, 1944:

> Well, after I telephoned you yesterday I went out and walked around New York a little, mostly in Times Square. I passed one theater and saw that the musical show *One Touch of Venus* (with Mary Martin, John Boles and Kenny Baker) was playing. I didn't think I could get a seat because this is one of the most popular shows in New York. I was able to get the one seat that was left and it was the best in the house. I had to pay six dollars for it, but it was worth it however, because it really was a swell show. I was also able to get to New York again today. This time we went to Radio City, took the tour through it, and also saw a Radio Show broadcast. I'm also beginning to know my way around New York. If we ever go down again when the war is over I'll be able to show you around.

A good number of the men who came from the greater New York area were allowed to visit home, with many taking along their buddies for a final home-cooked meal. A Battery's Walter Damiano was a native of New York and brought home his good friend Don Paschal. Prior to their departure from Camp Shelby, Paschal—ever the consummate scrounger—was able to gather thousands of wire clothes hangers from the barracks. He then sold a full truckload of the hangers to a Hattiesburg laundry, making the tidy profit of seventy-five dollars in the process. Damiano's mother helped Paschal cash the check, which he in turn later used as seed money to start a profitable laundry service as soon as they arrived in England. Robert Geiges was one who was able to link up with his wife for one last evening together.

The two weeks at Camp Shanks and in New York passed quickly and soon the time came for the 7th Field Artillery Observation Battalion to sail to England.

CHAPTER 2

England: The Battalion joins XX Corps and Readies for War

With heavy duffel bags in hand, the battalion formed ranks in the early hours of April 24, 1944. Departing their Camp Shanks barracks, the men were trucked to the Hudson River. There, a ferry took them to the New York pier where the British transport ship, His Majesty's Trooper *Arawa* awaited. The men unloaded at the pier only to find the unwelcome news that they had been selected to arrive a day early in order to perform cleaning detail on the ship. The men got to work, scrubbing seemingly every corner of the large vessel. The following day, the full complement of 3,000 troops, including replacement air corps personnel bound for bomber crew assignments in England, were loaded aboard.

It was hard to believe that the time had actually come to depart for Europe. Passing the Statue of Liberty, the *Arawa* set sail out of New York Harbor. Reflecting back one year later, a future issue of the battalion's newsletter wrote of this moment. The article also highlights some of the cynicism that the prolonged three-year stay in the states had caused with many of the men:

> No log of our service would be complete without a recollection of those last days at Camp Shelby, when opinion was 50-50 as whether we would actually go to a theater of operations or not. After three years of "Hup, two, three, four," twice-a-week inspections in ranks, retreat formations and parades, field problems, inspector general tests, and maneuvers we had many cynics and they were not convinced when we boarded the troop train on that Easter Sunday and began the journey to the Point of Embarkation (POE). When the locomotive failed while we were still in Mississippi, these cynics said, "The 7th will soon take Camp McCain and will have the situation well in hand." A new locomotive fixed that one. Then POE and mad preparations, learning a new way to make a roll, "over the side," and the "Broadway Soldier-Sailor Instructor," who repeated over and over again, "Now when you get to that transport." Again our cynics said, "Hooey." Then, that foggy morning when we went aboard and still our cynics said, "Aw Hell, it's a dry run, we've been sittin' here all day and you can tell by looking at this scow she's only a Hollywood set." That morning found us in convoy and drawing overseas pay (the anchor was up); we were on our way. Some stayed on deck until the last minutes to get a last look at the "Old Girl" – that great old girl who held high the torch of liberty, which was temporarily unlighted, but which we knew then would shine again, and which will, before long, light every corner of the world. Be it one year or ten more, it will be but the wink of an eye compared to the ages of darkness and oppression that then threatened the world."

The HMS *Arawa* sailed on through the Long Island Sound to form its part of a sixty-two ship convoy (designated CU 27) for the fifteen-day transatlantic voyage. As the 7th FAOB was the largest unit aboard the *Arawa*, Lieutenant Colonel Schwartz was designated as the commander of all the passengers.

Conditions on most troopships, especially the British ones, were awful. Typically over-crowded with passengers, fresh water was rationed and the men could only drink at stipulated intervals. The showers ran cold saltwater. Adding to the general discomfort, the men had to wear their life jackets at all times, which meant that they were constantly bumping into each other. The food was terrible and the primary diet was undercooked liver, old prunes, and an occasional boiled egg. The entire ship reeked with an ever-present, fish-like stench. Before every dusk, the ship's speakers would blare "Blackout, blackout, close all ports and outer doors; no smoking on deck." A soldier described that below the decks, nighttime resembled a morgue after a major disaster, with men sleeping on and under the mess tables, on the floors, and the lucky ones, in hammocks.

Battery B's Bill Williamson couldn't manage to sleep in his hammock and traded with a buddy who had a mattress. Williamson soon came to find that the mattresses were no great prize either. During the day the mattresses were stacked against the bulkhead and spread out on the decks at night. Rats would scurry over the men as they tried to sleep, resulting in ruckuses as the GIs attempted (always unsuccessfully) to kill the rodents. Williamson also recalls that the bread they were given was so soggy that some practical jokers would form them into baseballs and hurl them at the back of unsuspecting heads.

The food situation was so bad that Lieutenant Colonel Schwartz ordered A Battery Mess Sergeant Stephen Wandzioch down to the galley to try to improve things. The *Arawa*'s mess crew were all English cooks who were clearly unsympathetic to the American's complaints and dietary preferences. Tensions were such that fistfights almost broke out between the American and British cooks. When Wandzioch noticed that the British were baking bread with worm-infested flour, his complaints fell on deaf ears. He then went ahead and had his own cooks sift worms from the flour as best they could. Wandzioch was further horrified to see the British cooks boil liver in large vats of water. Instead of making any effort to rinse the vats after draining the liquid, they would simply heat up more water to make tea out of it, producing a foul brew full of grease. Also served were cans of World War I-era corned beef, with packing labels dated 1916-1918.

Kurt Rieth had this to say of his experience on the *Arawa* (though he likely downplayed hardships to appease his parent's worries):

[Mid-voyage, May 1, 1944]: There isn't a great deal we are allowed to write about this trip. I can tell you, however, that I haven't been seasick a bit, although a lot of the boys felt pretty bad the first few days. This of course isn't exactly a pleasure cruise and there is always some work to be done. Everyone is assigned a special job. Some of the fellows and myself spend a few hours each morning bringing supplies from the hold of the ship to the canteen. This leaves me with the rest of the day off. Some of the boys aren't so lucky and have jobs that last most of the day.

[One week after arrival in England, May 15, 1944]: That article you read about troopships is partly true but it wasn't quite that bad. We only had two meals a day, and they were rotten, but there was plenty of room to move about on the deck and we slept below every night. As you wrote, it was nothing like the previous trips we made but just the same I sort of enjoyed it. That made me about the only one, but I always liked being around the water.

Lieutenant Slessman was more critical in his assessment of the trip, and described the journey as "a long tedious voyage that was, for the most ardent sailor, a pain in the neck. . . The food was terrible, having a fishy aroma that made it very unappetizing. . .We had a few days of rough weather and there were plenty of sick people on board—a few like Lieutenant Douglas Smith were sick the moment they boarded the ship. I felt bad one day but managed to make every meal and keep it, which was a surprise to me."

One man other man who suffered terribly from seasickness was Jack French of B Battery. He was so sick that he spent most of the fourteen days in his bunk, too ill to barely move.

Robert Geiges, who would be later detailed to serve on one of the ship's anti-aircraft guns, also remembered the awful food. When assigned to cleaning duties the day before departure, Geiges said they must have scrubbed every inch of the ship except the galley, which was filthy throughout the voyage. The plates and cups were perpetually covered in a film of grease, leaving the men to believe that they were never actually washed. There was liver served with maggots, and bread covered with roaches.

On April 24, the same day that the HMS *Arawa* departed New York, another boat under a different flag set sail from the other side of the Atlantic. This was the German submarine U-473, which slipped out of her reinforced concrete pen in Lorient. In her second patrol under the command of twenty-seven-year-old Kapitanleutnant (Kptlt) Heinz Sternberg, the U-473's objective was to find an eastbound Allied convoy and sink as many enemy ships as possible. The U-473 was a VIIC Type U-boat that was commissioned on June 16, 1943 in Kiel, Germany. In the maiden voyage that began in January 1944, Kptlt. Sternberg received credit for one kill, sinking a 1,400-ton ship. Braving a vast array of antisubmarine ships and aircraft out to destroy her, the U-473 was now headed for the hunting grounds of the North Atlantic.[9]

In the first years of the war, German U-boats were on the verge of strangling England to win the war for the Atlantic. Thousands of tons of Allied shipping were sent to the bottom of the Atlantic by the marauding submarines and convoys proceeded at great peril. Beginning in 1942, the fortunes reversed against the Germans. Allied code breaking and radar and sonar advances now made the hunter the hunted. By the spring of 1944, the Germans were losing their U-boats at a rate greater than the Allied ships they were attacking. Although service on a German sub often resulted in a near suicidal fate for her crew (the U-Boat service eventually had a 75 percent casualty rate), the U-boats still kept coming.

While the Allies had gotten a clear upper hand against German submarines by the spring of 1944, Atlantic crossings remained a harrowing affair. There was always the threat that a U-Boat would surface at night in the midst of a convoy, fire her torpedoes, and escape into the darkness. In daylight hours they could attack submerged, with the only warning being a brief periscope sighting or incoming torpedo wake. To protect the convoys, American and British antisubmarine commanders needed to be vigilant every minute of every cruise. To accomplish his mission, a German U-boat skipper needed to be lucky with just one torpedo. Each convoy was protected by an outer screen of destroyers and destroyer escorts. Using sonar and radar, the escorts formed a protective perimeter around the convoys. The ships also maintained a zigzag course intended to deflect a U-boats aim as an additional countermeasure. All that said, if a submarine could penetrate the escort screen and launch a torpedo attack, it could reap catastrophic results. Despite the maximum dispersion of a convoy's ships, they still were packed so densely that even one errant torpedo was bound to hit a target. Each ship posted lookouts on constant alert and manned guns around the clock. On the HMS *Arawa*, there was a shortage of sailors and the crew looked to the 7th FAOB for help in serving her guns. Lieutenant Slessman: "Like all ships at that time, it was undermanned as far as regular navy personnel were concerned, so some of us were selected to man the various guns on the ship in the event of an attack. Having had more experience than most with artillery, I was given the job of running the various gun crews."

Ed Shock described his duty on a gun crew as well as life on the *Arawa*:

There were 3,000 troops on board, and most of them were sea-sick. After one day, I realized that I had to get up on deck—I'm a little claustrophobic. I volunteered to help man a six-inch gun on the upper deck. Another sergeant and another soldier from a different outfit joined me.

We were hoping we wouldn't have to fire it, as it was so caked with layers of paint we were afraid it would explode. We stayed with the gun twenty-four hours a day, except for meals. The food mostly consisted of liver boiled with cabbage. This, along with tea and biscuits, made up most of our diet. We had all of our gear up there with us as well.

The conditions for the fifty-three-man German crew of the U-473 were even worse. The tight space, high seas, and constant threat of air attack made for a miserable and perilous experience for all German submariners. Just as the U-boats had once nearly blockaded England, the Allies now tried to sink each German sub before they slipped up the French coastline en route to the shipping lanes. From the beginning of her patrol, the U-473 had a rough go of it. On April 28, they were attacked by a British Halifax Bomber that dropped six depth charges. Escaping unscathed, the sub was yet again attacked the next day by another bomber, this one dropping seven depth charges. Kptlt. Sternberg evaded his enemy once more, moving west into the North Atlantic in hopes of intercepting a convoy—an accomplishment that was becoming increasingly rare for the U-boats.

On May 3, U-473's destiny was fulfilled when it stumbled on convoy CU 27. In a submerged approach, Sternberg maneuvered his boat toward the convoy to select the highest value target possible. Sternberg's heart must have raced as he observed a large troopship that had strayed to the outside of convoy. Behind it were other freighters, including a munitions ship. The only catch was that there was a destroyer escort in close proximity to the fat targets. Sternberg had to act fast. Placing the periscope crosshairs on what may have been the HMS *Arawa*, Sternberg quickly called out range and directional data as his crew obtained a target solution. The U-473 fired a single T-5 torpedo. The torpedo launched true and set a dead course toward the *Arawa*. Ed Shock continues: "We were sailing among a convoy, in a zigzag pattern, and they were trying to keep our troopship in the middle of the convoy. Early one morning, we realized that our ship was on the outside of the convoy. Soon afterwards, an alarm was sounded aboard the ship, a submarine had spotted us and had launched a torpedo. We could see the torpedo coming straight at us."

The warship near the *Arawa* was the veteran destroyer escort USS *Donnell* (DE-56), which was on its fifth transatlantic convoy under the command of Lieutenant Commander F.C. Billings. The *Donnell* first detected the approaching U-boat on sonar. With the crew racing to battle stations, a lookout spotted the sub's periscope. Lieutenant Commander Billings ordered a course straight toward the sub while the crew armed and readied the racks of depth charges on the ship's stern. As they started to close in on the U-boat, a torpedo wake was seen heading toward the *Arawa*. Destroyer escorts are fast and highly maneuverable ships. Billings probably could have easily avoided the torpedo and then turned back to attack the nearby sub. In an act of supreme selfless courage, the *Donnell* instead set a course to intercept the inbound warhead. Charlie Wright of B Battery watched as the destroyer nearly turned over on its side as it made the maneuver. Ed Shock: "One of our destroyer escorts positioned themselves directly in the path of the torpedo and took the hit. We witnessed the explosion that was intended for our troopship. We later learned that several sailors had lost their lives in that incident. They were sacrificed for the sake of 3,000 soldiers. I surely hope that the army, or navy, has awarded them appropriately for their action."

A tremendous explosion erupted from the stern of the *Donnell*. The torpedo also set off some of the just-armed depth charges, causing them to detonate as well. The entire stern section of the destroyer escort was blown off, killing twenty-nine sailors and wounding another twenty-five. Three other escorts, the USS *Reeves*, the USS *Hopping* and the HMS *Samsonia*, raced over to the *Donnell* to provide assistance to the badly stricken ship. Additional destroyers turned to attack the U-473, leaving the rest of the convoy with precious little security. Lieutenant Slessman: "If that that torpedo had not hit that other ship, it would have hit us, as we were right in line with it. It evidently got away in spite of numerous depth charges dropped on it." The U-473 did escape from the attack of the remaining convoy's escorts, but Sternberg's getaway did not last for long.

Two hundred miles to the northwest, a flotilla of three British destroyers was on its way back to port after escorting an American cruiser to Murmansk, Russia, where it was presented as a gift from President Roosevelt to Joseph Stalin. The destroyers were part of the 36th Escort Group under the command of Captain Johnny Walker, an experienced anti-submarine officer credited with sinking over a dozen U-boats. Alerted by urgent signals from the CU 27 convoy, Walker calculated the U-473's most likely escape route. He ordered his destroyers, the HMS' *Starling*, *Wren*, and *Wild Goose*, to set an intercept course. Sure enough, the flotilla detected U-473 early on May 5 and began an intensive depth charge attack. In desperation, Sternberg dove his boat down to 656 feet, far deeper then the maximum depth it had been engineered to reach. The terror and sheer misery for the sub's crew can only be imagined. For twenty-three hours, the cat and mouse game continued, with neither side willing to give up. All told, the destroyers dropped 350 depth charges. While never mortally hit by a depth charge, there was nothing that Sternberg could do to shake off his pursuers. In the early morning hours of May 6, the heavily damaged U-473 was virtually out of oxygen and had exhausted the physical limits of her crew and battery charge. Sternberg had to surface, but he made the choice to do so fighting. The submarine blew its tanks and popped to the surface like a cork, taking the pack of destroyers by surprise. Sternberg was the first man out of the conning tower and immediately selected a target. A torpedo was fired and missed the HMS *Wren* by a mere ten yards. Sternberg readied his remaining three forward tubes for another attack when the guns of the three destroyers came alive and let loose a fusillade of cannon and automatic weapons fire. The U-473's bridge took a direct hit and Sternberg was killed. Still under fire, the remaining crewmen set demolitions charges and abandoned ship. The sub exploded and sank before the destroyers could reach and capture it. Of the U-473's fifty-three crewmembers, thirty were rescued to become prisoners of war.

Meanwhile, back aboard the *Donnell*, exceptional damage control measures were taken that saved the destroyer from sinking. The ship was towed to Dunnstaffnage Bay, Scotland, and arrived nine days after the attack. The damage to the *Donnell* was so extensive that she was deemed a "Total Constructive Loss," and her days as a warship were over. Still, the *Donnell* continued to serve the war effort. Reclassified as Accommodation Ship IX-182, the *Donnell* was outfitted as a power hulk. When the Allies took the port-city of Cherbourg, France in August 1944, all power-generating resources were destroyed. The *Donnell* was sent to the port, and was able to help power the city through that December. After the war, the *Donnell* was towed back to the Philadelphia Navy Yard where she was decommissioned and sold as scrap.

The eventual destruction of the U-473 occurred a long way from convoy CU 27, which was then closing in on the Irish coast. It is doubtful that any of the men of the 7th FAOB ever became aware of the final battle to sink the submarine, or even knew of its number, the name of its captain, or the fate of its crew. If they were able to reflect on it, some would see that the attack of the U-473 on the convoy typified, in many ways, the war that the 7th FAOB was entering. Kptlt. Sternberg must have been crestfallen when the *Donnell* took the torpedo he had intended for the troopship, though by sinking a destroyer escort he was actually reducing an immediate tactical threat to himself and his crew. The German submariners were not out to sink destroyers, they were after tankers, cargo ships, and most importantly, troopships. If the U-473 had hit the HMS *Arawa*, they could have prevented 3,000 American soldiers from invading their homeland. The attack of the U-473 was representative of their battles before them. The 7th would find the Germans to be an enemy who was technically and tactically competent, well equipped, highly courageous and so determined to defend their homeland that many would fight to the death against overwhelming odds.

The experience of the U-boat attack was barely behind the convoy when the seas turned against them. The weather for the first two-thirds of the cruise was reasonably calm, but that ended during the later part of the first week of May. The North Atlantic then turned ugly, and a major storm broke loose. Everything moveable was tied down and secured. Sideboards on the dining tables had to be put up so the men's plates would not slide off and crash mid-meal. The trip went from supreme drudgery to pure misery. Finally, after rounding Ireland, the English shore was a more than welcome sight as the convoy approached it on May 9, 1944.

The HMS *Arawa* sailed up the river Clyde and approached its pier in Liverpool, where a Scotch Highlander band and an American Red Cross welcome station greeted them. Eager to be at the end of their journey, the passengers crowded to one side of the ship to cheer the band, which caused the *Arawa* to cant so excessively that it made her impossible to dock. The men were then ordered below and the ship finally was secured to its slip. Finding their land legs after the rough journey, the battalion happily departed company with the *Arawa*. From the docks, they marched to nearby trains where they were jammed in and transported to Stourbridge, a suburb of Birmingham that is halfway between Liverpool and London. To prepare for the battalion's arrival, an advance party consisting of Major George Tucker, Lieutenant John Gott, and Corporal Quinton Otwell had taken an earlier voyage and had already had set up housing arrangements in the local community. Despite the prior planning, the actual billeting process was still a rather haphazard affair and not everyone had preassigned housing. As the GI's marched through the streets, English housewives stood at the garden gates of their yards indicating how many men they could house. The troops pealed off until everyone had a place to stay.

The subsequent one-month stay in Stourbridge was a pleasant one. On the down side, the British were already five years into their war and the GIs found that just about everything was rationed. Other than simple meals served by the battery cooks, food was scarce and even canteen candy bars were rationed at three per week. Care packages from home were valued more than ever. There were some adjustments that had to be made, with the men learning how to drive on the left side of the road and getting used to the increased daylight hours (in June, it remained light until 10:30 or 11:00 P.M.). The men in some of the more austere homes had to get used to making due with chamber pots instead of flush toilets. Jack French, billeted with Bob Dallman, remembers the night when he accidently dropped both the pot and its contents out of a second story window. Both French and Dallman snuck out the house and crawled around the small victory garden below until the pot was retrieved.

The troops were pleased to find that many of the English, most importantly the women, liked the Americans and a number of friendships were cultivated in the weeks that followed. Children were constantly asking for candy, with the refrain "Got any gum, chum" greeting the troops wherever they went. The men were issued English pounds, which were liberally spent in nearby pubs. As Kurt Rieth reported home, visiting pubs during off duty hours was a popular pastime:

> I don't believe that in any of my letters that I mentioned the English pubs. These of course are the British barrooms, but are much different from the barrooms back in the States. The atmosphere is much nicer and in the better ones you'll find young, middle aged and old people who come in to have a conversation and a few glasses of beer. There are some pretty wild pubs too, especially those frequented by too many soldiers. I usually drop into one for a while when on pass, but don't have more than two or three glasses of beer, because I don't like the [English-brewed] stuff.

Walter Damiano, a draftsmen in A Battery's sound section had this to say about an evening's experience in Stourbridge:

> We would go to the local pubs and drink some of their "bitter" ale or beer until they would call out "time please," that's when the bitters had run out, something which never took us long to do. On one particular evening, an officer from the 7th FAOB came into the pub and told us

we all had to leave because the good people of Stourbridge had decided to do something nice for the "Yanks," and would hold a dance for us. "Oh no!!" was the first reaction—they hadn't even called "time please."

We all gathered at a local hall and were introduced all around. Just before the dance started, a buddy of mine came up to me and showed me a bottle of scotch he said he found in the cloakroom. Since scotch was hard to get at the time, I never questioned his "acquisition."

During the course of the evening it was decided by those who organized the dance to have a Jitterbug contest, with that being the popular dance of the time.

I was very fortunate to have a good dancing partner, and boy could she dance. Her skills, along with my having drunk some of that Scotch, led us to win the contest. We were called to the center of the hall to receive our prize. After a delay, the master of ceremonies informed us that the prize, a bottle of scotch that was kept in the cloakroom, was nowhere to be found!

We settled for a pack of English cigarettes.

To the extent possible, some of the men were able to get out for excursions to the English countryside. Lieutenant Slessman recalled this of his Stourbridge experience. "I was fortunate to be able to make a few trips and visited places such as Shakespeare's home, various American Air Fields, Birmingham, and London. I struck up an acquaintance with a chap in the air corps and we planned to take a short flight across the Channel in his plane one Sunday, but as things turned out, I was unable to get away then. I later learned that he was killed over France, in late August [1944]."

One group of 7th FAOB soldiers who definitely did not enjoy their time in Stourbridge were the A Battery cooks. As told by Mess Sergeant Stephen Wandzioch, the living accommodations were nice enough, with the six cooks living in a big English country home with ten to twelve bedrooms that all had their own fireplaces. The problem was with the kitchen, which was in a separate building behind the main house. The kitchen consisted of only two small wood burning stoves and a sink. With those two tiny stoves, there was no way that the mess section could cook and serve hot food for 150 men. The severe fuel shortage in England compounded the problem as the cooks were prohibited from using their gas burning field ranges. However, no group of people in the world are more in the "make it happen" business than are army cooks. Wandzioch solved the problem by breaking down the brick ovens into a configuration that allowed for more direct heat to cook with. Also, the cooks were on duty around the clock to keep the men fed. To prepare breakfast, they would have to start at 8:00 P.M. and cook throughout the night to have the meal ready for the next morning. The system worked and the A Battery men enjoyed chow as good as could possibly be expected. As a reward for his ingenuity, Wandzioch was "billed good" for the damage inflicted in modifying the original brick stoves. Once the battalion moved to a tented bivouac later in their England stay, the cooks finally had access to the gas burning ranges that greatly simplified their work. Reflecting back, Wandzioch states: "Facing all the hardships of feeding the boys in England, my cooks did a wonderful job and I am very proud of them."

With the 7th FAOB in Stourbridge, the backdrop of the Overlord invasion of France was looming. Lieutenant Slessman noted that "this was prior to the invasion and every day great fleets of bombers would drone over our heads on their way to the continent, and it was quite a spectacle to see them in such large numbers." The battalion kept busy making preparations for their own eventual deployment to France. Vehicles had to be off-loaded from Liverpool and cargo unpacked, cleaned, and made ready for field operations. Once all their equipment was available, a full training cycle resumed, which was made all the more urgent for what would obviously soon be in store.

Security tightened even more, and the men were strictly limited in what could be reported in correspondence back home. Letters sent to the states were now in the form of "V-Mail" (Victory Mail). In order to save precious cargo space, the GIs had to write their letters on specially formatted V-Mail sheets. After being screened and censored from a unit officer, the V-Mail sheets were mimeographed, and then enlarged to postcard size after reaching the States. The mimeographing process required that the handwriting be quite large, or it would be illegible after reduction. Descriptions of the location the men were writing from could be no more specific that "Somewhere in England," or later "Somewhere in France," and eventually "Somewhere in Germany."

Each V-Mail was limited to one page in length, and there could be no mention of any operational activities. While these regulations made good sense at the time from an operational security perspective, they are frustrating to today's historians, as they greatly reduced the common soldier's on-the-spot reflections of their most significant combat experiences. Having to censor the mail was also no fun for the officers, who had to go through endless stacks of mail and blank out inappropriate comments. The one predominate wartime memory that Lt. Marlin Yoder would later leave his family was of his distaste for the necessary, but unpopular task of censoring mail.

It was during this period that the 7th Field Artillery Observation Battalion would become assigned to the XX Corps. From that point forward, the 7th FAOB's membership and function within XX Corps was its single most important command relationship for the remainder of the war.

XX Corps was one of three such organizations (along with XII and XIII Corps) that made up General Patton's famous Third Army. Like an army headquarters, an army corps is purely an operational and administrative headquarters. In World War II, the army eventually fielded twenty-six separate corps in the European and Pacific Theaters. The corps' primary source of battlefield power came from its combat divisions. The corps' armor and infantry divisions (each about 15,000 men in size), could be swapped around with other corps simply by assigning or transferring them to suit mission requirements. Depending on resources and Third Army objectives, there would be between two to six divisions assigned to XX Corps at any given time. In the course of the war, eleven infantry and nine armored divisions would serve under XX Corps control at one point or another.

While the composition of maneuver divisions would constantly change, the corps retained its own pool of special troops, such as artillery battalions, engineers, medical facilities, etc., which always remained permanently assigned.[10] As part of the XX Corps artillery, the 7th FAOB fell in this permanent category. For the firing elements, corps-level artillery was typically heavier in caliber then that assigned to the divisions. The corps-level artillery battalions would often be used for special fire missions that had corps level priority. XX Corps artillery would rely on the 7th FAOB to determine the location of German cannon.

The wartime study of conventional infantry and armor battalions actions is typically viewed in terms of specific battles that occurred at single geographic locations, usually no wider or deeper than several miles. Trying to understand the 7th Field Artillery Observation Battalion's history is quite different, as they would be dispersed throughout the entire XX Corps sector where the front could be anywhere between fifteen and seventy miles wide. As such, the history of the 7th Field Artillery Observation Battalion is actually one and the same of XX Corps operations.

Lieutenant General Walton H. Walker commanded XX Corps throughout its service in the Second World War. Walker, a World War I veteran with longstanding ties to his protégé, General Patton, looked rather like a bulldog with a short, squat frame and a broad face usually set in a ferocious scowl. Like Patton, Walker was the grandson of Confederate officers whose Civil War legacy instilled in him an early interest in a military profession. Also like Patton, Walker first attended the Virginia Military Institute and later secured an appointment to West Point, from which he graduated in 1912. In the First World War, Walker commanded a machine gun battalion and was decorated for heroism. After the war, Walker had a conventional army career, with command and staff assignments that had him serving directly under future army leader George C. Marshall.[11] Walker was a fifty-two-year-old colonel with twenty-nine years of service when World War II broke out.

Patton's biographer, Ladisals Farag, describes Walker irreverently as a "roly-poly tanker." It would seem that Patton was fond of him but did not always take him too seriously. In many ways, he was the shadow of the more illustrious master whom he idolized, sharing his passion for smart appearance, and his energy and drive. Unlike Patton, he was unostentatious, wearing GI Shoes and an ordinary webbing belt. Walker was approachable but it seems that he was never really liked. As Farag goes on to describe, "there was no General Walker popularity cult, no legends, and few anecdotes. His virtue in Patton's eyes was that he did what he was told, which meant that he survived in command of his corps."[12] In summary, Walker's leadership record should not be shortchanged. *Time* magazine gave this description of him in 1950: "Walker was not a colorful prima donna, or an affable diplomat, or a profound strategist, or an egoist with a flair for drama. He was rather a military fundamentalist in every sense of the word, he is an old pro."[13] Ultimately, he must be given credit for the overall excellent record of his unit, labeled by the Germans with a measure of fear and respect as "the Ghost Corps."

As well as marking the epic D-Day invasion of France, June 6, 1944 was also the day that the 7th FAOB moved out of the pleasant comforts of Stourbridge to set up camp at Salisbury Plains. From Stourbridge, Salisbury was a two-hour drive south, and near the eventual departure port of Southampton. While the battalion did not have a direct role in D-Day, the men did get a front row view of the huge air fleets flying overhead on the way to France. Slessman: "The day we moved to Salisbury was D-Day, and I will never forget the huge air armadas that flew over our heads for hours; fighters, bombers, transports towing gliders, in lines further than the eye could see. Everyone was exited and anxious to get started across the channel." Robert Geiges also recalled the incredible sight of endless wave after wave of bombers, transport planes and gliders. Jack French vividly remembered that the sky was black with planes and gliders. Kurt Rieth wrote the sentiments that would later be shared by others in a letter to his parents that was penned on June 6: "Today is the day that Allied forces started the invasion of the continent. I hope you haven't been worrying that we are in it, because we are still here in England. We can just hope for the best now, and feel if everything goes well the war will end much sooner."

With D-Day, all the men now put their thoughts toward the end of the war. Talk was so rampant, that Sergeant Wells of B Battery started a pool for the GI to submit their predictions for the exact date for the surrender of Germany. Ten marks per entry were to be paid to the winner.

The battalion's six-week stay in Salisbury Plains was generally regarded as miserable. The men cared little about the fact that they were posted in the shadow of historic Stonehenge, but rather that they were living in cramped and soggy pup tents. It rained constantly and the men had to sleep directly on the wet ground, with nothing but their blankets between them and the mud. Victor Salem, a tent mate of Kurt Rieth, recalled that every time something touched the canvas of the tents, the rain would drip directly in. The pace of training picked up considerably and included large-scale field exercises with other XX Corps units at the firing ranges of the English Army's Larkhill Base. The battalion used this time as well to fill their ranks up to full strength. A number of men, such as Hank Lizak (A Battery) and Tom Delay (Headquarters Battery) joined the 7th while in England. Lizak, who was initially trained as a radio operator for a tank destroyer battalion, arrived in England in late June and was assigned to the battalion on July 11. Delay came out of a replacement depot and was immediately tasked to be Lieutenant Colonel Schwartz's radioman. Although still weak in Morse code (he only learned how to code up to the letter "e"), Delay figured out he was saddled as the battalion commander's radio operator because he was the new guy and no one else wanted the job. The new men integrated quickly, established friendships, and soon were a part of the 7th FAOB team.

While the 7th received some new men, others were shipped off to other units. A need for experienced observers arose when a ship transporting the 12th FAOB was torpedoed crossing the Atlantic and lost fifty percent of its men. Battery A's Walter Damiano was on guard duty one night when he was told he had one hour to pack and be ready for shipment to the 12th FAOB. Damiano had been a member of the 7th from its origin and was devastated by the news. Without even the chance to say farewell to his buddies, Damiano was ripped away from his army family. Although Damiano eventually went to combat with the 12th, he never again felt the degree of closeness and pride as he did with his 7th FAOB comrades. (Fifty-eight years later, Damiano reflected on the only one possible benefit of the transfer. The 7th FAOB section that he had been assigned to was overrun in March 1945. Had he still been with the unit at that time, Daminao almost certainly would have been either captured, wounded, or killed.)

Not all of the battalion's field time in England was strictly devoted to training, and the opportunity for an actual combat mission came up. German V-1 "Buzz Bomb" rockets – launched from France and Holland—were hitting England hard. B Battery flash observers were sent to northern England to provide some help in trying to pinpoint the inbound missiles. Amos Robinson was sent along with the group to serve as their medic. Amos remembered that they stayed at an English Army camp somewhere in the north. One night during this mission the men had a chance to go back and visit London. It was decided that straws would be drawn and that the loser would have to stay back and guard the trucks. Robinson, whose medic status supposedly made him exempt from guard duty, somehow got roped into the draw and lost. (The results of the effort to locate the Buzz Bombs remain uncertain.)

While in England, some of the battalion's leadership had the opportunity to be present for a classic speech given by their future Third Army commander, General Patton. He made rounds to a number of the units that he would be commanding once Third Army became operational in France, and presented the highly colorful address that would eventually be immortalized in the opening scene of the classic 1970 George C. Scott motion picture *Patton*. The actual speech was considerably more profane than the Hollywood version, and hearing it from Patton's lips would be an event never forgotten by those present.

Getting passes to leave the Salisbury Plains camp and go into town was considerably harder to do than in Stourbridge. When they could get passes, the men were able to do such things as visit the ancient city of Salisbury and see its famous cathedral, go to the movies (where *Madame Curie* was playing), swim at the public pool and even overnight at the USO center there.

By early July, the battalion began to prepare in earnest for shipment to France. The men could not write home of what was going on, but some gave cryptic hints, such as in Kurt Rieth's letter dated July 14, 1944: "Don't be worried if you don't hear from me as regularly or as often as usual for a while. We expect to be very busy and I might not find an opportunity to write whenever I'd like to. Its getting pretty dark now and having no means of getting light, I'll sign off. Lots of Love, Kurt."

Equipment was cleaned and carefully packed in vehicles. To facilitate pending cargo ship loading operations, weight and dimension cards were calculated and posted on the passenger's side window. The movement day finally came on July 15. In long columns, the battalion's trucks pulled out of Salisbury Plains and headed to a marshaling area at Southampton. Once there, a final check of weapons and equipment was made. The GIs were issued K-rations, which were to be their sole source of sustenance until they reached France. Along with the K-rations, the troops were also passed seasickness pills, sulfa tablets, and vomit bags. Money was changed from English pounds and shillings to French francs.

On July 16–17, the battalion left the marshalling area for the port, where they began the task of uploading the vehicles by crane on a Liberty ship. Red Cross girls distributed coffee and doughnuts. That night, officers and men alike slept where they could, in vehicles or on piles of baggage and supplies. Jack French remembers using his backpack for pillow as he slept on a dock. An air raid warning sounded, but otherwise, it was a quiet night. The battalion had VIP company along for the voyage, as their Liberty ship was among the three vessels that would also transport General Walker and his XX Corps headquarters. The

7th FAOB would be among the very first XX Corps units to arrive in France.

By July 17, the loading was complete and the men were all aboard and ready to go. Tom Delay, a headquarters company radio operator who only joined the battalion three days before it left England, remembers taking a Dramamine tablet that night. The pill completely knocked him out and when he awoke the next morning he assumed they were now off the coast of France. Upon going topside, he was stunned to see they were still at dock! The ship finally moved out of Southampton only to make a twenty-four-hour anchorage at nearby Isle of Wight. The next morning, they joined a large convoy of more Liberty ships, as well as other big and small English transports.

Hank Lizak was assigned to guard duty on the ship. While walking the decks, he came across a Merchant Marine sailor whom he knew from radio school at Camp Hood. Having been discharged from the army due to his age, the sailor was able to get into the war by joining the Merchant Marines. The renewed friendship worked to Hank's great advantage, as Lizak was one of the few passengers able to eat in the crew's mess. This enabled him to enjoy food a bit more varied than the canned food-only diet that everyone else had to endure.

In the passage across the English Channel, sleek destroyers raced back and forth as they formed a protective screen and helped to guide the transports. The day was hot and clear, seemingly one of the few for that rainy English summer, and the men and sailors were relieved to see that the waters were calm. Lieutenant Slessman: "We joined a huge convoy of ships loaded down with troops like ours, with trucks sitting on the decks and in the holds. Much to my concern I noted that the ship immediately next to us was flying a red pennant signaling to all that she was an ammunition ship crammed to the top with high explosives." Late that afternoon, the convoy of ships was guided through mine-cleared channels along the French coast, and joined a massive fleet of hundreds of freighters and transports at anchor a short distance from Utah Beach. There were so many ships at Utah Beach that they seemed to disappear over the horizon in all directions. Cannon fire could be discerned in the far distance.

The 7th Field Artillery Observation Battalion had reached the war.

CHAPTER 3

Normandy: The Breakout into France

On D-Day, 175,000 Allied soldiers breached the Nazi's feared Atlantic Wall and began the long awaited invasion of France. In the assault's success, the casualties had been costly, especially for the infantry divisions that stormed Omaha Beach, as well as for the paratroopers who landed inland. Recovering from their initial surprise, the Germans poured tens of thousands of troops into Normandy to offer a better defense and to launch even more desperate counterattacks.

The Normandy campaign can be viewed in two distinct phases; the first was the original assault on the fortified beaches. The second, in which XX Corps participated, was the buildup of a lodgment area large enough for a base from which to launch the all-important breakthrough.

From June 7 to July 24, the American 1st Army fought south and southwest to secure a zone ten miles inland. In the process, they cut off a sizeable German force to the northwest on the Cherbourg Peninsula. To the 1st Army's left, the British 2nd Army was still battling to take Caen, an early D-Day objective that would remain in German hands for two more months. Greatly hampering the Allied advance was the German's highly effective defensive use of the endless network of damnable hedgerows, hardened dirt walls that ran throughout Normandy. Despite the initial success of D-Day, the Allied advance now seemed hopelessly bogged.

Both the Allies and Germans continued to buildup forces for the next inevitable chapter of the campaign. By the time that the 7th FAOB landed in France, more than 800,000 Americans were in Normandy and were facing an army of 750,000 Germans. At Caen, 600,000 British and Canadian armies were attacking a force of Germans that outnumbered them in both men and tanks. In sum, two million soldiers were now pitted against each other in a front that ran over one hundred miles. In the third week of July 1944, an Allied victory in France was by no means assured.

On July 20, the men of the 7th FAOB were still aboard their ships off Utah Beach, impatiently waiting their turn to disembark, when the weather turned against them. In order to form a protective harbor for the thousands of unloading transports, the Allied Navy had scuttled a large arc of derelict ships just offshore. The battalion soon learned however that the man-made port provided insufficient protection from a serious storm. The mild weather that had afforded the smooth channel transit became a violent storm, suspending all unloading operations for another forty-eight hours.

Eating only K-rations for a period of what became seven continuous days, the troops could do nothing but watch the beach from extremely cramped confines of the constantly rolling ships. The ships were so overcrowded that there was not enough space for all the men to fit below the decks, leaving those stuck above exposed to a driving rainstorm. Improvising as best they could, some of the 7th men removed a sheet of canvas that was covering a hold opening and used it as an ad hoc tent. Nighttime brought additional anxiety with the threat of German air raids.

Punctuating the horrors of the D-Day fighting, corpses of dead soldiers would occasionally rise to the surface and float by the ship. Jack French remembers there was an almost a pink tint to the water from all the bloodshed.

Finally, on July 23, the seas calmed enough to allow the ships' cranes to unload the vehicles onto "Water Hippo" transports and landing ship tanks for the short ferry ride to the beach. Most of the vehicles were off-loaded directly onto the beach while men were transported to a huge, specially constructed floating steel pier.

The men had the choice to disembark the Liberty ships from either a Jacob's ladder in the bow, or from a cargo net amidships. Tom Delay, who did not like heights, walked back and forth four times trying to decide between the two alternatives, not caring much for either. He finally selected the cargo net, as it was positioned directly over the canopy of a large truck, an object at least relatively soft and could break the fall should he slip. Bill Williamson remembers instructions he received while climbing down the rope ladder into the bobbing landing craft. At the end of the ladder, a sailor was urging the men to jump onto the barge only when it was descending into a wave. To hit the deck when it was rising could result in broken ankles.

As the transports moved toward shore, a disagreement arose between one of the landing craft crews and the beachmaster who controlled the inbound transport traffic. The storm interfered with the unloading schedule and increased the pressure to empty the ships as quickly as possible. This meant the trucks had to unload at a higher tide than the landing craft chief thought safe. Despite the concerns, the beachmaster gave a definitive "go ahead" order and the trucks were launched. Driving off the ramps, the men held their breath while the sea advanced up to the running boards of the trucks. As it turned out, they all made it up to the beach. It would have been a different story, however, had any of the trucks driven into a shell hole or hit some other obstacle.

Stephen Wandzioch on the movement to the beach: "I was on this landing craft with my kitchen truck-trailer and cooks headed for the shores of France. The operator of the craft told me he would drop the tailgate into three or four feet of water. We landed in about two feet. Thank the good Lord that my driver, Leonard 'Hog Head' Bamkin did a wonderful job of waterproofing the truck, and we hit the shore with no trouble at all."

Moving onto the Utah Beach, the men were stunned by the scope of the invasion effort and the evidence of the epic D-Day battle that took place there six weeks earlier. Most notable were the remnants of the German defenses—blasted emplacements where heavy cannon had been and pock-mocked reinforced concrete bunkers. Shattered equipment of every type that was destroyed in the June 6 fighting still littered the area, and the sandy beaches were pocketed with craters from shells and bombs. The men observed long lines of inbound troops streaming from the transports and toward the front lines and wounded men being loaded onto other vessels for shipment to England. They also got their first glimpses of Wehrmacht soldiers as large lines of passing German prisoners awaited transport to distant British and American POW camps. Kurt Rieth wrote home of his observation on the POWs at Utah Beach. Unimpressed at the shoddy appearance and lack of warrior qualities from these initial batches of German prisoners, he wryly reflected that the tougher ones would not be the first to surrender.

It was dark by the time most of the battalion was fully ashore. In blackout drive, which only provided the very dimmest of light to steer by, the vehicles moved forward to a bivouac field near St. Mere Eglise. Some of the vehicles were separated from the main body. Stephen Wandzioch's mess truck drove about a quarter of a mile off the beach when they came to a "Y" intersection. There were no signs or soldier guides to direct them. Wandzioch came across an old Frenchmen who pointed to the road to the left. They took the directions and sure enough linked up with the rest of the unit.

Not everybody made it off the ship that day. Headquarters Battery carpenter Ed Shock had this experience off-loading at Utah Beach:

> We were loaded on Liberty ships for the crossing, then transferred to landing crafts to unload at the beach. My truck was the last truck to be transferred to the landing craft, and the only one on that particular boat. When we got to the landing spot, it was dark, and the boat captain said he wasn't going to unload me until morning. I had to spend that night on the landing craft. Later in the night we were strafed by a German airplane. The boat captain told me to shoot at the plane with the little (.30 cal.) carbine in my possession. I soon realized that my little gun wouldn't have any effect on that plane, so I crawled under the truck axle and spent the rest of the night there. In the early morning, I was unloaded at an empty beach. I asked the captain where I was supposed to go, as my outfit had long since disappeared. He pointed to a road and said, just drive down that road. I drove for about three miles on a route that was lined with wrecked trucks, tanks, jeeps, etc. It gave me an uncomfortable feeling. Here I was, all alone in a foreign land, not knowing where I was going, or where my outfit was. After a while I spotted a jeep headed toward me—was it friend or foe? It turned out to be Sergeants Robert Siebels and Raymond Mitchell, out looking for me. I was really glad to see them, and they were relieved to find me—and my truck!

Corporal Charlie Wright records this memory of his first night in France:

Moving inland from the beach was visual and mental relief. The narrow road was welcome. Proceeding a short distance, we entered a rectangular field surrounded by hedge rows. It was twilight as we dismounted. The orders were fallout and dig in.!! I soon found a nice ditch alongside the hedgerow, requiring minimal digging. Needless to say, the first night in a combat area, what with the sounds of artillery and smalls arms fire, was nerve wracking. After a while I managed to go to sleep. The next morning, gear packed, I squeezed through the hedge to see what might be on the other side. WOW, surprise, surprise. There in a neat stack were about a hundred German anti-tank rockets. All I could think of was what if a round had dropped in here last night!

Although the battalion was still well behind the front lines, the act of spending the first night in a combat zone was nerve-wracking enough, and the muffled cannon fire further encouraged the men to dig deep foxholes before bedding down. Robert Geiges recalled that orders were given that if even so much light as a cigarette was seen, it was to be shot out. It was also disconcerting that the men were sleeping among huge stacks of artillery ammunition.

The town of St. Mere Eglise was the scene of a major battle in the opening hours of D-Day, when troopers of the 82nd Airborne Division fought hard to wrest it from German control. As daylight broke, the battalion had a close look at the devastation inflicted by modern weaponry in a full-scale battle. The village itself was shattered, and the surrounding fields were full of twisted trees, shell holes, active mine fields, burned out tanks, abandoned artillery, smashed vehicles of every description, and above all, vast amounts of discarded equipment, clothing, and litter. The smell of death and cordite hung through the air.

July 25 was an important transitional day for the battalion. In movement to the next staging location on the southwestern edge of the Cherburg Peninsula, the men would be exposed to sights that ranged from grand to horrific and leaving images that would never be forgotten.

That morning, the battalion moved out of St. Mere Eglise and drove fifteen miles west to the XX Corps assembly area in the vicinity of St. Jacques de Nehou. As the men readied for departure, they were able to witness the largest tactical air strike of World War II. The aerial bombardment was in support of Operation Cobra, an all out effort designed to break out of Normandy and into northern France. Looking skyward in awe, they watched squadron after squadron of Flying Fortresses and Liberators, medium bombers, and fighters fly past on their way to blast the German lines west of St. Lo. This enormous carpet-bombing involved 1,800 planes dropping more than 15,000 tons of explosives on the Germans. Combined with a front line artillery bombardment of 50,000 shells, this would be the largest expenditure of explosives in any single attack in the US Army's history.[14] Not all the bombs struck Germans, as 111 GIs were killed (including General Lesley McNair, Chief of the army ground forces) and another 500 were wounded when some of the missions went astray. Although the Germans in the target area were terribly battered, they were still able to repulse the approaching American infantry and armor assaults for the next two days. Additional American air attacks and artillery barrages followed, and finally on July 27, the German lines began to crack.

As the fighters and bombers flew endlessly overhead, the 7th FAOB continued their drive to St. Jacques de Nehou. On the route, the troops passed a number of the towns such as Montebourg and Valognes, which were completely destroyed beyond all recognition. For Hank Lizak of A Battery, more disturbing sights were soon to come. Advancing toward the front, he noticed a two and a half ton truck heading back toward the beaches with a cargo full of recently killed American soldiers—their uncovered and bloody bodies stacked like a cord of wood. The sight of these dead young soldiers, wearing the same uniform as he, was an unnerving and stark reminder of what fate may await him. Intellectually, all the men knew that death was a product of war, but that it somehow was only in store for the other guy. Now, viewed up close, battlefield slaughter was no longer an abstract concept. This terrible image remained with Hank forever, and he considered it the one time in the war that he was truly scared.

A more positive reminder of why the battalion was at war in France came in the reaction of the French people, who overwhelmed the Americans with the joy of their liberation. Throngs of Frenchmen crowded the roads to welcome the troops with open arms and open bottles. K-rations were gladly traded for fresh eggs and potent Cavados, a Normandy liquor powerful enough make even the strongest drinkers shudder. Stephen Wandzioch remembers this day:

> Ladies and young girls jumped on the running boards of the trucks and showered us with hugs and kisses. The expressions of these female faces showed joy and gladness, happiness and relief, and looks that will live in my memory forever, for I am sure they must have had one hell of a bad life under the German's rule. They must have felt a great relief that we were there and they were free once again.

Wandzioch and his driver stopped at a small town to fill up water cans when he came upon this scene:

> As we were pumping the water with the help of a Frenchman who spoke Polish, I heard the distant banging of drums and loud cheers that was getting closer. We looked up the road and saw a crowd of people coming down the street. As they passed us we could see the crowd jeer at about twenty-five or thirty naked women with shaved heads. I asked the Frenchman in Polish what was going on. He told me that these women had slept with German soldiers and were being run out of town. The people of the village were not at all concerned with whatever may happen to these women.

Edward Marinello made a similar trip with the 286th FAOB when they went into Normandy.

Although his arrival was two months after the 7th FAOB's disembarkment, he provides a compelling view on the thoughts of an inexperienced young soldier on his first journey into a battle zone.

> As soon as the men mounted, a convoy was formed that moved inland, and after a while the first roads sign introduced the town of St. Laurent. The mist was to lift slowly that day. The sixty or so vehicles continued to make their way over mauled roads, through destroyed towns and villages that before the invasion had never heard more than the crash of thunder, the crackle of lightning. As the trucks rumbled deeper into the ruined environment the men sat silently, perhaps pondering a multitude of things connected to the looming adventure, the dimensions of which they couldn't fathom, couldn't dismiss. The morning's haunting unpleasantness hinted at the brooding and brutal times ahead. In a real sense, the unsuspecting men were beginning a journey into themselves, an introspective look-see, as it were, preparing to meet, singly and together, challenges that couldn't have been imagined and would never be surpassed. At the end of that journey they would no longer be who they once were. It wasn't a matter of maturing, though it was that too. It was more that they would experience life as few men do, on its noblest, most testing levels. One result of the grand experience was to leave them with a sense of apartness from the vast majority of those who never shared in it.[15]

By the evening of July 25, the 7th FAOB reached its destination and pulled into an apple orchard near St. Jacques de Nehou, which was then about ten miles behind the front lines. This was to be their base of operations for the next eleven days. Wary of possible mine fields, the area first had to be cleared by mine detectors. While a lot of old coins, C-ration cans, and other assorted junk was dug up, the area was eventually declared as "safe" and the men were allowed to set up. Incorporating the naturally strong cover of the ever-present hedgerows, foxholes and slit trenches were dug, tents were raised, and vehicles carefully camouflaged.

The weather was wet and dreary and the conditions generally uncomfortable. Reminders of the relative proximity to the front came in the constant cannonade to the south and in the occasional drone of German Heinie bombers making their random nightly "Bed-check Charley" strikes. The battalion was still far enough to the rear that occasionally the men could drive to nearby streams to bathe. The overall experience at this assembly area served the 7th well by helping make an effective and gradual transition adjusting to combat conditions. The battalion made good use of their time at Jacques de Nehou to get their equipment in first-rate condition and to polish up on forward observation techniques.

On August 1, 1944, the Third United States Army officially became operational and took control of XX Corps. The legend of the Third Army would become synonymous with its colorful commander, General George G. Patton, Jr. His leadership of Third Army would forever give bragging rights to all 7th FAOB soldiers with the claim that they served with Patton. To understand something about the nature of Patton is to better understand the circumstances of how the 7th FAOB would be employed in the invasion of Europe. Patton is one of America's premier military heroes and is a fascinating character study.

Born to a well-to-do California family in 1885, Patton was a legacy of prominent Confederate officers. The Civil War had a major effect on Patton's family, as both his grandfather and granduncle were killed leading Virginia regiments in battles at Winchester and Gettysburg. Left destitute at the war's end, Patton's grandmother abandoned Virginia and resettled to California, where the former Patton family wealth was eventually rebuilt. As a young child, Patton was steeped in the lore of his family's military heritage and forever recognized a calling to be a great army leader. Although not formally schooled until he was twelve, Patton was closely tutored by his spinster aunt, and took a deep interest in Bible study and all aspects of ancient and modern history. Although brilliant in retaining oral studies, Patton suffered from dyslexia, which was then an unknown condition. While he would overcome the effects of dyslexia by sheer force of will, it forever made formal academic study extremely difficult for him.

Like his grandfather and father before him, Patton entered the Virginia Military Institute when he was eighteen. Desiring the guarantee of an army career above all else, Patton lusted for attendance at West Point, and with great effort, secured an appointment there in 1904. While he did well in leadership and athletic pursuits, Patton's dyslexia caused him to almost fail out of the Academy his plebe (freshman) year. Through his exceptional intellect and extraordinary personal drive, he persevered and was able to graduate in 1909 with a commission as a second lieutenant of cavalry.

Shortly after graduation, Patton married into an extremely wealthy New England family. Throughout his thirty-six-year long army career, money was never a worry for him. He had a compulsive drive to be the best in everything he did and never lost sight of his destiny to become a three-star general and command a large army in combat. Even as a young lieutenant assigned to horse cavalry posts at Fort Sheridan and Fort Myers, Patton would sometimes stand next to targets at rifle practice just to face the fear of having bullets whiz by his ears. He soon became bored with the daily grind of peacetime army life. But life as a cavalry officer did offer some major lifestyle benefits, as polo and equestrian competition were very much in the army officer culture of the day. At various stages in his career Patton, typically owned a personal stable of a dozen or so polo ponies that he would bring from post to post. In addition to being athletically gifted, Patton pushed himself to the extreme, and was selected to participate as an army representative to the U.S. Pentathlon Team in the 1912 Olympiad in Stockholm, Sweden. The events consisted of pistol shooting, a 300-meter swim, fencing, a 5,000 meter steeple chase, and a 4,000 meter cross country run. He finished the run in third place, but almost died from severe dehydration. Had he not performed poorly in the pistol shoot, Patton may well have won a medal.

Following the Olympics, Patton returned to the cavalry. In 1916, he finally had the opportunity to see some combat when serving in General John "Black Jack" Pershing's incursion into Mexico to attack bandit Pancho Villa. Villa had been raiding American border towns, and Pershing was charged to lead a cavalry expedition to bring him to justice. Patton finagled an assignment as Pershing's aide, and developed a relationship with the general that helped propel his career in the years that followed. While temporarily attached to a motorized patrol, Patton achieved national fame by killing one of Pancho Villa's key lieutenants with his revolver during an impromptu firefight. Years later, Patton's trademark became pearl-handled revolvers that he wore on his pistol belt. When asked why he carried revolvers, Patton's response was that he used such weapons to "kill his first men."

World War I finally presented Patton with his first opportunity to led men in real battle. Initially assigned as the commander of Pershing's headquarters staff, Patton seized the opportunity to be one of the first American officers selected to create the American Expeditionary Forces (AEF) fledging tank corps. Within one year he had gone from captain to colonel, and became the commander of the AEF's only light tank brigade. He pushed himself and his men unmercifully, creating a doctrine from scratch, fighting for equipment, and creating a elite fighting force in the process. Patton led the brigade into combat for the first time in September 1918 as American forces broke through German lines at St. Michel. In the battle, Patton could be found where the fighting was the thickest and he showed his troops great personal courage. Although beset with mechanical and communication problems, the American tanks acquitted themselves well in the battle and earned recognition for their future combat potential.

Patton's tanks were again in the lead when the AEF launched the Muese-Argonne Offensive in late September 1918, a campaign that led to Germany's defeat one month later. At a critically decisive point in the opening phase of the battle, several of Patton's tanks and a horde of leaderless infantry were pinned down in a ditch by unrelenting artillery fire and dozens of German machine-guns. To advance seemed like certain suicide and remaining in place was hardly better. With all seeming lost, Patton had an epiphany. Looking into the clouds above he saw a vision of his slain Confederate grandfather and granduncle beckoning him to move forward. Leading four infantrymen plus his orderly, Patton dashed into the curtain of enemy fire. The four infantrymen were immediately killed and Patton himself sustained a serious wound to his hip. The small charge sparked other Americans forward, and by the end of the day the German positions were turned and the Americans possessed the fields.

Patton's combat service in World War I was over, but he had established himself as one of the army's top experts on tank warfare. Patton's World War I experience also solidified his driving obsession for offense. Patton sincerely believed bold offensive warfare actually saved his own men's lives while being the surest way to victory.

In the aftermath of the war, the army was greatly reduced in size, and Patton was lucky to revert to a regular army rank of major. Despite the promise showed by the tank corps, the army refused to recognize armor as a separate combat arm. Poorly funded, the US Army tank corps was relegated to a secondary role until the eve of the Second World War.

In peacetime, Patton was a caged tiger, whose passion for reckless polo and equestrian matches were the only outlets for his need to again lead men in combat. Patton had a series of professional schooling and cavalry assignments in the inter-war years, with his enormous sense of drive rating notice from Army Chief of Staff General George Marshall, Secretary of War Henry Stimson, and even President Roosevelt. With the army's great mobilization of 1940-41, Patton's ship had come in. Finally promoted to general officer after thirty-one years of service, Patton took command of the 2nd Armored Division (where his draconian approach earned him the nickname of "Old Blood and Guts") and then the 1st Armored Corps.

Patton rose to real national prominence in the 1942 and 1943 campaigns in North Africa and Sicily. He brilliantly played the press, which further elevated his reputation in the public eye. The flip side of having such press attention came about when he was widely blasted for striking two shell-shocked privates at a hospital in Sicily in 1943. Disgraced and put in charge of the then "paper army" in England, he served in the role of a decoy to the Germans, who mistakenly thought he would be leading an invasion force to Calais. With the activation of Third Army on August 1, Patton, then fifty-nine, had the chance to redeem himself and fulfill his lifelong ambition as he readied to unleash his 315,000-man force for the greatest campaign in military history.[16] Carlo D'este, in his brilliant biography, *Patton, A Genius for War*, aptly characterizes the general with the following description:

> Patton was an authentic and flamboyant military genius whose entire life was spent in preparation for a fleeting opportunity to become one of the great captains of history. No soldier in the annals of the U.S. Army ever worked more diligently to prepare himself for high command than did Patton. However, it was not only his astonishingly breadth of professional reading and writing that separated Patton from his peers. But that intangible instinctive sense of what must be done in the heat of chaos of battle: in short, that special genius for war that has been granted to only a select few, such as Robert E. Lee and Field Marshal Erwin Rommel. Who but Patton would have tramped the back roads of Normandy in 1913 with a Michelin map to study the terrain because he believed he would someday fight a major battle there? Patton's great success on the battlefield did not come about by chance but rather from a lifetime of study and preparation. He was an authentic intellectual whose study of war, history and the profession of arms was extraordinary.[17]

By the end of July 1944, Third Army was ready to stand up and enter combat. On July 27, the First Army's breakthrough out of the Normandy pocket finally began to take full swing. Making excellent use of closely coordinated air and artillery support, the First Army pushed its infantry and tanks through

German defenses and around to their rear. Key road junctions were suddenly under American control, dooming German countermeasures. The American punches continued to land hard, and the German left flank became exposed.

General Omar Bradley, now in command of the 12th Army Group that included both 1st and Third Armies, saw a tremendous and potentially war-ending opportunity. With the 1st Army and the British holding the surviving Germans in place, Patton and the Third Army would blast south around their open flank, and then turn east and north in a daring dash to isolate the German 7th Army in the region between Normandy and Paris. The area where the Germans would be trapped was to become known as the Falaise pocket. This mission was well suited to Patton's aggressive approach, and the plan was put into action on Third Army's inaugural day.

XX Corps began its part of the Third Army attack on August 3, when its headquarters closed up to the front. The 7th FAOB's turn to move forward came on August 5, when they departed St. Jacques de Nehou. The battalion loaded up and drove one hundred miles south to the next XX Corps assembly area near St. Hilaire. Robert Geiges remembers this among the battalion's first movements in France. Despite some bad weather, the men had to drive with the windshields and overhead canvas tied down. While this would give them better visibility in the event of air raids, they also had to suffer the elements. While a lot of other units allowed their men to cut corners and keep the canvases and windshields up, Lieutenant Colonel Schwartz was a stickler for doing things the "army way." The men of the 7th got soaked while they watched their less vigilant comrades from other units remain dry. Over the next year however, that sense of heightened alertness would pay off, for indeed there were many instances where a 7th FAOB soldier's quick reaction saved men's lives during German aerial attacks.

As the 7th was pulling into position, Patton was pushing the remainder of Third Army through the breakthrough corridor. Once through this gap, Third Army forces were to fan out in four different directions to attack into the heart of France. Just the act of getting the Third Army into battle was a tremendous logistical challenge. An entire army consisting of 200,000 men and 40,000 vehicles was put through a "straw" of a narrow two-lane road at high speed. Once through the straw, full divisions came out intact and ready for battle. Great credit must be given to Patton and his Third Army staff for their excellent planning and execution of this difficult and vitally important accomplishment.[18] It was during this movement that many men of the 7th had their first view of their new army commander. Lieutenant Slessman recalls being in a monstrous traffic jam which was caused by a laundry unit that had somehow tied up a key intersection. The traffic suddenly started moving again and there was Patton, personally—and no doubt profanely—directing traffic and successfully clearing the jam. There was no question that this general meant business when he ordered his army to move forward.

Hitler, meanwhile, had his own plans to reverse the recent string of German Army misfortunes in France. Acting as he often did upon hearing bad news, Hitler rejected the advice of his generals who urged that the 7th Army be allowed cut its losses, retreat, and take up strong positions closer to the German border. Although badly beaten up, they still retained enough combat strength to make a formidable resistance along a number of more effectively defended river barriers east of Paris. This tactic would also buy the Germans time to make additional improvements along their heavily fortified "Siegfried" line that ran the length of the German border. Hitler would have none of this and instead demanded that his forces attack against the narrow apex of the Third and 1st Armies. His ultimate plan was to cut off Patton's vulnerable twenty-mile supply line and then destroy the Third Army in place. With Patton eliminated, the Germans could throw the Americans back to the more easily defended, hedgerow filled terrain of Normandy. Marshaling more forces, the German Army could then destroy the Allies in place and force any surviving enemy forces back across the English Channel.

Hitler launched this counteroffensive from Mortain on August 5. The immediate objective of the

German attack would be to take the city of Avranches on the west coast of the Channel. The attack was to be conducted by fresh troops from six armored divisions of the German 15th Army, units that had been previously posted to the northwest on the Seine. The only American combat unit in place in the Mortain sector to contest the six-division German spearhead was the 30th Infantry Division. Through Allied "Ultra" intercepts of German communication cables that outlined operational planning, General Dwight Eisenhower not only knew that the attack was coming, but in fact welcomed it. With overwhelming American air and artillery superiority, Eisenhower assessed that the impending German counteroffensive would enable the Allies the opportunity to draw out and destroy many more enemy troops. While the 30th Infantry Division dug in and braced for the German attack, Patton continued south to seek the enemy's flank and rear.

On the day of the German counterattack, the 7th FAOB's location at St. Hillarie placed them smack in the middle of the twenty-mile corridor that was the focal point of the assault. As the German tanks and infantry plunged into the 30th Division's front, bombers of the Luftwaffe struck at strategic targets in the rear, catching the 7th FAOB (along with the XX Corps and Third Army Headquarters) in their sights as well. This was to be the 7th's first direct exposure to sustained enemy attack. For two consecutive nights the 7th FAOB's assembly area was pounded by waves of Luftwaffe bombers trying to destroy a Bailey Bridge that the Americans had built across the Selune River.

XX Corps had established an anti-aircraft zone extending ten miles north and south of the river and eight miles east of St. Hillarie. A multitude of anti-aircraft weaponry was deployed to defend this airspace. The attacks came at night. The first German planes dropped flares to illuminate the targets for the following aircraft. The ground then shook with the impact of high explosive bombs as streams of tracers from American antiaircraft guns flew upward. The effectiveness of the anti-aircraft fire was occasionally evident when sudden bursts of flames could be viewed in the sky as the shells found their marks, followed by a wildly spiraling and spectacular crash of German bombers. Hank Lizak remembered that in at least one lull in the bombing, some of the more hearty men emerged from their positions and launched into singing such songs as "the Wabash Cannonball" and "The Rose of San Antoine." Rather than watching the fireworks above, most of the men were more intent on burrowing into the earth below. They crawled low in their foxholes and rode out the attacks as best they could, making the holes deeper in between the attacks. Amos Robinson recalls how his foxhole was burrowed into a hedgerow and had incorporated overhead cover, a feature he was glad to have built with all the explosions overhead. Not everybody had full trust of their foxholes. Ed Shock had opted to dig one large foxhole along with two of his buddies, covering the top of it with logs and brush. Describing the position, Shock recalled: "We were pretty proud of our project. Later in the night, the Germans began bombing a bridge close to us. We started thinking about being buried alive, so we bailed out of the foxhole. I spent most of the nights during those bombings under my truck."

Patton, with his Third Army Headquarters staff, was also in the same vicinity of the bombings. Carlos D'este, in "Patton, A Genius for War" describes the scene: "Bombs began falling nearby, and for many of the younger men of the Third Army staff it was their first taste of war. Most not on duty took shelter in nearby hedgerows. Patton sat in a deck chair in a nearby field, a cigar in his hand, cursing: "Those goddamned bastards, those rotten sons-of-bitches! We'll get them! We'll get them!" The word spread that if Patton was not afraid, there was no reason for anyone else to be either.[19] In all, over thirty German bombers were shot down in the air raids.[20] Although it was an arduous two nights, all the men from the 7th came through unscathed. After it was over, many joked about the numerous "uninvited guests" who dove into already occupied one-man positions at the beginning of the air raids. At any rate, the 7th had now been baptized by some real fire.

While the 7th FAOB was being bombed at St. Hilaire on August 6, XX Corps received their first operational mission, and it was to be a tall order. The primary mission was to extend the 12th Army Group's zone deep to the south. This attack would open up open maneuver room for a cascading army of tanks,

John K. Rieth

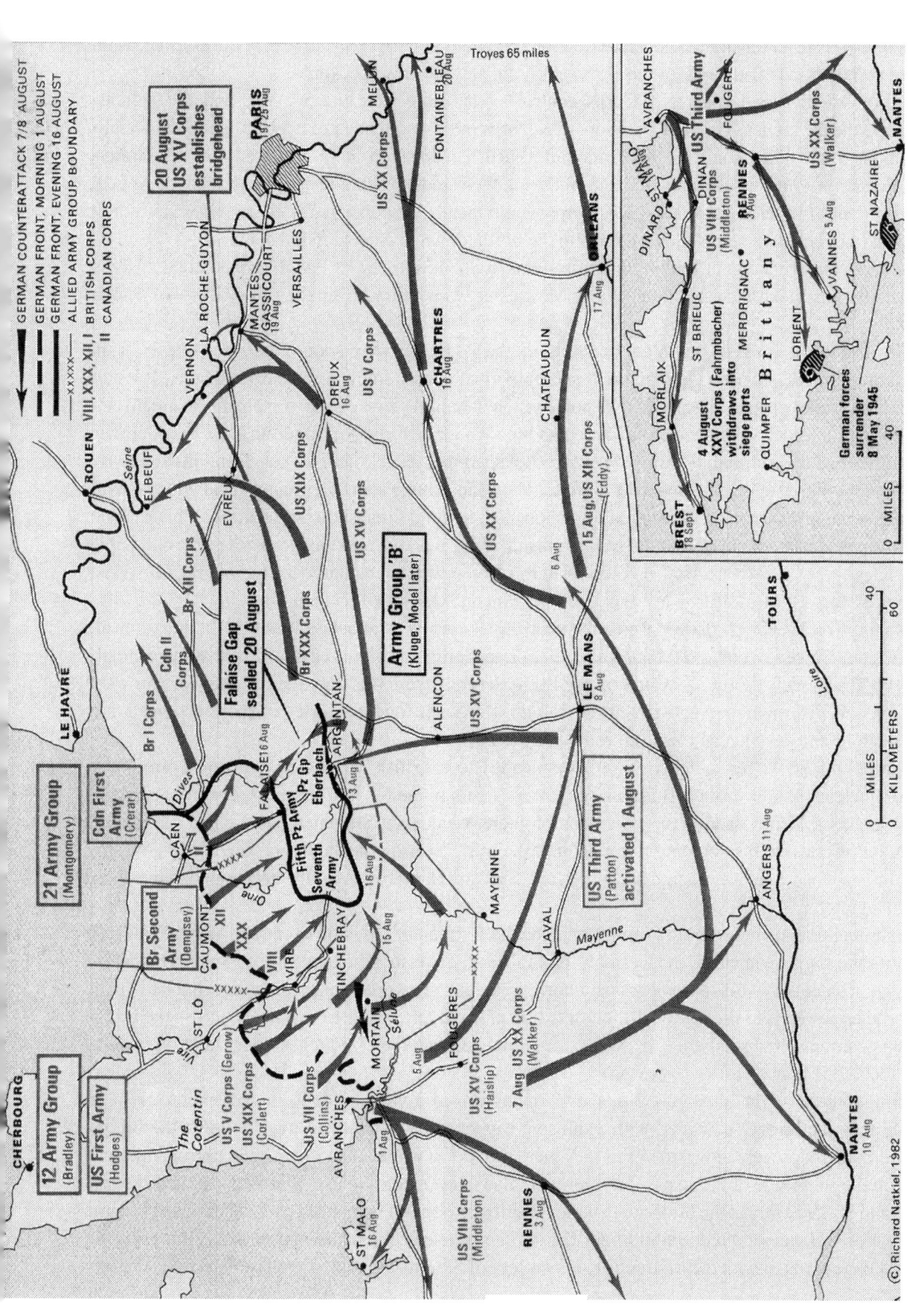

THE ALLIED BREAKOUT FROM NORMANDY

After two months of bitter fighting in Normandy, the Allies began an all out assault to break out of the Cotentin Peninsula in late July 1944. Third Army, activated on August 1, broke through the Avranches Gap into Brittany and Central France. Meanwhile, the Germans struck from Mortain in a failed attempt to cut off Patton. On August 7, XX Corps moved south towards Angers. Simultaneously, XX Corps shifted direction and moved northeast, taking Le Mans, Chartres and Fontainbleau as he race across France moved into high gear. Some 7th FAOB elements came within 15 miles of Paris by mid-August.

infantry, cannon and support forces to pour into. Once about 200 miles south of the invasion beaches, the corps would turn east and toward the general direction just south of Paris. Speed was of the essence, as the Allies were racing to cut off the rear of the German salient at the Falaise pocket.

The combat divisions under XX Corps control at this time were the 5th, 35th, and 80th Infantry Divisions, and the 2nd French Armored Division. XX Corps initially intended to concentrate in the vicinity of Vitre, about thirty miles south of the headquarters' current location at St. Hilaire. The 5th Infantry Division, already at Vitre, would take the lead on the southern most push, and capture the city of Angers, another thirty miles farther to the south. XX Corps would then be responsible for enormous seventy-mile wide zone that ran below the embattled Mortain in the north, down to Angers in the south.

Eager to leave the target of Luftwaffe bomb sights at St. Hilaire, the 7th FAOB moved out on August 7 and drove fifty miles south to a position near La Mortinanis, where they began their first offensive combat operations.

Following in the wake of the initial penetration, the 7th FAOB were soon close on the heels of the battered German forces. Broken German units and individual enemy soldiers were everywhere. It would be a couple of A Battery cooks that would take some of the battalion's first enemy prisoners. While driving on a dirt road en route to a water depot, Staff Sergeant Stan Wandzioch and Art Vogelsang saw two Germans dart across the road and run into a barn. The two cooks stopped their truck, as Vogelsang moved to the back of the barn while Wandzioch covered the front. Vogelsang spoke some German and called for enemy troops to come out and surrender. When nothing happened, he fired three shots in the air with his carbine, while Wandzioch shot a couple of rounds from his pistol. That worked, and the Germans came out, hands in the air. They turned out to be boys—no older than fourteen or fifteen, but large for their ages. The cooks turned the prisoners over to a nearby POW collection point and continued on their way.

In support of XX Corps main push to the south, B Battery was attached to the 5th Infantry for the attack on Angers. Angers, a city of 80,000, was an important communications center as well as main supply depot for the 7th Germany Army. Located on the Loire River, Angers was defended by the German's 16th Infantry Division. Throughout August 7, the 5th Infantry Division fought a series of sharp actions at key road intersections and at principal towns en route to the city.

In order to take Angers quickly, XX Corps needed to establish a crossing over the Loire River. Along with the lead infantry troops, B Battery observers set up in the town of Pruniers, directly across the river from Angers. While standing next to a church there, Lieutenant Slessman had a close call when a sniper's bullet just missed his nose and slammed into the wall, "scaring the daylights" out of him. Nearby American infantrymen were able to find the sniper, and Slessman later bypassed the dead marksman, whose body lay in a gutter.

A lightning dash launched from Pruniers enabled the 5th Infantry Division to capture an intact railroad bridge across the river. Somehow, the Germans had failed to detonate a boxcar full of explosives that sat on the bridge. Under heavy fire, a tremendously brave light tank crew drove onto the bridge, hitched up the boxcar, and then towed it to the safety of the north side of the river. Other troops raced across the bridge and took up position on the southern end. While the Americans had their bridgehead over the Loire, it was a tenuous toehold at best.

Throughout the night of August 7-8, the Germans staged a vicious nighttime counterattack in an effort to destroy the bridge. Loaded with explosive sapper charges intended to take down the bridge, fanatical German troops were blown to bits as they were shot down while attacking the thin line of American defenders on the south side of the span. The Germans also made extensive use of artillery in their defense of Angers, and blasted away at the bridge and at the American troops on both sides of it. These guns became the objective of B Battery's direction-finding. During the course of the battle of Angers, B Battery's fire adjustments were credited with the destruction of a battery of 88-mm cannon, as well as detecting a battery of medium caliber howitzers and one large railroad gun (which was out of range of the American cannon). With massive artillery support, the 5th Infantry Division was able to expand the bridgehead and infiltrate the city. By August 10, German resistance collapsed and Angers was in XX Corps hands. American forces were received as conquering heroes, with jubilant French citizens throwing flowers on their columns and offering the men wine. The German 16th Division was destroyed as a fighting force, with 1,834 enemy prisoners taken. The cost to the leading 5th Infantry Division units was heavy, with the 3rd Battalion of the 2nd Infantry Regiment alone losing 47 killed, and 99 wounded.[21] The reality of the American casualties in this first major XX Corps battle came home to B Battery flash observer Bill Williamson as he watched stacks of dead GIs being loaded on trailers. To the north, events related to the major German counterattack now underway at Mortain would result in major modifications to the XX Corps original mission.

Under VII Corps responsibility, the twenty-mile-wide zone between Mortain and the coast at Avranches continued to be the objective of the German 15th Army attacks. The defense by the 30th Infantry Division against this tide was among the most stoic and effective in the annals of the army's history. For three days, an overwhelming force of German tanks, infantry, artillery, and aircraft battered away on the 30th Division's defensive positions. A brief description of a segment of this battle demonstrates the value of forward observers as a decisive power on the battlefield.

One of the 30th Division's infantry battalions, the 2nd Battalion, 120th Infantry, was surrounded and cut off on Hill 317. The small American force on top of this critically important position was one that the Germans could not afford to bypass. Artillery observers posted with the infantrymen had a twenty-mile panoramic view that enabled them to pound the German rear lines with accurate artillery fire and air strikes. Two German SS Panzer Divisions spearheaded the attack against the 2nd Battalion. The attacks lasted five days and were relentless. So was the American artillery firing in response. German artillery could not be positioned without being observed from the hill, and battery after battery was destroyed or neutralized by the American guns. Despite the long odds and severe shortages of men, ammunition, food, and medical supplies, the 2nd Battalion was able to hang on by the narrowest of margins during the five-day siege. The 2nd Battalion held, but by the time the attacks were over, 300 of the 700 defenders of Hill 317 were either killed or wounded.

Field Marshall Kluge, responsible for the German Army Group making the attacks, begged to be allowed to retreat, but Hitler refused. In addition to suffering tremendous losses in men and equipment, Hitler's obsession to cut off Patton resulted in the exposure of the German left flank to a XX Corps counterattack.

On August 7, XX Corps commander Walton Walker ordered the 35th Infantry Division to turn north and hit the exposed German flank. Reinforcing the thin corridor, Walker also posted the French 2nd Army Division in the vicinity of St. Hilaire. Supported with elements from the 7th FAOB, two combat commands from the 35th Division ripped into the German 4th SS Panzer Grenadier Regiment.

For Lieutenant Colonel Schwartz (as well as the XX Corps headquarters staff), the command, control, and communication challenges were enormous. The 5th Infantry was fighting for Angers in the south, the 35th Infantry was leading an attack at Mortain, causing 7th FAOB elements to fight in two separate directions over a seventy-mile-wide front. One soldier especially busy was Tom Delay, the recent arrival who was given the unenviable job of being Schwartz's radio operator in the "Headquarters 1" command car. Simultaneously working two ten-switch radios, Delay had to be in constant contact with the widely dispersed A and B Batteries, as well as with Corps artillery headquarters. For the battalion as a whole, this is where the years of intensive training paid off. The line officers, NCOs, and men knew their business, and did whatever it took to execute the mission with minimal supervision from higher headquarters. The professional performance of the 7th FAOB and the XX Corps artillery group in their first days of combat is testimony to their arriving on the battlefield extremely well prepared.

The 180-degree change of corps direction wreaked particular havoc on B Battery, which was in the midst of enjoying the triumphant entry into Angers as they received new orders. B Battery was first to rejoin battalion headquarters at Laval, sixty miles to the north. After having gone through several days of heavy combat with little sleep, B Battery arrived at Laval at 2:00 A.M. Once there, new instructions were issued. The battery was now to proceed another thirty miles north to join combat commands being formed to attack the Germans engaged in the Mortain fight. B Battery was back on the road one hour later, and reached their combat commands by 8:00 A.M. Lieutenant Slessman had a harrowing experience on this journey when a German soldier jumped out of the brush and fired a burp gun at his jeep. He explained, "Fortunately for us, he must have been more excited than were we, as the shots went over our heads. I managed to get off a shot at him with my carbine and had the satisfaction at seeing him topple like a bag of wheat."

Accompanying the 80th Infantry division, who oscillated between XX Corps and XV Corps control, the 7th FAOB elements traveled all the way to the edge of the Falaise line. There, they briefly participated in an all out effort to destroy the Germans that were on the verge of becoming trapped. This battle then became the responsibility of XV Corps, so the 7th FAOB batteries pulled back to support XX Corps' march east.

From the north, the VII Corps' 4th and 9th Infantry Divisions also attacked the shoulders of the Mortain penetration. The Germans were now being hammered from three directions, and taking terrible losses from the combined heavy artillery and aerial attacks. Finally, on August 11, even Hitler realized that continuing the assault was futile, and authorized Kluge to pull the surviving members of the 15th Army out east through the Falaise gap. By then, it was too late for the Germans to save much of anything. The Germans lost about eighty percent of the men and vehicles they had thrown into the six-day Mortain assault. In a typical panzer regiments engaged in the campaign, nineteen out of twenty-two tanks were destroyed or abandoned.

The entire German front before Normandy was collapsing in one final, desperate and chaotic retreat through the ever-narrowing Falaise gap. In a disaster of unimaginable proportions, retreating German columns were blown to bits by American bombers, fighter aircraft, and artillery and tank fire of every caliber. Everywhere were dead Germans, horse teams, smashed tanks and abandoned vehicles. So awful was the smell of death that even pilots of piper cub spotter planes circling above the battlefield became sick.

While the Allies never succeeded in completely closing the Falaise pocket before many of the Germans had escaped, the damage inflicted was severe. When the seventy-five-day battle of Normandy was over, the cost to the Allies was 209,672 casualties, including almost 40,000 killed. The Germans lost the better part of 450,000 troops, with 240,000 of those either killed or wounded. Of the 1,500 German tanks that fought at Normandy, only 24 made it back across the Seine. The Germans also lost another 3,500 artillery pieces and 20,000 vehicles. Of all those Wehrmacht soldiers engaged in Normandy, only a small fraction escaped the Falaise cauldron.[22] Despite these losses, the Germans still had plenty of fight left, the degree of which XX Corps would find out within the next month.

CHAPTER 4

The 7th Field Artillery Observation Battalion at War

To best appreciate just how the 7th FAOB daily operations contributed to the overall combat mission, it is helpful to understand the battalion's organization and specific functions. One of the challenges of relating the 7th Field Artillery Observation Battalion's history is due to the expansive nature of its mission and location. The XX Corps front ranged anywhere from twenty to seventy-five miles wide on any given day and members of the 7th FAOB were everywhere in between. For most of the 7th FAOB's operations between August and November 1944, A Battery would generally be responsible for the northern part of the XX Corps zone, while B Battery would cover the southern sector. Lieutenant Colonel Schwartz's battalion headquarters would be located somewhere in the middle, with command posts placed where he could best communicate with both his subordinate battery commanders as well as the commander of the XX Corps artillery group. In this regard, the entire battalion was seldom concentrated and engaged in anyone particular action at one time. In other words, the battalion focused its efforts in support of XX Corps' most important priorities. Suffice it to say that wherever German artillery shells were flying the thickest, there served men of the 7th Field Artillery Observation Battalion.

Specifically, the primary missions of an American field artillery observation battalion from 1944 to 1945 were:

1- Locate enemy artillery.
2- Register and adjust field artillery.
3- Collect information/intelligence.
4- Coordinate survey operations.
5- Provide field artillery meteorological messages.[23]

The overarching function of the 7th FAOB was to find enemy cannon firing against XX Corps. Fire direction and counterbattery operations in the Second World War were critically important tools to commanders, as well over fifty percent of the war's casualties were caused by artillery fire. Reducing the effectiveness of enemy artillery would be a top tactical objective in every battle that XX Corps fought in. The Germans had excellent artillery and gunners who knew how to use their ordnance. Every German cannon and artilleryman that was either destroyed or suppressed supported the American army's primary objective: to enable the infantry to close in and defeat the enemy.

When further evaluating American casualties in World War II, the infantry suffered about eighty percent of all combat losses. Comparatively, while artillerymen made up only about five percent of American combat casualties, forward observers *overwhelmingly* suffered the vast majority of all artillery losses. Being a forward observer in the Second World War was dangerous business.

As described by Marinello, the FAOBs that served in the European Theater of Operations (ETO) became part of a "long, unbroken line of artillery observation battalions that stretched from the northernmost sector of First Army, later to be joined still further north by Ninth Army, through all of Third Army, and south into the breath of Seventh Army. Each of these armies had two or three corps, and each corps was assigned its own FAOB. Theoretically then, whenever a German cannon went off, there were both sound and flash devices attempting to record its location."[24] In actuality, FAOBs were rarely able to provide complete coverage over the elongated, irregular corps fronts that prevailed during the war. The structure of the FAOBs was based on the 1942 Table of Organization that had anticipated a corps front of 10,000 yards. In actual employment during the war, corps fronts often exceeded 40,000 yards. As a result, the deployment of FAOBs throughout the ETO frequently overextended the units to four times that of doctrinal planning. While the battalions adapted to these conditions as best they could, observation capabilities, security, command, control and communications were always tested beyond their intended maximum limits.

When directing artillery fire, 7th FAOB observers would generally reach out to the XX Corps Artillery batteries for shooting the missions. XX Corps artillery packed a heavy punch. At all times, the corps had its own organic artillery group which was comprised of headquarters elements and seven battalions, with each battalion controlling three firing batteries of four cannon. This gave corps-level control to eighty-four individual guns, generally ranging in types of 240- or 155-mm howitzers. These were among the most powerful field artillery pieces that the army had in its inventory. In addition, the corps would also integrate the fires of the attached artillery battalions of the various combat divisions that were assigned to XX Corps. During the course of the war, twenty-three separate artillery batteries served under XX Corps control, some for a period as short as one week, but most for at least several months.

Coordinating the employment of the various artillery battalions was a complicated process. To accomplish this task, the corps artillery commander created four to five field artillery groups controlled by a corps fire direction center (FDC). The FDC could allocate its assets to the divisions or control them itself. Corps artillery also tied into the divisional artillery, making it possible to coordinate every field artillery tube within the corps' sector. In the campaign through France, the corps' zones became so wide that one FDC could not control all of the corps' artillery. A field artillery brigade headquarters frequently served as a second FDC. The corps FDC system was highly efficient at massing artillery fires and proved to be extremely responsive and flexible. On one occasion during the Lorraine campaign, an infantry unit about to make an assault contacted XX Corps FDC with a request for artillery support. The FDC plotted the target and issued orders to the appropriate artillery battalion. The battalion in turn assigned the mission to a battery that delivered sixty-seven rounds on the target. The total elapsed time from receipt of request to completion of the mission was six minutes.[25]

To target German cannon, the mighty XX Corps artillery force turned to the 7th FAOB. The 7th's two "letter" batteries (A and B) were responsible for conducting the actual detection of enemy artillery and other targets of opportunity. From the days at Camp Shelby through France in October 1944, A Battery was commanded by Captain Robert Johnson. In late October 1944, Captain Johnson was transferred and was replaced in command by his executive officer (XO), First Lieutenant Slessman. B Battery, while deployed to Europe, was commanded by Captain Richard Clark and later by Captain Keith Chandler. Each of the two batteries was identical in terms of organization, equipment, and mission capabilities.

A and B Batteries consisted of headquarters and support elements which ran the command, control, and logistics for the battery, and the sound and flash platoons which performed the observation missions. At full strength, each battery had about 150 soldiers assigned. Key leadership in the headquarters portion of the battery included the commander, the executive officer, and the first sergeant. The commander was ultimately responsible for all that his battery was charged to accomplish. In an organization as diverse as a field artillery observation battery, the all-encompassing responsibilities included the tactical deployment and operations of the sound and flash observation posts (OPs), the security of the battery, communications, supply, maintenance, and the safety, care, and feeding of all its men. The executive officer was the principal assistant to the commander and would take over the battery in the event the commander was absent. For the most part, executive officers would generally be responsible for all battery administrative and logistical requirements. The first sergeant was the senior enlisted leader in the battery and served a vital role in its ability to function, as well as in boosting the men's morale and enforcing discipline. While the senior officer would command the battery, there was no doubt that it would be the veteran first sergeant (or "top") who ran the day to day operations that kept things going. A Battery veteran Hank Lizak has fond memories of his top, First Sergeant "Buzz" Bennet, an excellent leader with an untarnished reputation of taking care of his soldiers' welfare.

At the heart of the 7th FAOB missions were the A and B Battery sound and flash ranging platoons, each led by lieutenants. The two letter batteries actually functioned as a series of platoons, and not as a single, integrated entity. This required an enormous degree of autonomy and responsibility on junior noncommissioned officers and enlisted men who would independently select and operate the OPs with little supervision from battalion or battery headquarters. Interviewed in 2002, Don Slessman spoke of the high degree of intelligence of the battalion's soldiers and of the large amount of trust that he, as a battery commander, placed on them.

As implied by the name, the thirty-five-soldier sound platoons used a series of specially constructed microphones to record the sound disturbance caused by incoming artillery. Each sound platoon had four forward observation sections that would be posted as far forward in the XX Corps front as possible. Depending on the tactical situation, the OPs would be dug into foxholes or hidden in buildings. Each OP consisted of a squad of two to four soldiers, with at least one being on duty at all times. As soon as a German cannon was heard, the observer would call back to the sound ranging base with the warning "On the Way!" and click a field phone switch that would activate the string of six microphones buried in the ground over a stretch of about 3 ½ miles. In staggered series, the microphones captured the sound waves created by the cannon. Back at the sound platoon command post, the sound central base would immediately begin to amass the data. Key to the process was an oscillograph that produced a tape that registered the impulse of the incoming sound waves. One soldier would analyze the spacing between the impulses and pass it to another who worked a plotting board that overlaid detailed maps with a grid system. Based on the quality and quantity of the readings, the plotter used a T-Square to draw converging lines on the location of the German guns. A third soldier would relay this information to battalion headquarters where it would be passed to XX Corps artillery and sent to a firing battery.

Because command post (CP) duties required the men to work from a plotting board, run the oscillograph, and communicate by radio and field phones (tasks that at night needed the light from kerosene lamps), it was usually impractical to dig the CPs into the ground. As tents did not protect the men from shrapnel, open fields were forsaken as CP crews took refuge in the cellars of larger houses and solidly built churches. Even when CP shifts were off duty, the cellars were a haven where men sweated out a shelling, or where they relaxed and horsed around. Command posts would sometimes take on the air of a clubhouse.[26]Sound observation used four primary counterbattery techniques that depended on the tactical situation, environmental conditions, and known intelligence on the location of enemy cannon. While the degree to which each corps used a particular method varied, the techniques themselves were quite standard.

Sound counterbattery techniques were:

Map Data Corrected: This procedure was used when the exact location of sound ranging targets were confirmed with such information as recent photo intelligence. In essence, the Americans already knew exactly where the enemy guns were and it was the job of the sound OPs to detect when they were shooting. Firing data was based upon the established map plots and combined with adjustments from current sound base readings.

Sound Ranging Registration: Sometimes sound operations could make decent plots of enemy cannon but conditions precluded confirmation by secondary sources. Using sound range registration, surprise counterbattery barrages could still be fired on the offending guns. This technique required both skill and luck, and the tradeoff for gaining surprise was reduced accuracy. The enemy location was based on the best analysis of sound base plotting. Friendly artillery would then fire a registration round at a known location some distance away from the intended target, with the sound OPs tracking the location of the impact. Based on the sound data of the target and registration shells, a direct calculation was made between the two locations. A massed artillery strike would then be fired on the enemy battery, hopefully accurate enough to catch the gunners exposed and unaware.

Sound on Sound Adjustment: This technique was similar to sound ranging but was more precise. Based on initial sound ranging, one or two friendly artillery shells were fired on the target as near as data permitted. The position of each set of bursts was plotted by sound ranging and the deflection and range corrected before the next firing. This was continued until the sound data of registration shells and target were identical. This method was slow and lacked the element of surprise but had the advantage of greater accuracy. It was also more effective when the battalion was engaged in more static operations. If nothing else, this technique encouraged the enemy batteries to frequently displace. When the German guns were running from counterbattery fires, they could not shoot at American troops.

Coordination with Air Observation: All of the above methods were significantly enhanced when augmented with observation from spotter aircraft. Based on a general location from both sound and flash OPs, the spotter planes could then pinpoint the targets and take over responsibility for calling in counterbattery fire missions. This technique required good visibility and weather, a condition distinctly rare when XX Corps fought its hardest battles from September 1944 through March 1945.[27]

In addition to the skill level of the observers, the accuracy of sound detection depended on a number of environmental factors. The more battlefield noise, the more difficult it was to make decent plots. There were times when so many German and American artillery were firing simultaneously that the oscillograph could not identify single cannons. Weather and meteorological conditions also came into play, and if it were stormy or windy, the acoustics would distort the data. The observers quickly became experts in assessing the specific nature of winds, an acquired trait that stayed with the men forever. Marinello: "…For his entire life, an old sound man remains aware of winds. It becomes second nature to gauge them. Ten miles an hour, thirty. He's subjective about them, too. Winds are friendly, hostile, indifferent. Winds come as zephyrs. They come as gusts. It is the becalmed day that the old sound man likes best. It causes him to exult, "Boy, I wish the Krauts would open up now. We'd get every one.""[28]

The thirty-five-man flash platoons operated similarly to the sound counterparts, except that their OPs were responsible for detecting the visible flash of enemy cannons as they fired. As the sound platoons were the 7th FAOB's ears, flash were its eyes. The flash observers used a specially designed azimuth instrument, a kind of elaborate telescope with all sorts of markings that could be oriented to the stars. The telescope, in conjunction with other OP sightings, would determine the angle of the targeted cannon's point of origin.

Life as a flash observer had its own brand of dangers. To properly use the bulky M1 azimuth instruments, observers had to stand, resulting in their increased exposure to enemy fire.[29] Flash OPs were positioned where they could get the best visibility of the firing of enemy cannon—on high ground of the front lines. When possible, common aiming points were plotted, which enabled the discrete OPs to call their sightings off of a known location. Jack French, a B Battery flash observer, describes flash ranging techniques:

A flash OP consisted of three observers, was dug into a ditch or foxhole and was camouflaged. They were usually surveyed in. The length of time OPs were manned varied depending on the situation, but on average, they were often occupied for about three days. We used specially designed "BC" scopes for observing and also binoculars. As soon as we saw a flash, we set our scopes on it, and then would call it in to the Command Post. There would be three or four OPs spread out on the ridges. If more than one OP caught the flash, they could plot it and call artillery on it." French also commented on the danger of OP work. "We would draw artillery fire occasionally. On one occasion I saw a patrol of about six enemy soldiers, about 150 to 200 feet to my left, so we remained very quiet and let them pass.

These were some of the common methods of employment and missions of the flash platoons:

Flash Ranging Bases: When terrain conditions allowed, four or five observation posts, each separated by at least 2,000 yards were established. The observers were on the constant lookout for the flash of enemy guns. When detected, the OPs would report the azimuth from their locations. The flash base would plot the intersection of the angles and relay it for fire missions.

Orientation and Registration: The location of the flash OPs were surveyed both quickly and with pinpoint precision. Using these OPs as reference points, corps artillery elements could register spotting rounds at specified locations. When firing against enemy targets, adjustments were based on shifting the impact point from these known registration points.

Adjustment of Fire: With their eyes trained constantly on the battlefield, flash observers could direct fire on virtually any target of interest, artillery or otherwise. When at least two OPs could zero in on a specific target, fire missions could be far more accurate than conventional observation techniques.

Flash-bang: Flash observers were highly trained in calculating the distance of enemy guns based on the separation of the time in the flash of the cannon and the sound of its discharge. When combined with other observation techniques, flash-bang calculations could be surprisingly effective.

Compared with sound operations, about twelve percent of the 7th FAOB's total wartime plots of enemy cannon were made by flash observation (which was actually slightly higher than the ten percent average of other theater FAOBs.) The German's introduction of flashless powder in its towed artillery, combined with their using flares to mask their fires, made flash observation more challenging than pre-war doctrine had anticipated. The stormy or overcast European weather also frequently hampered collection efforts. Still, flash observation played a critical role in the overall counterbattery mission of the FAOB. In the direct mode, it remained highly effective against the bright flash of German "Nebelwerfer" rocket launchers. Combined with other means of observation, data from flash OPs were of overall great value in improving the accuracy of counterbattery plotting. The eyes of the flash observers themselves were among the deadliest weapons in the American arsenal. Their ever-present optic on the battlefield provided an invaluable source of intelligence and a highly responsive multiplier in directing artillery at any target of the commander's choosing.

Perhaps the most critical aspect of any field artillery observation function involves pinpoint accuracy of terrain survey. To be as accurate as possible, artillery gunners required absolute precision in matching maps with actual ground survey registration. This mandated exceptional land navigation expertise for those conducting the surveys. Both battalion headquarters and the sound and flash platoons had specifically designated survey squads that were tasked to lock in the exact location of OPs and other battlefield reference points. In supporting sound survey, there was the additional task of placing and digging-in the sound acquisition microphones. The sound platoons had two survey crews, each consisting of a single transit operator, two tape men, a rodman and one or two mathematicians going by the title of "geodetic computer." Transported in a weapons carrier and a couple of jeeps, the survey crews were equipped with twenty second

Gurely transit, a steel rod, six microphones, and metal tape. The soldier serving as the geodetic computer was to compute the survey data that determined the exact place of each of the six microphones. The complex computations were figured in conjunction with several tables of logarithm sines and cosines, tangents, and cotangents.[30] Paul Asman, who was the chief of the B Battery sound ranging platoon (until January 1945, when he transferred to the same function with A Battery), describes the importance of map related survey. "[Knowing] location was a big thing for us—knowing where we were, where our microphones were, where the firing batteries were, and where the enemy was. Our people did a lot of topographical survey. For the most part we were able to pick up from known benchmarks or from surveys made by the engineers, but we could also do sun shots, star shots, resections and the like. Often we would work all night at registrations of batteries as they pulled in after dark so they could be ready with dawn fire missions. Once registered, they could fire off the maps that we had which were very good and very detailed." Often the first Americans on the scene, the survey crews had to work over ground that was uncertain to be fully secured of enemy forces, frequently mined and shelled, and probably under hostile observation.

In the course of the war, the 7th FAOB surveyed 1,280,125 meters of terrain. The value of the FAOB's survey function far eclipsed its primary counterbattery mission. Under the direction of the survey control information center, the battalion provided extremely accurate map and survey data to all of the artillery units within XX Corps. This information was critical in improving the accuracy of all artillery fires. The army's post-war study of FAOBs concluded that the operations of survey control information centers were probably one of the most valuable innovations of World War II.[31] Another technique for determining the location of enemy cannon was the shell reporting (shell rep) teams, who could study the impact of the blasts and then estimate its source. Working as team, the reports of the sound, flash, and shell rep units would sometimes all come together for combined analysis. Advanced trigonometry was a basic skill. Plotting the German guns was a complicated process that used the best technology of the day and was executed by some of the smartest men in the army.

Jim Royals, serving as a heavy machine-gunner with B Battery, wrote of his experiences when he accompanied a shell rep team operation that also evolved into a flash observation mission. This action occurred in France, and typified the essence of what the line elements of the 7th FAOB did in a usual day's work. These were times when the OPs were located in places that Americans controlled during the day, and then would revert to no-mans-land at night. Royals recalled:

> I was attached to a shell rep team—about five in the detail. I was a heavy machine-gunner and stood watch in order to protect the crew. Sergeant Charlie Wells, Corporal Charles Sherrick and a lieutenant (either Lieutenant William Henry or Lieutenant Slessman), myself, and the truck driver, C.R. Kriesheimer, I believe.
>
> We went to the front line positions in an area held by infantry units. We would find shell holes and stop and get out and measure its width and depth to determine the direction the shell came from. All information was written down. We learned the difference between 88-mm shells and those larger—like up to 8 inches. I would keep look out and stay near the .50 cal. mounted on a tripod on the truck. At times I also helped to measure the holes by holding the tape and moving rocks, etc.
>
> Later in the afternoon we went in to a small town. It was almost empty of people. We set up a position in a barn-like building with a second story hayloft. The hay gave us a good place to rest and sleep. First we drove the weapons carrier truck in a garage enclosure beneath us. Then we fastened the door to keep anyone out, had K-rations and cold coffee, and sat down to rest. Not long after, we heard the sound of hob-nailed shoe heels on the paved sidewalks in the street—Germans were still in the town. We only whispered when we spoke.

About eight o'clock a couple shells came into the town, down a good ways from us. Then we decided that we may need the radio and power pack from the truck, so the driver and myself were designated to slip down the ladder and get to the door. The two doors were only a few feet apart. We very quietly opened the first door and eased outside and opened the second door behind the vehicle. Once inside we used the red lens flashlight to unhook the radio and get the power pack off. After peeking outside to make sure no one was near, we then moved the equipment into the second door. After re-securing the garage door from inside, we made two trips up to the loft with the commo gear. The lieutenant and sergeant hooked up the radio and placed a call to an outfit a few miles away. We were informed that the infantry unit was getting some 88s dropped on their positions. Our forward flash section asked us to try and get a fix on the enemy artillery firing the rounds. Sergeant Wells went to the end of the loft and looked through the cracks and could see flashes in the distance. He took the map and determined where the guns were located.

    Battalion headquarters got us connected to the field artillery in the rear. They lobbed a couple of shells toward the 88s and did some further adjustments. Once the enemy was bracketed by our spotting rounds, Wells called fire for effect, and all hell broke loose on the hill where the enemy was firing from. After about an hour, all was quiet again. The lieutenant gave headquarters a report on the results and all were pleased. We told a few quiet jokes and then took our naps, two or three at a time, while the rest stood guard. Next morning we headed back to our battery area. Leaving the town we passed an infantry unit. They came out in the road and thanked us for knocking out some of the artillery that had been firing on them during the past night.

    Now I know what hob-nailed boots sound like at night walking on pavement or wood flooring. We were lucky to have returned safely.

As well as performing the unique counterbattery finding mission, the observers of the 7th were also fully capable of directing fire on any other target of XX Corps priority. Every time XX Corps formed combined combat teams in mobile operations, 7th FAOB observers were present and prepared to adjust fire. Don Slessman recalls countless occasions where 7th FAOB observers would be in the very front of XX Corps lead combat units. As soon as enemy contact was made these observers would call in the American artillery response. Using conventional field artillery observation techniques, 7th FAOB observers would adjust fire on targets of opportunity or direct massive XX Corps elements in pre-planned fire missions. One such technique was the deadly "Time on Target," wherein each gun in the corps fired at the same target in a sequence that ensured every round arrived at the same split second. The firing of hundreds of shells within a moment's time resulted in unimaginable devastation to the target area and great shock effect on those few who survived it.

    The men found other ways to target the enemy when the weather failed to cooperate for sound and flash detection or when the big corps-level guns were not available. Whenever setting up in a new OP, Private First Class (PFC) Ray Peabody of A Battery's sound section would make the extra effort to make contact with the mortar platoon of nearby infantry units. While the mortars had far less range and punch than the heavier "tube" artillery, they were a critical resource in providing timely and close-in fire support to infantry company commanders. When the wind was too strong for sound detection, Peabody used his expert conventional forward observer skills to call in fire on whatever mortar targets were present. It was win-win for both Peabody and the mortar gunners as the enhanced fire direction also served to better protect both the infantrymen and the ever-at-risk OPs.

    In sum, if a German cannon, tank, vehicle, bunker, formation or even individual soldier was visible to the 7th observers, they were at risk of being on the receiving end of a murderous XX Corps artillery salvo.

Another important function of the battalion's observation mission that is easily overlooked was their excellent tactical intelligence collection capability. By being at the very front, the forward observers, especially those serving in the flash OPs, were often the eyes and ears of the XX Corps Intelligence Officer (G-2). The observers were trained to quickly send situation reports on their observation of enemy movements, as well as any other information the G-2 needed. The timeliness and quality of their reporting often made a critical difference in the commander's decision-making process during many battles. During the course of the war, the 7th FAOB would be responsible for the collection and dissemination of 2,443 intelligence messages.

There were times, especially during the Metz and Saar-Triangle campaigns, where the OPs would be dug into one place for weeks at a time. There were other occasions where the observation platoons would be constantly on move, changing OPs by the day. Marinello describes the process of finding good OP locations: "Choosing a proper site had a lot of elements. The best allowed the observer to see the enemy, preferably, without being seen himself. Everyone was astute enough to know that such characteristics were desirable. But such sites were rare. Sometimes it was good to have infantry all around, other times not. Certainly the observer didn't want to be on a bald, jutting ridge that might make it a can't-miss target. German artillery had a nasty habit of pounding away day and night as though they were on automatic. When it was all said and done, there was much that went into making or breaking a site. As the saying went, you knew a good one when you saw it.[32] The observation platoons had to be able to quickly transition from a static to a mobile mode. The platoons got to a point where it took only minutes for the thirty-five men to collect their gear, board the collection of jeeps, weapons carriers and single 2 ½ ton truck and move out."[33]

Whether they were flash or sound men, the OP observers were volunteers. Marinello: "Tender care was directed to the forward observers. They had no extra duties. With the sole exception of occasional assistance to the overworked survey teams, they were excused from other assignments, including guard duty and hauling supplies. This exclusivity had the effect of establishing an elite group that nobody resented. For the rest of the battery, it was enough that they didn't have to be sent up to the observation posts."[34]

The best firing data and battlefield intelligence that could possibly be obtained was useless unless it could quickly be analyzed and communicated back to the XX Corps firing batteries and G-2 section. To meet this critical requirement, each battery had a commo section of thirty-five communication specialists. The communication platoons were the one element that worked between the sound and flash outfits.

The commo platoons used a combination of radios and telephone wire depending on distances and the degree of mobility. Radios provided a greater degree of flexibility, but were limited to an eight to ten mile range depending on line of sight. For ranges up to twenty miles, Morse code systems could be used. While radios were obviously a major part of the communications link, their limited range and vulnerability to enemy signals interception and jamming operations often rendered them inadequate.

To operate a radio near the front meant literally to risk your life. The Germans had excellent radio direction-finding capabilities. If a radio operator was on the air for more then a few seconds, the enemy could pinpoint the exact spot of transmission. When there were no other higher priority targets being serviced at the time, the Germans were likely to fire artillery at the source of the radio call. This threat was clearly brought home to Battery B's Bill Williamson one day when he and Milton Spielberg were trying send a radio message from their command car located on a farm. Failing to get a response from their transmissions, Williamson got out of the vehicle to set up an antenna in the upper part of a nearby building. While he was doing so, two shells screamed into the area. The first shell completely disintegrated a nearby pear tree. A fragment from the second shell hit Private Daniel Moore in the face, shattering his jaw. After

Moore was evacuated, Williamson returned to the command car to find the seat that he had been sitting in to be completely riddled by razor-sharp shards of shrapnel.

Taking precautions against the enemy's radio direction-finding threat, commo operators limited conversations to the minimum while also sending their transmissions away from large clusters of troops.

To augment radios, an extensive network of field telephones served as a key part of the battalions' communication infrastructure. Large 2 ½ ton trucks were specially outfitted with gigantic spools of black commo wire. Wire had to be laid from the battalion to battery headquarters and then out to the OPs. In addition to establishing field phone lines, the sound platoon microphones also needed to be linked together.

Whenever the battalion halted, the communications section's wiremen had the thankless job of laying and retrieving wire over a chaotic battlefield. The wires were perpetually being cut, sometimes by enemy fire, or more commonly by bad weather and the endless passage of vehicles rolling throughout the combat zone. Each time the wires would go down, day or night and in every weather and combat condition conceivable, the wiremen would have to go out find the source of the break and splice it back together again. In performing their mission, the commo members would have to brave shelling, enemy patrols, and nervous American sentries as they wandered the battlefield in the endless cycle of laying, fixing, and retrieving wire. The bravest of the brave were polemen like A Battery's Carmen Kelly, who would have to shimmy up telephone poles and tall trees, often under the threat of enemy snipers. Hank Lizak remembers many occasions when local infantry patrols would halt the work of the wiremen because they were so close to the enemy lines that they were bound to draw fire. In the battalion's war stories that still spin among the vets sixty years later, some aspect of fixing broken commo wire seems to hold a common thread in many of the adventures.

Of course, it would have been impossible for the batteries' operational elements to conduct their work without an effective support apparatus. Under the battery commander and first sergeant's control were the food service section (a mess sergeant and six cooks), battery clerks, a supply section, motor section, machine gunners, and other support specialists. In addition, medics from the battalion medical platoon would be assigned on a permanent basis to each battery to handle routine or emergency medical care.

The 7th Field Artillery Observation Battalion headquarters and Headquarters Battery were responsible for the tactical employment and logistical sustainment of the line batteries. The battalion headquarters had both a fire direction as well as performing its battery support mission.

In terms of counterbattery operations, the battalion provided analysis of firing data, as it linked the observation batteries and XX Corps headquarters. The overall control of operations was dependent on the tactical situation. When good communication could be maintained, a centralized control approach maximized the corps' full counterbattery resources. Observation data was relayed by the sound bases to the battalion operations section for analysis. From there it was relayed to the corps' artillery counterbattery section. This enabled enemy battery and intelligence information to be plotted at one central point, integrating analysis of sound and flash FAOB data with photo intelligence, shelling reports, and air observation. To ensure a degree of flexibility, sound and flash ranging officers were authorized to call to the nearest divisional artillery battalion to attack targets of opportunity. When the situation was more fluid, the letter batteries were attached to either field artillery group or divisional control. While the decentralized control approaches were quicker and more responsive, it was at the cost of more thorough overall target analysis.[35]

The analysis of weather played an important role both in counterbattery operations as well as in directing friendly artillery fires. Such factors as wind direction, speed, and the density of the atmosphere all came into play when plotting artillery strikes. The battalion headquarters had its own meteorological detachment to keep constant track of these conditions and to report them to corps artillery headquarters for further dissemination to the firing battalions. To gather this data, the "met" detachment launched weather balloons on a regular basis as well as tracking instruments such as barometers and psychrometers. 7th FAOB veteran Sid Shafran discusses his experiences with the battalion's met section, and the hazards of sending up weather balloons in a combat zone: "I was a T5 in the met section in Headquarters Battery and we did send messages to the letter batteries that were usually relayed through artillery headquarters. One such contact occurred during the battle for Metz. Since we were stationed in Thionville it was decided that we were too far from the action for the messages to be effective. Several of us were sent forward to try to solve this problem. We set up and were able to send one message before we were kicked out of the area. It seems that sending up a balloon with a little Japanese lantern attached wasn't a very good idea. Most of the time that we were in combat the met section traveled with corps artillery headquarters. At other times we were with an Air Force Weather Detachment."

With the battalion under the overall charge of Lieutenant Colonel Schwartz, headquarters also had its own battery that was commanded by a captain. Like the line batteries, the Headquarters Battery also had an executive officer and a senior enlisted leader, Sergeant Major Henry Herman. Within the battalion, there were the following primary staff sections that were usually led by captains.

- The S-1, or battalion adjutant, ran personnel administration. The S-1 was responsible for strength accountability, requesting and processing replacements, pay, casualty affairs, awards, and general administration.

- The S-2 served as the battalion's intelligence officer. The S-2 was responsible for keeping track of the enemy situation and worked closely with the S-3 in advising the battalion commander on operational plans. The S-2 processed the intelligence spot reports sent from the line units up to the XX Corps G-2.

- The S-3 was in charge of operations and conducted battalion level counterbattery analysis. Taking direction from the XX Corps artillery G-3, the 7th FAOB Operations Officer assigned sectors for the A and B battery commanders to operate in and guided the overall direction-finding mission of the battalion. The S-3 also had its own communication section tasked with maintaining commo with XX Corps and A and B Battery headquarters. Among its responsibilities, the commo platoon relayed weather data from the meteorological section every six hours.

- The S-4 was responsible for all of the battalion's supply and logistics operations. In a unit as diverse and complex in function and organization as a field artillery observation battalion, this was an incredibly difficult responsibility, as soldiers had to be equipped, fed, and fueled over a large geographic area.

In Headquarters Battery, every soldier had an important job. Just as in the line batteries, there were cooks to make the chow, maintenance and ordnance technicians to fix the trucks, equipment and weapons, supply sergeants and personnel clerks to keep logistics and administration going, and heavy machine gun operators and weapons specialists to protect them all. Headquarters Battery also had some additional specialized troops. To maintain their faith, the battalion had its own chaplain (as Patton once said: "Even the Chaplain is important, for if we get killed and he is not there to bury us we would all go to hell!"). No matter what their specific job was, every enlisted soldier, NCO and officer in the battalion were members of an integrated team whose sum made for a highly significant force multiplier to XX Corps combat power.

Of all the specialized troops, few were more valuable than the battalion's medics. To keep the GIs healthy and treat them when they were wounded, the battalion had an excellent medical detachment of fifteen men led by Captain Louis del Bello. U.S. Army field medics in World War II were among the most heroic and important soldiers on the entire battlefield. They went through all the hardships that the common soldier faced, and their highly specialized training not only saved lives, but also kept the men as healthy as the abysmal front line conditions would allow. In the field, the medics set up aid stations at the battery headquarters. When possible, they treated those sick and lightly wounded and returned them to duty, while more serious cases were evacuated to higher echelon medical facilities. As testimony to the effectiveness of first-level emergency skills, ninety-six percent of the American casualties evacuated back to WW II field hospitals survived.

Roy "Doc" Barber retained some medical records for A Battery. He reports that in 232 days of combat operations, the A Battery medics treated 1,602 patients on sick call. Exposed to the elements in a bitter northern European winter, men frequently suffered from influenza with fevers averaging 102 degrees. The vast majority of sick call cases were treated at the aid stations, kept on limited duty, and recovered in a few days. The men of the battalion were greatly appreciative of the service of the medics. To this day, Stephen Wandzioch still considers medic Roy Barber to have been one of the "finest men he has ever met."

Although technically noncombatants, the mission of the medics was at least as dangerous as were the duties of others on the front. Amos Robinson has these memories as a Headquarters Battery medic:

> I remember one time when XX Corps was going so fast through Germany, some German soldiers were bypassed and were behind us. We thought that we might have to fight some of them. My captain told me that we would need all the help from our men if we did, and that I could use one of his two .45 pistols. I replied, "Captain, if we are attacked, my time will be spent doing the job that I was trained for, being a medic." Another time, we were in an empty schoolhouse and the Germans were shelling us heavy with artillery. Part of the building was shot up. We all went down to the basement. Somebody said that one of our men was missing. The Captain said, "Robinson, go upstairs and look for him." I went up and found him sitting down behind a stove in the kitchen. He was shell-shocked and did not want to move. I had to drag him to the basement. Before I got this done, another shell came in and blew the side off of the kitchen.

In sum, all of these collective skills and efforts were combined for the primary purpose of knocking out enemy artillery. Evaluating the battalion's effectiveness in the war was both a quantifiable and subjective process. On the objective side, the average 7th FAOB wartime plots of enemy artillery locations were accurate within a fifteen-meter radius of their targets, an amazing accomplishment considering the technology of the day. The collection and analysis of the firing data could often be relayed to XX Corps artillery gunners (or Air Corps bomber resources) in a matter of minutes. This meant that exposed German artillery could not shoot at XX Corps soldiers for more than a short while without drawing deadly fire in return. Except when protected in heavily fortified positions, the Germans had the option to either fire a few shells and immediately displace, or stand fast and risk destruction from an inevitable inbound barrage. To make matters worse for the Germans, the majority of their artillery pieces in 1944 were still horse drawn, further restricting their ability to quickly "shoot and scoot." Whether either being fired on by 7th FAOB direction or being forced to continually move, the effectiveness of German artillery directed against XX Corps was considerably reduced. What can never be calculated is the countless number of American lives saved from German artillery shells that were never fired because their gunners were either destroyed or suppressed by the presence of the 7th Field Artillery Observation Battalion.

The information collected by the 7th FAOB was only as good as the confidence entrusted in it by the corps' artillery commanders. If they did not have faith in the accuracy of the counterbattery plotting, they would not waste valuable ammunition firing at the proposed targets. In the early operations in France, the XX Corps artillery commander, Brigadier General Julius E. Slack, was initially distrustful of the army's counterbattery capabilities. To demonstrate how precise their operations could be, the 7th FAOB conducted a test and used their equipment to detect the known location of American batteries. Slack was presented with this data and was reportedly amazed with its accuracy. From that point forward he was a strong believer in the credibility of the 7th FAOB's ability to find German cannon. As a result, the battalion would become a critical force multiplier in every subsequent XX Corps campaign of the war.

Medic Clarence Brennan, who at forty years old in 1944 was probably about the oldest man in the battalion, penned the following poem. The ode was written for unit members to send home during Christmas time in 1944 and covers the spectrum of just about every element serving in the 7th Field Artillery Observation Battalion.

MEMOIRS AT CHRISTMAS TIME

They'll be wanting to know 'bout the Seventh O.B.
Our folks back at home want a full history,
Of just where we've been, and what all we've done,
Of the part that we played in the battles hard won.

So let's keep alive and fresh to retell
The work of a unit that's done its job well.
We're proud of the Seventh, the part we all play,
Our successes to date, many earned the hard way.

In reverence, we speak of our glorious dead,
Of citations for courage, as each one was read.
The sacrifices made by them all was supreme;
They were MEN, one and all…America's cream.
Let's never forget them, each man and his name;
No shirking of duty by THEM. . . They were game.

There are others amongst us, our Purple Heart men,
Who braved sudden death from mine, shell, and then
Continued on living, though the Reaper was nigh,
Their names we'll inscribe on our Honor Rolls high.

Then, too, are those men whose valor and deeds
When crises arose, fulfilled urgent needs.
To them went the Silver or Bronze Star awards,
"For service. . . achievement," thus the army records.

Our men on the outposts deserve a big hand
The job that they're doing's magnificent… GRAND
They brave both the weather and counter-barrage.
They're hard to locate, like a phantom mirage,
But they're IN there, and pitching, each hour of the day,
And what they observe brings our guns into play.
To our Ops. . . our watch-dogs . . .a hearty salute.
They locate Nazi guns, thus render them mute.

We mustn't forget our men who run wire,
Who, heedless of mines, and traps, muck and mire,

John K. Rieth

Go through with their lines while snipers and shell,
Are trying their best to blast them to Hell.

And equally gallant and brave. . . are the men
That make up our teams of survey. . . for when
Coordinates, azimuths, and similar work
Need speedy attention, they're not ones to shirk.
Then, too, there's our 'met" men. . . perform all day long,
Reporting the weather, when it's right. . . when it's wrong.

There's our men who do plotting. . . computing with speed,
They're precise and they're careful. . . supply what we need,
Stay close to their posts, to their tables and boards,
And the work they perform helps reduce Nazi hordes.

And none will ever question our tribute to those
Who, because of their work wear green fatigue clothes,
That's our men who, with wrench, hammer, and grease,
Keep motors performing, revive those that "cease."

This brings us to those who harness the other,
Not the medics. . . you're WRONG, so just take a breather
And THINK for a moment, you'll understand
It's our radio men. . . "The Best in the Land."

But what about those who are right on the trail
Of every shell bursting, this "info" to nail.
No overhead shelter, no bulletproof vest,
Just blood, flesh and GUTS, 'gainst the enemy's best.

The men on the switchboard deserve a big hand
They're tense and alert, under headphones and band.

This brings us 'round to some 'Overhead' men
Who handle all records with typing and pen.
Not hazardous work, but trying. . . and long;
No room for mistakes, no excuse for being wrong.

Have we covered them all? Let's check back and see.
To be sure, there's our medics. They work without fee.
No guns do they carry, nor glory they seek;
They're workers of mercy, for wounded and weak.

And by all means, let's mention our KPs and cooks
Not all they prepare agrees with the books,

But it's wholesome and filling, and clean, fresh and pure
So, the hell with the books, our food holds allure.
And they're workers, these men in our kitchens, we swear
We wouldn't be here, if they weren't RIGHT there.
So, Mother and Dad, when this message you get,
We hope it's the kind that you want. . . the best yet.
The Seventh is proud of your boy on its rolls
He's doing his part to accomplish our goals.

>
> Clarence E. Brennan
> Medical Detachment
> December, 1944

CHAPTER 5

Northern France: August 1944

After the German thrust to Mortain was contained, XX Corps continued its main offensive to the east. With the addition of the 3rd Cavalry Group and the 7th Armored Division in mid August 10, XX Corps further swelled in size, mobility, and combat punch. The speed and shock of XX Corps' operations in the weeks that followed would earn it the "Ghost Corps" nickname, a moniker given by the frustrated German intelligence officers who had such difficulty keeping track of its hard hitting divisions. XX Corps' attack through Northern France in August and early September of 1944 became a key element in creating the legendary status achieved by Patton and the Third Army.

With a substantive armor capability now assigned, XX Corps was ready to attack east. Heavy fighting was still raging to the north, as the Americans were hammering in against the Falaise pocket. To support this effort, Patton ordered the 80th Infantry Division to be detached from XX Corps and sent north to XV Corps. XX Corps continued onward to the east, with the city of Chartres, about 120 miles northeast of Angers, becoming Walker's next major objective.

Elements of the French Resistance also assisted the Ghost Corps' advance. In addition to attacking and harassing German forces from all directions, some Resistance units were also able to actually capture a number of towns in advance of the armored spearhead. Although the Germans were by and large headlong in retreat, they still put up localized defenses at some key road junctions, delaying the oncoming Americans with minefields and machine gun fire.

German resistance began to stiffen as XX Corps approached Chartres on August 14. With a population of 40,000 citizens and famous for its great cathedral, Chartres was an important objective for Third Army, as it was considered as a key gateway to Paris. Unbeknownst to XX Corps intelligence analysts, the city also served as an "absorption point," or rally location, for those German units retreating from eastern France. Among the city's defenders were the remnants of the 17th SS Panzergrenadier Division and 352nd Division, regiments of the 338th and 708th Divisions, and the staff and student cadre of a local German anti-aircraft school.[36] These flak gunners had a variety of dual-use weaponry at their disposable and would prove to be fanatical fighters determined to hold the city. As the fight for Chartres took shape, the 7th FAOB command element halted long enough for the battalion headquarters to set up a command post that would remain in place for three days. The CP was located on the grounds of an expansive manor house near St. Luperce. Despite the combat conditions, the battalion staff were evidently good guests, as the estate's owner, M.de Cosse, sent Lieutenant Colonel Schwartz a letter one year later expressing his appreciation of their liberation, and commenting on how he enjoyed the battalion's stay there.

Schwartz seemed to make an effort to set a good impression with the French people. In one of the battalion's reunions many years later, some of the 7th veterans still recalled with amusement the time that Schwartz, using terrible French, took the time to attempt to explain the workings of a 30 cal. carbine to a young mademoiselle. One soldier in particular that had close contact with Schwartz was his radio operator, Tom Delay. Initially wary of Schwartz's hard-line reputation, Delay ultimately found him a good boss to work for. Delay learned that as long as one did his job, Schwartz was not that hard to get along with. One of Delay's extra duties was to be alert for passing generals' command cars. While Schwartz would be focused on reading his maps, Delay would call out, "Here comes General Walker's car!" Schwartz would render the appropriate salute and continue on with his work without missing a beat. In one humorous remembrance, Delay recalls the time when they passed a group of French children who had somehow gotten a hold of some GI condoms and were blowing them into balloons. As they drove by, Schwartz commented, "How did those kids get all of that bubble gum?" Delay and Sergeant Major Herman exchanged glances and were able to keep silent while suppressing what would have been a good laugh.

At this point in the campaign, the men were allowed to include slightly more details of their operations in letters home. Kurt Rieth wrote this on August 14:

> Well at last we have been allowed to write where we are, although I suspect you may have guessed it already. The first thing, of course, I want to say is do not start worrying about me twice as much as you did before. Everything is going smoothly and I feel confident that I'll be all right. It's really quite an experience living in France now. You should see the people in the cities and villages, especially the ones we have just retaken when we drive through them. They line the streets waving and cheering with joy. As we happen to stop a few minutes, they rush into the house and bring out wine, cider, or cognac and pour us glasses of it. When we first landed, almost every town we went through was completely wrecked, but as we have been moving deeper into France most of the towns have very little damage.

The entire offensive through Northern France was a very fluid operation. Events often moved so quickly that sometimes the advance patrols of the 7th FAOB actually were ahead of the scouts who were supposed to have been in the very front of the XX Corps columns. Every veteran seems to be able to recall such experiences at one time or another. On occasion, hidden German troops would let the lead elements pass unmolested and then open up on unsuspecting troops in following echelons. In one such instance nearing Chartres, Headquarters Battery Supply Sergeant Geiges, along with other headquarters elements, came under heavy fire after following a lead XX Corps vanguard force. They were pinned down for a substantial period of time until an infantry unit came up and finally cleared the area.

There were times when the men would occasionally get lost and accidentally drive past the friendly lines and into enemy-held territory. This is what happened to Staff Sergeant Robert Siebels when he and his driver were traveling at night in a jeep looking for the battalion CP at the De Cosse manor. Getting lost while in blackout drive is an easy thing to do, and somehow they drove right past the American front line and straight into the German pickets. Suddenly, they were engulfed in a hail of enemy machine gun fire. As the jeep temporally slowed, Siebels jumped out. Despite the heavy fire, the driver was somehow able to turn the jeep around and race back to safety, leaving Siebels hugging the bottom of a ditch.

Although Germans were all around, Siebels was able to sneak himself to a nearby haystack where he spent the night. At daybreak, he began crawling down a ditch trying to make it back to the American positions when three Germans got the drop on him and forced him to surrender. Quickly searching him, they removed his pistol. To Siebel's great surprise, the Germans seemed satisfied with their prize of an American weapon and then allowed him to walk back to American lines with his hands in the air. More than half expecting to get a slug in the back, Siebels walked away very briskly, and then broke into a sprint as soon as he was out of close range. He safely made it back to the battalion CP, lucky to have the ordeal cost him no more than a pistol.

The battle for Chartres was brief but bloody. While the tanks and mechanized infantry of the 7th Armored Division pushed into the city, the squadrons of the 3rd Cavalry swung around and formed an arc around its perimeter. The Germans fiercely resisted, and the flak school's 88-mm and 40-mm cannon rained deadly fire on the American armor. For a time, the Germans held the upper hand and pushed the American tanks out of the city center. Colonel Welborn Griffith, the XX Corps G-3 (chief of operations), was among the Americans killed.

XX Corps artillery, many batteries of which were placed far forward, played a key role in silencing the German guns. The fire missions had to be registered with precision, as orders were given not to damage the ancient cathedral that was located in the center of the city. Walker threw the 5th Infantry Division into the fray, which tipped the balance of power. On August 17, XX Corps had taken Chartres.

Lieutenant Slessman was with the lead infantry units that entered the city. As soon as he reached the great cathedral, he realized the value of its tall spire as an observation post. Breathless after racing up the stairs, he found the surrounding countryside devoid of any visible enemy forces. Although not finding any Germans, Slessman did spot an interesting memento for his trip up the tower—an ancient key to some cathedral door. Common to every soldier's experience in the ETO was the collection of "souvenirs," be it enemy equipment or some other item of interest. Everyone did it. Slessman helped himself to the key, carried it throughout the war, and returned home with it. (Over the years, he found it increasingly difficult to live with the guilt of the acquisition, and later, on a vacation to France, made a special trip to Chartres to return the key to stunned church officials.)

On August 18, Walker received the order from Third Army to take over a defensive position from XV Corps at the city of Druex, twenty miles north of Chartres and only fifteen miles south of Paris. Reportedly, Walker cursed "loud and long" when he read the order, as it shifted the momentum of eastward attack from offense to defense.[37] The 7th FAOB's A Battery was assigned to the 7th Armored Division for this movement. The battery went into action so quickly that they had no time to make any detailed terrain surveys. Still they were able to plot a few enemy guns via sound ranging before the 7th Armored Division's lightning advance secured the assigned bridgehead. This day was the closest that the battalion would get to Paris (with the exception of rare and valued liberty passes that would occasionally be issued in the months ahead).

Fortunately, for the men of both opposing armies, neither side employed the horrific and deadly poisonous gasses that were used in the First World War. The Germans, however, were not above using non-lethal chemical agents to try to slow down the overpowering Third Army advance. On August 19, medic Roy Barber recorded that retreating Germans had sprayed the creosote (similar to tear gas) on the roads the Americans would soon be passing. An A Battery column subsequently drove through the area, kicking up the typical dust clouds the men had come to expect on the French roads. Suddenly, men began to choke as their eyes, noses and lungs began to burn fiercely. While most of the men recovered quickly, twelve of them required hospitalization, with some out of action for a period of up to five days.

Completing its missions at Druex and Chartres, XX Corps next objective would be to cross the Seine River. On the rainy morning of August 21, XX Corps moved out toward the river, twenty-five miles east. Under XX Corps control was the 3rd Cavalry Group, which led the advance, the 7th Armored Division, which had the northern sector, and the 5th Infantry, which was responsible for the southern zone. The northern route was mountainous and wooded and afforded good cover to German rear guard detachments. The retreating Germans used the terrain as best they could, and offered some resistance near Limour, halfway to the objective. The southernmost elements made fast progress, slicing through enemy armored cavalry screens and driving through heavy artillery fire to seize the city of Milly. By August 22, XX Corps was poised on the west side of the Seine.

Facing XX Corps was a force of 20,000 Germans, elements of the 9th Division, the 338th Division, three security regiments, an anti-tank battalion, and three battalions of 105 mm howitzers. The river itself provided the Germans with a strong obstacle from which to defend. The river in this area is 250 to 300 feet wide and lined with high hills on both banks. A tributary of the Seine, the Loring River, cut directly to the south, and through the town of Fontainebleau, which also was defended by German troops. At this time there were no bridgeheads across the Seine from Paris to the south, and it was up to XX Corps to make this first breach.

The Germans had carefully laid-in their artillery with extensive pre-registration plotting. When the Americans neared, they would be subject to extremely accurate artillery fire.

As the 7th Armored Division approached the river near Melun on the afternoon of August 22, heavy German artillery barrages forced them back behind the west bank hills. That night, American fighter-bombers pounded the German positions. The XX Corps attack was launched in earnest at first light. The 7th Armored Division attacked in the northern zone to secure three bridgeheads near Melun, while the 5th Infantry Division attacked in the south, first to take Fontainebleau, and then to cross there and at Montereau. Walker's plan was extremely bold, as he would few reserves available should any of the crossings fail. The performance of XX Corps artillery would be critical in supporting the attacks. For its part, the 7th FAOB would have to find and direct fire on up to eighteen batteries (about seventy cannon) of enemy artillery.

The 5th Infantry Division led off the attack to the south. Using the cover of the woods at Fontainebleau (historic hunting grounds of the French royalty), the infantry stormed into the town while other battalions approached Montereau, at the extreme south of the XX Corps sector. Finding bridges down at both locations, the infantryman charged ahead by either swimming through the water or by rowing across on abandoned boats. Once on the far shore, they were vigorously counterattacked by angry German infantry supported by tanks. Had it not been for the close fire support of XX Corps and divisional artillery, it is doubtful that any of the American footholds would have survived.

In order to achieve maximum surprise, the 7th Armored Division made their attacks at Melun without any prior artillery preparation on the German positions. While surprised, the Germans were also largely unmolested when the armored infantrymen appeared in their sights, and they fired away as soon as they saw them. Despite the heavy enemy fire, XX Corps troops continued to pour across the river anyway they could, either by swimming, wading, using assault boats or abandoned German craft. At one point in the battle, when a 7th Armored Division attack was faltering, General Walker personally reorganized the assault under direct machine gun fire. A number of his staff officers were wounded in the process. This type of command emphasis does make a difference, and eventually, the corps established five small crossings over the Seine.

Establishing a bridgehead is one thing, holding it is another. The Germans pushed back fiercely, throwing all the tanks, anti-aircraft guns, and artillery they could muster in the direct fire mode. XX Corps artillery fired constant box concentrations that completely smothered a specific geographic area with shellfire. These artillery attacks were very effective in breaking up German infantry assaults and taking out their cannon. In this action, XX Corps artillery fired their first ever combined "Time-on-Target" salvo. This massive strike completely destroyed an enemy four-gun battery of heavy artillery that had been blocking the advance of the armor.[38] While the fighting continued into the night, the rain poured down and continued through the next day. Although this restricted American air support, the muddy conditions also severely limited the German's ability to attack with their panzers. Engineers were able to throw up four pontoon bridges and reinforcements were quickly sent across. With the bridgeheads now secure, XX Corps had firmly broken across the Seine, and were free to continue the pursuit of the retreating Germans. XX Corps' breaching of the Seine sealed off Paris from the rear.

On August 25, Paris was liberated.

When fighting tapered off, the men were able to take some note of the spectacular town of Fontainebleau and the surrounding forests. Some weeks later, when he was allowed to write of previous locations, Kurt Rieth commented; "….I can mention now that I never got to Paris, but got as close as fifteen miles to it. At that time however, the city hadn't even been captured yet. I have been to Fontainebleau, however, which I think is the prettiest French city I've seen. We also took a ride through the beautiful forest where the French royalty in the old times had their hunting lodges."

Slessman had these observations, both on the countryside and the events that were happening to those French who had collaborated with the Germans:

> Fontainebleau was one of the prettiest cities I have seen and suffered little from the war even though we forced a crossing of the Seine River at this point. I had one OP right next to a champagne plant, and of course we had to sample their product, which was superb. While in this city I witnessed a rather unusual sight that took place one afternoon. I was on recon just north of the city for another OP when I chanced into a small town, where a large and very excited crowd of Frenchmen and women were gathered in front of a building. I asked a man what was happening and he at once grabbed me and hustled me into the building in front of which everyone was crowding. Inside I saw three very abject looking females, two without a hair on their heads, and the third in the process of having her hair shaved off by a very excited man. I later learned that these women had slept with German soldiers during their occupation and were being punished by the town citizens.

The 90th Infantry Division joined XX Corps at this time. XX Corps artillery forces were also beefed up with the arrival of three more field artillery units; a 105-mm howitzer battalion, a 105-mm armored howitzer battalion, and a 105-mm self-propelled battalion. On August 26, Patton directed that XX Corps swing toward the city of Reims, ninety miles northeast of Fontainebleau. Speed remained the order of the day throughout all of Third Army. Every possible mode of transportation, be it tanks, trucks, cars, and captured German vehicles, were to be used to get the infantry moving quickly forward. The troops were only allowed to dismount when maneuvering under fire.

Throughout the pursuit through northern France, XX Corps organized its field artillery assets to provide immediate support, while still affording maximum flexibility to the maneuver divisions. Generally, when the combat divisions were in the advance, the corps artillery battalions were not attached to the division. Instead, a field artillery group with three or four field artillery battalions was given the mission to follow the lead divisions closely and be on call to provide rapid-fire support. This way, the divisions in contact would be provided responsive heavy artillery assistance without being encumbered with the responsibility to move, position, and logistically sustain the units.[39] As always, the armored cavalry moved out first, now with the orders to seize Marne River crossings as soon as they could. At Chateau Thierry, the scene of a major World War One battle, a company of tanks and a platoon of infantry were able to cross over a bridge just before the Germans destroyed it. XX Corps artillery again saved the day, supporting the small force as they repulsed a counterattacking battle group from the 9th SS Panzer Grenadier Division. Soon, a relief force crossed to the south and the Germans were driven away from the river. More XX Corps units pushed over the Marne and Chateau Thierry fell on August 27.

The remarkable speed of the Third Army attack often made as much chaos for the American commanders as it did for their foes. There were many instances when the combat echelons would cut off large numbers of German defenders. When the headquarters and support elements would follow to set up their respective command and operational posts, the area would often still be full of marauding enemy forces. In some cases, the Germans would be more than happy to surrender, in others, they would fight desperately as they tried to break through and rejoin their retreating comrades. To counter this, the American units would use the corral system of defense. Like the covered wagons of the old days, troops would fan out in 360 degree circles and pre-plot artillery registrations all around, fully prepared for an attack from any direction at any time. A number of bitter skirmishes were fought under these circumstances.

In one such action in the pursuit across France, B Battery observer Charlie Wright ended up starting a battle of his own after he and buddy Bob Brown happened across an abandoned bazooka and stockpile of rockets. Charlie recalls the impromptu fight:

Bob Brown, who hauled me around in a jeep, and I were joy riding along a dirt lane when I spied a bazooka at the side of the road. "Hold it Brownie" I said as I slid out of the jeep as he stopped. There was this bazooka, and numerous rockets that we picked up to check out. Low and behold, maybe 150 or so yards away, were a squad of five or six German soldiers. Dropping to the ground, I said "Load me Brownie!!" Quickly he thrust a round into the tube and hooked the wire; FFFssshhhhTTTT BLAM!!! The round fell a little short and the Germans dove over the other side of the raised tracks. A fresh round in, Brownie said "do it again," so I did. As fast as he could load I dropped several rounds over the tracks. Then, hearing the sound of a speeding vehicle, we turned to see Lt. Col. Schwartz's command car roaring by. Dropping everything, we climbed back in the jeep and headed back. Easing into the command post, we could hear the colonel excitedly telling of the battle he had just seen. Well, they were going too damn fast to have seen anything, and needless to say, we weren't about to fess up!!

In the chaotic, lightning paced advance through northern France, it became inevitable that men would occasionally become separated from the battalion by either getting lost or left behind. This happened to B Battery's Jim Royals, whose resolution of his misadventure led to the intervention by none other than General Patton himself. Royals relays this remarkable story:

During a 7th FAOB convoy move, I was dropped off to direct the vehicles to make a left-hand turn at a dead end intersection. I was then supposed to be picked up by the last vehicle in the convoy. The time of day was late in the afternoon, just prior to dusk. I waited on the one spot for an hour after the last of the convoy passed by. Not one vehicle stopped to pick me up. A heavy rain started to come down. As I was getting cold and wet, a French family, in a house only about 150 feet away, called to me and invited me to come over for a warm drink and to dry off by their heater. I said I could not leave my position, as I was to be picked up. The Frenchman of the house came down and offered to stand watch for me while I went inside for coffee. I believe I finally accepted the offer. I walked to the house and the lady handed me a hot cup a cup of coffee. I positioned myself where I could see the intersection and the man standing in the road. *No truck* came by to pick me up. After about ten minutes standing by the heater and looking out the window, I left the house and returned to the intersection. I stayed there in the steady drizzle of rain, until well after dark. The man returned to his house. As the rain became heavier I got down in the ditch and found a sewer pipe, about twenty-four inches in size, going under the road. I slid in the sewer pipe, but kept my head in position to detect any vehicle approaching. No truck came by. I stayed part of the time in the sewer drain and as the rain would lighten up I would come out and sit on the shoulder of the road. Later that night I heard artillery shells land not too far away, so I slipped back in the pipe with several inches of water now at the bottom, and even took a short nap. Still, no truck came by to pick me up.

As daylight was approaching the next morning, I heard an engine running nearby. I crawled out of the pipe and only a few feet away saw a U.S. soldier on a motorcycle reading his map. I walked over toward him and he was shocked to see me there. I explained that I was put out to mark the route, but was not picked up. He suggested that I could ride on the motorcycle with him and he would help me find my outfit. Because of the exposure to the rain and cold all night, I had a severe cold with chills and fever. He took me to an outfit a few miles away, where throughout the day they tried to get information on the location of the 7th FAOB. They had no luck, but got me a ride on a mail truck that eventually got me to Third Army Headquarters.

I arrived at Third Army Headquarters at about 7:30 P.M. with a severe sore throat, chills, and fever. As the mail truck dropped me off, the driver told a sergeant that I was sick and was trying to find my outfit. The sergeant had me sit in the hall while he went to find a medic to help me. As I sat, I could hear talk coming from the end of the hall. I was sitting there and the three men came walking down the hall toward me. Suddenly I noticed a nice shiny pair of boots standing in front of me. I got to my feet, looked in the man's face, and realized that it was General George Patton. He asked what I was doing sitting in the hall. I explained that I was sick and was trying to find my outfit, and also that a sergeant had gone to look for help. The general yelled at his staff to get me some immediate help, directing that a doctor to come and treat me and to also see that I got a hot meal. In a couple of minutes I was examined by a doctor and told that food was being prepared for me. I was given a shot for the cold and tablets to take and was directed to the mess room. Then I was given dry clothes, dry underwear, and was able to shave and get dressed. I was ordered to eat and to get right to bed. I rested well as a result of the shot and the tablets.

The next morning, the doctor again examined me and I had a hot breakfast. About 10:00 A.M., I was put on a truck and taken to my outfit, which was several miles away. I was dropped off and then reported to the CQ (charge of quarters). As I had been absent for three days, the commanding officer thought I was AWOL and restricted me confined to quarters. He seemed very upset and told me that I may face court-martial charges. I was ordered to remain in my tent until he decided what action to take. As well as still being somewhat sick, I was now greatly worried that I was considered AWOL. I knew that I did the job I was given and that I stayed and waited to be picked up as ordered.

A while later, as I lay in the bunk, the CQ came and told me to get dressed and to report to Major Chandler (the battalion executive officer). I was feeling pretty low and didn't know what to expect as I entered the tent used for the officer's mess. I was applauded by hand clapping of a few of the officers. Then Major Chandler said all was squared away and asked me to have chow with the officers. I could only say yes and thank them. But curiosity was getting the best of me. I asked one of the officers why the change of the commander's attitude? He replied that General George Patton had personally called to the battalion to confirm my story and to make sure that I got to my outfit. Even Lieutenant Colonel Schwartz apologized for the mistake and for not believing me. From that incident to the end of the war, I always felt General George Patton was a very good person who really cared for the men under him.

Royals concludes his story with the following commentary:

I am not to be glorified, or decorated for my going through the difficult time to find my outfit and rejoin them. I am putting this down on paper to say to any other soldier who gets lost or left behind: *don't ever give up*. There is always a way and people who will help you. I was lucky and will always be grateful to the many different people and soldiers who helped me.

And to stand face to face with General George S. Patton and to get his help was something as well. With all that man's responsibilities, he took the time to make the call and make sure that the truth was told. I will always thank and admire him.

For all of his bluster as a hard disciplinarian, episodes such as this give evidence to Patton's deep sense of commitment that it is an officer's fundamental responsibility to care for the well-being of his troops.

Others were less favorably disposed toward the Patton legend. One of them was Edwin Marinello, who gives this mixed review of the Third Army commander:

> Patton's bravery was a given. He was willing to come up to the line and stay for hours. By all accounts he was arrogant and self-centered. Of those parts our guys never got a hint. Always he was a houseguest minding his manners.
>
> He exuded pride in himself and his army. It rubbed off on the men. They sensed being the best and that the Krauts were in fear of them. But as the piles of dead kept rising and he didn't let up in his attack mode, they began to see him as an egotistical bastard.
>
> It didn't sit well that Patton delighted in war. The men wanted the war to end in the next minute. He wanted it to go on and once over he probably wanted to start another. It wasn't just the publicity, the larger than life image, the dress, the adulation and the glory that spurred him. He enjoyed the blood part, too. Sure, he wasn't going to get himself killed, but he saw nobility and honor in others bleeding and dying and of them he was proud. . . To Patton's appellation of "Blood and Guts," the GI rejoinder was, "Yeah, his guts, our blood![40]

In the course of the war, and especially during the August pursuit through France, the 7th was responsible for taking a good number of enemy prisoners. One had to be careful in dealing with prisoners, for although Germans were surrendering to the Allies by the thousands, there were still enough Nazi fanatics in their ranks to make this a dangerous proposition. Hank Lizak recalled the following time when he and Cpl Kurt Rieth were in their jeep when a German NCO approached, wanting to surrender. Rieth, whose family immigrated to the U.S. from Germany in the late 1920s, spoke German with native fluency. As Kurt was explaining the process of how he would be brought to the rear, the German suggested that he had other comrades who wished to surrender as well. Rieth cautiously followed the German to a nearby wood-line. Lizak was more than surprised when Rieth returned a short while later with a dozen other prisoners in tow. Once captured, prisoners would be sent to local POW collection points manned by military police, and later transferred to camps in either the United States or England.

On August 28, the 7th Armored Division moved out toward Reims in columns of seven separate task forces (each column composed of a company of tanks, a company of armored infantry, a squad of combat engineers, and a section of tank destroyers.) En route, the 7th Armored Division overran a German artillery brigade, an infantry regiment, and a separate battalion. The tankers and mechanized infantryman then bypassed Reims to the north and cut off its garrison from escape. Meanwhile, elements of the 5th Infantry Division assaulted into the city, and captured it while meeting heavy sniper fire.

In taking Reims, XX Corps captured an airplane factory, an ordnance depot, and huge German supply dumps. While XX Corps lost only thirteen killed and eighty-six wounded, 1,847 German prisoners were taken, with another 446 killed.

Capturing German supplies started to become increasingly important, as the Americans were quickly outstripping their own logistical lifeline. Supply Sergeant Geiges was becoming concerned with the difficulty in keeping up the supplies for headquarters. One thing he found frustrating was the amount of

John K. Rieth

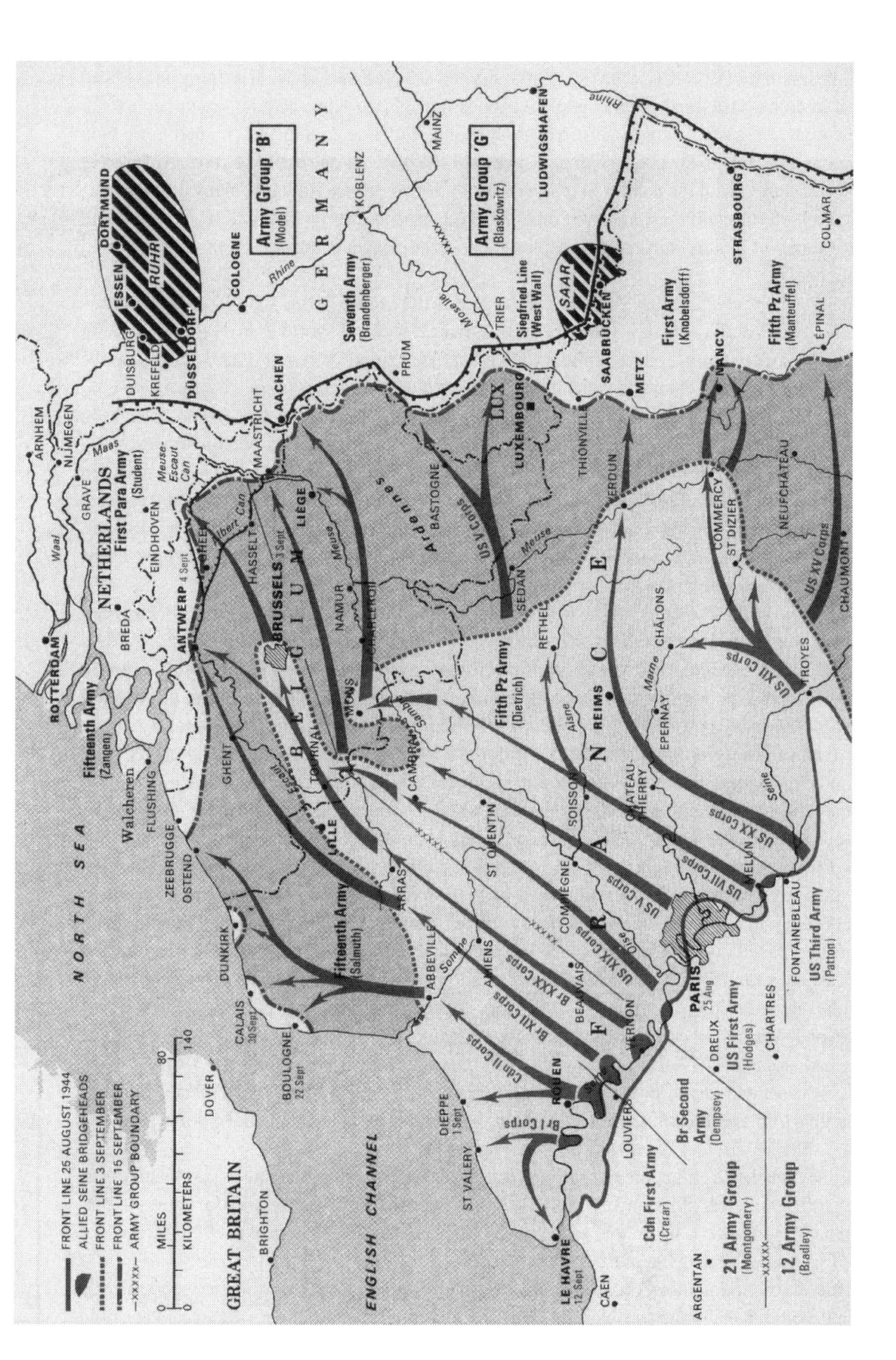

ADVANCE TO METZ

From Fontainebleau, XX Corps moved northeast, taking Reims on August 28, 1944. With the Germans in full retreat, Verdun—the site of World War One's greatest battlefield—was captured on August 31. Third Army was stopped here not by the Germans, but by a critical shortage in fuel. When the advance resumed again on September 5, the Germans had regrouped along the Moselle River. As XX Corps neared the fortified city of Metz, the German Army was well prepared to confront them. The pursuit phase was over and the battle for Metz would be a bloody and prolonged fight.

time required to fix simple problems with the soldiers' weapons. If a soldier had to turn in a rifle for repair, he would be defenseless until he had it returned. Although not an ordnance specialist, Sergeant Geiges became competent in doing basic repair work on the weapons himself. He also acquired quite an arsenal of weapons that he kept in his supply truck. If there was a problem that he couldn't fix, he had more than enough extra weapons available to swap out with a soldier until the original one could be repaired. Geiges was also becoming concerned with the condition of the men's uniforms. Since England, many of the troops had been cleaning their clothes with gasoline, and many of the garments were wearing thin. With the end of summer and beginning of a rainy fall season, keeping the men in clean and serviceable uniforms would be a growing challenge.

The next major natural obstacle that awaited XX Corps was the Meuse River. XX Corps was ordered to cross it in the vicinity of Verdun, which was the site of the greatest battle of World War I. Although the 7th Armored Division, 3rd Cavalry Group, and 5th Infantry Division faced some sharp rear guard actions on the way to Verdun, the lead XX Corps elements were at the outskirts of this famed garrison city by August 31.

The city of Verdun sits on both banks of the Meuse, a large and swift river that would have been difficult to cross without the assistance of the French Resistance. The Germans had previously destroyed all of the city's bridges, saving one central span to allow the withdrawal of the many thousands of troops still trying to escape from the west. For insurance against a quick American thrust, the Germans had posted two Panther tanks and several machine gun squads by the bridge, as well as rigging it with explosives. Just as the 7th Armored Division tanks were approaching the western outskirts of the city, French partisans assaulted the bridge and were able to cut the demolition wires, saving it from destruction.

As was usually the case, 7th FAOB forward observers were in the XX Corps vanguard. B Battery's Lieutenant Slessman was with the lead armored cavalry elements and was among the first into Verdun. He recalls an old bearded Frenchman with bad breath who hugged him and presented him with a medal. Slessman also recalls seeing the Panther tanks that were guarding the bridge. The American armor soon appeared and a sharp tank battle ensued, with the superior German panzers knocking out several American tanks before they themselves were finally disabled. With the 5th Infantry Division following up, Verdun, and more importantly, the Muese River, were under American control by the evening of August 31.

Although the German ground troops had lost the single bridge span across Verdun, the Luftwaffe was still intent on dropping it into the Muese, and attacked it in heavy bombing raids on September 1. A huge traffic jam resulted from the mass of vehicles trying to clear the bridge. Lieutenant Slessman was smack in the middle of the bridge when the city was attacked by a sortie of over 100 German planes. Some of the drivers ahead of him panicked and abandoned their vehicles, further trapping those stuck behind them. While anti-aircraft fire blazed away, an enemy plane broke through and dropped two 1,000-pound bombs that narrowly missed their target and landed in the river on either side of the bridge. Slessman remarked that although no one on the bridge was injured in the attack, "many gray hairs were cultivated."

Moving beyond Verdun, the Americans had to approach warily, because many of the large fortifications that had stopped the Kaiser's Army in 1916 could still be used against XX Corps. That, however, was not the case, and the all-out German retreat went on. On the night of September 1, most of the 7th FAOB were able to make it ten miles east of Verdun, where they stopped and bedded down for some badly needed rest.

By the time they reached Verdun, they had traveled over 600 miles, set up seventeen command posts, and surveyed over 100,000 meters of ground. 7th FAOB soldiers were at virtually every major action fought by XX Corps, and had yet to suffer a battlefield casualty. By all measure, the soldiers of the 7th FAOB could now be considered seasoned combat veterans.

In the first few days of September, the sound and flash platoons set up to cover the ground to the east of the city. Using the old but elaborate French forts from World War I, (some four floors deep and bristling with artillery turrets on top), the flash sections had excellent fields of observation far to the east, now seemingly clear of enemy forces. Logic begged that the advance resume immediately, as to not allow the Germans the opportunity to regroup. Lieutenant Slessman went on a hasty recon and made it almost to the Moselle River, which was to be XX Corps' next major objective. With little organized enemy resistance to oppose them, all those making XX Corps reconnaissance patrols urged an immediate pursuit to the river.

The August 1944 race across Northern France would be the highlight of Patton's career and was the campaign that made his name what it is today. Third Army's lightning advance will always stand in military history as a preeminent example of the power of a relentlessly aggressive offensive. This stunning victory would come at a price. The Third Army was now to become a victim of its own success, as a lack of gas could no longer allow it to keep pace with its enormous fuel expenditures. The first signs of the severity of the problem were evidenced on the march to Verdun, where the 90th Infantry Division was left behind at Reims because XX Corps did not have the gas to keep them going. By the time XX Corps had cleared Verdun, they barely had enough fuel left to cook their own food.

The math of the logistics dilemma shows that this was an inevitable problem that could not be avoided. As more and more Allied soldiers landed in France, they consumed more fuel. As they advanced farther forward, it took more fuel just to get the basic supplies to their destined units. The Allied logicians simply did not have the capacity to move all the fuel from England, through Normandy, and to the front in sufficient quantities. In essence, Patton's Third Army needed 400,000 gallons a day in order to sustain the advance. By the end of August, he was only getting 30,000 gallons. At Verdun, the XX Corps offensive through northern France had ground to a halt.

While waiting for enough fuel to be brought up to resume the advance, the men of XX Corps had an opportunity to view the expansive Verdun World War One battlefields, where over 700,000 German and French troops fell between 1916 and 1917. To preserve it as a shrine, the French had left much of the old battlefield as it was at the end of the war. (To this day, much of the area around Verdun is still off limits, due to the high amount of unexploded munitions that remain lying throughout the woods.) The troops also freely helped themselves to the large quantities of supplies that the Germans had to leave behind on their hasty retreat. Kurt Rieth on September 6: "Well I don't have to worry so much about keeping warm when the weather starts getting cold around here. We managed to get some swell jackets from a captured German warehouse. They are leather on the outside and fur on the inside. They must have either been used by aviators or in fighting in Russia. They are all white on the outside which makes me think they were used for fighting in snow." Hank Lizak remembers being with Kurt when they came across the jackets. Hank picked up an excellent coat that he managed to send back home and then wear every winter for the next ten years. Getting good German battlefield souvenirs was a top priority for every GI fighting in Europe, with pistols, Luftwaffe daggers, and other weaponry being high priorities. A few days later, after departing Verdun, Rieth secured some more booty. "I managed to pick up some more armament for myself the other day. We passed some knocked out German armored cars and decided to look them over. They had plenty of equipment in them, and I got myself a Schmeiser machine pistol. I would still like to find a Luger but I'm pretty satisfied with this."

The few days break around Verdun also gave the 7th a very badly needed rest. The battalion had been operating under sustained combat conditions for over a month with virtually no breaks. For the past several weeks, they were living off adrenaline, and now the weariness was beginning to show. It wasn't just gas that Third Army was short of. The fuel crisis had slowed down all logistical support, making it hard to supply the men with decent rations. To compensate for the lack of food, Amos Robinson remembers the fate of a chicken that one of the medics had somehow acquired as a pet. Over a period of several weeks, the hen and his private became close companions. The chicken would always sit next to the soldier in the truck while moving, and constantly follow behind him wherever he walked. At the height the logistics shortfalls,

Amos and a buddy were tiring of subsisting off of tins of captured German sardines and began to think of better uses for the bird. When its master was away, Robinson and his pal killed it, put a rod through it, and put it over a fire. When they thought it was done, they tried to eat it, only to be amazed at how tough it was. Simply unable to consume it, they buried the remaining evidence. The poor private who owned the chicken was reduced to tears when he realized it was gone, and Robinson forever regretted the event.

The men of the 7th FAOB had come a long way since landing in Normandy barely one month previously and 600 miles traveled. They were now hardened combat veterans possessing the confidence that they could perform their mission well. Kurt Rieth penned this letter in August 1944, and reflected on his one year anniversary in the army; "It just occurred to me a little while ago that one year ago today I left for the army. I never thought that in one year I would cover so much territory and see so much. I'll never forget that first day how we were rushed around and how lost I felt. It's amusing now when I think back about the strange ideas I had of army life."

By the first of September, General Dwight Eisenhower took over as the Supreme Allied Commander (SHAFE). His strategy at that time was to move his two army groups (the 12th Army Group under Bradley which controlled Third Army and XX Corps), and British Field Marshall Montgomery's 21st Army Group onward to Germany in a broad front. One of the effects of this approach would be to restrict the tempo of Patton's Third Army, which now had to keep a more coordinated pace with other army groups. Also in early September, Eisenhower gave priority to Montgomery's "Market Garden" plan, which called for a bold airborne-led strike into Holland, and crossing over the Rhine River at Arnhem. While Market Garden would not have a direct tactical impact on Third Army, the priority of resources made it that much more difficult for XX Corps to sustain the logistical flow of ammunition and gasoline.

It would not be until September 4 that XX Corps would have enough petroleum stockpiled to resume its march eastward. Patton's plans were typically bold and ambitious. XX Corps was to drive into the heart of Germany and establish bridgeheads over the Rhine River between Frankfurt and Karlsruhe. Once the Rhine was bridged, the Allies would be clear to go onto Berlin and win the war. If they could keep up a similar pace achieved in attacking through northern France, it was optimistically hoped the war could be won by Christmas.

Two big obstacles remained to be breached before Third Army could reach the Rhine; the first was the mighty Moselle River, and the second was the Siegfried Line (or West Wall), a continual network of bunkers and defensive works that ran the length of the German border. Given Third Army's experience of blasting through tough natural obstacles in northern France, there was no reason to believe the prospects of moving against these targets would be particularly difficult to quickly overcome. XX Corps' next mission orders were both vague and extremely ambitious. First, they would take the fortified city of Metz and establish a bridgehead across the Moselle, and from there, sweep into Germany and take the Rhine. This was asking a lot from a corps that held a forty-five-mile wide front with only three divisions (the 5th, 90th, and 7th Armored).

Despite the long journey ahead, it was generally thought from Eisenhower on down to the lowest ranks that the war could still be brought to an end before Christmas. Rieth on September 1, 1944: "Well I'm afraid another summer is slipping by, and I hate to see it go. I don't look forward to spending a winter in France, especially since we sleep out in the open. About half the time now I sleep in the back seat of the car. You can't quite stretch your legs out, but it's warm and softer than on the ground. I feel pretty confident, however, that by the time it gets real cold this business will be over with."

The American Army was about to be disabused of this optimism at Metz.

CHAPTER 6

Metz I: Meeting Europe's Strongest Citadel

If XX Corps was able to get a slight rest while waiting for gas at Verdun, the benefit to the Germans was exponentially superior. By the end of August 1944, most senior Allied commanders had written off the Germans as a credible fighting force. Calculating the huge numbers of enemy killed, wounded, and captured, as well as the material lost, it seemed impossible for the Germans to be able to rebound from their disaster in Normandy. The Wehrmacht would prove this assumption to be very wrong.

The German Army on the western front was about to be retransformed. Now on the border of defending the Fatherland, the backbone of the German Army was dramatically restored. The Germans had always been adept at their ability to reconstitute shattered combat commands, and in early September of 1944 they would again show their capacity to restore units that had been on the brink of annihilation only a short time before. Many of the more fainthearted German soldiers had already surrendered in the disastrous route through France, and those that remained were among their toughest troops. The ranks also swelled with hundreds of thousands of new recruits as the Germans lowered conscription standards to bring in younger teenagers and older men. Even the average German soldier was a more formidable enemy now that his homeland was directly threatened. Slave labor was put to use in improving the decayed Siegfried Line as well as putting greater muscle into war industries.[41]

Despite the intensive Allied bombing that destroyed Germany's greatest cities, German war production was at an all-time high. Germany re-outfitted its panzer units with the latest tanks, and those of far superior quality than the standard American counterpart of the day, the M-4 Sherman. While the Allies would enjoy vast superiority in its number of tanks, that advantage was reduced when one Tiger or Panther tank could easily disable four Shermans. When XX Corps encountered the Germans next, it would meet a different enemy than the one they rolled over in August.

By September 4, Air Corps transportation airlifts had replenished XX Corps with enough fuel reserves to resume a measured advance. Per its standard operating procedure, XX Corps first deployed its 3rd Cavalry Group, which moved toward Metz. This fortress city of Metz, sitting on the eastern side of the wide Moselle River, would play a big part of the next chapter of the 7th FAOB's history.

Located squarely on the historic invasion route between Germany and France, Metz had been a fortified city in some fashion or other since the 1500s. As artillery began to improve in the early 19th Century, the ring of forts around Metz expanded to the high ground farther to the outskirts of the city. In the 1870 Franco-Prussian war, thousands of German troops were lost while attacking Metz from the same ground that XX Corps would approach from seventy-four years later. Following a German siege, the French surrendered Metz and shortly thereafter lost the war to the Germans. Metz is part of the Lorraine province (mixed with German and French culture) that along with the Alsace, was ceded to Germany at the war's conclusion.

Under the Kaiser's control from 1870 to 1914, the Germans were responsible for a massive build up of the Metz defenses. By the time construction was completed, the Germans incorporated forty-three intercommunicating forts (an inner line of thirteen and an outer ring of thirty forts) on both sides of the Moselle. Additional fortified networks also spanned north to Thionville, twenty miles above Metz, as well as south along the Moselle. The forts contained guns of various heavy calibers, and were completely interlocked to provide coordinated fire on every conceivable approach to the city.

The pre-World War I construction of these forts were marvels of German engineering that stealthily blended the works into the terrain. For close defense, a typical fort consisted of infantry trenches, shellproof bunkers, a number of observation posts, and two types of heavily fortified artillery batteries. To fire at distant troop concentrations, the forts had 100-mm cannons individually mounted in rotating turrets. For counterbattery action, the forts had 150-mm cannon housed in equally well-protected individual turrets. The turrets themselves were made of thick, hardened steel, and could withstand direct hits from the heaviest ordinance available. Where possible, the gun batteries would be placed on the reverse slope of the hills, making them much more difficult to spot. Even the barracks were sheltered underground, with deep tunnels connecting all parts of the fort. These subterranean garrisons were self sufficient, with complete food service, medical, and electrical generators present. Deep moats and fields of barbed wire, covered by strong points holding machine-guns, surrounded the perimeters. Viewed from the distant exterior, all that could be seen of these huge forts (many of which consumed hundreds of acres and could garrison thousands of soldiers) was a deep irregular trench and a few stubby gun turrets on strips of concrete.

Although fighting swirled through the Lorraine throughout World War I, the Metz fortified belt was so strong that the Allies never even contemplated trying to attack it.

In the course of the German occupation of France from 1940 to 1944, the Germans paid little attention to maintaining the forts, and instead spent their resources in building the Atlantic coast wall. That changed in August 1944, after the Allies began to breakout of Normandy. German engineers focused hasty renovation efforts on a number of the most strategic forts. Artillery was refitted and made serviceable, barbed wire was re-strung, and forts were stocked with food and ammunition. Although the Metz forts were a far cry from their peak condition twenty-five years earlier, they were more than capable of extracting a heavy toll on the advancing invaders.

In addition to the advantage of defending the forts, the Germans had used Metz as a military school center before the First World War and again since 1940. In comparison to the Americans' lack of detailed information of the Metz forts, German senior commanders and NCOs alike knew every fold of ground throughout the area and literally had textbook solutions on how to best defend it.[42] The Germans had a force of about four of the XIII SS Panzer Corps under the command of Lieutenant General Walther Krause to man the forts in the Metz-Thionville sector. Despite the SS designation, few of these troops were true SS, but rather a hodge-podge collection of garrison/student units, and other forces that had been rounded up when the Germans closed the roads out of Metz at the end of the August free-fall retreat.

The fortresses in and around the city of Metz were defended by the 462nd Mobilization Division. Before the invasion, the 462nd Division served as the headquarters for a number of military school and garrison units. Most notable among these schools were 1,800 cadets of an officer candidate regiment, comprised primarily of hard-core, veteran NCOs from the Russian front. These Nazis were superb soldiers and could be expected to fight to the bitter end. Although recently commissioned as officers, they would be reinforced with 1,500 soldiers gathered from retreating columns and fight at Metz as a cohesive regiment and an extremely effective fighting force. The 462d Division was also rounded out by a 1,500-man regiment made up of an NCO academy, as well as 600 men from the garrison's 1010th Security Regiment.

The other prominent German forces that would oppose XX Corps were the 17th SS Panzer Division, which took up positions southwest of Metz, and the 559th Division that defended along the Moselle north from Metz and up to Thionville. There were also additional units in the XIII Panzer Corps that had been halted from the August retreat, and sent back to man the east bank of the Moselle. All in all, General Krause had about 14,000 troops and a varied array of armor and artillery to man a twenty-five-mile wide stretch of line. Although the Germans were spread thin and weak in anti-tank defense and armor support, these factors were offset by significant strengths. The Germans were occupying excellent defensive terrain, possessed some of the strongest fortifications in the world, and had cohesive command and control. Most of the units were assessed as having generally good morale.[43] As A Battery's Hank Lizak would relate, to the men of the 7th FAOB, "Metz would be another name for hell."

The continuing Third Army fuel crisis contributed to the appalling lack of intelligence that the Americans had of the German situation and forces. To try to fill these gaps, a 3rd Cavalry Group reconnaissance-in-force mission was launched on September 2. Taking advantage of captured German aviation fuel to fill the armored cars and light tanks, several squadrons broke through German lines and made a bold seventy-mile dash to the north and east toward the Moselle. One of the cavalry platoons was actually able to make it all the way to the west bank of the Moselle at Thionville, which would soon become the northern end of the XX Corps sector. The surprised German garrison there suffered losses, but quickly recovered and drove off the lightly armored troopers with their overwhelming firepower. Other patrols made it to the Moselle eight miles above Metz. In one of these forays, the commander of the 3rd Cavalry, Colonel Drury, was ambushed and captured. With no hope of additional help, and now low on gas themselves, the remaining 3rd Cavalry elements pulled back to friendly lines. Other than the reports that no bridges were intact and that resistance was stiffening, little information of real solid intelligence value was gained in this operation.

The 7th FAOB continued with their observation mission during this period, and by September 4 completed two sound and flash installations, as well as sixty miles of survey.

By September 5, XX Corps had distributed enough fuel to continue the advance west and was ready to move out. While the XX Corps leadership had some limited knowledge of the Metz forts, the general tendency was to hope for the best and dismiss the forts as probably obsolete and incapable of offering determined resistance.[44] Walker's basic plan was to have the 5th Infantry Division attack Metz head on, while the 90th Division would attack Thionville to the north. Once Thionville was secured, the 7th Armored Division was to then cross over the Moselle and race for the German border. The 7th FAOB's A Battery and battalion headquarters were located with the main thrust to the north, while B Battery was attached to the 33rd Field Artillery Brigade and the 5th Division for the intended crossings at Metz and to the south. The 3rd Cavalry Group led the advance on the morning of September 6. One squadron made it to the Moselle at Arnaville, ten miles south of Metz, before being forced back by heavy German artillery fire. None of the rest of the group made it to the river that day.

On September 7, the bulk of XX Corps combat power neared the river and went into action. To the north, the 90th Infantry pushed in strength toward Thionville, the 7th Armored Division reached the Moselle north of Metz, and the 5th Infantry Division pushed up the Metz area forts and the ground southwest of the city. The battle then began in earnest.

The Germans were not about to let the Americans approach the river unmolested. To disrupt their advance as much as possible, the Germans launched a surprise armored counterattack designed to thrust deep into the XX Corps left flank. This punch landed the night of September 7-8. The lead unit selected for this attack was the 106th Panzerbrigade Feldherrnhalle under the command of Colonel Baeke. The 106th Brigade had previously been shattered on the Russian front, pulled out, reorganized, and re-equipped with the latest tanks. The 106th included an armored infantry battalion, a tank battalion consisting of thirty-three Panther tanks and eleven self-propelled assault guns, plus a company of engineers and service troops. The Panzers were also supported by the infantry of the 59th Regiment of the 19th Volksgrenadier Division and several batteries of 88-mm artillery.

As XX Corps' 90th Infantry Division moved forward, they were completely unaware of this powerful armored threat that was now staged to attack only a few miles to the northeast. On the evening of September 7, the Division Command Post was set up at Briey, seven miles west of the Thionville objective. The Germans initiated the attack from the village of Auden-le-Roman and quickly broke through the 90th Division's front lines. The American infantrymen had little in the way of armor support or anti-armor weapons at hand, and the panzers simply rolled over them. Within minutes, half of the German tanks were able to race through the 90th Division's command post at Briey before the division staff had even realized what was happening. The division commander, Major General McClain, was awakened at gunfire not more than twenty yards away as the Americans and Germans blasted away in the darkness.

The 90th Division artillery staff was completely surrounded. Private Norbert Altman, of the 7th FAOB's A Battery who was detached to the 90th Division artillery headquarters that night, went into action so quickly that he went through the remainder of the night minus his pants. Undetected by the Germans, the divisional artillery staff was able to exfiltrate out of the area and sneak back to friendly forces.

By the dawn of September 8, XX Corps began to take action to stem the attack, but there was still great confusion among the assorted American elements as to the scope and degree of the German penetration. One such unit that was still completely in the dark of the German attack was the 7th FAOB command section. Just before the attack began, Lieutenant Colonel Schwartz, Captain Johnson, the A Battery Commander, and a recon party moved forward to coordinate the following day's operations with the chief of the 90th Division's Artillery Brigade. Expecting to link up with the 90th Division command post at Briey, they arrived only to find the area filled with knocked out and burning tanks and half-tracks, both German and American. Just as they were trying to piece the events together, a French civilian called out a warning from a cellar window to warn of a large German tank that was about to turn a corner ahead of them. Seconds later, the gun barrel of the tank came into view. Tom Delay was working the radios in the back seat of Schwartz's vehicle when the event unfolded. The command car was on a narrow street headed directly for the enemy tank. Schwartz turned to his driver and barked, "Sandy, let's get the hell out of here!" The driver needed little extra motivation, and put the vehicle in a sharp U-turn. Given the poor turning radius of a command car, Delay still can't figure out how they turned around as quickly as they did—the car literally scraped paint off a house as it came around. Schwartz and his party were able to dash out of the village before the Germans could react, and then spent the next few hours evading the panzers until they were able to make it back through 90th Division lines.

With daylight, the Americans sent spotter planes in the air and were finally able to get a better feel of the extent of the German penetration. The Germans had pushed deep into the 90th Division sector, but as a result, their own flanks were now vulnerable to American counterattack. While General Walker sent in tanks and tank destroyers of the 7th Armored Division to meet the Panzers head on, additional American forces struck hard at where the German attack had originated from—the village of the Auden-le-Roman.

Colonel Baeke had left behind some of his infantry and 88-mm guns to protect Auden-le-Roman, a key road intersection which the Germans needed control of should they have to retreat. Aware of the concentration of enemy cannon, A Battery's Lieutenant Fearn Field ordered a flash observation post set up at Mercy le Haut, just west of the German guns at Auden. As recalled years later by A Battery's Victor Salem, Lieutenant Field was an aggressive West Point graduate who always pushed himself and his men as far forward as possible. His flash chief, Master Sergeant Emeric Ujczo, seemed to sense a need for greater caution that day and made a point to ride out to the OP with Lieutenant Field. By all accounts, Master Sergeant Ujczo was an excellent noncommissioned officer who commanded great respect by the entire battery. Tall, handsome, and still in his early twenties, Ujczo quickly rose to the top of the enlisted ranks through his naturally strong leadership skills.

Once at the OP, Field and Ujczo proceeded to direct counterbattery fire against the 88s. The German

88-mm was perhaps the most effective field cannon used by any army in World War II. This gun was a high velocity, flat trajectory weapon that could fire armor-piercing shells at directly observed targets, or be elevated and fire high explosive shells against either troops or aircraft. The shells traveled faster than the speed of sound; one heard it explode before one heard it fired.[45] One of the rules of artillery observation is that if you can see the enemy, there is also a good chance they can also see you. In this case, the Germans detected the A Battery OP and opened fire on it. Master Sergeant Ujczo was killed by shrapnel from an air burst, becoming the 7th Field Artillery Observation Battalion's first casualty of the war. Ujczo had been in the battalion almost since its activation three years earlier, and his loss hit hard among the battalion, particularly on Lieutenant Field. According to Salem, Lieutenant Field felt largely responsible for the tragedy and came away from the experience a changed man. For the most part, Field would take much greater caution when sending men into harm's way in future operations.

By midday, the German attack had completely run out of steam and Baeke withdrew the remnants of his shattered force. When darkness fell on September 8, the Germans had suffered thirty tanks destroyed or captured, plus sixty half-tracks and one hundred other assorted vehicles lost.[46] While the 90th Infantry Division was battling the panzers before Thionville, the 5th Infantry, with support from the 7th Armored Division, was trying to secure a bridgehead over the Moselle just south of Metz. The lead elements were stopped when they ran into German strong points near Gorze, a few miles west of the Moselle. Bypassing the German salient, the American columns moved farther south to the small west bank village of Dornot. En route, they encountered heavy enemy artillery fire and deadly minefields scattered throughout the area.

Lieutenant Slessman writes of B Battery's experience during this movement forward.

On September 6, we finally got underway again and I went forward with a tank battalion of the 7th Armored Division down the big highway through Etain and Conflans without a bit of opposition. My purpose for accompanying the armor was to be on the lookout for "Jerry" artillery so that if shells began dropping, I could ascertain ahead of time from what general direction they came and how much and what size guns so that we could employ bases more efficiently if they were needed. It wasn't long before I found what I was looking for, because when we approached the Moselle River we received a warm reception from the vicinity of Amanvillers, where they knocked off five of our tanks with some accurate artillery that poured down upon us. We knew at once that the Germans intended to contest every foot of ground from here on, so our unit immediately set to work. Upon my initial reconnaissance I probed forward as far as the town of Gravelotte, not knowing whether the Germans were dug in the town or to its east. Upon entering the town on foot, I found it deserted of civilians with a roadblock in the center of the town. Deserted as it appeared, I felt as though there were plenty of eyes watching me, so I zigzagged my way out of the town as fast as possible and went south along the high ground that bordered the Moselle just south of Metz itself. I passed one fort that was not occupied by either side at the time, though the Germans came back into it in force days after. That was Fort Driant, where we lost so many men later in trying to take it.

Simply getting to the Moselle was a difficult challenge. Only one primary road ran from the central XX Corps down toward the river. The Germans commanded the high ground covering the road and their artillery was zeroed in on the approach. One town that was of some tactical importance in this sector was the small village of Gorze. At the edge of a defile, Gorze was situated on a road intersection two miles west of the river and one mile south of the German fortified lines on the west bank hills before Metz.

The Germans initially defended Gorze so fiercely that it was bypassed by the vanguard elements of the 5th Infantry Division's 11th Infantry Regiment. Skirting the town, a small force made it to the Moselle

River. Engineers with three assault boats linked up with the infantrymen. Trying to catch the Germans by surprise, the Americans immediately launched a platoon's worth of infantry on the boats. The Germans were ready however and let loose a fusillade of heavy machine-gun fire. Most of the men on the boats were killed and none of the survivors made it across.[47] Additional 11th Regiment forces were massed in front of Gorze and the town was taken by storm. While a clear route to the Moselle was now established, it would continue to be the subject of heavy bombardment by the German guns. The 7th FAOB's B Battery had the job of protecting this vulnerable and highly dangerous sector. In the weeks to come, B Battery would use Gorze for both command and observation functions as its sturdy stonewalled buildings offered some measure of cover and protection from the ever-menacing German cannon.

Charlie Wright was one of the first B Battery men to follow the infantry into Gorze. As such, he was tasked to ensure that a sector of buildings was completely clear of enemy forces. In addition to looking for any Germans, it was Charlie's practice to also keep an eye out for any caches of left-behind booze. In any case he had to be prepared for anything, for one never knew what he would find in these situations. With his carbine at the ready, Wright carefully checked room after room. Entering one bedroom, Wright took in a surprise when he came upon a dead woman covered with a sheet. The gun-shot corpse had obviously been an attractive young woman. Wright briefly speculated her fate; was she hit by a stray shot, murdered by the Germans, or perhaps had she had been a Nazi officer's consort killed by revengeful French citizens? Wright continued on with his sweep of the town, but long since wondered about the source of this mystery.

With B Battery of the 7th trying to find a way to reduce the German shelling, XX Corps continued forcing a crossing of the Moselle south of Metz. The 5th Infantry Division began to converge attack formations at the town of Dornot in the early morning of September 7. The Americans intended to use the same audacious tactics that worked so well in crossing the Seine on August 22. The plan of attack was to load up infantry squads on whatever boats could be made available. Under the blanket of smoke screens and heavy artillery support, the strike force was to paddle across the river, secure the far bank, construct pontoon branches, and continue the advance on the other side.

The attack was scheduled to begin at dawn, but chaotic conditions delayed it several hours. The staging area at Dornot was under continual German artillery fire, creating a real urgency for B Battery to make good counterbattery direction plots. Things quickly turned nightmarish for the Americans. Heavy rains and even sleet fell, making the roads into a slippery morass. Several trucks carrying ammunition were hit and set on fire. Unlike previous river crossing operations in northern France in the past month, XX Corps would be hampered by a severe shortage of artillery ammunition. As a result, the infantry had to attack with limited artillery support, and with every fire mission needing to be called with the greatest possible accuracy.

Through a curtain of fire, F and G Companies of the 11th Infantry Regiment rowed across the Moselle in tiny twelve-man assault boats. By early evening, four rifle companies and some heavy weapons platoons were on the far side of the river in a 200-yard wide perimeter that would become known as Horseshoe Woods. Ahead of them, on the crest of a hill, lay Fort St. Blaise, one of the large forts protecting the southern approach to Metz. F and G companies silently advanced up to the outer perimeter of the gigantic fort. Gaining entry into the fort was no simple matter, as it was protected by a dry thirty-foot deep moat, five separate barbed wire fences, and a high spike-studded iron fence. All entry points were enclosed in thick concrete. While the Americans considered their options, all hell broke lose. A heavy German artillery barrage opened up in concert with well-hidden snipers. One of the *Scharfschuetze* marksmen fired a shot that killed the F Company commander. Next, a large enemy infantry force attacked on both sides of the 200-man force. With no possible alternatives remaining, the survivors of the two companies retreated back to Horseshoe Woods where the real drama would soon begin.

The displays of heroism during the two-day defense of the Dornot bridgehead could in itself fill up a

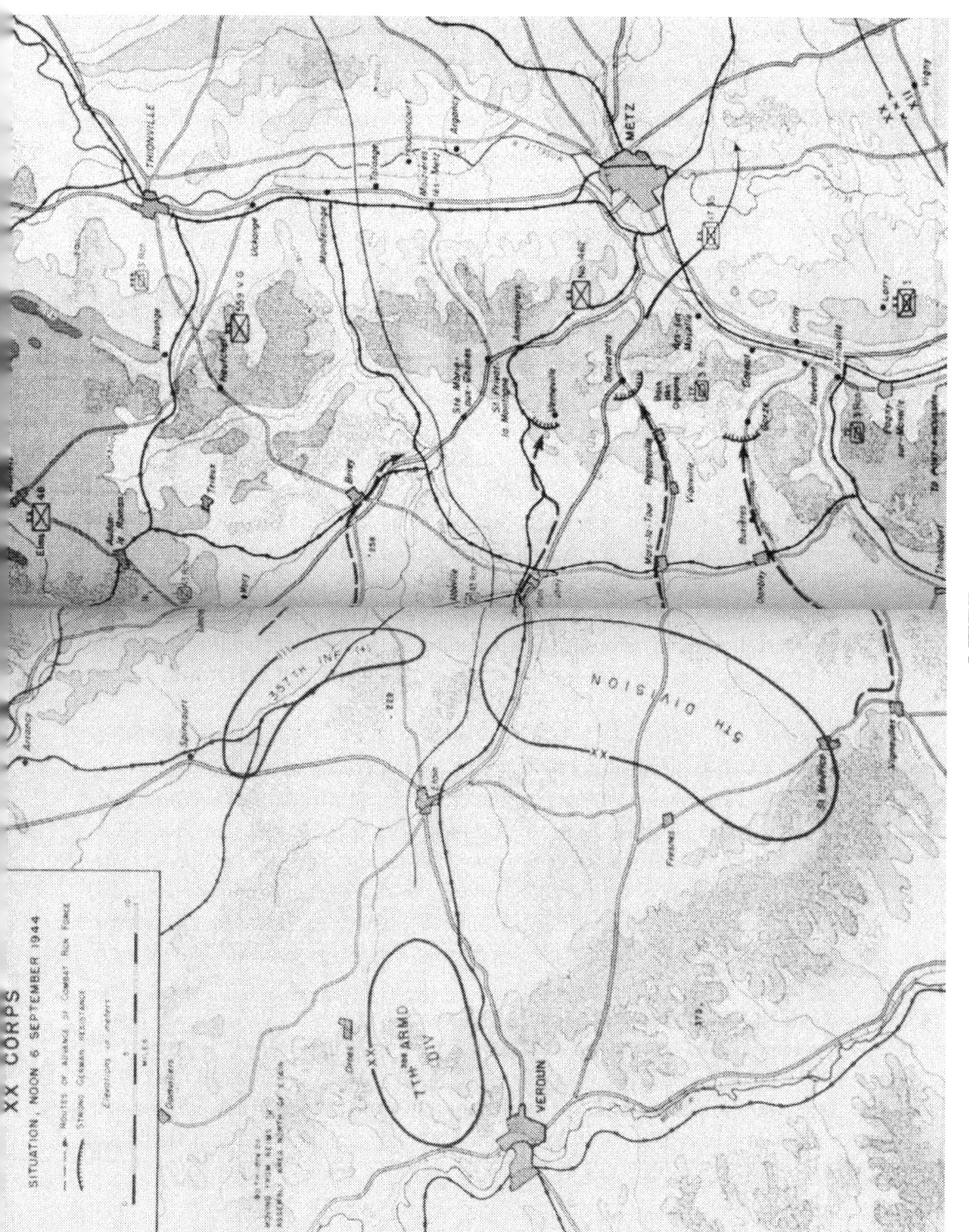

METZ

This map, taken from Kemp's "The Unknown Battle - Metz," depicts XX Corps arrival on the Metz front in early September 1944. Expecting a quick river crossing, XX Corps was stopped by the German's use of massive fortifications. To the south, the 5th Infantry Division eventually crossed at the Arnaville bridgehead only to have further progress on the east bank of the Moselle River halted. A strong line of forts, including Fort Driant between Dornot and Gravelott, allowed the Germans to hold their ground before and after Metz. A two-month stalemate was broken when the 90th Division crossed the Moselle above Thionville, moved south and met up with troops of the 5th Infantry Division heading north from the Arnaville bridgehead. Metz was surrounded and the surviving Germans were eventually forced to surrender.

book, but a brief sampling of some of the exploits are presented here. For over twenty-four hours, the tiny perimeter was subject to a constant artillery fire and thirty-six separate German armor-supported infantry charges launched by the 17th SS Panzer Grenadier Division. The intense and deadly accurate German shelling made it impossible to bring up reinforcements. In the night, German tanks would drive right up to the perimeter and spray the woods with cannons and machine guns in hopes of provoking a response that would better reveal the defenders position. The American fire discipline was excellent however, as they waited until the charging enemy were almost upon them before opening up. Hundreds of terribly wounded men bore their agony in silence in order to further cloak their location. In one instance during the first night, two privates volunteered to man an advance post. Ignoring orders to withdraw as the Germans closed in, they stuck to their posts where they were eventually killed. As dawn broke, the evidence of their heroic stand lay in the bodies of twenty-two dead Germans that were found strewn over their position.

Ammunition and medical supplies ran low, and the awful weather precluded any chances of air support. Although hundreds of Germans were killed in the struggle and many more wounded, their overwhelming numbers and firepower sealed the fate of the battle. There was no hope of maintaining the bridgehead, and the best that the beleaguered Americans could hope for would be to avoid complete annihilation. On the night of September 11, a massive barrage of XX Corps artillery blanketed the woods and allowed the shattered task force to row back across the Moselle. The four-day action had been terribly costly, with some 945 American soldiers killed, wounded or missing. For all practical purposes, the 5th Infantry Division's 2nd Battalion, 11th Infantry, had virtually ceased to exist.[48] The sacrifice of those lost at the Dornot bridgehead had not been in vain, as the German obsession to wipe it out it had allowed the 5th Infantry Division to successfully make and secure a crossing several miles farther to the south. With the fighting in Horseshoe Woods going full swing, Major General S. Leroy Irwin, the 5th Infantry Division commander, was able to better coordinate an effort to cross the Moselle at the town of Araville. With nine battalions of XX Corps and four battalions of division artillery pounding the surrounding fortifications, two battalions of the 10th Infantry Regiment swarmed over the river and seized a high ridge 3,000 yards east of the river.

The Germans reacted swiftly, and replied with a full-scale artillery attack of all calibers, both from the Metz area forts as well as from well-concealed mobile batteries. B Battery set up a number of sound and flash locations on both sides of the river amidst the steady rain of German shells. Lieutenant Slessman: "The next two days I completed my recon along the river establishing a flash ranging base that overlooked the river and looked down upon Metz, itself. Those were not easy days as Jerry was very temperamental about that high ground and raked it continuously with artillery and mortar fire, thus making the recon very laborious as the shelling forced one to embrace Mother Earth about every tenth step. I was lucky so far as the shelling went and, outside of scruffing my knees and elbows from hitting the ground, was no worse off for my efforts."

While most soldiers would do what they could to instinctively get away from artillery impact areas, the mission of the 7th FAOB required its men to actively seek them. Lt. Warren Sockwell was assigned duty with shell rep teams on the Araville bridgehead for a period of two weeks. As soon as a shell landed, he and his team would jump into the still-smoking crater to try to determine the characteristics of the round and the direction it came from. Each time he did so, Sockwell could only pray that the next shot would not land again in the same place. Sockwell considers this as among the most dangerous times he spent in the entire the war.

The effectiveness of the American counterbattery fire was limited by both the German batteries' stealth and tremendously fortified locations, as well as from severe XX Corps ammunition shortages. Between September 9 and 10, XX Corps artillery tubes had fired over 10,000 rounds, resulting in critically short ammunition reserves. In addition to effectively using their artillery, the Germans also mounted an aggressive armored counterattack from the south. One of these panzer strikes may well have proven disastrous for those American troops on the east bank of the Moselle, had not a last-minute P-47 airstrike drove off the oncoming tanks.

Although restricted by ammunition reserves, XX Corps maximized its artillery capability by modifying efficient command and control practices. The 33rd Field Artillery Brigade, which had just joined the corps along with five additional heavy field artillery battalions, was given control of all corps artillery in the 5th Division and 7th Armored Division zones. The XX Corps artillery assumed control of all artillery in the 90th Division zone. This allowed the 33rd Field Artillery Brigade to mass nine to thirteen artillery battalions for short but intensive fire against German attacks, a combat power that was critical in separating German infantry from their tank support, and allowing each assault element to be thrown back individually.[49] An example of how this artillery lash-up could be marshaled was recalled by Lieutenant Slessman, who was able to adjust fire to great effect one day in the 5th Division sector:

> During the three weeks that I remained in B Battery as flash officer, our life was so full of exciting occurrences that I can scarcely begin to relate all of them in this letter. Our OPs were under almost constant fire and the men stuck it out for the most part with stoical calm. I divided my time between the plotting center where I spent most of my time talking on the phone to the OPs, and the rest of the time at one of the five OPs looking for a choice target at which to shoot. On one occasion I had the luck to see about two hundred Jerries file onto the Metz airfield several miles across the Moselle, where they leisurely prepared to bivouac for the night. With great haste I called for fire from the 5th Infantry Division Artillery and soon adjusted a battalion of artillery on the edge of the field. The Jerries took to cover as we had anticipated and in about five minutes reappeared and carried on as before. This was just what we had been waiting for, so we let them have it with four battalions. The results were gruesome, bodies literally flying into the air. They must have lost about two thirds of their number.

For the next several days, the bridgehead was gradually expanded, and constantly attacked by the German infantry and artillery. By September 14, two Bailey Bridges had been set up over the Moselle River, which ultimately secured a foothold over the river south of Metz. Still, this position was under continual fire from Fort Driant, a monster fort on the west bank of the Moselle near Metz, and hemmed in by strong German forces in all directions. Although the 5th Division had successfully crossed the Moselle, the ring of fortifications protecting Metz was still virtually intact. Not counting the men lost at Dornot, the Americans lost thousands more men in the nearly ten days it took to establish one comparatively small bridgehead over the Moselle, and one which was situated in country that was extremely difficult for expansion by armor. In sum, a little over one week of fighting had cost the 5th Infantry Division over 5,000 men, and took out virtually half of the division's fighting strength.[50] The enormity of these losses was made clear to Charlie Wright. From his position in Gorze he watched on as hundreds upon hundreds of replacements marched on in neat columns of four down the road to the Moselle crossing points. Wright noted how clean and new their uniforms and equipment looked in contrast to the battle-hardened veterans. Wright also knew that every new man marching into the fight meant that another had been killed, wounded, or otherwise disabled. The toll was simply staggering.

With the 5th Infantry and portions of the 7th Armored Divisions hammering away at Metz from the south, the 90th Division attempted to close in on its northern objective—to secure a bridgehead at Thionville. After regrouping from the German's September 8-9 armored counterattack, the 90th Division's 357th and 378th Regiments moved into Thionville, which the Germans had left undefended as they withdrew across the Moselle. Following this movement, they destroyed the last bridge that remained north of Metz. By September 12, the 90th Division was in firm control of the west bank of the Moselle to the north of Metz, but also was in no condition to consider crossing.

It would take the bloodbath of direct assaults for XX Corps to finally appreciate the strength of the fortifications directly before Metz on the west bank of the Moselle. Incidentally, this is the same ground upon which two German field armies were mauled in unsuccessful assaults against Metz during the 1870 Franco-Prussian War.

Throughout the first week of the battle, American patrols had pushed close to the west bank forts. Although little meaningful tactical intelligence on the enemy situation had been gained, Walker concluded that therein lay the enemy's center of gravity. He summarily assumed that assaulting these forts would be the most direct key to capturing Metz. In response, the bulk of the 90th Division was pulled away from Thionville, and sent south toward this objective. Any thought of a quick dash over the Moselle River in the northern part of the XX Corps sector was now gone.

General Walker was now faced with a problem that would curse both his corps and the rest of the Allied forces for the next six months—the severe over extension of his combat forces. The lines that the Allies had to maintain, a distance that ranged all the way from the English Channel in Holland to the Swiss border, required far more men than could be transported and sustained on the continent. This also led to a critical lack of reserves that would be able to either exploit a breakthrough in the German lines or to check a serious counterattack from the enemy. In the 90th Division area, its three infantry regiments were spread over twenty miles, from before Metz in the center of the XX Corps area, north to Thionville. Through mid September, the extreme left of the 90th Division, which was also the left-most element of Third Army, was "hung in the air" and not connected to the 1st Army in Luxembourg. Had the Germans had the notion or capability to counterattack from this gap, Walker would have been in serious trouble.

Patton, desperate that XX Corps had yet to achieve a decisive breakthrough beyond the Moselle, put increasing pressure on General Walker to make some progress quickly. As further backdrop to this sense of urgency, Montgomery's Operation Market Garden offensive to gain a Rhine River foothold in Holland was becoming the primary Allied objective in Europe. This operation would take priority over Third Army in consuming precious logistical resources. On September 12, General Bradley ordered Patton to hold on the west bank of the Moselle and to set up on the defense. Patton was appalled. He begged Bradley to let him go all out in the offense, and expressed confidence that he could soon make it to the Rhine: Patton urged, "Don't stop us now, Brad, but I'll make a deal with you. If I don't secure a couple of good bridgeheads east of the Moselle by the night of September 14, I'll shut up and assume the mournful role of the defender." While Walker did get a bridgehead secured at Araville by September 14, he certainly was not making any progress in expanding it.[51]

Patton would do everything in his power to remain on the offensive, and the XX Corps leadership would continue to bear his wrath every minute that the advance forward stagnated. The next phase of XX Corps efforts would be to breakthrough beyond the relatively thin bridgehead across from Araville, centered ten miles southwest of Metz. The predominate terrain feature to the east was the high ground known as Hill 396. The hill was taken after hard fighting on September 15, and the next objective was to cross the shallow Seille River, a few miles farther east. To penetrate the Seille, XX Corps would first have to take a line of three villages that protected the access to the river. From north to south, these villages were Pournoy, Coin, and Sillengy. Once the towns were captured, then the Americans could cross the Seille and attack against the next major eastward objective, a series of fortifications called Fort Aisne.

The mission was given to the 7th Armored Division, which would advance in two parallel combat commands, CCA and CCR. B Battery of the 7th FAOB was tasked to direct counterbattery support for this mission. The weather continued to be as big an obstacle as did the Germans. It had been raining constantly, which not only reduced air cover, but also made travel over anything but hardened roads impossible. The tanks and armored personnel carriers of CCAs moved out on the morning of September 16, but were greatly hampered by the lack of serviceable roads and supporting infantry. Some progress was made by CCR in the south, but German infantry and artillery entrenched near Sillengy stopped them hard. Patton was not pleased, and threatened Walker that he would invade Germany with the rest of Third Army while XX Corps remained behind to contain Metz.

On September 17, the 5th Infantry Division was thrust into the fight to support the 7th Armored Division's embattled combat commands. The Germans easily predicted the attacks and realigned their defenses accordingly, moving in reinforcements from the relatively quiet northern sectors. On the left side of the American attack, an advancing battalion of German infantry landed squarely on the border of the 10th and 11th Infantry Regiments in bloody hand-to-hand combat that greatly disrupted the 5th Division movement. In the center, CCA received a modicum of artillery support in trying to take the tiny town of Marieulles, finally winning the objective after much hard fighting and many losses. On the far right, CCR suffered heavily from German artillery concentrations as they continued to renew the attack on Sillengy.

Heavy rain and fog made observation difficult for the 7th FAOB flash team. Compounding the bad weather, the constant German shelling made it difficult to even survey the OPs before the actual sites could be selected and manned. The work of the survey teams took much longer in such conditions, as the men were frequently having to "hit the dirt" to avoid the incoming bursts. For his work between September 15 and 17, Staff Sergeant William Jessel, the B Battery Survey Chief, was awarded the Bronze Star Medal. His citation read: "Staff Sergeant Jessel displayed exceptional technical skill, determination and energy in the performance of a mission of great responsibility. Assigned the task of carrying survey control to four flash ranging observation posts near Gorze, Staff Sergeant Jessel reconnoitered for suitable survey routes, and by his courageous behavior under enemy fire, inspired his men to a successful completion of the problem. His aggressive action enabled his unit to locate and neutralize many enemy gun positions."

Despite the hazardous conditions and terrible weather, some effective counterbattery work was being carried out. Lieutenant Slessman: "Our flash base was quite successful there, as we located dozens of enemy batteries and adjusted our own artillery on them. I had one close call at an OP one day when Jerry apparently saw me climb the hill. He fired 88s at us for ten minutes, cutting limbs from an overhead tree and one fragment stuck me in the waist, where it was stopped by my ammunition pouch. I have carried a bent carbine around as a lucky piece ever since."

At great effort, a combined force from the 5th Infantry Division and 7th Armored Divisions were finally in position to attack the towns of Pournoy, Coin, and Sillengy on the morning of September 18.

The Germans defended the three towns with the 37th and 38th SS Panzer Grenadier Regiments. With the Seille River to their backs, they had nowhere to escape, and would be forced to fight to the death or surrender in the attack they knew was imminent. The 5th Infantry Division's 2nd Battalion, 10th Infantry would attack Pournoy and the 1st Battalion's 2nd Infantry would take Coin. To the right, CCR of the 7th Armored Division would be assaulting Sillengy for the third consecutive day.

For the next five days, these XX Corps troops hammered away at their objectives with the utmost of heroism and determination that could be asked from any soldier. Likewise, the German defenders countered with equal bravery and fortitude, and both sides battled away with all they had.

The 38th Armored Infantry Battalion, with supporting tanks, launched the first attacks against Sillengy. As soon as they left the nearby woods, the Americans were blasted by German artillery. Some of the tanks did make it into the town, but were pushed back when they ran out of ammunition. Using the last two reserve platoons, the battalion again fought its way into the edge of town, only to be thrown out the next morning by vicious German counterattacks. On September 19, the fighting again seesawed around the town when the exhausted 38th Armored Battalion again resumed the attack. The battalion commander was killed, as was his executive officer when he stepped up to resume command. A third officer moved in to take command only to be wounded. The 38th Battalion covered itself with glory that day, but at a cost of seventy-five percent of the unit. They never were able to take and hold Sillengy, and its shattered survivors were withdrawn and replaced by CCA on September 20.

The 5th Infantry Division attacks against Pournoy and Coin were held off in hopes that Sillengy would be the first of the three towns to fall. Finally, on September 20, the 1st Battalion of the 2nd Infantry began their assault on Coin. Advancing in the face of heavy tank, artillery, and infantry fire, they fought their way into Coin by nightfall, and were able to make it to within a few yards of the Seille River. For them to advance farther it would now require the successful attack of 2nd Battalion, 10th Infantry Regiment on Pournoy a few miles north.

Even before the fighting had started, the 10th Infantry Regiment was suffering from thirteen days of continuous combat that had cost them 700 men, or about half their effective strength. The terrible weather had conspired to take out additional men with the painful malady "trench foot," a disabling cold weather injury that would plague XX Corps soldiers for the next seven months. Although the 1st Battalion was now up to strength by being filled with new replacements, the exhaustion and shock effect on the units' leadership and few surviving veterans was telling.

After leaving its final staging area in the woods, the 1st Battalion of the 10th Infantry (1/10th Infantry) had to cross over two thousand yards of open fields to reach Pournoy. As soon as they broke cover, they were hit by withering artillery, mortar, and machine gun and rifle fire from both the front and their exposed right flank. With the support of some tanks and tank destroyers, they braved the enemy firestorm and were able to make it into the outskirts of the village, although losing two of their four company commanders among the many who were killed and wounded. Once in Pournoy, the Germans continued to throw everything they could at the battalion. After fierce hand-to-hand fighting and fending off numerous counterattacks, the battalion secured about one third of the village by evening. Fending off German tanks with bazookas through the night and the next day, the 1/10th finally had control of the village by September 21. By this time, of the 800 men who began the attack, only 450 were left.

Throughout September 21-22, the Germans continued to aggressively counterattack. XX Corps and 5th Division artillery were superb, and their accurate firepower succeeded to keep the Germans from overwhelming the threadbare toeholds of the battered American infantrymen. The German artillery fire was relentless, and caused one American to later comment that "we were shelled just once at Pournoy; and that was all the time." B Battery of the 7th FAOB did their very best under these extremely hazardous conditions, and its men suffered from the same hellish German shelling as did the infantryman in the foxholes and cellars right next to them. The battery's sound ranging base was able to make several confirmed plots of enemy artillery, much of which were from mobile batteries that were well protected in the casemates of nearby Fort Aisne.

By September 23, it was clear that any further efforts against the Seille line were hopeless. Even if the 5th Infantry and 7th Armored Division's attacks could cross the narrow river, there were simply no reserves available for further exploitation. Shortly thereafter, Pournoy was abandoned and the 5th Infantry Division withdrew to a defensive line farther to the west. The 7th Armored Division crossed back across the Moselle and was subsequently pulled entirely out of XX Corps control. XX Corps gave up trying for any near term victory to the south of Metz.

CHAPTER 7

Metz II: The Attack on Fort Driant

As September advanced, Walker's options for breaking the Moselle line and taking Metz continued to narrow. He did not yet have the resources to force a crossing north of the city, and the bitter fighting to expand his bridgehead to the south did nothing but increase the casualty lists. His boss, Patton, was in no mood to receive excuses, and Walker was left with his last alternative—a direct push into the strongest area of the Metz fortification system.

The fighting throughout September had left a strong pocket of German defenses on the west bank of the Moselle in a line that ran from the industrial town of Maziers-les-Metz (seven miles north of Metz), to the high ground directly across from the city, and another five miles to the south. The bulk of this convex shaped line, especially the sector than ran in the high hills, was protected by a series of damnably impregnable forts. From north to south, those included Fort Deroulege, Fort Plappeville, Fort St. Quentin, Fort Jeanne D'Arc, and Fort Driant. The effect of the large-caliber artillery fired from these forts simply could not be ignored. In particular, the guns of Fort Driant were situated so that they were firing into the backs of the Americans to the south on the east bank of the Moselle on the Araville bridgehead.

Coming into the battle, the XX Corps leadership lacked solid tactical intelligence on the specific location and disposition of these forts. The 7th FAOB, with their unique counterbattery observation capabilities, would play a big part in trying to make up this shortfall. Seventh FAOB command and control was initially set up by establishing the battalion and A Battery's command post in a sheltered gully near the town of Jarny, sixteen miles west of Metz. For more forward operations, A Battery set up a sound base at the town of Malmaison, only a short distance from the enemy-held Fort Jeanne d'Arc, the largest of the Metz area fortifications. The Malmaison area would become the most heavily shelled sector in the entire forty-mile wide XX Corps zone of operation. The continual German shelling ripped up the telephone wire communication links between the various 7th FAOB elements. Hank Lizak, who was part of A Battery's "wire gang," recalled that the teams often had to go out to patrol and splice the wire lines up to nine or ten times per night.

Even out farther than the Malmaison base were the sound and flash observation posts, which had to be established as far forward as possible—often as close as a few hundred yards from the forts and other German positions. Because the German forts were so well camouflaged, the value of the 7th FAOB OPs during this phase of the campaign were critically important. Jack French remembers that the forts were virtually invisible to aerial observation and that most fire and bombing direction were based on observation from the high-powered flash OP telescopes. Given the constant volume of inbound heavy artillery, mortar, and sniper fire, this was extremely dangerous work. On September 15 alone, three A Battery men were hit by shrapnel and evacuated to the rear. These losses included Private Wesley Welch, who sustained a fractured leg, Tech Sergeant Tennis Mullins who was hit in the hip, and Corporal Lester Paulsen, Jr. with multiple shrapnel wounds in the arms and legs.

For the observers serving on the outposts and moving with the infantry, there was the perpetual danger of German raids and counterattacks. One such occurrence was on September 16, when a mobile German strike force made a spoiling attack against the 90th Infantry Division's 357th Infantry. The bitter fight that followed resulted in seventy-two American causalities.

While the infantry was looking for weaknesses in the fortified system, XX Corps artillery was doing what they could to blast the German defenders into submission. An enormous amount of precious ammunition was expended in this effort, much of which would later turn out to be fired in vain. In concentrated artillery barrages, the American artillery commanders used the full weight 155-mm and its heaviest 240-mm cannon to attempt to destroy the forts. The primary targets were Forts Jenne d'Arc and Driant. For all their might and the thousands of rounds expended, XX Corps artillery was unable to even disable a single German cannon. It was not that the 7th FAOB plotting of these forts were inaccurate, but rather that the forts' defensive capabilities were incredibly impenetrable. Many of these heavy shells scored direct hits on the German turrets, only to bounce off with as much effect as had they been pellets from a boy's BB gun. At best, the noise of the impacting American fire would sometimes cause the German gunners to withdraw to deep chambers inside the forts, only to resume their positions once the fire subsided.[52]

XX Corps' stalemate at Metz was by no means the only instance of the Allied stall along the western front. Far to Holland in the northeast, Montgomery's bold Operation Market Garden had failed to breach the Rhine and had resulted in the near annihilation of the British 1st Airborne Division at Arnhem. General Courtney Hodges' 1st Army was able to reach the German border, but was having as little success in penetrating the deadly Siegfried Line as had XX Corps made against the Germans at Metz. Near Aachen, thousands of Americans were caught up in a terrible cauldron in the Hurtgen Forest. Charging through the Hurtgen's dense woods against thick German bunkers, two divisions lost up to eighty percent of their front-line troops in September attacks that gained virtually no ground. In the remainder of the Third Army sector, just to the south of XX Corps, Patton's XII Corps was now contained in the aftermath of its brief success in taking the city of Nancy in mid September.

To address these challenges and reset strategic priorities, Eisenhower held a conference with his army commanders at his Versailles headquarters on September 22. The Allied forces were still beset with critical supply problems, and above all else, Eisenhower needed Antwerp in Belgium as a deep-water port. This would be his primary objective, followed by an offensive into the German industrial Ruhr Valley. These top priority missions would go to the 21st Army Group and 1st Army. Given the limited logistical support remaining, the Third Army would be relegated to staying put along the Moselle and assume a defensive posture—the operational antithesis to Patton's very soul. Making matters worse, XX Corps' 7th Armored Division, whose participation was so critical in the race across France, would be transferred to 1st Army while Patton's entire XV Corps would be lost to the 6th Army, which had landed in southern France. Not only was Patton thrust into a defensive and secondary role; he was losing a major portion of his combat power should he somehow regain the initiative.

On September 25, Patton was forced to accept this turn of fortune in orders passed to his senior subordinate commanders. Blaming supply problems as the core reason, he ordered his army to assume a defensive posture, but while also concealing any obvious signs of this to the enemy. He forbade such typical defensive activities as digging trenches and setting up barbed wire and mine fields. Instead, the Third Army would have forward outposts that would be backed up by mobile reserves readied to counterattack. Once this suitable line was secured, Third Army would again be set to resume the offensive.

Patton also sought and received permission from Bradley to make some "minor adjustments in his present lines." As a secondary objective, he intended to retain the flexibility to drive a wedge into the Metz fortified perimeter. Even though forced to maintain a defensive stance, Patton still planned to continue localized attacks to keep the Germans off balance. This strategy laid the groundwork for the ill fated attack against Fort Driant, an operation that would turn out to be XX Corps', if not one of the entire U.S. Army's, greatest debacles of World War II.[53]

Of the five primary forts that remained on the western bank of the Moselle, Fort Driant continued to present the biggest thorn in XX Corps' side. In addition to lobbing heavy shells throughout the XX Corps sector, Fort Driant became a beacon of German resistance, and a target that Patton and Walker insisted had to be destroyed. Sitting on a high hill and occupying over 350 acres, Fort Driant was a huge triangular-shaped defensive work built in 1899. In a full war footing, it could hold up to 2,000 troops. A deep infantry ditch surrounded the fort, while hardened machine gun emplacements guarded two batteries of three 100-mm guns and two batteries of three 150-mm howitzers that were armored, parabolic, steel turrets. A fifth battery of two 100-mm guns protected the fort's southwest approach.

The central barracks contained underground communications, a hospital, and power generators. Five concrete bunkers overlooked north and south approaches and more than one hundred armored artillery observation posts were scattered among the barracks, bunkers, and perimeter. All of the barracks, facilities, and gun turrets were connected by a maze of tunnels that ran below the shrub-covered exterior. Deep barbed-wire entanglements both surrounded the fort and ran through it, with special concentrations around the five separate artillery batteries.[54] Fort Driant was designed so that even if an attacking force was able to penetrate into the fort, they would have a hard time trying to gain access at the defenders well-protected deeply inside it. Not only was the fort difficult to penetrate, but its German defenders were a battalion from the much vaulted officer candidate regiment, by far the most determined and capable enemy that XX Corps would face in the Metz campaign.

The first serious attempt to reduce Fort Driant was an air campaign boldly named "Operation Thunderbolt," which began on September 17. Bad weather and competing missions reduced the scope of a previously intended grand bomber attack on the monstrous forts. Still, the operation did result in a large number of medium bombers and fighter aircraft dropping large amounts of ordnance. Many of the 7th FAOB veterans retained vivid memories of watching P-47s swooping down to drop napalm and high explosives on the fort, all without inflicting any apparent serious damage to the target.

In mid September, Colonel Yull, the commander of the 5th Infantry Division's 11th Infantry Regiment, began to hatch an audacious plan that called for his 2nd Battalion to storm and capture the fort. It was this battalion that had been badly decimated in the Dornot bridgehead on September 7-8, and had recently been reconstituted with new replacements. The 11th Infantry had taken its share of casualties from the guns of Driant, and its leadership was eager to silence them for good.

Like the previous attacks in Metz, the first assault on Driant was hastily conceived and executed. Although some accurate renderings of the fort had finally been obtained from French engineers, the attacking companies were briefed from rudimentary drawings and maps. On September 27, the rainy weather broke and renewed air strikes were launched. Taking advantage of this support, two companies of the 11th Infantry were readied and a XX Corps artillery concentration from eight large-caliber batteries was fired.

German artillery retaliated in kind, resulting in a bloody day for the 7th Field Artillery Observation Battalion. Lieutenant Slessman, who was transferred from B Battery Flash Chief to A Battery XO on September 25, recalls how, two days later, he was helping to post some of the Malmaison Base sound observers to their forward base. At Sound Outpost #1, he dropped off Private Harold Lorman and watched as he walked up the hill to his post. Lieutenant Slessman continued on his way, and stopped by to check on the OP on the return trip. There he learned that Lorman had just been hit. Slessman immediately contacted the Battery CP and dispatched medic Roy Barber, who quickly set out with a litter and jeep. Barber remembers: "We drove on grass in a valley near Gravelotte. I followed the wire over the hill to the foxhole where Private Lorman lay. He had been hit by a mortar shell in the right upper chest and neck, I am sure he died instantly. We put his body in the litter and drove to an appointed spot where the grave detail picked him up." Barber recovered Lorman's body while under heavy fire. (Private Lorman was the only 7th FAOB killed in action to be permanently interred in Europe. Today his body rests at the Lorraine United States Military Cemetery).

Barber continued to have a busy day. Upon returning back to the A Battery command post, he learned that another A Battery sound section had been hit hard by the heavy German shelling and had taken additional casualties. Barber got his jeep driver and went out the OP, which was on flat ground near a road intersection. Three of the men, Private William J. Miller Jr., Sergeant William R. Hicks, and Tech 5 (T/5) George H. Carlton all had serious shrapnel wounds and had to be evacuated to the 315th Clearing Station, a transfer point en route to rear area hospitals. The threat of German artillery never let up. Hank Lizak was standing guard at A Battery Headquarters alongside Private Charles Arnatz. As they were casually talking, an enemy artillery barrage descended upon them. Following the explosions, a rain of shrapnel whizzed by their ears, reminding Lizak of the noise made by angry bees. Arnatz called out that he was hit—a jagged chunk of metal was lodged deep in his thigh. "Doc" Barber treated Arnatz, as well as Corporal Elbert B. Snarr, who had less serious shrapnel wounds to his hands. Barber was able to remove the shell fragments; he bandaged them, and quickly returned them back to the line.

That night, Roy Barber made some quick mental calculations and came to the troubling conclusions that if the German shell fire could continue to kill and wound the men of the 7th at the same rate they did that day, there would be few troops still left standing by Christmas. He was rather relieved the next day when the first patient to be seen was Hank Lizak, whose only requirement was to get some medication for a bad cold. Barber was awarded the Bronze Star for his valiant efforts on September 27 in rendering aid to the wounded while under heavy fire.

While the 7th FAOB OPs were getting hammered by German artillery, XX Corps preparations to take Fort Driant went into high gear. From dawn until 2:30 p.m., XX Corps artillery fired away until their gun tubes were red hot. Confident that no enemy could withstand such pounding without being killed or rendered ineffective, the men of two 11th Infantry rifle companies launched forward in their attack on Fort Driant. Under the cover of a heavy smoke screen, the 300 or so infantrymen slugged their way up to a barbed wire obstacle that stood before the main ditch on the northeastern perimeter of the fort. Meeting heavy rifle, machine gun, and mortar fire from some previously hidden bunkers, the attack stalled. Although tank destroyers were brought up to fire at some of the German positions, their fire did little more than chip off tiny bits of concrete from the thick bunker walls. By nightfall, it was clear the attack wasn't going anywhere, and the Americans broke off contact, losing eighteen men in the day's fighting.

The 5th Infantry Division commander, Maj. Gen. S. LeRoy Irwin, would have preferred to have cut his losses and not pursue renewed attacks. After all, his division had taken some 3,056 casualties in the preceding three weeks and he needed more time to rebuild the infantry battalions that were so badly decimated in the Dornot crossings. Walker, clearly not appreciating the strength of the German fort, unfairly blamed the attack's failure on a lack of aggressive leadership at the unit level and called for an additional assault to take place. Patton, unsurprisingly, sided on the argument of offense and directed that a stronger attack be launched.[55] The bad fall weather continued to get worse, and the second attack was held off until October 3. In the next attempt, the Americans would greatly increase the amount of engineer and tank support. Under the command of Lieutenant James Blanchard, a hand-picked composite tank company was formed that consisted of eleven medium tanks, five light tanks, four self-propelled howitzers and two tank-bulldozers. The engineers had a deep supply of satchel charges, pipe-like bangalore torpedoes, flame-throwers, and special "snake" explosive tubes, longer versions of bangalore torpedoes laid by the tanks that were designed to destroy the rows of barbed wire entanglements. One other infantry company was added

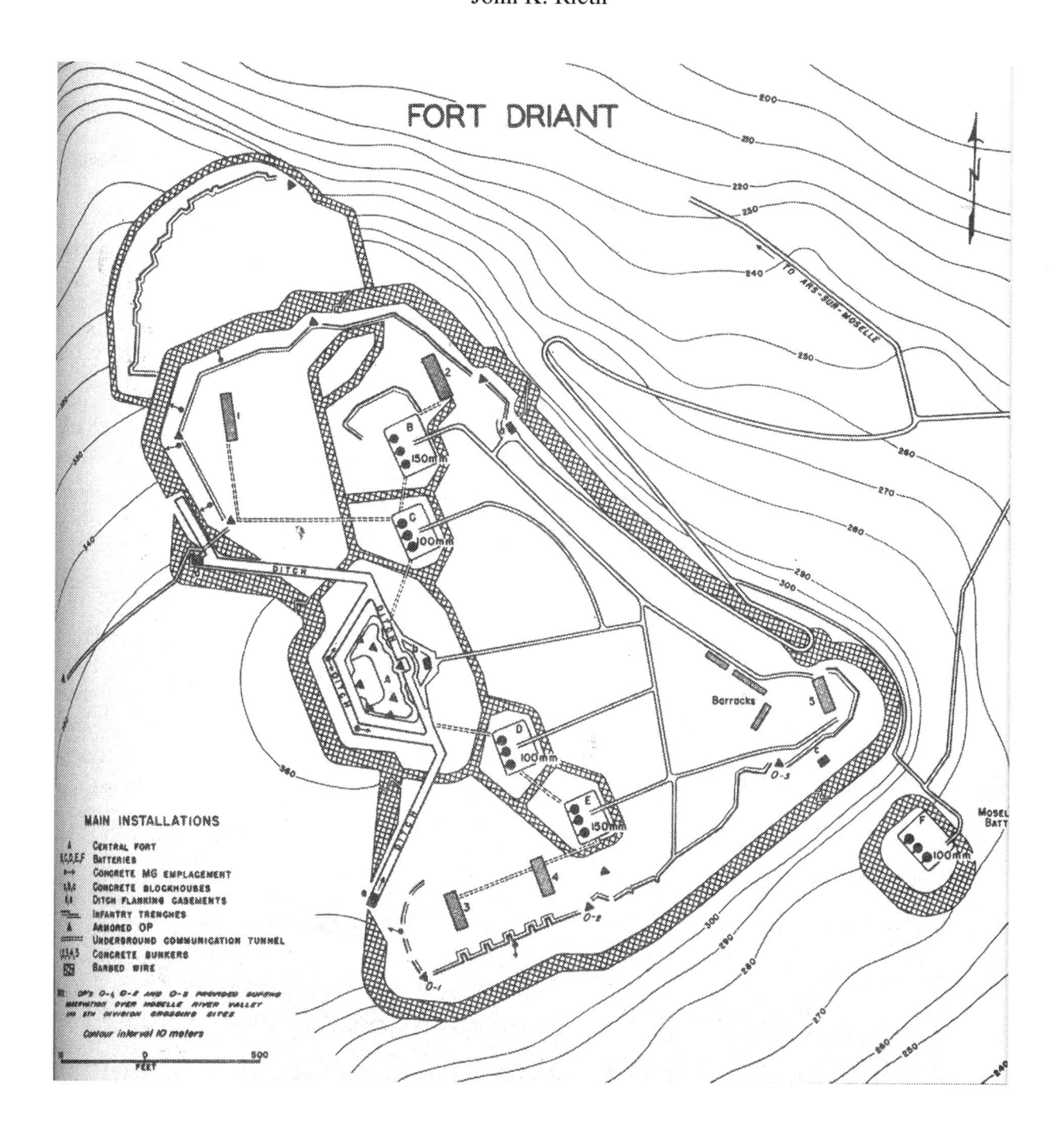

Fort Driant

For over two months, this monstrous fort proved impervious to the most intensive XX Corps heavy artillery bombardments and infantry assaults. Air Corps bombs and napalm also had little effect. The German guns inside the fort hammered away into the backs of the Americans holding on the east side of the Moselle. General Patton was fixated on taking Driant from the beginning of the Metz Campaign, but it would continue to hold out until the very last days of the siege.

to the mix, and they would be deployed as an immediate reserve. Improved blueprint drawings of the fort were also obtained that showed the intricate catacomb network of tunnels that ran underneath the fort. It was now realized that even the maximum explosive power of massed artillery and bomber attacks could only accomplish so much against this target. Victory would be achieved by sending in infantry to breach inside the fort and kill their foe by rifle, grenades, and bayonet.

The attack was to be led by another corps-wide artillery bombardment and major airstrike. Again the weather failed to cooperate, which limited the amount of air support to some napalm bombs dropped by a few fighter-bomber sorties. The XX Corps and 5th Division artillery battalions fired with all their power, but with little more effect than was delivered on the attack of September 27. Start time, or H-hour, was at noon, and the lead two companies of the 11th Infantry led the attack.

Assaulting on the southwestern corner, B Company of the 11th Infantry attacked through several enemy bunkers, crossed the ditch, and was able to reach its objective, the underground barracks just inside the fort's interior. Once there, however, the engineers had no success in using TNT to blast into the barracks, and the exposed company continued to take losses. E Company attacked against the northwest corner of the fort, but was unable to reach the fort's deep moat before being caught in a withering crossfire of German machine guns. The two engineers' tank dozers that were assigned to fill in the ditch both broke down, and E Company was stopped a few meters short of the fort. Despite their ability to penetrate into the fort, they hung on as tenaciously as could possibly be expected. Bearing fire for four consecutive days, E Company valiantly stood at this position, losing fifty-five of their original 140 men.

The other portion of the Fort Driant battle opened at B Company's position at the southwest quadrant of the fort. As the infantry concentrated outside the wire, tanks blasted at the defenses. The lead tank, commanded by Lieutenant Bauer, made it into the fort only to be hit by a Panzerschreck rocket. Bauer, along with his gunner and loader, was killed. Using shell craters for cover, the infantry moved forward and was soon on the fort's exterior. Steven Ambrose, in his classic book *Citizen Soldiers*, gives us a gripping account of the drama that followed. A slightly edited portion of the fight for Driant is provided here:

> An intense firefight ensued. Germans popped out of their holes like prairie dogs, fired and dropped back. They called in their own artillery from other forts in the area. The efforts of the engineers using TNT continued to fail, as the heavy walls of the casemates were as impervious to TNT as to shells and bombs.
>
> On top of the casemate, a courageous private named Robert Holmlund found a ventilation shaft, and despite the heavy fire, was able to drop several bangalore torpedoes down the opening. (Holmlund would not live the see the Distinguished Service Cross he earned for this act, as he was killed before the battle for Driant ended.) Germans who survived evacuated the area, and Captain Anderson, the B Company Commander, led the first Americans inside the fort. They were only able to take a couple of barracks rooms before the Germans counterattacked.
>
> The subterranean battle was a new dimension in the horrors of combat. In the confines of the tunnels and underground chambers, the nerves, eardrums, and bodies were shattered by the mind boggling noise created by the explosions of grenades, rifles, and machine gun fire that reverberated in the thick masonry walls. The air was unbreathable; men in the barracks room had to take turns at gulping some fresh air from firing slits. The stench was a mixture of gunpowder, gas fumes, and excrement. The wounded could not be treated properly. Fresh water was nonexistent.
>
> B Company was stuck there. It had neither the equipment nor the manpower to fight its way through the maze of tunnels. It couldn't go back; being on top of the fort was more

dangerous than being in it. At dark, American reinforcements, accompanied by a half dozen Sherman tanks, crossed the causeway and assaulted another casemate, but they were badly shot and forced to withdraw when the Germans came up from the tunnels and filtered into their rear. These small, local counterattacks could be devastating. Four of the Shermans were knocked out by panzer faust shells. One tank was captured when the supporting infantry withdrew without informing the crew.

Captain Jack Gerrie, the commander of G Company (which had been almost wiped out at the Dornot crossing three weeks earlier and was now filled with replacements) led the reinforcements. On October 4, Gerrie tried to knock down the steel doors at the rear of the fort. Direct cannon fire couldn't do it and protruding grillwork made it impossible to put TNT charges against the doors themselves. The Germans again called down fire on Driant, which forced G Company to scatter to abandoned pillboxes, ditches, shell holes, and open bunkers, anywhere they could find shelter. That evening Gerrie tried to reorganize his company, but his efforts were hampered by the Germans, who came out of the underground tunnels—here, there, everywhere—fired, and retreated, causing confusion and further disorganization in G Company. Gerrie could count about half the men he had led to the fort the previous evening.

At dawn on October 5, German artillery commenced firing at Driant. After hours of this, Gerrie wrote a report for his battalion commander, and sent it out of the fort by a runner: "The situation is critical; a couple of more barrages and another counterattack and we are sunk. We have no men, our equipment is shot, and we just can't go on. . . We cannot advance. We may be able to hold till dark but if anything happens this afternoon I can make no predictions. The enemy artillery is butchering these troops. . . We cannot get out to get our wounded and there is a hell of a lot of dead and missing….There is only one answer the way things stand. First either to withdraw and saturate it with heavy bombers or reinforce with a hell of a strong force, but eventually they'll get it by artillery too. The Germans have all of these places zeroed in by artillery… This is just a suggestion, but if we want this damned fort let's get the stuff required to take in and then go. Right now you haven't got it." This report was so compelling that it moved right up to General Walker, who showed it to Patton, saying the battalion commander wanted to withdraw.

Never, Patton replied. He ordered Fort Driant to be seized "if it took every man in XX Corps, but he could not allow an attack by this army to fail.[56]

Over the next three days, Third Army ignored Gerrie's advice. As the shattered 11th Infantry was gradually relieved the 5th Infantry Division threw troops from the 10th Infantry regiment into the attack, with similar ghastly results. No sooner than they recaptured some of the ground lost by the 11th Infantry, two platoons from 1/10th Infantry were wiped out, with the B Company commander and two of his forward observers being captured. With the impasse on the surface continuing, renewed fighting went on in the tunnels underneath. Every time a limited gain was made, the Germans would effectively block or counterattack it. The fumes from the welding and explosions became so unbearable that at times the tunnels had to be evacuated, with dozens of men rendered disabled by the gassing. More troops from the 2nd Infantry Regiment were brought in, contributing only by adding more numbers to the growing casualty lists. To the increasingly beleaguered American grunts, it seemed like the Germans had every advantage—surprise, expert knowledge of the ground, shelter from both their own and American artillery, and secure communications.[57] Many of the GIs thought they would never get out alive. During the whole operation, a vast concentration of American artillery had been amassed to counter the enemy batteries that were slaughtering the desperate infantrymen trapped on the fort. In spite of ammunition shortages, virtually the whole corps artillery became involved, including the heaviest of the pieces, the mighty 8-in. and 240-mm howitzers. Some of the fire was directed by forward observers operating from tanks that were specially assigned for this purpose. Although they were able to cause casualties among the Germans that emerged from the tunnels after nightfall, the American artillery did little real damage to the gun turrets themselves, as even direct hits harmlessly bounced off. On occasion, there were instances when the German turreted cannon were somewhat neutralized in dramatic direct fire duels with XX Corps 155-mm self-propelled guns. These big cannon would move close to the targets and fire so intensely that the German gunners would be forced to retract their guns into their emplacements for at least a short period of time. On a few occasions over the course of the Metz campaign, some of the turrets were damaged to the extent that they could not again be raised.[58] As Ambrose concludes, it was the attackers on top of the fort that were the ones under siege, and the lowliest private among them could see perfectly clearly what Patton could not; that this fort had to be bypassed and neutralized, because it was never going to be taken by direct assault. Patton finally relented. Still, not until October 13, ten days after the attack started, were the American troops withdrawn.[59] The actual evacuation was carried out on the night of October 12–13. In addition to many dead, the Americans left behind six tanks, which were later destroyed by American artillery. In the few areas that they had controlled, the engineers set over 6,000 lbs of explosives in order to destroy as much as possible of the fort's facilities. The last troops left the surface of the fort just before midnight under the cover of a massive XX Corps artillery barrage.

In the attack, the 5th Infantry Division lost 64 killed, 547 wounded, and 187 missing—about half of the attacking force. Of the survivors, many had been temporarily disabled by gassing or simple exhaustion. Third Army had received its first unquestionable defeat.[60]

CHAPTER 8

Metz III: The Objective Taken

If the strong German defenses weren't bad enough, the weather also continued to turn against the Americans. Fall is the rainiest season in the Lorraine, with an average monthly total of three inches for September, October, and November. In autumn of 1944, it was abnormally wet, and the area experienced almost twice the rainfall as usual. The cold temperatures and torrential rain caused many health maladies for Third Army. At the beginning of early October, the total strength of Third Army was down to 220,000 men; 18,000 of whom were out of action with influenza, trench foot, and other weather related ailments.[61] The weather not only made life miserable for the men, but also greatly reduced mobility, observation, and the use of overwhelming American air superiority.Patton was miserable and frustrated. His Third Army's mission was to take Lorraine, but with the stubborn German defenders, the sheets of cold rain, the thick mud that clung to boots and tank treads, and the now flooded Moselle River, he could not do so. Patton expressed his ire in a letter to the Secretary of War: "I hope that in the final settlement of the war, you insist that the Germans retain the Lorraine, because I can imagine no greater burden than to be the owner of this nasty country where it rains every day and where the whole wealth of the people consists in assorted manure piles."[62]

Following the attack at Fort Driant, and with the exception of an attack at Maizieres-les-Metz, the XX Corps sector largely fell into a relative lull for the rest of October. The Third Army still suffered logistical and manpower shortfalls, which reduced the options for Patton to regain the initiative. Summing up the situation, XX Corps was responsible for manning a fifty-mile wide front with only two infantry divisions (augmented by armored cavalry). Opposing them were four understrength German divisions that were protected by a combination of well-fortified positions and the swollen Moselle.

XX Corps used the mid October lull to catch up on much needed rest and training. After weeks of sustained combat, the badly battered infantry units were taken off line and sent to rest camps in the rear. Hot showers and laundry services were made available. Replacements, which had literally been sent in as cannon fodder, began to be properly integrated into their gaining units.

If there was any benefit to the Fort Driant catastrophe, it was that the American commanders, from Patton on down, finally realized the futility of direct attacks on well prepared fortifications. While the German positions were contained and monitored by outpost lines, the majority of the XX Corps maneuver troops were pulled back to begin a crash training program designed to figure out a means to more effectively reduce the Metz garrison. A training base was established in the old Maginot Line forts west of Thionville. There, the troops practiced how to attack fortified positions, benefiting from lessons that had been learned the hard way in the preceding weeks. A wide variety of methods were tried out in order to avoid any future Fort Driant-like disasters.

While many of the infantry battalions had some respite in October, the 7th Field Artillery Observation

Battalion enjoyed little rest. Artillery on both sides remained in contact, and the mission of the 7th was critical in monitoring German artillery activity. The sound and flash OPs continued to be manned, and in general, battalion operations continued to be sustained at peak levels. Both line batteries continued to improve their positions while survey parties were constantly checking and enhancing control and registration points. Across the XX Corps front, an extensive and highly integrated artillery observation system was established that tied together seventy ground observation posts and sixty-two airborne observers.

The grind of the Metz campaign was beginning to wear on the men of the 7th FAOB. Lt. Don Slessman was normally upbeat when writing to his wife, Joyce. In the first month of combat, his letters reflected a positive tone as he minimized the dangers and optimistically predicted a quick end to the war. His letter dated September 21, 1944 evoked a more pessimistic and war weary attitude: "My dearest, Another day is almost by and I always regard each day as one day closer to the time when we can again be with each other. Though our separation has only been six months, it seems has if I have been fighting for six years. Perhaps I shall seem different to you when I get home - I know I am more serious than before, and perhaps have changed in other ways - but my love for you will never change darling." In an other passage, Slessman wrote of his transition from B to A Battery, and his regret of leaving his flash platoon team behind: "My old gang made me feel good - they got together and told me I was the best officer they had ever had in the Army. It made me get a lump in my throat as I am very fond of them all and hated to leave them. That compliment was better than any medal that could have been awarded to me."

As always, the battalion's forward observers were in-between the shelling of both armies. From his B Battery flash OP one morning, Bill Williamson looked on as a huge 155-mm self-propelled cannon lumbered up just behind his position. The gun's crew fired several rounds and then took off down the road in search of a new site. The Germans had good counterbattery detection observers of their own and quickly determined the location from which the cannon had fired. Within minutes, a cascade of shells rained down around the OP, despite that the offending gun was no longer there. Bill remembers thinking, "thanks a lot!" to the traveling gunners.

In the first several weeks of the Metz campaign, the 7th FAOB Battalion and A Battery headquarters had set up their command posts in a deep gully near the town of Jarny, ten miles directly west of Metz. Nicknamed "Yellow Jacket Hollow," the torrents of rain made life and operations in the muddy gulch intolerable. If there was any consolation prize to being near Jarny, it was in the huge stock of German liquor that was left behind when the area was liberated by the Americans. Walker was generous in distributing much of this supply to his appreciative troops.

Finally realizing that their stay before Metz would not end any time soon, a more effective and permanent command and control center was sought out. On September 25, both Headquarters and A Battery relocated. The battalion CP moved three miles northeast to Hatrize, and A Battery set up another five miles farther toward the front in an industrial complex known as "Mine Ida," near the hamlet of St. Marie aux Chenes. For those men that were not on duty in the flash and sound OPs, the new location afforded some improved shelter and comfort. Lieutenant Slessman described the new A Battery CP: "…Our command post was located in a home on the edge of a small village named St. Marie. It was formerly the home of the superintendent of one of the many ore mines in this section of the Lorraine. We enjoyed for the first time in many months a real bathtub, carpets, easy chairs, and steam heat." For a period of two more weeks, the B Battery CP would continue to hold in the hotly contested bridgehead on the southeast bank of the Moselle.

In spite of the combat conditions, the army did what it could to keep up the morale of the forward troops. The USO contributed greatly, as did a number of stars from home that helped support its efforts. Some of the entertainers risked going quite close to the front, and one who paid a visit to XX Corps on September 24 was none other than "Der Bingle" himself, crooner Bing Crosby. Kurt Rieth saw his show and reported this in a letter to his parents: "Well I saw Bing Crosby last Sunday and enjoyed it very much. He put his show on in a clearing in some woods, using the back end of a truck as a stage. He had a comedian, two beautiful girls, and a guitar and accordion player with him. Bing sang a few of the songs he made famous and he had a swell comedy act with the comedian. One of the girls called one of the soldiers up on the stage and put her arms around him and started singing. He was a little embarrassed at first but got over it quickly and got quite a kick out of it. He's sitting beside me now and we're still kidding him about it and calling him the great lover." On occasion, movies were also shown in the vicinity of the battery CPs.

Those local Lorraine citizens who had not evacuated the area were grateful to be out of Nazi rule and were very appreciative of the American presence. Wishing to interact with an American soldier, the owner of the mine that A Battery occupied asked the commander to send a GI over to his home for dinner. Due to his German fluency (most residents of the Alsace-Lorraine are bilingual in French/German) Kurt Rieth was selected to represent the battalion in a dinner with the owner and his family. For the most part, the citizens in the war zone had it tough in trying to keep themselves fed. In writing a response to his mother's question on local food sources, Rieth wrote this on October 15: "No, there isn't much to eat that you can buy fresh from the French people. It's really pitiful when you see how little they have to eat. They take a few vegetables from their gardens, cook them and call it a meal. Most of them have only enough meat for one meal a week." The troops did what they could to help out the near starving locals. Hank Lizak relates: "We got to share our rations with the local people, mostly children. When we were all fed, the kitchen would feed the children while we would give them our gum and candy rations."

The battery mess sergeants did yeoman work in getting food to the forward troops under the most trying of circumstances. The quality of food in combat conditions is a critical health and morale issue, and the 7th FAOB cooks rose to the challenge as best they could. A Battery mess sergeant Stephen Wandzioch earned a well-deserved Bronze Star for his efforts during the Metz campaign. The following portion of his citation well describes the work of the cooks during this period: "Due to the scattered locations of various parts of his battery, Sergeant Wandzioch, serving as mess sergeant, encountered a difficult problem in feeding the men. With the sound and flash platoons operating along the Moselle River, the sound central at Gravelotte, the flash control at Hagondagne, and Battery Headquarters ten miles from any of them, getting hot food to them was extremely difficult. Sergeant Wandzioch solved the problem by setting up three separate kitchens, personally carrying rations to each daily, often dodging German artillery bursts to do this. This plan operated so successfully that the men of his battery had three good hot meals a day."

In B Battery, Jim Royals had quite an adventure one day when he, along with Sergeant Arthur Gerrow, were assigned to deliver food to an outpost near Nancy. As usual, a heavy rain was falling. Nearing the OP, Royals realized a rear tire was flat. While Gerrow continued on foot toward the OP, Royals stayed back to change the tire. Just as Royals had loosened a few nuts with the lug wrench, he heard a tank rumbling down the street parallel to his. When the tank made a U-turn and began to head directly back toward the jeep, Royals noticed a swastika marking on the turret. Fortunately, it was raining so hard that the German tank crew apparently didn't see Royals, as he was certainly within close range. Royals immediately jumped back in the vehicle and raced across the road and into a nearby orchard. Sergeant Gerrow suddenly reappeared and directed Royals to "get the hell out of there!" Despite the fact there were only two or three lug nuts barely holding onto the flat tire, Royals hoped for the best, put the jeep in four wheel drive, and took off out of the orchard and back toward Gorze. A few miles later they came upon a couple of Americans from another unit. Sergeant Gerrow found that one of the soldiers was from his native Chicago, and convinced them to help change the tire. When Royals and Gerrow were finally back at battery headquarters, they turned the flat tire over to Motor Sergeant Smicker and received a new spare, their adventure over. Reflecting back on that day, Royals writes: "I still remember seeing that tank coming and the swastika on the side of it. It was so close. I was glad it was raining hard that day. I thanked the Lord in my own little way. Just another close call."

No matter what a soldier's task was, danger was never far away. On September 26, the day after A Battery moved into the new command post at Mine Ida, a near disaster occurred. Don Slessman:

A V-1 or buzz bomb dropped about five hundred yards from our CP and mowed down about ten houses flatter than a pancake. It made quite an impression on me, and from then on, we watched every one that flew over our area, and quite a few came our way too." The buzz bombs were especially frustrating in that they were launched from so far away, there was little that could be done to stop them.

On October 11, a significant realignment took place when the 286th Field Artillery Observation Battalion relieved the 7th FAOB's B Battery from the Pagny bridgehead on the far side of the Moselle. Ed Marinello of the 286th writes of his battalion's introduction to the front lines:

The men of B Battery had come five thousand miles from the sapping mugginess of Mississippi to the penetrating dampness of the Lorraine to set up operations in a field outside the town of Villecey-sur-Mad, itself a mile or two behind the booming front lines then facing the prized city of Metz.

It was twilight when the twenty trucks and jeeps turned off into the wet fields. Sound platoon settled for a clearing where it set up its command post, encircling it with nearly twenty two-man foxholes. The men promptly jumped out and started to dig in. They used collapsible shovels that were strapped to the waist, something commonly done on maneuvers in South Carolina and Tennessee, but later abandoned in France where cellars soon became the abodes of choice. Though the soft dirt was easy to dig, the work kept getting interrupted by incoming shells. The holes measured roughly between six to seven feet long, four feet wide and at least two feet deep, and were covered over by tenting material and logs. Kept warm in a bedroll with an extra blanket and a steady supply of cigarettes, Lucky Strike and Philip Morris among the brands, the miserable little excavations were to become as cozy as the bunks at Fort Bragg. When the kitchen staff announced it was too late to cook that night, the men set up large pots of water to heat C-ration cans. After which they stood around or sat on logs eating and speculating about what was coming. This as German shells combed the fields and XII Corps artillery responded. For the rest of the war, the pulsating pattern was to remain unchanged. Sort of like dinner music.

The first days of combat were taken up absorbing the sulfur and adjusting to violent sounds. When night came, the men never felt more together, never more alone. . . From the first days they went about their work with utmost seriousness. There was no need for the battery commander to lecture that the game was now played with big chips. What had to be done was done promptly and expertly. The distance from home, accentuated by a strange tongue and signs that spoke in kilometers and not miles, was contributing. . . As strangers the guys surely wouldn't have been able to ease into the strange and detonating environment as smoothly. As each acted in concert with his buddies, the superior training of Fort Bragg and Camp Shelby became evident.

…The men gradually conditioned themselves to the impure air, the dead animals, and the chewed up landscape. The conditioning was no less evident in coping with the awful weather and muddy roads, despite nature's nasty trick of waiting until they arrived to [drop] record rains that turned into record snows. It is one thing to read in the daily press or hear over the radio of inclement weather and another thing to live it.

It would be several days before we could begin to pass on the proximate artillery teams a stream of data pinpointing enemy cannons, crucial data, it must be realized, since our work went on unabated night and day. But before we could make ourselves felt, tormenting the Krauts while rejuvenating our comrades, as was to become our wont, we had to learn the ABC's of combat.

Their initial hours outside the woods overlooking Metz became the first time they actually observed their enemy. Marinello continues: "...They appeared in flashes. They came out of something, dashed for cover. These men were out to kill us. We could only stop them by killing them first. The way they flitted about, not exposing themselves for an extended time, made them our teachers."[63] After helping to guide the 286th FAOB into their new positions, B Battery of the 7th FAOB consolidated some of their positions and established a new CP at Gorze. Gorze was virtually a stone's throw directly southwest of Fort Driant, where the 5th Infantry Division's failed attack was winding down.

By October 12, the 150-mm guns of Driant began to hammer Gorze unmercifully, driving the men deep into the cellars and to whatever cover they could find. The fire made command operations at Gorze untenable, and on the next day portions of B Battery pulled back to finally set up a more permanent CP in the tiny village of Tronville, three miles to the northwest. Observers remained in place and were forced to absorb the heavy shelling.

Jack French, who was a member of B Battery, recalled this of his experience in flash observation post during this time frame:

I was in B Battery at Gorze in the flash section. There was a great deal of shelling on the hillsides and we were on duty every four hours. A cave-like entry into an old bunker from WWI gave us a place to sleep while we were off duty. Our command post was on the ground floor of the Village Hall. The Burgermeister that lived upstairs had been drafted into the German Army but his wife and daughters still lived there. [*Following the 1940 invasion of France, the citizens of the Lorraine province were considered German subjects, and many were drafted into German service.*] They were very nice to us, and one day, Mrs. Putsch cooked us a rabbit dinner (we got the rabbits). We dressed the first one and she started to wave her arms to tell us to stop. The village barber dressed the second one and he left the head attached because the meat around the jowls was supposed to be the best part of the rabbit. Quite a revelation for a bunch of young GIs. Mrs. Putsch died a few years ago but my wife and I still keep in touch with the daughters.

Gorze's City Hall, which stood at the intersection of two roads going into the town, was put in service as a flash OP. Charlie Wright remembers a large stone monument that stood in front of the building that was marked "Le Rock," and how the blatantly obvious label seemed so odd. One night Jim Royals was pulling guard duty in the building while observers Sergeant Wells and Corporal Gerrow were watching for flash activity. Royals was leaning against a railing at the top of the stairs on the second floor when the Germans began their regular evening shelling. An officer called for Royals to come down and take shelter in the cellar as the shells began to hit closer. Royals dashed downstairs as a large shell exploded just outside the building. Another GI tumbled head over foot down the stairs as glass shattered and shrapnel ripped into the stories above. After the shelling had stopped, Royals returned to his previous position on the second floor. There he found the railing he had been leaning on was completely sheared off by a large piece of shrapnel. Royals kept a fragment of the jagged metal as a reminder of what a close call he had that night.

Bill Jessel, a B Battery flash observer, also recalls the heavy pounding they were subjected to at Gorze, which he considered some of the worse shelling of the war:

A small nondescript rural town seemingly deserted, Gorze lay deep in the Moselle Valley and in close proximity to the guns of Metz fortresses. A single road was bordered with typical masonry row houses, interspersed with farms and outbuildings. From the course of events we could only assume our presence was more than casually observed by the enemy. The 5th Infantry Division employed three artillery spotter planes that were well hidden in a copse of trees at the far end of the town. The crews went to great length to further camouflage the aircraft. No sooner than they had finished their work when a pinpoint barrage descended on the spot and in an instant destroyed all three planes. This event, plus the casual rounds that harassed us nocturnal cave dwellers convinced us that we were indeed props in a shooting gallery.

> Returning to the town on the day after a specified survey operation, we found our way blocked by a single 5th Infantry Division jeep that was stopped in the middle of the road. Unable to pass, I dismounted and went forward to offer assistance. When I reached [the driver] I saw that he was the victim of a direct hit by an artillery shell. The arms of the driver's mangled remains still clutched the wheel. The area remained under fire and the body could not be removed until after nightfall.

In addition to the never-ending shelling, the threat of mines posed a perpetual danger. The Germans set out thousands of mines throughout the Metz sector. Given the amount of travel required in performing their mission, it was only a matter of time before the 7th FAOB men or trucks were bound to hit them. A mine-related tragedy struck B Battery on October 24, 1944. Charlie Wright provided the following details:

> B Battery Sound Platoon was dug into a hillside in the Rezonville area. We had a sound OP located at the crest of a hill overlooking a large valley. The area was under fire from large mortars on the far slope.
>
> Our phone lines to the OP were blown out several times. After dark, Lt. Don Peterson sent me out to the OP to establish radio contact. Sergeant Julius Bagsby and Corporal Robert Schaaf drove me to the OP where I then went back down to the road to locate the parted line. Although the dirt road was partially frozen, a drizzle had set in which began to thaw the mud. Later in the evening I was picked up and brought back to the sound central CP. Cold and wet, I was enjoying some warm food when the line was knocked out again. Lieutenant Peterson was going to send me back out but Sergeant Bagsby said that he and Corporal Schaaf knew the area the fire was hitting, and to let me thaw out, they would take care of it. Needless to say, I was pleased. Traveling back on the road I had just come from, they went out and fixed the break. On the way back their truck ran over a mine. Bagsby was killed and Schaaf was badly bruised and knocked out. Schaaf regained consciousness and was able to make it back to the OP where help was called for. Lieutenant Peterson, who loved and respected all his men, personally went out and brought Sergeant Bagsby's body back in. In the many years since, I think of Sergeant Bagsby often, knowing he gave his life for mine.
>
> [Bagsby was initially buried in a field cemetery in France. In 1949 his remains were re-interred in the Nashville National Cemetery.]

A longer-range but omnipresent threat came in the form of a gigantic German 280-mm rail gun that targeted Third Army in October. Mounted on a railroad car, this monstrous cannon fired an enormous shell that weighed 660 lbs with a range of twenty-five miles. So large were the barrels on the rail guns that twenty-five men could easily stand shoulder to shoulder on top of them. The rail gun first made its presence known on October 5 at 3:00 A.M. In what sounded like a freight train descending from the sky, six of the gigantic shells hit near the XX Corps artillery command post at Jarny. Seventh FAOB shell report teams were dispatched to examine the house-sized craters. Robert Geiges was on one of the teams and remembers finding the first four craters with ease. The fifth shell was a dud and landed in the mud of a deep ravine. The sixth shell was tougher to find. One soldier in search of it looked up at the top of a ridge-line and found the answer. The shell had hit near the top of the ridge and carved a crevice through the top of it. The projectile then exited the other side of the ridge, and exploded in the air, completely defoliating a large number of surrounding trees. The nature of this particular hit gave the shell rep teams a good idea of the direction from where the gun was firing.

The German rail gun was targeting various Third Army command posts throughout both XX and XII Corps sectors. One dud round penetrated twenty-seven feet into the ground. The 7th FAOB set into motion trying to find the gun, with both A and B Batteries making some plots. When it fired again on October 7, the 7th FAOB was able to direct some heavy caliber fire missions in return. It is uncertain whether these counterstrikes hit their mark, but the rail gun was silent for the next two weeks.

On October 17, the rail gun again reappeared, firing at least twenty shells into Jarny, as well as into XX Corps and Third Army Headquarters and XII Corps sectors. A number of casualties were taken at the XX Corps command post, with one of the shells sending a piece of shrapnel that ripped completely through General Walker's staff car (which he was not in at the time). There was tremendous pressure both on the 7th FAOB and the 286th FAOB (in the XII Corps zone) to find the location of the huge cannon.

Although engaged in combat operations for less than two weeks, the 286th FAOB was quickly becoming a veteran unit. After first taking position at Villecey-sur-Mad, B Battery of the 286th displaced and relocated south, closer to primary XII Corps thrust outside Nancy. On October 13, the 286th B Battery sound platoon CP was severely shelled and they suffered their first combat loss when Private Sal Mingione was killed by shrapnel. Despite the heavy shelling, the battery produced some excellent locations on the German guns that had been targeting them.

Marinello, with the 286th B Battery sound command post, remembers the tremendous amount of artillery fire that both sides were slinging the night of October 17. This provides a highly detailed account of sound operations in the heat of battle as well as the hunt for the rail gun:

> It started out as the kind of ordinary day we had come to expect in the Lorraine. Rain was steady, of course. Shelling no less. Toward twilight the rain abated, the shellings only somewhat. Later when the rains stopped, the shellings returned to their original fury. The resumed level didn't help anyone's mood.
>
> Some men found refuge in sleep. One that couldn't climbed out of his foxhole and headed for the CP tent, hoping to relieve the loneliness by throwing the bull or reading by the kerosene lamp. The artillery barrages raging during those moments couldn't be bargained. Like it or not, they were coming in torrentially with brute force and without end. The result was that the night, that night more than most, was characterized by a noise level so shattering that the oscillograph wasn't able to separate the lines on the tape. Thus each time a piece of tape was ripped off, the CP staffer eyed only a mish-mash of entanglements that made no sense. It was as though dozens of people were screaming at the top of their lungs, the tumult so dinning that nobody could be understood. Similarly burdened that night were the flash observers unable to distinguish from among the clashing, multitudinous flashes."
>
> In the midst of this terrific bombardment, the German rail gun nicknamed by the Americans as "Big Bertha" let loose and fired into XII Corps territory. Almost immediately,

the field phone rang at the sound CP. The first calls came from officers at battery and battalion headquarters, wanting to know what could be done to find the big gun. While asking legitimate questions in patient tones, the calls only heightened the pressure on the sound men who were doing all within their powers to get a legitimate plot. More desperate calls came from area artillery units, who were begging for culpable targets in order to make the terrible German shelling—not just from the 280-mm rail gun—stop. To all the inquiries the answer was the same: sound hadn't been able to achieve anything verifiable. To shoot at the scrambled plots on the board was to waste ammunition. It wasn't our fault, we pleaded. Nobody could be expected to make sense out of nonsense. Only if the gods were to favor us with a let-up in the shellings, enough for a clear reading to form, could we come up with worthwhile data. But that was a distant hope, not a commitment. In all the back and forth about discernable plots, the CP guys were contemplating Big Bertha not at all. It didn't make sense that she would be on our collective minds when even the puniest result wasn't forthcoming. Insofar as we were concerned, the artillery guys would have to settle for any cannon, a single reading suggesting that B Battery was alive though with a weakened pulse.

The field phone again squawked, this time the caller was the commander of XII Corps artillery, Brigadier General John Lentz. Although speaking in polite tones, Lentz minced no words; he wanted to know about Big Bertha, and what sound platoon was doing to snare her. Lentz's call was fielded by Sergeant Pete Wait, an unflappable Cornell graduate who kept a cool head in the madness of the German barrage. When responding to Lentz's questions, a flash of the simple obvious occurred to Sergeant Wait. The combined noises of the sector, American as well as German, were keeping the sound detection system from working. If all the XII Corps artillery would stop firing for a period of time, the noise would be cut in half, and a relative clearing may be able to catch the German guns on the oscillograph's tape. The proposed plan was not without drawbacks, as the gap in the American fire across a corps front would give the German's a break from their pressure, and put at risk frontline infantry depending on the unrelenting support to keep the enemy at bay. However, the benefits of getting more accurate fire data were obvious to Brigadier General Lentz, and he immediately ordered a fifteen-minute halt to the American fire.

After two minutes, our sounds became less until the front half-quieted. To the uninformed GI on the line the attenuation must have been ear-shattering. It had to baffle him in one minute, anger him in the next.

The first minute of the deception went by with the happy Krauts hammering away.

A second minute and a third. So far they were oblivious to what was happening.

Another minute. By then there was no doubt that the enemy was being caught off guard.

The oscillograph hummed. From the less cluttered tape, the one that spoke German, cleaner readings were immediately evident. Sense was replacing nonsense. The CP crew was in action from the first second, calling out the spaced pulsations and plotting the diabolical coordinates. The first plots were "Qs," four intersecting lines, good if not spectacular. The success in those early minutes was about to eliminate the night's stigma.

Over the first seven or eight minutes, though, Big Bertha failed to appear. As successes piled up, the men wondered if Lentz's sole measure of success was our locating her. When ten minutes went by without her appearance the feeling was that our success was going to be limited.

The duped Germans kept at it with the rest of their artillery, shelling like mad!

The machine kept humming and the plots piled up. The scheme had worked. Several plots were perfect, which meant the Germans were going to pay for their shenanigans that night. But only three minutes were left of the fifteen-minute window, and still no sign of Bertha. Then suddenly, out of the blue, it happened!

The OP called in "Here she is, here she is!" From their position, there wasn't any doubt she had let go. Her monster sound carried by the OP and began to hit the mikes and register on the oscillograph. The markings were the biggest we'd ever seen, making the tape easy to read.

Sergeant Wait personally called the location of Big Bertha to a grateful Brigadier General Lentz. The fifteen-minute firing moratorium had ended and all hell again broke loose, this time, with the American guns having accurate firing data. The immediate objective was the rail gun, and XII Corps artillery serviced it with Time-on-Target (TOT) barrage. Every long-range cannon in the corps, from 155-mm "Long Toms" on up, fired in a sequence that ensured each round landed in the same instant. Other fire missions then focused on the multitude of other enemy batteries that had been blasting XII Corps through the night. While the TOT silenced Big Bertha for the evening, she was not yet destroyed. The next morning an aerial reconnaissance flew over the area and reported a collection of large craters, but no sign of the gun.[64]

In the next two days, the rail gun again reappeared, firing into XX Corps and near Patton's headquarters. For all his bluster and his ability to act unfazed when under artillery fire, Patton very much detested being shelled. The pressure on the forward artillery observation battalions to locate the rail gun now came from the highest levels. On October 18, Lieutenant Slessman was sitting at the A Battery CP when he answered a call on the field phone. On the other end of the line was General Patton himself, directing in no uncertain terms that the 7th FAOB do something about knocking out that gun.

This time it was flash that was able to contribute. When the big gun fired, an A Battery flash OP got lucky and was able to make an excellent "3 P" plot of the piece. Based on the plotting, it was determined that the Germans were using a distant railroad tunnel to hide the cannon. The gun would be towed out to a firing site and then pulled back under the cover of the tunnel for reloading. Using both the flash and sound data, Slessman was able to calculate the pattern of when the cannon would be inside the tunnel. As the location of the tunnel was outside the range of even the most powerful American cannon, it would be up to the Army Air Corps to attack the rail gun. Reaching out from XX Corps resources, Slessman was able to coordinate with the XIX Combat Air Command who dedicated some P-51 fighter-bombers for the task. Based on the 7th FAOB analysis, the Air Corps commanders could predict when the cannon was in the tunnel and launched their attack accordingly. Using great skill, the P-51 pilots were able to skip-bomb their ordnance directly into the enclosure. From that point on the rail gun was silenced. Many weeks later when the Germans were retreating, Lieutenant Slessman was able to go by the tunnel and confirm that A Battery's direction-finding was responsible for knocking the gun out.

The American observers at the outposts also remained vigilant for any sign of enemy activity. Lieutenant Slessman described just one example of what was occurring every day along the 7th FAOB OPs. Taking a break from his administrative duties as A Battery XO, he went to the neighboring town of St. Privat, which was then a front line infantry outpost location. He went up the steeple of the village church spire, which served as an excellent position from which to observe the German positions in the valley and the next village a mile to the northeast. While there, a nearby tank destroyer outpost reported some undue activity in a certain house in the town of Amanvillers, one mile south. Slessman then watched the house closely for the next hour, and confirmed the high degree of traffic that suggested that it was some sort of German headquarters. Calling in fire from a 155-mm battery, Slessman was able to adjust ten direct hits on the home, most of which exploded inside the thick walls.

Later that month (on October 25) Lieutenant Colonel Schwartz advanced Lt. Slessman up from XO to take over command of A Battery from Captain Johnson. The A Battery command car was comprised of Slessman, First Sergeant Buzz Bennet, driver Hank Lizak, and Kurt Rieth as the radio operator.

Just to the south of the 7th FAOB and XX Corps boundaries, the 286th FAOB was beginning to get into the rhythm of maintaining daily forward observation post activities. In the passages that follow, Ed Marinello gives a detailed and personal glimpse of an OP mission near the town of Arracourt, on the east bank of the Moselle, fifteen miles south of Metz. Marinello, initially assigned to the 286th B Battery's command post, volunteered for duty with one of the unit's four observation posts. Marinello wrote the following passage:

Just as soon as Lieutenant Watson approved the make-up of the new observation team, Sergeant Wait scheduled our debut for the next day, October 31. My enthusiasm ran high since I considered the assignment real soldiering. Forward observers were almost always positioned with the infantry and at times up ahead to take advantage of a view. The result was that, not infrequently, they constituted America's first line of defense in a sector.

The night before, our team prepared by cleaning our carbines, collecting extra ammunition including grenades, checking out the telephone and radio, and packing Ten-in-One rations, bedrolls and blankets. Waking the next morning to rain, we loaded into two jeeps. On that dreary, slow morning, the jeeps bounced along abused roads, past the congested might of Third Army. Once through Jurvecourt, we rode for another mile until we reached the bottom of the hill on which the observation post was located. Shouldering the necessary supplies, the new team began ascending the hill, staying to the grassy side of a muddy path. Dotting the slope were foxholes of the 2nd Cavalry and the recently arrived 26th Infantry Division.

At the top of the hill we entered into protective woods where we paused to consider our next move. From there we could see the Germans, but they couldn't see us. About a hundred yards from the woods, situated on a projecting, almost defiant ledge with a panoramic view of everything German, was the observation post that we had come to occupy. From where we stood to where we had to go, the Germans had an unobstructed view. Certainly we were within rifle shot. The obvious strategy was to dash across one by one, not together. We loaded up. First one, then the others followed widely spaced, hitting the ground every ten yards or so until we made it across. Dropping into the hole, we were greeted warmly by the outgoing crew, who lost no time in shouldering their supplies and departing, doing what we had done, except in reverse. Reaching the woods, they quickly descended from the hill and into the waiting jeeps.

The first requirement in taking over an OP was to check in with the command post. This I did pronto, informing them that the new team was in place and operational. Next, to orient our position, I took out a detailed military map to determine exactly where we were. Now and then the Germans chucked shells in our direction and our guys responded in kind. This activity continued well into dusk. Around the time of the first yawn, the shift work began. Two hours on and four off. The 'on' observer sat up, one ear on the Germans, the other on the phone to the CP. Meanwhile his partners slept.

This particular OP was situated in a rock outcropping that was a partial cave, which provided a fair degree of overhead protection. The cramped space of an OP, any OP, required that each man limit his movement while showing an extra dose of tolerance for his roomies. Idle daylight hours were employed writing letters home and mostly shooting the breeze either with each other or the infantry guys. Nights in the OP were long and hard to endure. The one awake had no company. He sat in the dark, cannons his company. He didn't speak normally. Instead he whispered to somebody staffing the CP, a someone who wasn't experiencing the same night and aloneness. The CP guy was in a warm cellar with as many cups of tea or coffee as he liked, this as he wrote home by the bright kerosene lamp. Besides, if he wanted to talk there were two others on duty whose eyes he could see and whose expressions he could judge. The observer had light. His real company was himself. It was why he daydreamed a lot.

As shells landed near and far, the observer calculated the distance. The close ones had a message, the same one all the time, which was that the only thing that mattered was getting through the night alive. When morning came, it came with incoming shells and coffee brewing on the Bunsen burner. The chilly, penetrating air brought on an urge to pee, which meant having to climb out of the hole and walk a decent distance. Then coffee and washing, the men using their steel helmet as sinks, securing water from the five-gallon reserves.

On the second day of this forty-eight-hour mission, Marinello received some disturbing news from a neighboring infantryman. Supposedly, a German patrol had been captured the previous evening. Interrogations revealed they were the reconnaissance element for a much larger force that would attack the position that night. Marinello passed the information to the rest of the team, and they remained as alert as possible. Armed only with light carbines and a few hand grenades, they would be dependent on the infantry to repel an enemy attack. The OP began the evening shifts with a heightened sense of alertness, and other than occasional, routine shelling, Marinello's first watch quietly ended at midnight. Waking his relief, he immediately went to sleep. Only minutes later, he was shaken awake as the Germans unloaded a massive barrage on the hill.

Marinello continues his account:

Without lead-in, the Germans had commenced an artillery barrage of unprecedented fury and were to sustain it over a long period of time. Had it not been for the cover of the natural rock formation, the fledgling team would have been among the first dead." The unrelenting barrage lasted for hours, with one observer on duty calling a constant chant of "on the way, on the way!" After three hours of living hell, the shelling suddenly stopped at 3:30 A.M. The OP's relief quickly transformed to terror as the sound of the artillery turned into that of approaching tank treads. The three observers crawled as far back into the tiny cave as possible, as tank after tank rumbled past their position. Had a follow-on German infantry thought to throw a grenade into the opening, all three would have been killed. As it turned out, the panzers continued down the reverse slope of the hill and into a well prepared kill zone manned by the 26th Infantry. The OP listened to the fight at the bottom of the hill, and it soon became apparent that the Germans were driven off. When daylight came the hill was back in American hands, and control of the OP transferred to a new team.[65]

Such was the life of a forward observer manning a front line observation post.

As grueling as the weather conditions, combat losses and stress, and logistical shortfalls were for the Americans, they were also taking a toll on their enemy. Just as Third Army had to sacrifice troops and logistics for the 21st and 1st Army efforts to the north, the German defenders at Metz began to strip away resources to support defensive operations near Aachen and in Holland. In great secrecy, the Germans pulled large numbers of troops off line in order to prepare for the great Ardennes offensive that would be launched in December. The quality of the German troops facing XX Corps began to deteriorate, with some of more effective troops being removed from the Metz sector and being replaced by lessor quality units. One new such German organization, the 416th Infantry Division, had no combat experience and was mainly comprised of elderly men. Having virtually no offensive capability, they German high command derisively nicknamed them the *Schlagsahne* (whipped cream) division.[66] Although the Germans were significantly weakened when compared to their strength in September and early October, they still held the key fortifications and easily defended terrain. Furthermore, Hitler was paying close personal attention to the defense of Metz. While the garrison's eventual destruction may have been inevitable, their continued resistance bought the Germans extra time to prepare for the upcoming Ardennes offensive. With this in mind, Hitler gave express orders that Metz would hold out until the last defender fell—surrender or retreat would not be options.

On an individual German soldier level, the most demoralizing aspect of having to fight the Americans was to face their overwhelming might in artillery. As Don Slessman has described in some of his experiences, any time that the Germans became careless and or otherwise visible to American forward observers, they were subject to devastatingly powerful and accurate artillery barrages. Over the many weeks of the Metz campaign, American artillery fire took a heavy toll in terms of actual losses of men and on the nerves of those who survived them.

The later stages of the Metz campaign showed the American Army at its best in adapting to adversity. To make up for the shortfall of heavy-caliber ammunition, XX Corps surveyed and employed tanks, tank destroyers, and mortars to replace conventional artillery. Extensive use was also made of captured German ordnance. One Time-on-Target mission fired in XX Corps' zone was executed with captured German 105-mm howitzers, Russian-made 76.2-mm guns, French 155-mm howitzers (also captured from the Germans), and German 88-mm antitank guns. Eighty percent of the artillery ammunition expended by XX Corps in the last week of October was of German origin.[67]

The logistical crisis that severely impacted XX Corps' operations in September and early October also began to ease. The French railroad system was quickly rehabilitated and put to military use. Although the railroads in Normandy had been badly damaged prior to and during the invasion, those in central and eastern France were relatively undamaged by Allied aircraft and had been abandoned almost intact by the retreating Germans. During the October lull, Third Army brought its railheads as far forward as Nancy. For a time, Third Army personnel actually operated the trains themselves. The French civilian sector provided rolling stock and trained personnel to supplement Third Army's quartermasters.[68]

Third Army's intelligence picture also improved during the October lull. Through the Ultra codebreaking system and other sources, the German order of battle was now well known to Third Army's G2 and would remain so throughout the campaign. Ultra revealed that the Germans, too, were rationing gasoline. Even the panzer divisions were partially dependent on horse-drawn transportation. XX Corps headquarters received detailed plans of the Metz fortifications, obtained from archives in Paris, and supplemented by French officers who had built and manned the citadel. The most encouraging intelligence received in October revealed that the Germans were withdrawing many of their best units from Lorraine, including Fifth Panzer Army.

On October 18, Eisenhower held a top-level strategy conference with Montgomery and Bradley that would set into motion the final stages of the Metz campaign. Beginning in early November, a general allied advance would proceed. While priority of efforts would still go toward the 21st and 1st Armies targeting the Ruhr, Patton's Third Army would be ordered to proceed to the Saar Basin (with the caveat, "as logistics permit"). After breaching the fortified West Wall, Third Army would launch an attack toward the Rhine, and cross in the vicinity of Mainz.[69] Patton was ecstatic to be unleashed to resume the offensive, and the Third Army staff immediately went into motion to begin planning. XX Corps' combat strength would be nearly doubled, as they received control of the 95th Infantry Division, and the 10th Armored Division.

The first steps toward resuming the offensive came about in an attack against the Maizieres-les-Metz.

Maizieres was an industrial mining town of 3,000 residents located on the west bank of the Moselle, eight miles north of Metz. Maizieres marked the northern extreme of the German salient on the west side of the Moselle. Beginning in early October, the 90th Infantry Division had made piecemeal attacks against the town. With many of the buildings being constructed with thick stonewalls, the Germans were able to establish a number of strong points in the town, the center-most being the Maizieres' city hall. The shortage of artillery ammunition had previously made an all out American assault impractical, and the situation resulted in both German and American troops sharing the town in a mutual stalemate.

With the arrival of Brigadier General James van Fleet to command the 90th Division, as well as increased artillery ammunition stocks, a renewed effort was made against Maizieres on October 29. As the only unfortified approach to Metz began to crack, the 90th Division also used this operation as a further means of validating their previous weeks of intensive training. The attack began with one of XX Corps most powerful artillery concentrations of the war. The 7th Field Artillery Observation Battalion was given credit in a War Department film, *Combat Bulletin Number 31*, for A Battery's direction of the massive strike. XX Corps guns blanketed suspected enemy artillery positions while also providing a rolling curtain of fire that crept ahead of the advancing infantry troops. XX Corps' counterbattery fire was particularly effective, as the German's artillery response in the battle was reduced to a few scattered rounds.[70] The attack itself was conducted by several companies of the 90th Division's 357th Infantry Regiment. In well-rehearsed and closely controlled operations, assault teams methodically cleared designated objectives. Still, the German defenders fiercely contested the town, and the fighting was particularly brutal at the city hall. By October 31, Maizieres-les-Metz had fallen. Although the final attack had cost fifty-five American casualties, the Germans lost the better part of a battalion. In taking Maizieres, XX Corps had opened a way to outflank the fortified salient to the west, while gaining valuable experience in learning how defeat an enemy well entrenched in an urban area.[71]

By the first of November, XX Corps' plans for the final attack on Metz began to take shape. In essence, it called for the 90th and 5th Infantry Divisions to encircle Metz from the north and south, while the 95th Infantry Division would contain the western salient. To accomplish this plan, the 90th Division would bridge the Moselle in the vicinity of Thionville (fifteen miles north of Metz). Once a bridgehead was established, the 10th Armored Division would cross over and immediately swing northeast toward the Saar River. The big forts were to be contained or bypassed, and frontal assaults against them would be avoided if at all possible.

While XX Corps was to encircle Metz, Patton ordered his other major maneuver element, XII Corps (contained by the Germans at Nancy, to the south of XX Corps) to cross over the Seille River and then move toward the Rhine.

The XX Corps portion of the plan was launched in great secrecy and used battlefield deception ploys. Nicknamed "Operation Casanova," 90th Division and 10th Armored Division silently crept to the north. Unit insignia on uniforms and vehicles were removed or altered, fake radio nets were established, and sound deception simulated movements of vehicles through different parts of the corps sector.

In early November, the 7th FAOB prepared for the operation. While both A and B Batteries initially remained in line, the battalion headquarters took part in the movement north, displacing thirty miles up to Frisange, Luxembourg. During this time, Tom Delay remembers when he field-stripped his carbine in the command car. The weapon somehow accidentally discharged, sending a bullet through the canvas roof of "Headquarters 1." Lieutenant Hughes casually walked over to the command car and asked Delay if he was hunting for ducks. Fortunately, the .30 cal. round made only a tiny hole, which Delay was able to quickly cover up before it was noticed by Lt. Col. Schwartz.

Preparing to support the attack, many XX Corps artillery battalions established new positions to cover the crossing sites. When the artillery units moved, remaining batteries increased their rate of fire, while rubber guns replaced the real ones that were relocated. Likewise, registration in the new area was limited to one gun per battalion and masked by the fire of units already in the area.[72] Exercising great care to keep themselves hidden from the Germans, the 90th Infantry Division moved to their staging areas above Thionville. The American logistical system made sure that the offensive would not stall this time for lack of gas, food, or ammo. According to Headquarters Battery's Sergeant Geiges, Eisenhower had baited Patton by asking him if he had enough supplies. Patton supposedly retorted, "You know damn well I do!" Geiges and the rest of the 7th FAOB battery supply sergeants worked overtime to ensure all of the trucks were filled to capacity with extra equipment. To make sure they didn't run out of fuel again, jerry cans full of gasoline were strapped in every conceivable place on the battalion's vehicles.

Weather continued to work against the American effort as the Lorraine suffered from its worst floods in thirty-five years. Twenty of the past thirty days were filled with rain. The weather virtually negated American air superiority. The XIX Tactical Air Command, which had flown 12,000 sorties in the golden days of August, flew only 3,500 in November. There was no air activity at all for twelve days out of the month.[73] The rain delayed the attack for several days, and then continued to pour even harder. Finally, on November 8, Patton could not bear waiting any longer and ordered the attack to occur despite the now flooded Moselle and lack of air support. Overruling the objections of the XII Corps commander, Patton launched the all out attack to start on November 9. Just before the attacks were launched, Patton paid a personal visit to the front line and had this to say to a collection of 90th Division officers: "I've been going up and down the line today giving hell to everybody, but I don't need to chew out you bastards. I just stopped by to say hello, because I thought you'd be insulted if I didn't. There's nothing I can tell you sons of bitches. You bastards sure know how to fight."[74] The XX Corps attack began with a battalion-sized demonstration south of Thionville at Uckange. Crossing the flooded plain of the Moselle, elements of the 377th Infantry Regiment established a small beachhead on the enemy side of the river. With the Germans distracted here, the main event would take place seven miles farther north at two 90th Division bridging sites.

Favoring stealth over brute force, the American planners delayed firing artillery support until the very moment of the attack. The Germans had long come to appreciate the certainty and power of the American's pre-attack artillery concentrations. Accordingly, they assessed their best defensive positions covering the likely river crossing points as most vulnerable to artillery attack. General Balck, commander of German Army Group G, had ordered his units to hold the front with a minimum of strength until the anticipated artillery barrage had passed, whereupon they were to rush forward in force to meet the American assault waves. Exploiting this tactic, the Americans began the crossing without preparatory fires. As there was no artillery barrage, and since the Germans otherwise failed to predict the attack, Balck's defensive scheme was unhinged at the outset of the operation.[75]

Once the attack kicked off at H-Hour, massed battalions of XX Corps artillery were unleashed to fire on every known or suspected German artillery position. On October 29, a rare break in the weather enabled XX Corps aerial observers to confirm many of the plots provided by the 7th FAOB. As a result of the combined analysis by the XX Corps artillery G-2 staff, the American counterbattery fires were extremely effective in neutralizing much of the potential German artillery response.[76] The terrible weather and the flooding of the Moselle also offered the Americans some advantage, as it inundated the German minefields on the east bank and lulled the defenders into a false sense of security. As one prisoner later explained, "We were all sure no one would attack in such weather."[77]

The main 90th Division effort would be to establish two primary bridgeheads north of Thionville near the small towns of Malling and Cattenom. Crossing over the swollen river in assault boats during the early morning hours, the lead battalions swarmed over the far bank. The surprise was complete and the initial objectives were quickly taken. One enemy fort that could not be bypassed was the mammoth

Fort Koeingsmacher that sat astride the lower crossing at Cattenom. The battalion from the 19th Volk's Grenadier Division responsible for defending the fort was caught completely unaware. American infantry from the 358th Regiment gained control of the interior trenches even before the Germans realized they were under attack. XX Corps had learned from the mistakes of the failed Fort Driant assault. Rather than facing the Germans head on in the labyrinth of tunnels, engineers first destroyed observation posts and then blew up the exits, trapping the enemy inside. Gasoline was poured down ventilation shafts and ignited. Although it took two more days of fighting, the surviving Germans inside Fort Koeingsmacher surrendered, with minimal casualties to the Americans.

While the first American infantry troops scored their share of successes on the east bank, they still were bedeviled by the raging Moselle behind them. Facing artillery fire and the strong current of the river, XX Corps engineers worked frantically to build pontoon bridges in order to get some armor into the attack. At Malling on November 11, Patton's birthday, a bridge was completed. Everyone held their breath as the first vehicle, a badly needed tank destroyer, lumbered across. As it neared the far side of the river it suddenly veered to the side and snapped a suspension cable, sending the bridge tumbling downstream. Patton later recorded that the entire company of exhausted engineers "sat down in the mud and bawled like babies."

The situation at the bridgehead started to get desperate. While three regiments of infantry had made the crossing, they had only a few light 57-mm anti-tank cannons with them. Soon the GIs were critically short on ammunition and other supplies. As well as enemy fire, exposure to the cold and rainy weather also took its toll, and within forty-eight hours, six of the engaged infantry battalions were down to fifty percent strength. If the Germans were able to make a concentrated armor-supported counterattack, the bridgehead may well have collapsed, and with it the loss of most of the 90th Infantry Division.

Once again, XX Corps artillery was magnificent. The 7th FAOB did its part by managing a highly effective counterbattery program. While the infantry and engineers did face some German artillery fire, it was at a greatly reduced amount. Away from the shelter of the main Metz fortification system, German artillery was now far more vulnerable to the XX Corps guns directed by the 7th FAOB. XX Corps had massed seventeen artillery battalions (about 300 cannon) that pulverized German counterattack efforts and shelled virtually every building in the assault area.

Meanwhile, liaison aircraft and amphibious trucks helped keep the bridgehead supplied as best as possible. Low flying observation planes dropped ammunition, food, batteries, and medical supplies. When the weather finally cleared somewhat, the U.S. 8th Air Force sent over 1,000 four-engine bombers to conduct saturation bombing. However, the poor weather forced the airmen to bomb by radar, which significantly detracted from the accuracy of the attack.

Having previously stripped the Moselle sector of armor support, the Germans were slow to react. However, by November 11, the Germans were able to bring up an armored battle group from the 25th Panzergrenadier Division that had been refitting at Trier. In the early morning hours of November 12, the German counterattack landed on the 359th Infantry. The American infantrymen did their best to check the oncoming panzers, with twenty battalions of XX Corps and 90th Infantry Division artillery contributing greatly. The 733rd Field Artillery Battalion fired their "Long Tom" cannon so fast that some of the men were afraid that the barrels of the guns would drop off.[78] Still, the tanks rolled on and a scratch force of headquarters service personnel were scraped together to make a desperate final last stand. In a near Hollywood-scripted scene, a pair of American tank destroyers came up at the last moment and the German attack was repulsed. At first an orderly retreat, repeated American counterstrikes turned the German withdrawal into a rout. The Germans left behind 400 dead, 150 prisoners, and scores of tanks and assault guns.[79] The arrival of the American armor marked the final completion of a serviceable bridge across the Moselle; the bridgehead was at last secured. Patton and Walker were on hand to witness one portion of this battle. Patton turned to Walker and commented, "Never in all my life have I seen so many dead Germans in one place.[80]"

With the 10th Armored Division now crossing the Moselle and the repulse of the last German counteroffensive capability, the fate of the Metz garrison was now sealed. At Thionville, another bridgehead had been established, and an ad hoc task force of troops from 95th Infantry, supported by tanks and tank destroyers, set a path south for Metz. Designated by the name of its commander, Colonel Robert Bacon, the task force moved off in two columns, destroying or bypassing all enemy troops found in their way. The infantry rode on any vehicle possible, avoiding enemy strong points and dismounting as little as possible. By the evening of November 17, Bacon's task force had reached Fort St. Julien, three miles from the city center. Author Steven Ambrose, in *Citizen Soldiers*, wrote the following about the capture of this fort:

> St. Julien was one of the old Vauban forts. It sat on dominating terrain and commanded the two main roads leading into Metz from the north. Surrounded by a moat twelve meters deep and twelve meters wide, with high thick walls and a covered causeway, it had a garrison of 362 Germans. They had no heavy weapons, but with their machine guns and rifles they could prevent American movement on the main roads. St. Julien was the one fort that had to be taken.
>
> The assault began at dawn, November 18, in the fog. By noon, Task Force Bacon had fought its way to the moat. For the next hour, the 75-mm cannon on the Shermans, plus the 15-mm self-propelled cannon, supported by 240-mm howitzers from behind, pounded the fort.
>
> At 1:00 P.M., the infantry jumped off and began to dash across the causeway. The Germans stopped them with heavy small-arms fire. Two Shermans moved forward to spray enemy firing slits with their .50 caliber machine-guns, and a second attempt by the infantry was successful. But then the GIs ran into an iron door that locked access to St. Julien's interior. The tanks crossed the causeway and fired point-blank at it, but the 75-mm shells just bounced off. A tank destroyer with a 90-mm gun drove up. It fired six rounds at a range of less than fifty yards. They had no effect. With the machine gun fire from the Germans keeping the Germans back from the firing slits, a 155-mm howitzer was wheeled into place. The big gun slammed ten rounds into the door, but still it held.
>
> The Americans decided that if they couldn't blow the door down, they could destroy its stone facing. The 155-mm gun then fired twenty more rounds into the door's mounts. Finally, the door collapsed inward with a mighty crash. Infantry moved through the opening, bayonets fixed. They were met by Germans with their hands up.

German veterans, when asked to comment on the Americans as soldiers, invariably begin with a criticism; that whenever GIs ran up against opposition, they hunkered down and called in the artillery. In the German army, the infantry solved its own problems. But most GIs would consider their use of high explosives something to praise, not criticize.[81]

To the south of Metz, the recently refitted and rested 5th Infantry Division attacked north from the Araville bridgehead that had been secured back in September. The overall plan was for the 5th Infantry Division to swing east and then north, bypassing the outskirts of Metz to link up with the 90th Infantry Division that would be closing the pincers on the city from the other direction. The 5th Division's attack kicked off on November 9. Hampered by the stiff German resistance, as well as the bad weather, the Americans made slow but steady progress. Continued exposure to the elements caused rampant cases of trench foot, with some battalions losing forty percent of their combat strength alone to this disabling ailment.[82]

Finally by November 17, the three American infantry divisions began to converge in Metz; Task Force Bacon and elements of the 90th Infantry Division from the north, the 5th Division from the south, and the 95th Division nearing the Moselle bridges to the west. As street fighting ensued in Metz itself, XX Corps' artillery laid interdiction fire on all German escape routes east of the city.[83] Although Hitler had officially declared Metz a fortress, meaning that it would hold out to the last man, the local German commanders decided to make no further investment in the city. They abandoned the second-rate division fighting in downtown Metz and broke contact, withdrawing to the east. On November 19, 90th Division and 5th Division linked up east of Metz, completing the encirclement of the city. Although some of the forts held out for several more weeks, General Kittel, the commander of the German garrison in Metz, surrendered on November 21. (The last forts to surrender were the two that gave XX Corps the most grief—Fort Driant and Fort Jeanne d'Arch. These forts were not in American hands until December 13.) At the end the twelve-week battle, XX Corps was the first military force to capture Metz by storm since 451 AD.[84]

In comparison to XX Corps' experience in racing through Northern France in August 1944, Metz would be remembered for the exact opposite. As Ambrose summarizes in *Citizen Soldiers*, "In August, Third Army had advanced almost 500 miles, from Normandy to the Moselle River. From September 1 to mid-December, it only advanced twenty-five miles east of the Moselle. The Siegfried Line, which Patton had said he would reach on November 10, was still a dozen or so miles to the east. In crossing the Moselle and taking Metz, Third Army had suffered 47,039 battle casualties."[85] (It is estimated that the opposing German forces lost about 150,000 troops killed, wounded, and missing in the same time period.) Given the intensity of fighting around Metz, it is surprising that it is still considered a relatively obscure action in the relative scope of World War II history. One of the few serious studies on Metz was published by Anthony Kemp in his book, *The Unknown Battle" Metz, 1944*. Kemp explains this phenomenon:

> Apart from the official history, the story of the struggle on the Moselle and the battle to capture the fortress city of Metz has never (previously) been detailed. Generals Bradley and Patton gave it scant notice in their memoirs, and it is almost as if a discreet veil of silence has been drawn over the whole affair—which is an injustice to those that fought and died there. It was certainly not an episode of which those responsible for the direction of the campaign could be particularly proud, as the only glory going was won by the junior officers and enlisted men of both sides.[86]

The nature of the initial battle for Metz did not favor the operational style of the Third Army and XX Corps leadership. Certainly, Patton and Walker made significant errors in the September–October phases of the battle. They grossly underestimated their enemy's strength and intentions, failed to appreciate the challenges of terrain, and allowed their forces to engage in piecemeal attacks. To be fair, Walker could not help the logistical shortfalls initially facing him, but he failed to adapt a flexible operational plan that recognized these problems. Perhaps worst of all, from early September through mid October, Walker, at the insistence of Patton, blindly attacked the Germans at their strongest points, and without the reserves required to exploit any gains that may prevailed.

An analysis of the later phases of the Metz battle also shows XX Corps and the U.S. Army performing at its best. In the wake of the early October Fort Driant fiasco, XX Corps finally realized that a radically different approach was needed to assure a victory at acceptable costs. The benefits of refitting and retraining the line units would prove critical in the November successes. Furthermore, General Walker must also be given credit for the execution of the final attack that actually took Metz. Using surprise, mobility, and the effective massing of combat power, XX Corps decisively took its objectives.

By all accounts, XX Corps artillery, of which the 7th Field Artillery Observation Battalion played an integral part, performed magnificently at Metz. In terms of sheer battle power, from November 9 to the 22nd, the corps artillery controlled some 350 cannon of various calibers that fired a total of 137,000 shells.[87]

Most importantly, the artillery's ability to mass its fire at critical points was tactically decisive time after time. Although initially hampered by a lack of ammunition and thwarted by the impervious Metz forts, the 7th FAOB's counterbattery program became extremely effective in the later stages of the battle. The Battle of Metz taught the army a number of valuable lessons on how—and how not—to attack strong points. In fact, the study of Metz has been a core part of the curriculum for many years at the U.S. Army Command and General Staff College at Fort Leavenworth, Kansas. In the final analysis, one thing that cannot be called into question is the fighting ability, determination, and courage of the soldiers that fought it—both American and German.

PHOTOGRAPHS

William Jessel, Fort Bragg, 1941
Jessel, like other men who first joined the 7th FAOB, was initially issued World War I surplus equipment.

Camp Shelby, Mississippi
The troops were billeted in quarters like these during the battalion's two year stay at Camp Shelby.

Destroyer Escort USS Donnell
This picture was taken only moments after the Donnell was hit by a torpedo that was headed for the HMS Arawa, the 7th's troopship. Much of the Donnell's stern was blown off by the explosion.

Lieutenant Colonel James P. Schwartz
A strict disciplinarian, Schwartz commanded the 7th FAOB from training at Camp Shelby through the end of the war.

Headquarters Staff, 7th Field Artillery Observation Battalion
Lt. Col. Schwartz is pictured kneeling at the center.

Battery A Mess Sergeant Stephen F. Wandzioch
Wandzioch serving Christmas turkey, December 25, 1944. He was very nearly killed that morning when a German ME-109 barely missed his truck in a straffing run.

The Battery A Cooks
Mess Sergeant Wandzioch is standing at upper right. Photo was taken in Colmen, France, December 1944.

7th Field Artillery Observation Battalion Medical Detachment
This picture was taken in June 1944 at Salisbury Plains, England. Standing (L-R): S/Sgt. Pollack, Cpl. Barber, Pfc. Duke, Pfc. Glennon, Pvt. Nutter, Pfc. Huffaker, Pvt. Surges, Capt. Del Bello (detachment chief), T/5 Brennan. Kneeling (L-R): Pvt. Arnaiz, Pvt. Russo, T/5 Robinson, Pvt. Rank, Pvt. Semon, (unknown).

John K. Rieth

Tech Sgt. Kurt Rieth
Picture at left was taken in Colmen, France, December 1944. At right is during occupation duty in Mondsee, Austria, June 1945.

Battery A Men
(L-R): Leo Walman, Hank Lizak, Ed Piatkowski

Lt. Don Slessman
Slessman commanded Battery A from October 1944 through the end of hostilities. He is pictured in late 1944 holding Battery A's mascot German Shepard.

Lt. Marlin Yoder, Headquarters Battery
Yoder transferred to the 7th from the 286th FAOB.

Battery A Officer's: Lt.'s Slessman, Gott, Sockwell

Senior Brass Visit XX Corps, October 1944
MG Irwin, Commanding General, 5th Infantry Division (pointing), briefs LTG Patton (left), MG Walker (in dark jacket) and Army Chief of Staff General George Marshall (right) on a planned attack at Metz.

The Road to Metz: Fall 1944
These B Battery observers stand by a road marker for Metz. XX Corps' Metz campaign was marked with some of the most bitter fighting of the Second World War.

James Rutledge adn Arthur Sutliff
Battery B soldiers stand by a knocked-out German tank.

Flash Observation

B Battery Flash Observers William Jessel and Al Mongiovi in action. 7th FAOB Flash Observers used specially designed azimuth-telescopes to try to detect the firing of enemy cannon.

John French

French was a flash observer with Battery B. At left he is with the 2 1/2 ton truck he drove throughout the war. At right he is seated on a "liberated" motorcycle.

Battery B Flash Survey Squad
7th FAOB survey sections were tasked to determine the exact locations of observation posts and sound ranging equipment.

Battery B Men Relaxing Over a Bottle
(L-R): Godseu, Rutledge, Sutliff, Johnson and Ryan

7th FAOB Crossing the Danube River at Regensburg

German Prisoners of War
The deeper XX Corps pushed into Germany, the more war-weary German troops surrendered by the thousands. This picture was taken by B Battery's William Jessel.

7th FAOB Troops in German Uniforms
After finding a cache of German uniforms, these B Battery men posed for a picture taken by William Jessel. (L-R): Howard, Koulec, Hoyt, Sfreddo, Tansey, Williamson, Maturo.

B Battery Marching in Parade, Simbach Inn, Germany, May 20, 1945
Three days after this parade, the 7th FAOB moved into Austria for occupation duty.

Ed Piatkowski at Ludwig's Palace, Chimsee
From June 10 - July 18, the 7th FAOB was posted at the German resort center at Chimsee, Germany. Some men served as tour guides for GIs visiting King Ludwig's elaborate palace on a large island.

Medic Amos Robinson
At the Regensburg-Danube crossing, late April 1945.

Mondsee, Austria
The 7th FAOB was posted in this idyllic Austrian resort town from May 28 - June 9, 1945.

Headquarters and Headquarters Battery, 7th Field Artillery Observation Battalion
July 2, 1945, Chiemsee, Germany

Front Row: (l to r): T-3 Windsper, Sgt Weaver, Anderson, Brannock, Pfc. Rose, Pimaggia, T-5 Rapp, Griffin, Combura, Cook, Ramsay, Shock, Lane, Zettle, Ostrum, White, Peck, Lokken.
Second Row: T-3 Kenderdine, S-Sgt Murphy, West, T-Sgt Callahan, Montgomery, M-Sgt Ballman, M-Sgt Allred, CWO Roeske, Lt Sprague, Lt Whipple, Lt Peterson, Capt Sotry, Lt Col Schwartz, Capt Johnson, Lt Slessman, Lt La Vanway, Lt Smith, Lt Harper, Lt Ostensen, 1st Sgt Skelton, T-Sgt St. Romain, S-Sgt Clark, Ezinga, S-Sgt Wardwell, Geiges, Randle.
Third Row: Cpl Baker, T-5 Mateoli, Zlotkowski, Close, Lizak, T-4 Kutniewski, Ball, Drane, Cpl Ward, T-4 Peck, Muzyczka, Know, Puhr, Rogiere, T-5 Kramer, Cpl Lunsford, Bratcher, Bahr, Kolodzik, Tatro, T-4 Otwell, Cpl Salinas, T-5 Severns, T-Sgt Hicks, M-Sgt Herman.
Fourth Row: Pfc Alarcon, Grisham, Weigel, Kebbe, Pvt Blascak, Pfc Purdy, Sweenie, Hasselbach, Mason, T-5 Kinsella, Pfc Sennett, Waddington, Cpl Capp, Scallon, Pfc O'Shaughnessy, Hughes, Dale, Huffman, Smith, G, DeGirolamo, Elsperman, Lisanti, Barnard, Hoskins.
Fifth Row: T-4 Alter, pfc Eggleston, McGarry, Fuhrman, Duke, Pvt Nutter, Pfc Danniel, Ray, Grabowski, Napier, Pvt O'Neill, T-5 Rivers, Pvt Sullivan, Pfc Graham, T-5 Shafran, Pfc Zehring, Sargood, Pfc Devore, Russo, Day, Vought.
Absent: S-Sgt Fraser, Lindsey, Pollock, T-3 Cohen, Sgt Loste, Peters, T-4 Battistelli, Hoag, Mays, Cpl Fouquet, Weaver R, Barber, T-5 Crouch, Gamble, Groman, Leftheris, Morris, Schroeder, Smith V, Thomas, Wesler, Pfc Huffaker, Semon, Surges, Babb, Barlow, Carter, Creekpaum, De Lay, Doyle, Gohonio, haines C, Holloway, Meyer, Rudy, Schum, Talbott, Unger, Vinceslio, Pvt Lauffer, Rank, Arnaiz, Fordna, Kutch, La Marea, Chin, Moschiano, Peterson.

John K. Rieth

Battery A, 7th Field Artillery Observation Battalion
July 2, 1945, Hafling, Germany

Front row (l to r): Pfc Patterson, Yates, Altman, T-5 Mullins, Pistilli, Cpl Reina, S-Sgt Kozak, Ziebro, Vandzioch, 1st Sgt Bennett, Lt Zur Schmiede, Capt Clark, Lt Hawkins, Lt Johnson, S-Sgt Setzer, M-Sgt Assmann, T-Sgt Holmes, S-Sgt Webb V, M-Sgt Tyritz, T-4 Mercer, Cpl Haines, Sgt Martin, Pfc Zuniga, T-5 Koerschner, Pickett, Pfc Dougherty J, T-5 Waldman.
Second Row: Pfc Caswell, T-5 Pleak, Cpl Burrell, Stasiowski, Pfc Webb W, T-5 Dowden, Cpl Kopp, T-5 McGahee, Finnell, Sgt Webb O, T-5 Logan, Pvt Kelley, T-5 Roll, Czarnecki, Storms, Pfc Gallo, Pvt Untied, T-5 Dougherty L, Pfc Urban, Sgt Wright J, Pfc keefe, Pvt Prescott, Pfc Hudson, T-5 Rogge, Sgt Dressler, T-5 Zot, Pfc Howard.
Third Row: Pfc Huebert, Rosner, pvt Clover, T- Landry, Cpl Chabalowski, Pvt O'Connor, T-5 Fuller, Pfc Elnick, Somers, Pvt brown C, Pfc Molton, T-5 Felts, pfc Makosky, pvt Shinkle, T-4 Raymond, Koon, Cpl Eskinazi, Pfc O'Brien, Pfc Beasley, Andrews, T-4 Ciolek, Pfc Hillery, Wright S, Pvt Rainey, Cpl Woods, Pvt Kozma, T-4 Joyner, T-5 Bermes, DeForest, Sgt Zygarowski, T-5 Gentile.
Fourth Row: T-4 Richardson, T-5 Shagam, Cpl Sutera, Pfc Westenzweig, Pvt Johnson, T-5 Deeg, Riccolo, Rankin, Pfc Fagan, Prewitt, Cpl Mulford, Pvt Legg, T-5 Solomon, Pvt Jenkins, Cpl Brown E, Sgt Albrinck, Cpl McCoy, Pfc Mdkean, McIntire, Cpl Baier, T-5 Taylor, Pfc Massias, Cusano, T-5 Mcgauhey, Cpl Hinman, Pfc Trepkus, Hasenjager, T-5 Robinson, Pfc Stephens, Brady, Simonse.
Absent: Lt Ostensen, lt. Wackernagel, T-5 Castanza, Hynson, Sgt Hilzinger, Maher, Cpl Munson, O'Malley, Scott, T-4 Castriotta, Fogel, Galbreath, Kedenburg, Murray, Rieth, T-5 Bereswill, Bostwick, Cirincione, Corsi, Lubay, Perrino, Piatkowski, Radosky, Sabre, Pfc Culley, Dokulil, Flaherty, Freeman, Kliebert, Druger, Maney, Paschal, Pillar, Pooley, Pfretzloff, Starrett, Surgos, Pvt Daniel, Hagan, North, Walsh.

Battery B, 7th Field Artillery Observation Battalion
July 1, 1945, Eggstadt, Germany

Front row (l to r): Cpl Bitticks, Pfc Javor, Monofer, T-4 Schmieker, Cpl Valentine, Ryan, Pvt Taylor, Sgt Chism, Pvt Howard, T-5 Godsey, Pfc Mussell, Blankenship, LaFrenz, Sgt Haust, T-5 Gilbert, Pfc Rau, T-4 Tomlin, Weizer, Cpl. Van Reen, Pfc Johnson, T-4 Blake, Sgt Strous, Pfc Gamble, T-5 Noble, Pfc Zaino.

Second row: T-5 Weidler, Pvt Bradley, Pfc War, T-4 May, Pfc Fallon, Cap Hartley, Stonebrook, Pfc Puczylowski, T-4 Smith, S-Sgt Tansey, Bethea, T-Sgt Benson, M-Sgt Clem, Lt Ofenstein, Lt Malloy, Capt Bowden, Lt Henry, Lt Sockwell, 1st Sgt Taylor, M-Sgt Gerrow, S-Sgt Jessel, Fowler, Pfc Eldredge, Palmer, Pvt Giglistti, Pfc Kidd, Hyatt, Hitchens, Pvt Feichtel, T-5 Ottersen, Small, Pvt Karcher, Pelliggiaro, Cpl Gies, Pfc Gossner.

Third Row: Cpl Robers, Pfc Peterson, T-4 Cohen, Pfc Kelly, T-4 Tolliver, Pfc Tkachuk, Sgt Rutledge, Pfc Jurgens, Neal, Cpl Gingorelli, Pvt Saczawa, Pfc Wright C, T-5 Tallman, Cpl Joeris, T-5 Franklin, Pfc Roach, Hawkins, Cpl Jarrell, Sgt Mongiove, Cpl Clemmensen, T-5 Horton, Pfc McCombs, Wisniewski, T-5 Karpman, Elsrode, Pfc Setter, T05 Goodwin, Pfc Lyon, T-5 Anthony.

Fourth Row: Pfc Williams, Peters, Williamson, Blessing, Boucher, Pvt Mathus, T-5 Gilliland, Zimmerschied, Pfc McCann, Fanchor, T-5 Powers, Siebels, Cockrell, Sgt Vlahakis, Pfc Bennett, O'Neal, French, Sgt Caouette, T-5 Walker, Pfc McCutcheon, Larkin, Uniacke, Cpl Wollenberg, T-5 Letendre, Royals, Pfc Joyce, Donato, Manalili, Cpl Houldin, Gos, T-5 Kustermann, Pfc Fleischman.

Fifth Row: Pvt Hoyt, T-4 Spielberg, Pfc Semon, Gour, Jackson, Trickey, Swisher, Cicilli, Yourkavitch, Jachetta, Sgt Turner, Cpl Schorock, Pfc Kawalec, Pvt Maturo, T-5 Warren, Hershkowitz, Sgt Montemarano, Pfc Waddell, McCaffrey, T-5 Foulkes, Dallmann, Sgt Sutliff, Pfc Pacheco, Elijah, Elliott, Cpl Strausbaugh, Pfc Libby, Sgt Harding, Cpl Barber.

Absent: S-Sgt Sfreddo, T-4 Domicholo, Jones, Cpl Tucker, Pfc Dawson Kreisheimer.

Home: The 7th FAOB, aboard the Liberty Ship S.S. Leidy arrives in New York Harbor, August 26, 1945

Group Picture 2003

Front row, left to right: Jess Grisham, Jack French, Walter Ball, Jerry Peterson, and Arnold Price. 2nd row: Don Slessman, James Royals, Charles Wright, Leo White, Robert Geiger, Thomas Delay. 3rd row: Art Vogelsang, Bill Williamson, Walter Damiano, Warren Sockwell, Joe Puczylowski, Ed Shock.

CHAPTER 9

To the Saar and the Ardennes

As the Battle of Metz was winding down, the 7th Field Artillery Observation Battalion's priorities shifted toward Third Army's next objective—crossing the Saar River. To strike into the heartland of Germany, Third Army still needed to penetrate three more major obstacles; the Saar River, the West Wall fortifications along the German border, and the Rhine River. It was now the race for the Saar that mattered.

The 10th Armored Division led the XX Corps march to the Saar, and the bulk of the 7th FAOB was attached to this effort. On November 20, elements of the battalion moved twenty-five miles northwest along the east bank of the Moselle River to the town of Sierck. The XX Corps zone of operations quickly ballooned to near unmanageable levels. Although the fighting around Metz was largely reduced to mopping up operations, German artillery in the area was still meddlesome. Portions of the two 7th FAOB letter batteries were called back to Metz on November 22 to support the 90th and 95th Division's fight to eliminate the final enemy resistance.

Writing in their V-Mail letters back home, the soldiers in the 7th FAOB could only make veiled references to what had been going on. Kurt Rieth wrote home on November 21. In addition to hinting at operational developments, he described the newest member of A Battery, a German Shepherd named "King":

> Well as you can see by the papers, things are moving along a little faster over here. I believe the next few weeks will tell just how long this war is going to last. We've got sort of a mascot in the battery now. He is a young German police dog. When we move, he rides in the back of the car with me and barks at the civilians. The only thing I have to watch is that when I talk on the radio he doesn't bark into the mike. [Writing two days later, Rieth gives a fair description of the countryside:] I'm getting darn sick of this country with the muddy streets and manure piles. It seems every time we pull into a new area at night we park beside a manure pile and when I get out of the car I step into it. Well, it may be over before too long and I can sit back and laugh about it.

The countryside abounded with stray dogs. Despite regulations forbidding pets, it was a forgone conclusion that many of the animals would be adopted by the troops, many of whom badly missed pets of their own back home.. In addition to A Battery's King, other mascots included Headquarters Battery's "Irish," A Battery's "Steamshovel" and B Battery's "O.P."

Robert Geiges still retains fonds memories of his dog, Irish. Geiges came across the small chocolate-colored spaniel in the middle of a noisy duel between U.S. and German artillery batteries. Passing the booming American guns, he spotted the panicked dog trying to hide under some branches in an effort to shield itself from the outgoing and incoming artillery fire. Trying to calm the dog, Geiges gave it some food. The dog, of course, followed his new found friend back to the battalion command post. One thing led to another and the dog quickly became adopted by all of Headquarters battery, with Robert as its primary keeper. Throwing regulations aside, even Lt. Col Schwartz and First Sergeant Skelton took a shine to the dog, with Skelton naming it Irish, as its coat resembled that of an Irish Setter.

After a period of several weeks with the battery, Irish seemed to be unwell, a condition Geiges attributed to bad Army food and an unhealthy lifestyle of riding around all day in military vehicles. In the best interest of the dog, Geiges reluctantly decided to give him to a couple of French boys he spotted on the roadside. The boys happily agreed to take the dog. Driving away, Geiges looked in the rear view mirror and saw Irish pull away from the boys and chase after the convoy in breakneck speed. The dog actually caught up with the Geiges' truck and ran abreast to it for a good period of time. Geiges couldn't stand it any longer and pulled the truck over to let Irish back in the cab. From that day on, Irish had renewed vigor and acted in high spirits.

Irish was an inseparable companion of Headquarters Battery. Every time headquarters would displace, Lt. Col. Schwartz would ask if Irish was accounted for. There were several occasions where a battery deployment was delayed until the dog was found. Geiges recalls that Irish was very much in demand as a guard dog. On many nights soldiers pulling guard duty would approach Geiges and ask if Irish was available. The dog was ever-alert to strange sounds and smells and served as welcome companion to weary and nervous sentries. Irish remained with the battery through the entire war.

Jim Royals also has found memories of B Battery's mascot, OP. OP earning his name for his abilities as a watchdog. As well as being a faithful pet, the observers would post the dog at front line observation posts where they appreciated his alertness in softly growling at nighttime disturbances.

These pets were important part of the 7th FAOB lore and helped the soldiers cope with the ever present hardships of combat life.

Marinello provides us this description of the this combat as Third Army moved on past Metz and towards the Saar:

> At destruction, Third Army worked twenty-four hours a day. There was no rest. Nothing was to be left standing. Only with a steady pounding could the Hun be dislodged. The GIs kept attacking, the gritty foe held on. The result was that the landscape was destroyed. Craters dominated. Houses and churches were rubbled. Steel tracks of undiscriminating tanks mutilated roads and fields beyond imagining. Heavy trucks got caught in the muddied ditches and ripped themselves free. Like a frontiersman's campfire in uncharted territory, burning tanks lit the night. Tanks and half-tracks smoldered into dawn. Cows and trucks turned over on their side.[88]

With Metz finally contained, infantry followed the armored push toward the northeast. By November 27, XX Corps closed up all along the Saar River to the east and west and finally stood at the West Wall defenses. Lieutenant Slessman recalled the final stages of the Metz battle and the movement toward the Saar:

> We operated several bases along the river at various points and finally crossed the river with the 95th Division. We followed the 95th Division down the east bank of the Moselle but it became evident that the Germans had withdrawn most of their mobile artillery as we encountered only mortar and tank fire. Upon a junction with the 5th Infantry Division in Metz, we turned at once to the east with a new armored division, the 10th, our objective, to cross the Saar-Moselle Triangle and secure at least one bridge intact across the Saar River. Our advance was

rapid, resistance spotty and disorganized, until we reached a point about five miles from the river. Our only mishap was the loss of several when their jeep hit a Tellermine. The armored division ran into considerable artillery near the border town of Waldweis, so we went to work again and had a pretty hot time of it for a while. The 90th Division finally broke through and drove to the river. We followed them closely and set up a sound and flash base along the Saar River just north of the city of Saarlautern. The Germans really saturated us with artillery fire and we lost quite a few trucks, though we were luckier with our men.

One of the instances that Lieutenant Slessman referred to was when an A Battery jeep hit a German mine on November 21. Tech Sergeant Raymond Golden and Corporal Herve Souliere were seriously wounded and had to be evacuated to a rear area hospital. Lt. Don Little was also hurt, but was treated and returned to duty.

Another incident noted in the Slessman account occurred on November 27. A group of A Battery flash observers that included Victor Salem, Max Rosner, and Frank Riccolo were moving toward the front in a ¾ ton truck. After cresting a low rise, they stopped and took a break to eat a snack. In hindsight, they later realized that they had silhouetted themselves against the gray sky to become perfect targets for a nearby German observation post. While opening a can of cheese, Victor Salem recalls the entire area suddenly filled with exploding enemy mortar shells. He turned to run down the far slope of the hill. It was like being caught in a slow motion nightmare, with each step becoming bogged down in the thick mud while trying to race to safety. A mortar shell actually struck his foot, sending him sprawling and causing him to lose his helmet. To Salem's happy surprise, the shell was a dud and he arose to sprint into a nearby ditch that was occupied by Rosner and Riccolo. Looking back, they saw that their truck had not been so fortunate, and was left burning in flames. In an emotional release to their close call, the three burst into hysterical laughter. Every year for the next five decades following the incident, Victor Salem would always pause on each November 27 to reflect on his luck that day back in 1944.

Moving forward required advanced reconnaissance missions—almost always a dangerous task. Charlie Wright of B Battery remembers a forward patrol comprised of various battalion elements led by a full colonel from corps artillery. Wright was detailed as the colonel's radio operator. The colonel was an extremely tall and lanky officer who wore a custom holster that carried his pistol at the mid-thigh level. Traveling in a small convoy, the patrol moved toward German lines when a battery of 88s began to open fire on them from the cover of a nearby wood-line. The entire party jumped out of their vehicles and into a ditch as high velocity shells exploded all around. Still under fire, the colonel pulled out a flask of whiskey, took a swig, and then offered Wright a sip. Wright initially declined, but at the colonel's insistence, helped himself to a good gulp or two. The colonel then suggested that someone get on the radio and put some counterbattery fire on the German guns, and further added that the ordnance be set for a tree burst. Moments later, shells screamed overhead and exploded into the tops of the trees that had been hiding the enemy cannon. Tree bursts are particularly murderous against exposed troops, as spear-sized shards of timber add to the lethality of the shrapnel. As quickly as the attack began, the German guns were silenced. Wright later explored the site of the German battery where he found both shattered cannon and dead gunners. In one gruesome scene, Wright noted a dead German soldier who had both the top of his helmet and skull sheared off with seemingly surgical precision.

The men were shelled so often that many developed some kind of sixth sense to predict that an attack was coming. Hank Lizak relates the time when he and Kurt Rieth were out fixing some broken commo wire. For some odd reason, Rieth suddenly felt uncomfortable and recommended they get out of the area. Lizak agreed and they quickly drove away in their jeep. Immediately after they left, the ground they had been standing on erupted in explosions from German shells.

In moving toward the Saar, the Third Army advanced on a broad front of nine divisions spread out over seventy miles. Had Patton instead concentrated his three armored divisions into one corps for a knockout blow, he may well have breached the West Wall before the Germans had time to regroup and defend it in strength.[89] Instead, the wide advance again allowed the Germans time to rest and rebuild their forces behind a strong defensive works. Despite the gains across the Moselle, Third Army would be denied any decisive breakthrough.

On November 3, the 95th Division captured an intact bridge across the Saar River at Saarlautern, but then encountered some bitter enemy resistance. The German troops were now fighting on their own soil and the intensity of their efforts showed. The Americans discovered that the town of Saarlautern itself was part of the West Wall. In Saarlautern, the fighting was literally house-to-house and pillbox-to-pillbox. To try to speed up the slow infantry advance, XX Corps' heavy artillery fired in direct support of small units. The 8-in. and 240-mm pieces adjusted their fire on individual buildings on one side of the street, while American infantrymen advanced on the opposite side. On December 5, the 90th Division forced a crossing of the Saar at Dillingen and encountered similar opposition. Casualties mounted as the Germans brought to bear the heaviest artillery fire that Third Army had yet experienced.[90]

With the toehold across the Saar, the 7th FAOB was finally on German soil. On December 3, Battalion Headquarters and Battery A set up a command post in Hemmesdorf, Germany.

The area in which XX Corps would focus their next series of operations became known as the Saar-Moselle Triangle. The topography of the area would play a critical role in the next several months of fighting. At the northern tip of the triangle was the German-held city of Trier. Trier, an ancient city with a history of Roman conquests, sat at the convergence of the Moselle and Saar rivers. The capture of Trier would be a tremendously significant objective for XX Corps, and would be the ultimate focus of its efforts over the next three months. The left angle of the Triangle was the Moselle River, which ran along the pre-war border of Germany and Luxembourg. The triangle's right angle was the Saar River. The base of the Triangle was a German defensive line that ran from east to west, twenty miles south of Trier. This line became known as the Orscholz Switch. The eleven-mile-mile long Orscholz Switch was an extension of the West Wall, or Siegfried Line, the defensive barrier that ran the length of the German border. The Switch linked the two rivers, and (from west to east) included the towns of Weis, Berg, Nennig, Tettingen, Sinz, and Orscholz. These small towns were incorporated into the line's defenses, and would all become parts of one bloody battlefield in the weeks that followed.

Unlike the Maginot Line or the Metz fortifications, the West Wall did not consist of gigantic underground fortresses and heavy artillery emplacements. In many ways the West Wall was a more difficult challenge to breach than were the forts of Metz. Rather than a collection of forts that could be bypassed, the West Wall was a belt of well-concealed tank obstacles, barbed wire, integrated pillboxes, extensive minefields, and fortified buildings. The nature of the defenses also made it much easier to camouflage and blend in the surrounding terrain. The tactical intent of these defenses was to inflict such heavy losses on the attackers that even a localized breakthrough would be wiped out by armored counterattack. The Orscholz Switch was a particularly strong segment of the West Wall line. Author Nathan Prefer gives an excellent description of this line in his book about this campaign, *Patton's Ghost Corps*:

> The Switch consisted of a defensive position two miles in depth protected by dragon's teeth [triangular shaped concrete barriers] and antitank ditches. The defenses themselves were pillboxes and concrete bunkers reinforced by field fortifications. In addition, the many small towns and villages in the zone were to be converted into strong points by the German defenders. These consisted mostly of concrete and stone buildings, which in many areas, tripled the defenses available to the defending forces. The entire position was on high ground

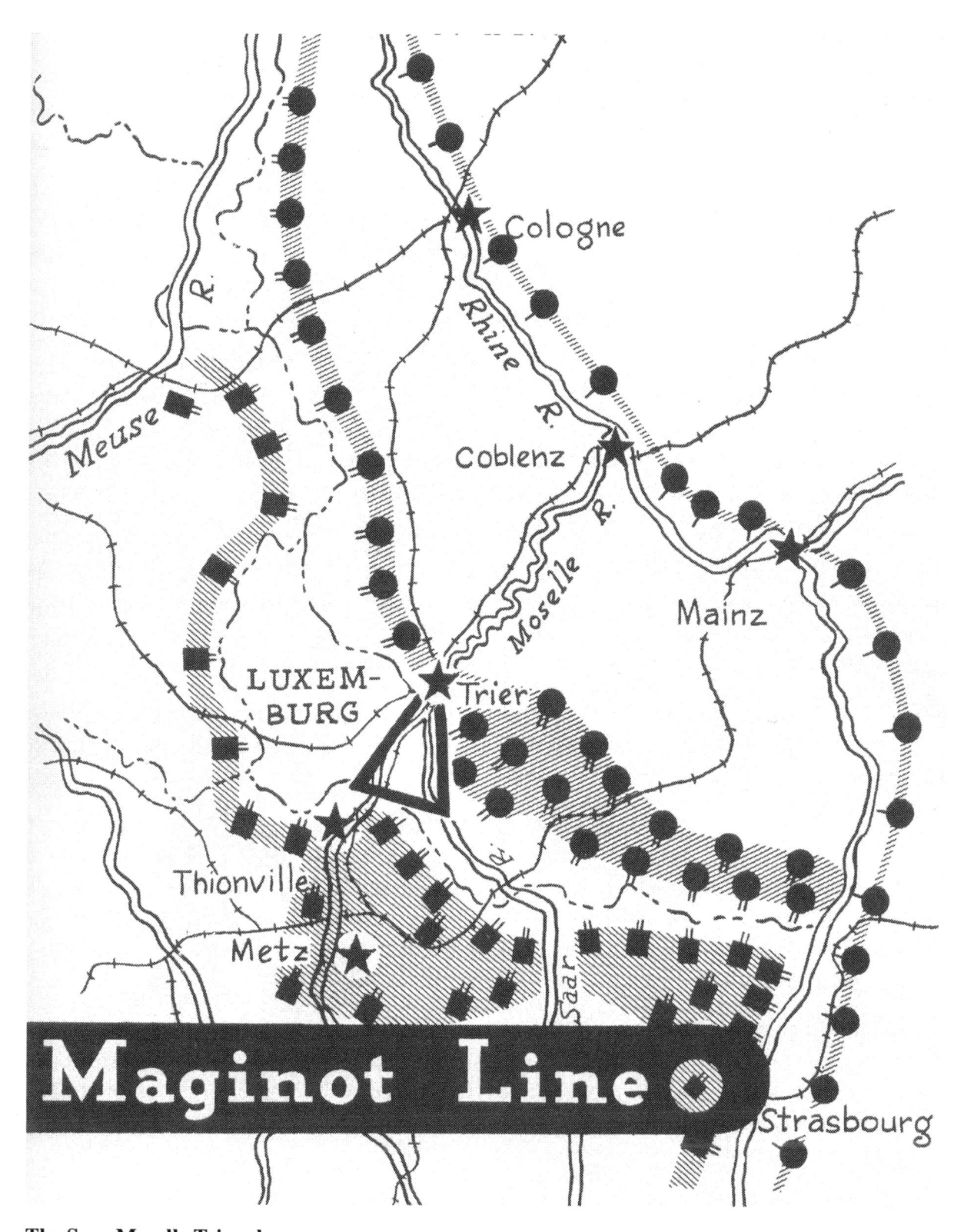

The Saar Moselle Triangle
This map depicts the pre-1940 disposition of the French Maginot Line Forts (in squares) and German Siegfried Line (also known as the Westwall and depicted in circles). The Saar Moselle Triangle is at the map's center. Trier is at the apex of the triangle with the Moselle and Saar Rivers forming the left and right angles. To protect the all-important Trier from a southern attack, the Germans constructed a strong defensive line 20 miles south of the city that linked the two rivers. This base of the triangle became known as the Orscholz Switch. From December 1944 through late February 1945, XX Corps hammered away at the Saar Moselle Triangle while the remainder of the Third Army was consumed with the German Ardennes Offensive to the northwest of Trier.

that formed the watershed of streams feeding the Saar and Moselle Rivers. An added bonus for the defenders was the several dense woods scattered throughout out the area. All the major roads in the area converged on the town of Saarburg, toward the center of the triangle on the west side of the Saar River.[91]

As XX Corps was pulling into position before the Switch, they were subjected to some of the fiercest German artillery fire that they would receive in the course of the war. Much of this fire came from the newly established 404th Volks Artillery Corps. The Volks Artillery Corps was a new German concept designed to give greater artillery punch and mobility to augment the organic firepower of the standard divisions. These artillery groups contained about seventy-five different cannon of various calibers, and could be moved relatively quickly to mass firepower and to support threatened sectors.[92] The German artillery fire was especially severe on the XX Corps bridgehead areas. The Saarlautern Bridge alone received over 3,000 shells in a twenty-four-hour period. It was up to the 7th FAOB, in concert with the XX Corps Counterbattery Intelligence Section, to find these guns and direct fire to knock them out. Throughout the sector, A and B Batteries worked around the clock to set up and operate sound and flash installations. The 7th also received some help from temporary attachments of the A Battery of the 286th FAOB and the B Battery of the 288th FOAB. The 7th FAOB's efforts were responsible for over 613 plots of enemy guns. In addition to the all-important flash and sound plots, the corps' counterbattery intelligence section analyzed aerial reconnaissance photos, shell reports, and POW interrogations to get an inclusive picture of German battery positions. On one day alone, XX Corps fired 19,404 shells against German artillery positions. The results of the counterbattery fires were extremely effective, as the German artillery fires began to noticeably slacken.[93] Elsewhere in Third Army, and in support of XII Corps, the remainder of the 286th FAOB was posted to the northwest of the 7th FAOB in Luxembourg. Ed Marinello describes a particularly bitter counterbattery duel during this period.

> The battles were fought in the mud and the cold and the night. I cite this particular example because I believe it was typical and because it showed the heroic qualities of both sides. I recall it vividly. The episode involved an artillery unit during the Luxembourg snows in the winter of '44-'45. It took place on a hill outside of Beaufort, a small town overlooking the Sauer River on the other side of which, being Germany itself, the enemy was situated in strength. At some point, a group of 155-mm howitzers, taking advantage of the Sauer to come up closer to the front, moved in behind our sound observation post and without delay started pounding away at the Germans. After a long time of blasting away, the gunners took cover in anticipation of a response. The Germans obliged, raining shells on them (and on us!). Once the counterbattery stopped, the not-to-be-fazed GIs came out of their foxholes in a bad mood and resumed blasting once more. Then they once again took cover. The Germans retaliated and the pattern was set. First one, then the other. The afternoon's unfolding lasted a long time, when in a burst of wild impulsiveness, the gun teams climbed out of their holes to man the cannons again to resume hammering away, this as shells continued to explode all around them. They had lost control! What made it worse was that the Germans didn't back off either, accepting the challenge. The result was simultaneous counter-batteries during which everybody could get killed. It lasted an eternity. Then suddenly the German shells stopped coming in! Had they given up? Or were they all dead?
>
> The adrenaline-elevated GIs were not instantly aware [that the shells had stopped]. They were to keep at it, punctuating their fury with shell after shell. When finally they noticed, they still didn't let up, banging away until their aching arms cried out to be rested. Only then,

first one team, then another, halted, to finally drop on the ground. In the next moment they lit cigarettes and began to crack jokes. The jokes were at the expense of the Krauts, who that afternoon had earned their grudging respect.[94]

It was important to the Third Army that something be done to reduce the power of the German artillery, as Patton was planning for a new offensive to begin on December 19. Veteran units, such as the long-suffering 5th Division, were pulled out of the action for reorganization and training. Patton received another corps headquarters, III Corps, and some fresh units that included the 87th Infantry Division. Third Army's objectives for the December offensive were the same as they had been in August: to seize bridgeheads across the Rhine in the vicinity of Mannheim and Mainz. Preparations for the American attack continued through mid December, until interrupted by one of the most spectacular surprises in modern military history—the German Ardennes offensive (also referred to as the Battle of the Bulge).

On December 16, 1944, Hitler launched the last great German offensive of World War II. Allied intelligence had completely failed to anticipate the attack, and the Americans could not have been more surprised. In what was presumed to be a sleepy sector in the Ardennes Forest, the Americans had posted a thin line of five badly spread out divisions. Scattered along the German border, these grossly overextended units covered a vast 100-mile long front. In the greatest of secrecy, the Germans had amassed a huge force of thirty divisions and 1,000 aircraft prepared to overwhelm them. Hitler's intent was to regain the initiative, split the Allied armies in half, and to retake the Channel port of Antwerp. With that success achieved, some German leaders dreamed a peace could be negotiated with the Americans and British.

In the early morning hours of December 16, German panzer forces, led by seemingly unstoppable King Tiger tanks, rolled over stunned American outposts and main line positions. Many American troops remained firmly dug-in and made heroic stances. Others were completely overwhelmed by the sheer power of the German onslaught. One division, the newly arrived 106th Infantry, was trapped in the Schnee Eifel and lost 7,500 men captured.

Hitler had counted on three elements to assure a German victory. The first was for bad weather in order to negate American airpower; the second was for tactical surprise; and the third was for a slow American response in bringing sufficient reinforcements into the battle. The Germans were able to get two out of three of these factors on their side. The weather that December truly was awful, with heavy snowfall and cloudy skies that completely restricted an Allied air response for the first critical days of the offensive. As a result of good operational security and deception, compounded by Allied intelligence failure, the Germans did indeed achieve as complete a surprise as could have been hoped for. It was in the third element the Germans miscalculated, for the American response was far swifter than imagined.[95] While the 7th FAOB did not have a direct combat role in the Battle of the Bulge, they did contribute by helping to transport troops and material in support of the American surge.

On December 16, Third Army first received fragmentary indications of trouble in the 1st Army's sector to the north. When it became apparent that a full-scale German counteroffensive was under way in the Ardennes, Patton canceled the December offensive that he had planned to launch three days later and immediately shifted the direction of his army to the north. Patton's leadership in the Battle of the Bulge was among the finest moments in his military career. Patton was one of the few senior American leaders who actually anticipated the threat of a German counteroffensive in the Ardennes. As a result, he already had contingency plans that resulted in a speedy Third Army response to contain the attack. Third Army had control of three corps at that point, the XX, III, and XII. Two of the corps (III and XII) were ordered north into the Ardennes to help stem the German offensive. This movement left XX Corps holding virtually the same line that had previously been manned by all three corps. To make matters worse and even more difficult for Walker, XX Corps was stripped of the 10th Armored Division, which was sent racing to relieve the 4th Infantry Division and to shore up the right shoulder of the salient. In addition to losing armor and infantry forces, five artillery battalions were also detached from XX Corps and thrown into the Ardennes melee.

The reorientation of a field army from east to north involved routing 12,000 vehicles along four roads, establishing a completely new set of supply points, and restructuring the Third Army's entire signals network to support a new army headquarters in Luxembourg. Third Army troops entered the Battle of the Bulge on December 22, and four days later the lead armored forces were poised to relieve Bastogne.[96]

Ambrose records that over the years, a great deal of lore has been written about the Battle of the Bulge, and much of it, deservedly, centers on the grit and fighting spirit of the American GI. Of at least equal importance is the heroic logistical effort that it took to get sufficient American forces into the fray to turn back the Germans. On December 17, alone, 11,000 trucks and trailers carried 60,000 men, plus ammo, gasoline, medical supplies and other material into the Ardennes. In the first week of the battle, Eisenhower was able to move 250,000 men and 50,000 vehicles into the fight.[97] A number of the 7th FAOB vehicles and men took part in this effort. Wire trucks were reconfigured to hold men and cargo, which they transported non-stop to the Ardennes. Driving unmerciful hours in the miserably cold weather, the men of the 7th contributed in an unsung but vitally important mission. Jim Royals of B Battery was a part of this effort and wrote: "I remember the trip heading to the Ardennes and the Battle of the Bulge. That was some convoy. General Patton would sometimes be at an intersection and wave us on. He would give that old high sign—go fast sign—pushing his hand up and down. I am a member of the Battle of the Bulge Association and get the Bulge Bugle regularly. They sent me a nice certificate. I show it with pride."

During the darkest moments of the battle, the front line divisions became critically short of men, and some 7th FAOB men, such as John Powell, John Clements, Frank Bauler, and Meyer Friedman were transferred to the infantry. B Battery flash observer Jack French recalled how these men were rushed off to the infantry with no time for specialized training. Not everybody survived. At least two 7th FAOB alumni who had been transferred to other units, Lt. Goffman and Staff Sgt. Donvito, were killed in action before the end of January 1945.

On December 20, the realignment of Third Army forces mandated the retreat of XX Corps back across the Saar River. This meant that the 7th FAOB's Battery Headquarters and A Battery CP's had to leave Hemmersdorf, Germany to recross the Saar, and return to France. The Germans added to the misery of the retreat by firing heavy artillery strikes at the river crossing sites. The new battalion CP was set up at the small town of Filstrof while A Battery established winter quarters in the village of Colmen. At the time of the movement to Colmen, Rieth wrote of one of the more humorous experiences he observed: "We are near an outfit now that has a generator, and we ran a line from it to the radio and have it playing again. There are a lot of animals wandering around this town; pigs, cows, horses, and goats. This morning one of the boys tried to ride a horse. He's quite a short fellow so he brought the horse alongside a wall so he could get on. Just as he jumped for the horse's back, the horse moved away and took off down the road with him hanging on his side. First his helmet came off and then he flew off into the mud. We call him the 'Lone Ranger' now."

Although the move across the Saar to Colmen was only a few miles in distance, the negative impact on morale was great. The symbolism that they were retreating out of Germany was a disparaging indication that the war was still a long way from being over. Writing several months later (when censorship restrictions were lifted), Kurt Rieth had the following additional comments about this retreat: "I am enclosing nine more photos in this letter. They were all taken a few days before last Christmas, and didn't come back from Signal Corps until now. We were in the small village of Colmen in the Lorraine at the time, right on the border with Germany. That was the only time we ever had to retreat during all of our operations in Germany. Those were pretty discouraging days and also some of the toughest ones we ever had." The men's concern of having to withdraw back across the Saar River was a legitimate operational gripe as well, for having to retake it many weeks later would prove a much more difficult and costly endeavor.

It was during the Battle of the Bulge that one of the American Army's great tragedies of World War II descended upon a sister unit of the 7th FAOB— B Battery of the 285th Field Artillery Observation Battalion. Like the 7th and 286th FAOBs, the 285th was one of the observation battalions that formed a continuous link of counterbattery acquisition forces that ran across the length of the Allied front. During the course of the war, a number of soldiers rotated between the two units, and many men of the 7th had good friends serving with the 285th. Indeed, the battalion commander of the 285th FAOB, Lt. Col. Archer Fruend, had briefly commanded the 7th FAOB back in the early Camp Shelby days. It would be B Battery, 285th FAOB that would bear the infamous distinction of being the victim of the horrific "Malmedy Massacre."

On December 16, 285th B Battery commander Captain Leon Scarborough received orders transferring his battery from VII to VIII Corps control. Captain Scarborough left ahead of his unit to coordinate taking over the sector of operations being vacated by the 16th FAOB. On the morning of December 17, B Battery, now under its executive officer, Captain Roger Mills, began its move south to link up with Scarborough in Luxembourg. The convoy was comprised of the standard FAOB battery complement of thirty jeeps, weapons carriers, and 2 ½ -ton trucks. Nearing Malmedy, an engineer officer warned Captain Mills that there may be German armor ahead. Knowing the battery had deployed forward guides to serve as route markers, Mills decided to press ahead on his established route as to not abandon his men.

B Battery was indeed set on a collision course with the lead elements of SS Kampfgruppe Peiper, an elite armored battle group that was the spearhead of the 1st SS Panzer Division's concentrated attack. The German penetration had moved far faster than the Americans had imagined and the lightly defended trucks of B Battery were doomed. The two forces met at a five-road intersection two miles southeast of Malmedy. German tanks and half-tracks took the trucks under cannon and machine gun fire. The Americans were taken completely by surprise. Most of the vehicles not destroyed by the fire were run off into ditches or collided with each other. The German tanks quickly moved through the wreckage of the convoy, pushing abandoned vehicles off the road, and firing machine guns at ditches to encourage the survivors to surrender. As the GIs had no heavy weapons available, they quickly gave up and were ordered to the intersection to form a hasty POW collection point. About ninety of the 285th FAOB men had been captured. Added to this group was a collection of other American prisoners, bringing the total POW count at the intersection to 150 men.

The GIs were herded into a snow-covered field where they were held for several hours, assuming they would be taken back to POW camps in Germany. The reason for what happened next remains uncertain, but the consequences were unquestionable. Whether it was due to a perception of an escape attempt or through wanton cruelty or convenience on behalf of the Germans, SS guards suddenly opened up with machine gun and rifle fire. Many of the terrified GIs not immediately cut down ran for the woods. About seventy or so escaped, while eighty-two were murdered in cold blood.[98] Tech 5 William Summers was a survivor of the atrocity, and he reported this to the *Stars and Stripes* on December 18, 1944: "Those of us who played dead got away later, but we had to lie there and listen to German non-coms kill with pistols every one of our wounded men who groaned or tried to move. Those dirty ____. I never heard of anything like it in my life. Damn them. Give me a rifle and put me in the infantry. I want to go back and kill every one of those ____." Left in a no-man's land, many of the bodies lay in place for at least a month. Lieutenant Slessman had occasion to travel to Malmedy in the aftermath of the massacre and witnessed the frozen bodies of its victims in the killing ground. Like others who saw the evidence of the murder first hand, he came away from the experience much more embittered toward the enemy. The survivors of the 285th FAOB's B Battery were eventually shipped off to other units, with a number being transferred to the 7th FAOB. Captain Scarborough, with no company left to command, was sent to the 7th FAOB where he eventually took command of their B Battery at the war's end.

In Patton's effort to stem the German offensive, the Third Army attacked into the southern shoulder of the German penetration with fury. Some elements of the 7th FAOB were directly in the Ardennes fighting. Charlie Wright had this to recount of an experience during this period.

> It was during the Battle of the Bulge when I was caught in an OP along with three wire men. My last orders were to hold your position. I didn't realize that we were cut off by enemy armored forces, and we were not too far from the scene of the Malmedy Massacre. I tried to contact battery headquarters for orders but to no avail. Then, to my amazement, I heard my own voice, proper radio procedures and all, calling for Milton Spielberg, whom I had been trying to contact. Over and over, a German mimic was transmitting "Baker 7, calling Baker 7." Milty reasoned I was not receiving him, but the German was. As Spielberg later told me, "I knew your voice too well pal, he wasn't fooling me.

The spiritual side of Patton ran deepest when he was in his greatest battles, and he devoutly believed that God was responsible for his successes. In battle he would call on God to assist him and in the aftermath of victory he would always give credit to the Lord. During the most desperate days of the Battle of the Bulge, Patton sent out a wallet-sized card with a Christmas greeting that was distributed to each Third Army soldier. On the back of the card was a prayer written to call for heavenly intervention to bring about the clear weather needed for tactical air support. Charlie Wright carried his card throughout the war and he still retains it as of this writing. The front of the greeting read:

> *"Headquarters, Third United States Army. To each officer and soldier in the Third United States Army, I wish a Merry Christmas. I have full confidence in your courage, devotion to duty, and skill in battle. We march in our might to complete victory. May God's blessing rest upon each of you on this Christmas Day. Signed, G.S. Patton, Jr., Commanding, Third Army."*

On the reverse side of the card was printed:

> *"Almighty and most merciful Father, we humbly beseech Thee, of Thy great goodness, to restrain these immoderate rains with which we have had to contend. Grant us fair weather for Battle. Graciously hearken to us as soldiers who call upon Thee that armed with Thy power, we may advance from victory to victory, and crush the oppression and wickedness of our enemies, and establish Thy justice among men and nations. Amen."*

Whether it was through Patton's request for divine intervention or through luck, on Christmas Eve the skies began to clear. Pilots of both sides took to the skies. On Christmas Day, the German Luftwaffe ME 109s attacked 7th FAOB units. In one instance that day, a number of A Battery men had attended a special Christmas worship service. Ed Piatrowski went to the church in a 6x6 truck, and was about to climb back into it after the conclusion of the service. Staff Sergeant Fred Kozak, the A Battery motor sergeant, suggested to Ed that he instead ride back to the battery in his jeep. By doing so, Piatrowski missed being in the truck that was strafed by a German plane just moments later. Injured in the attack were Corporal Michael J. Woods, Sergeant Leonard Albricnck, Sergeant John Petrovits, and T/5 Frank Zot. Fortunately, none of the wounds were serious, and all the men were treated and returned to duty. (Ed Piatrowski changed his name to Ed Miller at the end of the war. His family paid a steep price in the war, as Ed's older brother was a radioman and gunner on a B-17, and was killed in a bombing raid over Berlin in May 1944.)

More German planes swarmed over A Battery headquarters at Colmen. At least ten ME 109s bombed and strafed the battery, with one of the attacking planes being shot down by the heavy anti-aircraft fire that the Americans sent in return. Hank Lizak was in back of a 6x6 wire truck when the attack caused his driver to pull off the side of the road. There was a mad scramble to get out of the truck's cargo hold, with the large reel of commo wire impeding a speedy escape.

Battery A mess sergeant Stephen Wandzioch also had a very close call in the air raid. In order to provide the men with a little Christmas cheer on that cold morning, Wandzioch and First Sergeant Bennett were out on a mission to find some cognac to mix in with the daily ration of grapefruit and orange juice. On the way back to the battery headquarters, a German plane pulled behind the mess truck and was lining up for a gun run. Wandzioch then turned left at an intersection just in time, for a split second later the road he had been heading on was ripped apart by the plane's cannon and machine gun fire. Not only did Wandzioch make it back intact, but he also prepared a first class turkey dinner for his men that day.

As described by Kurt Rieth's letter home on Christmas, Wandzioch made good on the delivery of the booze as a supplement to the day's feast. "Another Christmas is almost gone and though the distance between us is great, I know we were together in our thoughts. Anyway, I know we will enjoy the future Christmas's together all the more. We had a big meal this afternoon with turkey, cranberry sauce, mashed potatoes, carrots, asparagus, and peas. For dessert there was fruit cocktail, apple pie, and of course, coffee. This morning, before the dinner, we had a drink made of cognac and grapefruit juice. We also received some cigars which I am smoking now." Later that afternoon a signal corps photographer took photographs of the A Battery men. For many of the soldiers who did not own cameras, these pictures were probably among the few they acquired in the course of the war.

The B Battery chow trucks on their way to supporting the Christmas celebration were also attacked by German planes. Jim Royals remembers fishing chunks of shrapnel out of the gravy in his Christmas dinner.

The clearing in the weather that resulted in these German airstrikes also allowed the Americans to become airborne as well. At this point in the war the Americans had better planes and a lot more of them. Battalion radioman Tom Delay remembers watching with great relief low flying P-47s and contrails of bombers at higher altitude on the way to hit the enemy. For the first time since the offensive began, American aircraft were able to pummel the exposed German panzers as the tide of the battle began to turn. The 101st Airborne Division's defense of Bastogne, now supported by aircraft and Patton's tanks, sucked nine German divisions into a hopeless attack. At the height of the offensive, the Germans were able to create a salient that reached forty miles wide and sixty miles deep. By December 27, the German offensive had reached its high water mark. Although the fighting in the Ardennes would continue until January 28, 1945, there was now no longer any doubt as to its outcome. The losses suffered by the combatants are difficult to fathom. Of the 600,000 American soldiers who fought, almost 20,000 were killed, 20,000 captured, and 40,000 wounded. About 800 American tanks and other armored vehicles were destroyed or lost.[99] The Germans suffered even worse. Of the 500,000 men they put into the battle, 100,000 were killed, wounded, or captured. In addition, the Germans lost nearly all of the tanks and aircraft they committed to the offensive. The difference was that while the Allies could replace their losses, the Germans could not.[100]

7th Field Artillery Observation Battalion Christmas Card - December 1944
In December 1944, the 7th FAOB printed up these unit Christmas cards for each soldier. Kurt Rieth wrote on the back of his card: "Dear Mother and Dad, Someone in the battalion drew this picture and they made up a bunch of them so every man could have a few. The picture is supposed to represent our sound and flash sections picking up the location of enemy guns. You also see some of the places we've been at."

CHAPTER 10

The Saar Moselle Triangle: Against the Westwall

Toward the end of 1944, the composition of the XX Corps' combat divisions was dramatically reduced from the powerful force that had taken Metz in November. The 10th Armored Division and the 5th Infantry Division were sent up north to help stem the German Ardennes Offensive. This realignment left only the 90th and 95th Infantry Divisions, the 3rd Cavalry Group, and XX Corps artillery to hold what had previously been the entire Third Army line. Fortunately for XX Corps, the German offensive came no closer than twenty miles to the north of the edge of the Saar Moselle Triangle. Had they been able to make a serious move against XX Corps, there would have been few forces left to stop them.

For those 7th FAOB troops not involved in transporting forces and equipment into the Battle of the Bulge, this was a relatively static period. The lack of serious movement allowed the battalion to begin publishing a weekly newspaper. After a contest to pick a name, the paper was titled "Seekers News." Lieutenant Colonel Schwartz had this to say in the first issue:

> This first issue of our Battalion newspaper represents the culmination of over three years of wishful thinking on my part. I have directed the editor to limit the paper to what the command says they would like to read and know about their outfit; namely, news of personalities, achievements of various sections and batteries, and what's going on in the battalion in general. For this splendid issue one, I wish to acknowledge my appreciation to the editor, the battery assistant editors, the artists and all the others who have so cheerfully given long hours of unstinting effort in its production.

Although security and censorship restrictions limited the paper in providing any meaningful operational data, it served as a means to recognize soldiers getting awards, passes to Paris (rare and highly valued prizes), news of births back home, the welcome of new replacements, and other humorous anecdotes.

New Years Eve of 1945 came in with a literal bang. All of the Third Army FAOBs took part in selecting targets for a New Year's Eve salute to the Germans. To honor the arrival of the New Year, General Patton ordered that every Third Army artillery piece fire on a likely German target at the strike of midnight on December 31, 1944. Following these mighty salvos, forward observers throughout Third Army listened to the screams of many enemy wounded during the early morning hours on the first day of 1945.[101] In response, the Germans returned their own salute to Third Army on New Year's Day. The Germans correctly forecasted that many American units would enjoy a large holiday-style meal around 1:00 P.M. That afternoon, in the 286th FAOB, Edward Marinello was away from the B Battery CP in Waldbillig, Luxembourg in support of a sound survey team mission. The survey was hampered when a group of

American P-47 aircraft mistook them for Germans and attacked them repeatedly (amazingly without loss to the survey members). Returning to Waldbillig in a dark mood, but eager to partake in the New Year's feast, the team became stunned at the vast destruction inflicted on the town while they had been gone. Survivors of the severe German artillery bombardment described the shelling as among the most blistering and prolonged they experienced in the entire war. The Germans had cleverly timed the attack to catch as many American troops as possible out in open chow lines. In Waldbillig alone, forty-five Americans were killed or wounded. B Battery of the 286th suffered two men killed and two seriously wounded.[102]

At the beginning of the new year, the 7th FAOB started to get in some replacements to make up for combat losses, illnesses, and men transferred to other units. (A number of 7th FAOB veterans were sent back to the States to serve as the cadre for newly created field artillery observation battalions. Before the war ended, the army would activate twenty-five field artillery observation battalions.) Among those arriving were Lt. Marlin Yoder and Jess Grisham. Grisham's journey was typical of that of an average ETO replacement. Drafted in June 1944, he was trained as a battery clerk and shipped to England in mid December. After transiting several replacement depots, he arrived at a final holding station in Metz. In early January, Grisham and five other men were picked up by a 7th FAOB truck and transported to battalion headquarters at Filstrof. Initially, all new replacements were assigned to Headquarters Battery, where they went through a streamlined orientation course on the unique operations of an observation battalion. Along with Grisham's group, another eleven men were sent to A Battery and nine more to B Battery.

Grisham describes his initial experience with the 7th FAOB:

Activity at Filstrof consisted of orientation each day and working with a survey team. I was assigned to a farmhouse with Sergeant James Brannock and Private Joseph Jachetta. We slept in an area between the farmer's quarters and his cows—the cows were the only source of heat. It was cold as hell, snow up to my waist—so cold that the old farmer had moved the family privy into his barn. One day I found it, and no longer trudged through the snow to our slit trench. Many others of us did the same. The old farmer soon discovered the full house and went raving mad to First Sergeant John Skelton. The sarge put a 'keep out sign' on the outhouse and it was back to the basics.

As a result of the Battle of the Bulge, keeping the men supplied with fresh rations also became more difficult. Master Sergeant Jerry Ballman, the Headquarters Battery motor sergeant, provided this account:

Somewhere in France, just across the border from Germany, rations were temporally slowed down and we hadn't had meat in a while. We somehow found out that a French farmer had a German's cow, and no longer wanted it. Captain Del Bello, the battalion medical officer, gave it some sort of cursory inspection and said it would be OK to eat.

First Sergeant Skelton shot it with his .45 pistol. We then hung it up using the hoist on back of the battalion motors truck. We then backed a weapons carrier under the animal and one of the cooks butchered it, with the entrails, hide, and other byproducts dropping in the truck to be hauled away and buried.

It wasn't allowed to hang very long and the decision was made to cut the whole thing into steaks. Soon you could smell the meat frying all over the area. The smell was about the only good thing about it because the meat was so dammed tough you could hardly eat it! That was our first and last attempt to supply our own meat.

Other encounters with local livestock had happier endings. One snowy night in late January, an agonized villager braved the curfew restrictions and burst into the headquarters aid room with an urgent request for medical help. Captain Del Bello and three other medics followed the farmer to his barn where the emergency turned out to be a mother cow in the midst of difficult labor. The four medics helped pull the new the calf out into the world and the crisis ended well for all concerned.

Kurt Rieth wrote this of life at A Battery headquarters on January 5: "We've had continuous cold weather for quite a while now, and everything is frozen. There is always just enough snow to keep the ground covered. The streets are very slippery and last night the ground was covered with food where the fellows had fallen down with their mess kits and spilled their meals all over the landscape. It's a funny sight to see a man slip, watch his coffee go up in the air, and come down on top of him."

As a result of the realignment in American lines in response to the Battle of the Bulge, XX Corps became the only American corps directly facing a path to the Rhine River. In early January, the Saar Moselle Triangle became of greater emphasis to Patton. The initial fighting along the base of the triangle (the Orscholz Switch) started back in mid November 1944. The 90th Infantry Division, after breaking through the Moselle north of Metz, came up against the West Wall at the Orscholz Switch and made the first serious attempts to breach it. Battalion-sized attacks were launched at the (far left) Moselle portion of the sector in the town of Berg, and in the village of Tettingen, three miles farther east. Realizing the threat to Trier, a key staging area for the Ardennes Offensive, German Field Marshall Von Rundstedt rushed in reinforcements. The 90th Division attack was thwarted before any serious progress was made. The positions remained in place for the next two months, and the Third Army response to the Ardennes Offensive was to put off further attacks until mid January 1945.

On January 7, XX Corps lost the 90th Infantry Division, which was replaced in line by the 94th Infantry Division. The 95th Division was kept occupied by holding Saarlauten bridgehead across the Saar, and would be in defensive mission for the next several weeks, unavailable to further participate in offensive operations. Although the recently returned 10th Armored Division was also technically based in the XX Corps zone, they were so badly shot up from the Battle of the Bulge that they were unavailable to support XX Corps operations. As such, the 94th Division became XX Corps' solitary maneuver force. With the exception of lightly armored vehicles from the 3rd Cavalry Group and a handful of tank destroyers, XX Corps was virtually devoid of any significant armored support. Despite the lack of resources, General Walker wasted no time in putting the newly arrived 94th Division to the test, and on January 10, ordered them to make limited objective battalion-sized attacks against the German defenses.

Facing off against XX Corps' 94th Division were the better part of three enemy divisions. First was the German's 416th Infantry Division, which XX Corps had faced and soundly thrashed at Metz. Now in line at the Triangle, the 416th was substantially rebuilt and fully manned with three regiments of about 10,000 troops. Also occupying the Orscholz Switch was the 256th Volksgrenadier Division. German infantry was further augmented by a miscellaneous collection of fortress battalions originally designed to defend the triangle, as well as the previously discussed 404th Volks Artillery Corps. The biggest threat to XX Corps was from the 11th Panzer Division, which was in reserve and posted in nearby Trier. The 11th Panzer was a veteran armored division that had seen extensive action on the Eastern Front, and in southern France. The division was reconstituted prior to the Battle of Bulge, where they remained in reserve and were not engaged. With full strength in men and equipment, the 11th Panzer was rated as one of the best divisions at that time in the entire German Army.

In the offensive, conventional military doctrine usually requires that the attacker hold at least a three-to-one superiority in manpower. At the Triangle, the Germans were defending a well-prepared fortified position with a force that was larger in infantry strength, and far superior in armored capability. The weather was also in the German's favor, as the snow and freezing rain restricted American airpower. In the face of freezing January temperatures, the Germans had better cold weather clothing and shelter for their troops than did the Americans. The only advantage that XX Corps possessed was in the numerical and qualitative superiority of its field artillery resources. In terms of calculable odds, the chances of success for the initial XX Corps attacks did not look good.

While the 94th Division had been in some defensive-type fighting in Brittany in the fall of 1944, they did not have the offensive experience that other XX Corps maneuver divisions had achieved. With the 94th Division leadership eager to prove themselves, Third Army and XX Corps Headquarters would be watching with close eyes.

The first series of 94th Division attacks were planned to begin on January 13. General Maloney, the 94th's commander, was restricted by Walker's orders to not commit more than one battalion at a time. Although not specifically mentioned in the description that follows of the bitter fighting, XX Corps artillery and the 7th FAOB played an important part in virtually all aspects of the fire support to the 94th Infantry Division operations. In its routine operations, the 7th FAOB worked in close concert with corps spotter planes. On some days, as many as twenty enemy batteries were located and placed under fire by XX Corps guns.[103]

An initial XX Corps objective was to take the town Tettingen, which was midway between the Moselle and the center part of the Triangle's switch. The 1st Battalion of the 376th Infantry Regiment 1/376th conducted this attack. The assault surprised the defending elements of the German 416th Division and the Americans quickly established control of the town. Seeking to exploit their success, the American battalion then advanced toward the next town of Butzdorf, which was only a few hundred meters farther north. There, German resistance stiffened and the Americans began to take considerable casualties as they fought off several small-scale enemy counterattacks. Holding at Butzdorf, the limited American attack had accomplished its objective. Whether the 94th Division could hold Butzdorf for good remained to be seen. Like an ignited fuse, the attack at Tettingen and Butzdorf set into motion the explosive counterattack of the powerful 11th Panzer Division based twenty miles north.

With the 1/376th attacking at Tettingen, the 94th Division also had the 3/376th move against the extreme left of the Switch. The objective would be three small towns—Weis Berg, and Nennig—that stood within a several mile radius of each other on the east bank of the Moselle. Like their sister battalion's attack at Tettingen a few miles to the east, the 3/376th assault initially caught the Germans by surprise. However, the heavy smoke screen that was employed to cover them from the Germans also caused confusion among the 3/376th. In the town of Weis, one American platoon was isolated and badly cut up, and all of its non-wounded survivors captured. The bitter weather—it was eight degrees Fahrenheit below zero—caused machine guns to jam and froze the hands of the men who struggled to clear them. To offset the misery of the weather and strong German resistance, the American infantrymen were well supported by artillery. They continued to press the attack and by the end of the day, all three towns were under American control.

To further solidify the day's gains, the last battalion of the 376th Regiment (2/376th) took a strategic wooded area to the southeast of Tettingen. By January 16, it appeared that XX Corps, via the heroic efforts of the 376th Infantry Regiment, began to make some progress in chipping away against the Siegfried Line. As the American troops consolidated their forces in the newly established towns, German General von Wietersheim, commander of the 11th Panzer Division, set out to reverse all American gains.

On the evening of January 14, the 11th Panzer Division departed Trier for the Saar Moselle Triangle with the orders to counterattack the 94th Infantry Division and to retake the towns that the 376th Infantry had captured. A severe ice storm slowed down the panzer's arrival, but on the night of January 16-17 the American troops waiting in their foxholes could clearly hear the ominous sound of engines and track treads as the enemy tanks were moving into attack position. The GIs laid out all the antitank mines and guns that could be mustered, and braced to meet the inevitable attack. They did so with the knowledge that there

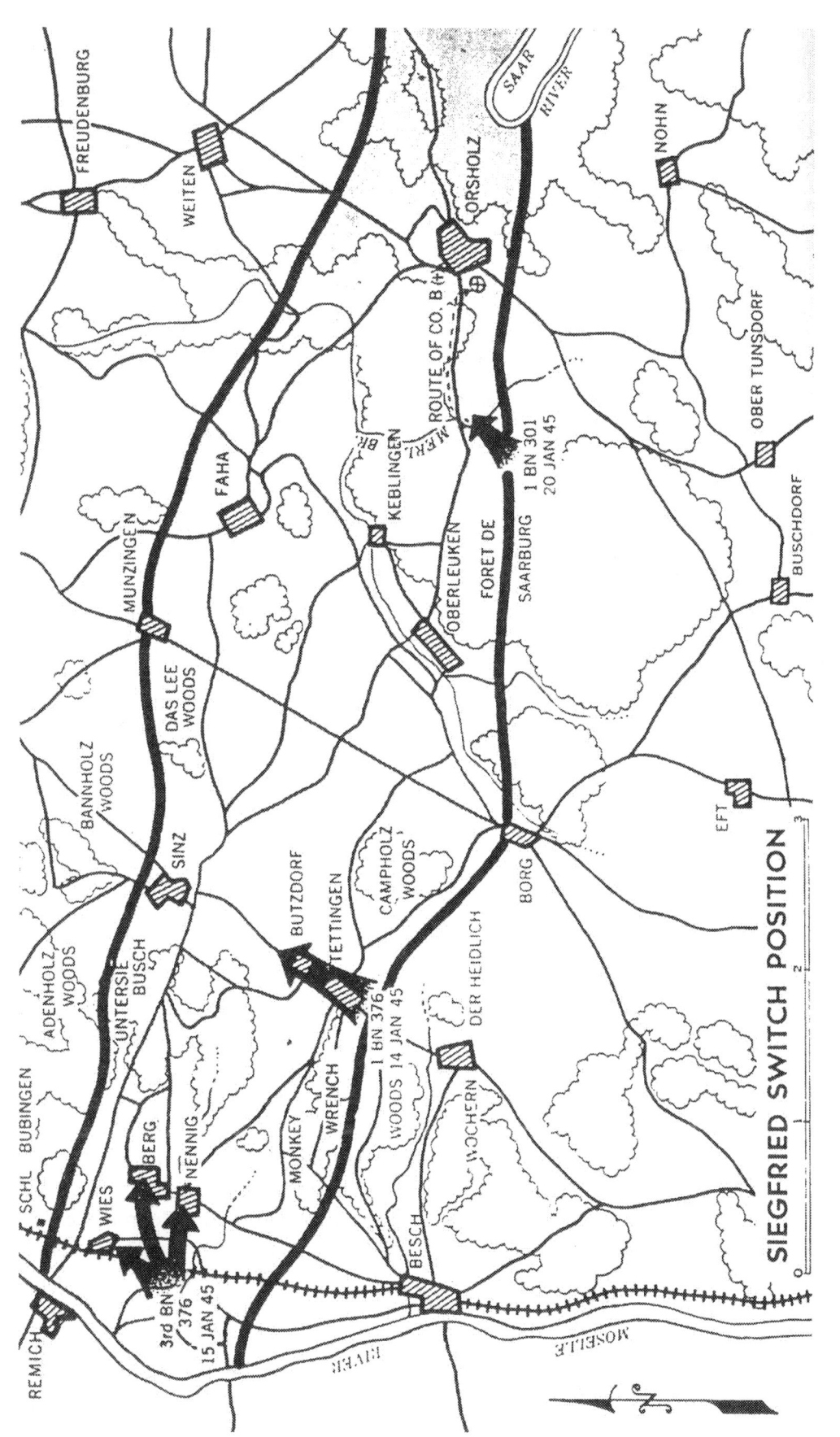

The Orscholz Switch

Located 20 miles south of Trier, the Orscholz Switch was a strong defensive line that connected the Moselle and Saar rivers. This line served as the base of the Saar Moselle Triangle. Ten miles long, the Switch was two miles in depth. Within this line, the Germans had carefully concealed bunkers that were linked with field fortifications and minefields. From January through February 1945, XX Corps' 94th Infantry Division was bled white trying to penetrate the Switch. This map depicts the initial 94th Infantry Division attacks in mid-January. Fought in the coldest of weather, the battle became a bitter contest of attacks and counterattacks where progress was usually measured in yards.

would be little hope of any American tanks on hand to support them.

With dawn on January 17, the Germans let loose with a twenty minute artillery barrage that blew apart Butzdorf and Tettingen. The better part of a German regiment, supported by fifteen tanks and self propelled guns, attempted to storm the towns that were held by only three infantry companies. Antitank mines and bazookas were able to knock out the first tanks that entered each town, but the German infantry swept forward and was able to occupy several of the buildings. Despite the odds, the Americans counterattacked and by the end of the morning had pushed the Germans out of the town. Five German tanks were disabled. The Germans regrouped and continued the attack just before noon. The German tanks fired point blank into the shattered buildings, driving the Americans into the cellars. Some M-10 tank destroyers and Third Cavalry light tanks tried to get forward, but the superior German armor held them at bay. (Episodes like this finally led the army to conclude what shaped their post-war armored doctrine—the best way to beat an enemy tank was by building a better tank of your own.)

German infantry again charged Butzdorf. The attack was supported by fire from three directions, making it impossible for the Americans to send in reinforcements. Inside the town, both sides fought ferociously. In one instance, three brave mail clerks that had been used to ferry in supplies got a hold of a bazooka and some rockets and proceeded to knock out four German tanks. Despite the heroic defense, by the end of the afternoon it became clear that further efforts to hold Butzdorf were untenable. After suffering heavy casualties, the two companies defending the town were withdrawn. The 94th Division was able to reinforce its troops in neighboring Tettingen, and that town held.[104]

In spite of the new presence of large German armored forces in his sector, Walker still wanted to press XX Corps attacks forward. Walker realized he would need armor of his own to win, and appealed to Patton for help. Patton agreed, and sent the newly arrived 8th Armored Division to XX Corps control. However, there was a catch in using the armor, as Third Army directed that at least two thirds of its combat forces (Combat Commands, or CCs) remain in reserve. Thus, only one tank and mechanized infantry battalion could be used by XX Corps at any one time. Worse still, XX Corps would only have the services of the armor for a forty-eight-hour period. The first 8th Armored Division element to support XX Corps would be Combat Command A, and it was scheduled to arrive on January 21.

While awaiting the armored reinforcements, the rest of the 94th Division was not idle. Two of its three infantry regiments (the 301st and 302nd) had yet to be engaged, and were presently put into motion. The 302nd Regiment replaced the battered 376th Infantry on the western end of the line, with the 376th moving back to recuperate as divisional reserve. The 301st Regiment was ordered to the far eastern end of the Switch, where they would be ordered to attack the village of Orscholz. Orscholz, near the Saar River, was a key anchor of the German line as well as the namesake of "Orscholz Switch." By rolling up the Moselle and Saar borders of the Triangle, it was hoped the German line would collapse. Orscholz would be a tough objective, as it sat on dominating high ground and was protected by the Saar River to the east, thick forests on either side, and a line of strongly held pillboxes and mine fields that covered possible American approaches.

The 94th Division attacked Orscholz on January 20, a full twenty-four hours before the 8th Armored Division would be available. The plan called for an all out attack from the 1/301st Infantry. A and B companies would advance abreast, with C Company in reserve. The attack ran into trouble from the very beginning. A long march through a blinding snowstorm delayed the movement and separated the two rifle companies. While B Company was able to penetrate the first series of German defenses, A Company began to take terrible losses from a minefield they had stumbled on in the thick snow. While A Company was thrown back with heavy losses, B Company was quickly isolated and surrounded. Lieutenant Colonel Miller, the battalion commander, was killed while trying to renew the attack. When Company C was committed from the reserve, they too ran into a minefield and lost sixty men killed or wounded in a matter of minutes. For the next twenty-four hours, B Company fought valiantly against overwhelming odds. The Americans had to battle both German gunfire and the weather. It was so cold on the night of January 21 that a number of men froze to death. Virtually out of ammunition, medical supplies, and troops still able to fight, the survivors of B Company, and other assorted squads that were trapped along with it, could do nothing but attempt to escape. XX Corps and divisional artillery laid a heavy smoke screen to serve as cover as the beleaguered Americans tried to exfiltrate back to friendly lines. The Germans were too strong and the effort was too late. The retreating force was completely overrun by attacking Germans and 240 American soldiers were captured. The 1st Battalion of the 301st Infantry was virtually eliminated as a fighting force.

With their left flank holding at Orscholz, the Germans could now focus on eliminating the remaining American foothold that had been gained on January 14. The 11th Panzer Division was present in complete force, and prepared to retake Berg, Nennig, and Siegfreid Line positions west of Tettingen. The German attack came at dawn of January 20, and hit just after the 302nd Regiment relieved the 376th.

At dawn, a terrific German artillery and rocket barrage descended on the American positions. German tanks and infantry then emerged from the woods and set upon their objectives. Ninety-fourth Division and XX Corps artillery could only do so much against the enemy tanks, but were able to raise hell on the accompanying infantry. Without close-in infantry support, the German armor was rendered more vulnerable to defending bazooka fire. As a result, the German tanks were not be used as aggressively as they otherwise could have been. Still, the German attack made progress against the outnumbered Americans, and eventually the panzer grenadiers were able to fight their way into Berg and Nennig. The fighting swung back and forth, with each side gaining and losing ground in the towns.

To help relieve the struggle for Nennig, American troops moved against German bunkers outside the town. In action here, Master Sergeant Nicholas Oresko, a platoon leader of C Company, 1st Battalion, 302nd Infantry, would later be awarded with the Medal of Honor. Single handedly, Master Sergeant Oresko charged a concrete bunker, knocked out its machine gun, and then killed its six occupants. Although severely wounded in the hip, he charged a second bunker and took out another machine gun and a half dozen more Germans as well. He then refused medical evacuation until the position was fully secured.

By the end of the day on January 22, the Germans held about half of Berg and Nennig. Losses on both sides had been enormous. Enemy fire and cold weather injuries such as trench foot and frostbite had whittled L Company, 302nd Infantry, down to a force of eighteen effective men (from a full strength of 150). The Germans suffered badly as well, with the both the 110th and 111th Panzergrenadier Regiments reduced to fifty percent strength. One battalion, the 3/110th was so decimated that it was disbanded and its survivors distributed to other units.[105]Finally on January 23, Combat Command A (CC A) of the 8th Armored Division was in position to support the 94th Division. XX Corps had only forty-eight hours to make the most of this resource. Its objective was to clear out for once and all the German penetration at Nennig and Berg, and to take the tactically significant town of Sinz. Sinz was two miles north of Tettingen and sat at an important road network. Furthermore, Sinz was located at the rear extreme of the fortified West Wall. If XX Corps could penetrate there, the Americans would finally be clear of prepared enemy defenses. Breaking out of the West Wall was of supreme strategic value, and would finally allow Third Army to resume a mobile offensive.

The heavy losses and overall exhaustion of the 94th Division's infantry battalions would hamper the American attack at Nennig and Berg. As such, the 8th Armored Division would have limited infantry support as they moved forward. In Berg, the Germans had made a strong point out of the town's medieval castle, and threw heavy fire from its thick walls into the armored infantryman and tankers. Losses among the American leaders were extremely severe, resulting in one battalion being led by a staff captain, some companies commanded by second lieutenants, and platoons and squads run by junior enlisted men. Once again, highly accurate and overwhelming American artillery support made the difference in saving the day, and by January 25, Berg was secured.

With Berg taken, XX Corps directed its main effort at Sinz. Leading off the attack were two infantry battalions of the 94th Division. After reclaiming Butzdorf, which had been lost ten days earlier, the Americans set off for a ridgeline overlooking Sinz. The lead battalion stumbled into a minefield and then was beset by German artillery fire, stalling the attack just outside the line of departure. The second battalion, followed by another reserve battalion, was able to avoid the German mines and moved forward toward Sinz. Midway, they too were stopped by German defenses. Finally, the 8th Armored Division's CC A, having finished at Berg, came to the support of the pinned-down infantrymen. B Company of the 18th Tank Battalion detected a fifteen-tank ambush that the Germans had set up. A bitter tank vs. tank battle erupted, ending with the Americans destroying four German Mark IV tanks and two antitank guns. With the armor support at hand, the American advance finally was able to enter Sinz. Clearing the town was a costly process, and 18th Tank Battalion lost ten tanks in doing so.

Although the Americans now held Sinz, it was a tenuous toehold at best. Only two infantry companies had been able to make it into the town, and both of those had suffered over fifty percent losses. The forty-eight hour window on using CCA of the 8th Armored Divison had expired just as the town was taken. Despite pleas by the 94th Division Commander, the CC A was ordered to return to the 8th Armored Division, where they were to immediately be assigned to another army command. Once again, XX Corps was devoid of any serious armored support. Realizing that there was no way to defend Sinz with the forces available, the 94th Division gave up the hard fought town and retreated to the high ground to the south.[106]

After two weeks of extremely grueling and courageous fighting—primarily on behalf the 94th Infantry Division—the XX Corps position against the Saar Moselle Triangle was virtually unchanged. In other XX Corps developments, the 95th Division, which did not have a major role in the January operations, was ordered to join 9th Army in the north on January 26. To replace the 95th Division, XX Corps was given 26th Infantry Division. Although the 26th Division was a veteran outfit, they were badly mauled during the Battle of the Bulge, and were sent to XX Corps primarily to rest and refit. It would be some time before they were available to resume combat operations, and it would continue to fall on the weary shoulders of the 94th Division to hold the XX Corps line.

With only one over-committed and now under-strength division available, it should have been obvious that continuing XX Corps advance against the Orscholz Switch would be folly. Still, Patton was impatient and did everything he could do to get more forces to launch a strike for Trier in early February. Complicating the Allies' flexibility was the Supreme Commander of Allied Expeditionary Forces' renewed sense of caution in the aftermath of the Battle of the Bulge. General Eisenhower was determined that he would not again have insufficient forces readily available to react to another major enemy counterattack. Accordingly, he established a substantial theater reserve force that took entire divisions away from the control of the front line armies. Patton wrote the following in his diary: "Reserve against what? This seemed like locking the barn door after the horse was stolen. Certainly at this period of the war no reserve was needed—simply violent attacks everywhere with everything. . . .the Germans do not have the resources to stop it."[107] Despite Patton's pleas, additional troops would not be made available and Third Army would have to wait until at least mid February before they could launch any major advance. Patton fumed at the thought of remaining on defense and his frustration was evident when he visited XX Corps and 94th Division headquarters on January 30. Rather than using the occasion to compliment the division on their heroic efforts attacking the Triangle, he instead berated them with the accusation that they had suffered a higher number of cold weather casualties than direct combat losses.[108]

Patton's ire may have better served his soldiers had it been focused on the Allies' logistics staff rather than the poor men who suffered due to inadequate boots and cold weather gear. Trench foot was the worst of the cold weather ailments, and its disabling effects greatly impacted Third Army. Continued exposure to cold and wet conditions caused portions of the feet to actually freeze and blacken, killing flesh, causing intensive pain, and making it impossible to walk. A case of trench foot could disable a soldier for weeks if not months. Part of the blame for the high rate of non-combat casualties must go to the Quartermaster, European Theater of Operations, who had refused to order a newly developed winter uniform for the troops because he believed that the war would end before cold weather came. Not until January was there an adequate supply of jackets, raincoats, overshoes, blankets, and sweaters. As a result, 46,000 troops throughout the European theater were hospitalized, the equivalent of three infantry divisions.[109]

Ed Marinello writes of the clothing and other means that the men of an FAOB used to try to stay warm that bitter winter.

> What the GI was expected to wear during cold periods was a bulky, restrictive overcoat that reached well below the knees. Instead most GIs took to wearing a combination sweater/jacket plus the element that made the difference; long johns. As a result, overcoats were stored in trailers along with each man's duffel bag that contained a second shirt and pants, a half dozen pairs of socks, underwear, handkerchiefs and writing material. When milder weather came, the heavy coats, as well as gas masks, were removed and dumped on the roadside to make room for the wines and liquors that were being looted as Third Army began capturing towns in greater abundance... Despite the fountain of liquor, heavy drinking rarely became a problem of any magnitude.[110]

While the weather remained cold in early February, it warmed just enough to change the snow into freezing rain, and turn the frozen ground and roads into a hellish quagmire of deep mud. Movement on vehicles and on foot became even more of a challenge. If there was a side benefit for the infantry, at least some of the German land mines were now becoming visibly exposed and could be more readily avoided.

The first two weeks of February were largely a static situation for XX Corps. However, the lack of movement did not necessarily mean quiet. Although not active in offensive operations, the 94th Division conducted a number of "reconnaissance in force" missions designed to chip away bit by bit at the West Wall. Artillery on both sides was active and the forward observation mission never relaxed. For the 7th FAOB observers manning the flash and sound OPs, there would be no rest or let up on the misery. There was the constant exposure to the weather, the ever-present danger from German artillery, and the perpetual threat of deadly small unit raids. For those in the remainder of the battalion supporting those in the OPs, the conditions were also miserable. Many 7th FAOB members' duties involved moving around large portions of the XX Corps sector. Imagine driving around for hours on end on the coldest winter day in a convertible with the top and windows down—and no heat as well. These men did this day after day and week after week in one of Northern Europe's worst winters on record.

Battery sick call attendance grew dramatically during the winter months. A Battery Medic Roy Barber's log shows that on some days close to 40 men would receive treatment. The most common aliments were influenza, gastritis, and minor lacerations.

In addition to wounds and cold weather related injuries and illnesses, the medics had to deal with a host of other medical issues that could be expected from 550 men exposed to harsh outdoor life. Some conditions were of course beyond the medics' abilities to treat and the GIs would be sent to specialists or higher echelon hospitals. At one point in this campaign, Charlie Wright came down with a terrific toothache. He found an army dentist set up in a village and waited in a long line to be seen. The dentist happened to also be a former famous college football star whose name Wright immediately recognized. Wright had no sooner opened his mouth than the dentist barked, "Do you want it filled or pulled?" Wright elected to have it filled. The building had no electricity and the drill was powered entirely by a contraption that consisted of a corpsman pedaling a stationary bicycle. With the corpsman pedaling like mad (and without the use of Novocain), the former football hero set to work on Wright's tooth. His work turned out to be a first rate job and the filling remained in place sixty years later.

Even in combat conditions, the grind of regular army life continued for the average 7th FAOB GI. Kurt Rieth on January 31: "We've got an inspection coming up today by the colonel and we've already swept the room about twenty times so it will look clean. It's probably no use however, because there's bound to be something wrong. There are no civilians around here to wash our clothes, so I had to do a little washing myself yesterday. I boiled the things and managed to burn a hole through an undershirt, but everything else came out white." Several days later, Rieth wrote about the process of trying to take a bath: "I just got through giving myself a bath and I feel in the right mood for writing a letter. It's really a lot of work trying to get the time and equipment to take a bath, but it's worth it. First I had to build a fire in the stove, and then walk about sixty yards and lug back the water, and finally find a tub big enough to get into. As the saying goes over here, however, a man should take a bath every six months whether he needs it or not."

The relative lull on the battlefront allowed the 7th FAOB to send some men back to rear areas for a well-deserved rest. The Red Cross showed movies and brought up doughnut trucks as well. To occupy free time, some of the men took up cards or became involved in other projects. Kurt Rieth described these activities in letters dated February 9 and 15:

> It's a pretty dreary day outside and it has been drizzling since yesterday. This is mostly farming country around here, with small hills rolling up and down and little villages in the valleys. They've been giving passes every now and then to men in the outfit to Paris and Metz. The boys that went to Metz didn't have much fun, but the ones that went to Paris said they had a swell time. A few of the boys found a hotel full of wine the other day and brought back quite of bit of it. We've been fooling around trying to build a radio lately and also a gasoline engine we can use to generate electricity. I doubt if the radio will work, but anyway, we have a lot of fun trying.
>
> We had a moving picture this morning, but it was pretty bad. One of those silly murder pictures where they seem to make up the story as they go along. Tomorrow, the Red Cross doughnut truck is scheduled to drop by and that's all for the program this week. I've been to the city of Thionville a few times recently. It must have been very pretty before the war, but now many buildings are destroyed. Most shops are closed, but we did manage to get a glass of beer, and another fellow got some film for his camera. Now that the ice has thawed everything is mud again, just like last fall. Another two weeks however and things should dry up and then we might start rolling forward again.

Marinello writes of February from the perceptive of a 286th FAOB Sound CP in Luxembourg (which was posted to the northeast of the 7th FAOB's sector):

> February '45 turned out to be a crazy month. The early part was weighed down in a series of snowstorms. But suddenly the weather turned mild with the first hint of spring that led to a thawing so that the rivers rose. During those teasing days, something truly remarkable occurred. The men became rejuvenated and started doing things they hadn't done in months. Without orders coming from above, they spruced up their trucks and jeeps, changed the motor oil and spark plugs, lubricated joints and most amazing of all, thoroughly cleaned out the back. And not only was the laundry done more often, but everybody shaved![111]

To further fill some of the down time during this period, some of the more musically inclined troops in the 7th FAOB formed an ad hoc band and gave impromptu performances using "liberated" instruments. The March 9 edition of "Seekers News" reported the following: "MUSICAL NOTES: The fact that M Sgt. Paul Asman, Sound Chief, A Battery, is an accordion virtuoso was little known until a short time ago. His latest concert was given in the cellar of A Battery's CP before a large audience. Wonder if those Jerry shells had anything to do with the size of your audience, Sergeant? Speaking of music, a lot of hidden talent was discovered in A Battery recently, among them being; Lt. Wackernage, PFC Dokulil, PFC Webb, PFC Velasquez, pianists; Tech 5 Rieth, violinist; Cpl. Barber, cornetist; and PFC Surges, accordionist. A first class jam session was held last week, with the above mentioned taking part, plus vocalist Pvt. Harry (Sinatra) Flaherty."

While some of the men were able to get breaks that February, the fighting continued at the front. The XX Corps' more aggressive "limited attacks" occurred on February 7-10 in a renewed effort to take Sinz and the woods surrounding the shattered village. XX Corps artillery support featured prominently in supporting this operation. While the 94th Division did make some progress in gaining ground around Sinz, it was at the high cost of men and tank destroyers. Still, significant results began to show from these incremental attacks. It was now becoming apparent to both German and American commanders that the previously elite 11th Panzer Division was quickly being destroyed in the defense of the Triangle. When in the defense, German doctrine called for their armored forces to be deployed as a mobile counterattack strike force. Now, one month into the Saar Triangle campaign, the 11th Panzer was being completely decimated while being used in a primarily defensive role. The German high command back in Berlin realized that this losing battle of attrition was forever ruining the assault capability of this highly valuable resource. On February 15, the remnants of the 11th Panzer were pulled out into reserve status, and with that, XX Corps' strongest adversary was knocked off the battlefield.[112] The 11th Panzer Division was too badly shattered to be refitted, and for the remainder of the war would no longer be an effective fighting force. The reduction of German armor forces in the Triangle would play a significant factor in the events that transpired next.

CHAPTER 11

Breaking the Siegfried Line

Although long in coming, the gradual hacking away of the West Wall defenses at the Triangle was beginning to show signs that XX Corps was finally on the verge of real progress. Walker knew he would need armored support to make and then exploit a strategically meaningful breakthrough. Looking for those resources, Walker noted that the 10th Armored Division had been refitting for the past month in the XX Corps zone and should finally be ready to resume combat operations. Patton enthusiastically agreed with Walker's proposal and appealed to Eisenhower for permission to use them in an attack against the Triangle. Eisenhower made a conditional agreement that the 10th Armored could be used by XX Corps, but only on the guarantee that the 94th Infantry Division would first have to achieve a clear breakthrough on their own. Only then could the tankers be fully released to support a XX Corps attack.[113] The attack was planned to begin on February 19. For the first time in the campaign, the 94th Division would not be restricted to piecemeal single-battalion-level assault. The entire weight of all three infantry regiments (nine battalions), augmented by four battalions of tank destroyers, and all of XX Corps artillery, would be used to overwhelm the German defenses. Another highly valued resource that would be attached to XX Corps control was the 5th Ranger Battalion. These elite troops were the army's toughest fighters and would be on hand to take on any special mission requirements that XX Corps had. The general objective of the attack would be to penetrate through all possible portions of the German defensive network. Close coordination was made with the 10th Armored Division, which would be committed to exploit a clear infantry-led penetration of the Switch.

The artillery preparation for the attack was a critical part of the plan. The big guns of XX Corps artillery would fire deep into the German rear areas to hit enemy artillery locations, as well as supply routes and command and communication nodes. In addition to neutralizing German artillery, these fires would also disrupt the enemy's ability to reinforce their front or to counterattack any American gains. With XX Corps artillery blasting the German rear areas, the 94th Division Artillery would concentrate on smashing the enemy's front line positions with rolling barrages in direct support to the infantry assault.[114] The 7th FAOB was to plot the German artillery positions so that the XX Corps gunners could effectively neutralize them. In addition, the battalion also had to be able to react and move forward once a breakthrough had been achieved. In the week before the attack, A Battery survey and wire laying teams pushed as far forward as possible to make ready a rapid response. These efforts were conducted so close to enemy lines that they had to be done in the early morning fog and at night.

In terms of counterbattery fire, each known enemy battery location would be attacked by three battalion volleys as soon as the assault began. Once the battle got underway, five battalion-sized barrages would hit each fixed German battery every hour at irregular intervals.[115] With the three infantry regiments moving abreast, the 94th Division jumped off at 4:00 A.M. on February 19. To maximize the shock effect, several of the XX Corps artillery battalions held their fire until thirty seconds after H-hour, and then fired

15,000 rounds into their pre-designated targets. Although German intelligence had predicted the attack, the sheer power of the American artillery rendered any coordinated defense impossible. Some of the American rifle companies were able to pour over their objectives, while others were caught in minefields and met strong resistance. At Oberleuken, in the center of the Switch, the 5th Ranger Battalion ran into an electronically detonated mine field and dug-in infantry defenses. The Rangers were thrown back with heavy losses. Overall though, most of the advance went according to plan and the American infantry surged forward. Sensing victory, Walker gave the order for the 94th Division to attack with reckless abandon and destroy all opposition in front of them. Hit across the entire front, the Germans were overwhelmed. The huge German command and control bunkers that had defied XX Corps for months were overrun, with most of their defenders killed or captured. The devastating XX Corps artillery fire into the rear areas further reduced any initiative that the Germans otherwise may have hoped to regain. Even if the Germans had been able to react, the removal of the 11th Panzer Division eliminated any serious threat from an armored counterattack.

One reason that the attack went as well as it did was due to the relative lack of German artillery fire. The 7th FAOB counterbattery program deserves much direct credit for this accomplishment. Reviewing 7th FAOB survey plots after the battle, the XX Corps counterbattery report cited at least thirty-eight damaged or abandoned German cannon that could largely be credited to the battalion's direction-finding.

By early afternoon, Walker decided that the 94th Division had achieved the level of breakthrough required for the commitment of the 10th Armored Division. He passed the final request to Third Army, and Patton immediately approved it. Assembled in the town of Perl on the left flank of the Switch, the 10th Armored Division would be ready to enter the battle early the next morning.

XX Corps' success on February 19 was all that could have been hoped for. By nightfall, the Switch line had been fully breached, all objectives (except for Oberleuken) were taken, and eight miles of key terrain and prepared defenses were now in American hands. The next day would bring the tanks, and XX Corps was poised to finish off the remaining Germans in the Switch and beyond.

The 10th Armored Division attack was configured to move in two combat command spearheads. The tanks moved forward at 9:00 A.M. on February 20 and passed through the lead elements of the 94th Division. The first armored combat command raced up the center of the Triangle and pushed deep into the German rear. At the end of the day, they could see the spires of the Trier Cathedral off to the north. Additional armored forces split off to the west to assist the 94th Division in clearing the remainder of the Switch. While the German front was collapsing, a number of pockets held out and fought back savagely. One last Switch objective was the town of Orscholz, where German defenders had so severely repulsed the 1st Battalion of the 301st Infantry one month earlier. This time, the town was attacked from the rear with the assistance of tanks. In late afternoon, both Orscholz and Oberleuken had fallen, marking the end of organized German resistance in the Switch. The 2nd Armored task force moved up along the Moselle on the eastern portion of the attack zone. They also accomplished their objectives, and linked up with a 2nd Cavalry force that crossed the Moselle seven miles north of what had been the Switch line.

In a little over two days of intensive combat marked by extreme aggressiveness, XX Corps had reduced over one half of the Saar Moselle Triangle. The quick progress made by the 94th Infantry and 10th Armored Divisions came with a high cost in casualties. Between February 19 and 21, the 94th Division alone lost about 1,500 men killed and wounded. The 10th Armored Division and other XX Corps units took heavy losses as well. In return, the Germans lost 1,000 killed, 2,000 wounded, and many more thousands taken prisoner. Vast amounts of vehicles and other irreplaceable material were also destroyed or abandoned. In a more inclusive tally of the thirty days of Switch line combat, XX Corps destroyed not only the 11th Panzer Division, but also the 416th and 256th Infantry Divisions as well. Those few German organizations that did survive the final American offensive raced back to safety across over the last remaining Saar bridges at

Saarburg.

On January 21, Patton visited Walker at the 10th Armored Division's headquarters on January 20. Patton was very well pleased with the progress of the attack and ordered Walker to immediately cross the Saar and take Trier. Now that enemy resistance before them collapsed, the Triangle itself was no longer of tactical importance. What mattered now was crossing the Saar River, the last natural barrier before the Rhine, which was the primary objective of all Allied aims at that time in the war. For the first time since September, Third Army had a chance of reaching the German heartland in one big push.

In every sense, these recent developments were Patton's type of warfare. For Patton, the actual taking of Trier had spiritual significance that was equal to its strategic value of sitting on the junction of the Moselle and Saar rivers. Trier's ancient legacy went back to the days of Roman conquerors. Patton compared his triumphant journey toward Trier in 1945 to that of Caesar's legions centuries earlier. He wrote that he "could smell the coppery sweat of the legions" and was immensely proud to be following in Caesar's footsteps at the head of his own army."[116] In order to take final control of the east side of the Saar River, Saarburg still needed to be captured. The city was the largest in the Saar Moselle Triangle. Most importantly, two last two intact bridges still spanning the Saar were there. The 10th Armored Division raced for Saarburg on the remaining hours of January 21 in hopes of somehow taking a bridge intact, but mine fields delayed their movement. The Germans waited until they could get out as many troops over the river as possible, and then blew up the bridges just before the Americans could reach them. XX Corps would now have to cross the Saar by boat and then build their own bridges.

Despite having just completed three days of heavy fighting, XX Corps would have no time to prepare for a proper river assault operation. When swollen with late winter thaws, the Saar is a mighty river with a strong current and steep banks on either side. This is one of Europe's great wine producing regions, and the same steep hills that grow such wonderful grapes also served to aid the defenders' naturally strong positions. Behind the river, the entire region is very hilly, and the Germans had an expansive line of West Wall bunker defenses skillfully interwoven in the difficult terrain. Compounding staging challenges, the limited road network was insufficient to support the massive amount of XX Corps traffic that would have to traverse the area. Furthermore, those roads that did exist were carefully plotted by German artillery that would be firing on the far side of the Saar.

All focus would be on getting forces to the west bank of the Saar and then cross over in whatever boats could be made available. Speed was essential. Although the assault would have to be made in a haphazard manner, no one wanted a repeat of what happened at Metz. Above all else, the Germans could not be given the chance to regroup and prepare a well-coordinated defense on the east side of the Saar. But just as they had been doing ever since mid September, XX Corps would again be attacking into prepared enemy defenses.

One vital advantage that Mother Nature gave to the Americans on the morning of February 22 was a thick fog that blanketed the Saar River and obscured their movements from the enemy. In a letter penned that day, Kurt Rieth describes the fog and alludes to the increased tempo of operations: "It's high time I sat down and wrote you another letter. I've meant to do it for the last two days but just didn't have time to get around to it. Today the weather was beautiful although it was rather misty. I was on some high ground this morning and all of the valley was covered with blankets of mist and here and there other hills would stick up through the fog. It was about the same effect you would get flying in an airplane. Excuse the sloppy handwriting but I'm hurrying the letter. Lots of Love, Kurt."

In a hastily designed plan, the 10th Armored Division, along with one regiment of the 94th Division, was ordered to cross the river at Ockfen, north of Saarburg. Once over the Saar, they were to swing directly north and then take Trier, only ten miles away. At the same time, the remaining two regiments of the 94th Division would seize two bridgeheads south of Saarburg at Taben and Stadt. This effort was to divert the

German's attention from the main effort toward Trier, and to serve as a springboard for future operations into the Saar valley.

The first big hurdle was trying to get enough boats and bridging material to the launching sites. The roads were completely clogged, and the engineers had trouble getting the small ten-man boats to where they were needed. On the morning of February 22, the 94th Division's 302nd Regiment at Taben was the first element ready to go. As quickly as boats were taken off the trucks they were put into the water and rowed toward the east bank. The thick fog allowed the first boats to make it over without being detected by the Germans. Scrambling over a high retaining wall, the lead infantry squads completely surprised several enemy bunkers. The Germans reacted with an immediate counterattack that was wiped out by the first use of American artillery in the battle. Although the Germans were now alerted, XX Corps had their first troops over the Saar.

Just up river at Stadt, the 301st Regiment began their crossing. Here, the Germans were aware of the assault from the beginning and proceeded to lay plunging machine gun fire into the river. XX Corps artillery launched suppressive fires in return as both sides shot blindly away into the fog. Braving the bullets and shrapnel that churned into the water, the infantry climbed into their tiny boats and paddled against the strong current toward the other side. Within a short time, only six of the initial sixteen assault boats still remained in operation. The handful of Americans that made it over breached barbed wire entanglements and scaled the steep heights before them. Cresting the embankments, they then charged the concrete machine gun bunkers that continued to lay deadly fire into them and their comrades crossing over in the last surviving boats. With the midday sun burning off the last of the fog, the tempo and accuracy of the German direct and indirect fire picked up. More boats were brought up and despite the increasing casualties, a battalion was able to make it over to the far side.

A few miles farther to the north, the 10th Armored Division was having a more difficult time in their attempts to cross the Saar at Ockfen. By being more forward deployed, it was much harder for the assault boats to link up with the armored infantry battalions making the attack. Patton was on the scene and became enraged when he found out that that the delay was due to a 10th Division bridging train having gotten lost. Author Nathan Prefer records the meeting in *Patton's Ghost Corps*: "Patton's furious temper vented itself once again, this time on Walker and Major General Morris (the 10th Armored Division commander). To Walker he said, 'You should have seen that it was in place. So should I. We have all three fallen down on the job.' By the time he departed XX Corps, his anger had increased to the point where he blustered that 'General Morris will lead his division across the river in the first boat, or, if necessary, swim!'"[117]

As ordered, the attack began as soon as the boats were on the scene. By this time the fog had cleared off and the Germans were already putting heavy fire on the designated launch points. A smoke screen was needed to ensure some measure of success, but as it turned out, the smoke generators failed to work properly. With no cover whatsoever, the first wave of two infantry companies still attempted to make the crossing in broad daylight. To even get to the river, the infantry first had to cross several hundred meters of open ground. The effort was suicidal as infantry, engineers, and boats alike were chopped to pieces by concentrated enemy mortar, artillery, and machine gun fire. During the dash toward the river, each of the companies took severe losses, with one of the commanders killed and the other seriously wounded. Even had the infantry made it to the edge of the river, the sacrifices would have all been in vain, as every single one of the assault boats were destroyed before they could even be launched. A renewed 10th Division attack would have to wait for darkness.[118] As the battle got underway, German artillery was impacting in all three of the crossing sites and throughout the XX Corps zone. Given the speed of the XX Corps' advance over the last three days, the 7th FAOB simply did not have time to set up and register sufficient plots of enemy artillery positions to be able to support the first day's crossings.[119] As the fighting continued, the 7th scrambled as hard as possible to set up sound and flash OPs on the high ground overlooking the west bank of the Saar. Once in place, the battalion made a number of accurate plots that were then serviced by XX Corps artillery battalions. While XX Corps absorbed quite a bit of German artillery fire during the crossing operations, it would have been worse had it not been for the 7th FAOB's counterbattery direction. In the days that followed, the results of the 7th FAOB work was as impressive and important as any operation they participated in during the entire war.

The 10th Division tried another attack the night of February 22-23. Screened under the cover of darkness, this time the boats and the infantry were able to reach the eastern bank before being detected. Once there, all hell broke loose as machine guns from the German bunkers fired into the river. The tracer bullets that helped guide the machine guns also belied their positions. Moving forward, the American infantry stealthily crept up on the bunkers and were able to overwhelm several before dawn.

Although the three XX Corps bridgeheads were by no means secure, the Americans had at least some measure of a foothold on the east bank of the Saar by the early hours of February 23. In order to get bridges across the river and to bring on the tanks, the German forces still pouring fire into the crossing sites needed to be destroyed. The most pressing German strong point that had to be eliminated was the town of Ockfen, which was directly opposing the 10th Armored crossing. Eight battalions of 10th Armored Division and XX Corps artillery were mobilized together for one devastating barrage. In a short but terribly intensive five-minute concentration, 140 cannon blasted away as quickly as their gunners could fire them. An observer noted that "it looked as if the town just blew up." Infantry then attacked the town and captured its shell-shocked survivors. While the town of Ockfen may have been taken, the surrounding area was still full of Germans. For the next three days, fighting raged back and forth over the hills.[120]

The Americans needed some heavier firepower and a lot more ammunition in order to turn the tide. Although some tank destroyers were able to be ferried across the Saar, the lack of tanks and supply trucks became a critical shortfall in shoring up the slim east bank toehold. Unless something could be done to expand and ensure the stability of the American penetrations, the engineers would not be able to lay down bridges and the three XX Corps bridgeheads would remain at great risk. XX Corps faced a similar situation back at Metz in September, when the 5th Infantry Division failed to immediately expand the Arnaville bridgehead. That delay allowed the Germans to contain the American Moselle crossing for the next eight weeks. That situation could not be allowed to be repeated on the Saar.

An overarching American objective was to stop the flow of German reinforcements to the front. The XX Corps intelligence staff found a point where the Germans were most vulnerable to disruption—the road intersection in the town of Zerf, which was four miles beyond the 94th Division crossing at Stadt. The roads bisecting Zerf linked Trier to the front line defenses directly west. If the Zerf intersection was blocked, then the German units defending along the Saar riverbank could be cut off and destroyed. Taking Zerf would be difficult. Although only several miles away, the terrain between the bridgehead and the objective was very mountainous and greatly favored the defense. Even if armor could have been brought across the river, it would have been impossible for the tanks to make it through the thick woods. Fortunately for XX Corps, they had on hand an elite unit that was ideally trained for mountain operations—the 5th Rangers.

In the aftermath of their disastrous attack in the minefield defenses of Oberleuken on February 19, the Rangers had regrouped enough to resume further operations. The 5th, along with the 2nd Ranger Battalion, was one of only two such units in the entire ETO. These elite commandos played a major role on D-Day where they scaled the Normandy cliffs to attack the beach's strongest fortifications. Since D-Day, and to the Ranger's great frustration, the two battalions were used more often as conventional infantry rather than for missions more tailored to their highly specialized capabilities. The attack at Oberleuken highlighted how easily the Ranger's unique skills could be squandered by executing costly missions that could just as well have been done by regular line infantry units. This lack of proper utilization was about to change. The deep infiltration role envisioned by General Walker for the Rangers at Zerf was exactly what this unit was in business for.[121]

The Rangers advanced into the 94th Division bridgehead at Taben. The process of just crossing the river was difficult enough, as twenty-four men were lost to German artillery fire before they even reached the front. Heavily laden with all the ammo and antitank mines that they could possibly carry, the Rangers kicked off at 2:00 A.M. on February 23. German troops manning the front lines were either overrun or bypassed as the Rangers slipped deep into enemy territory. Making scattered contacts, the Rangers reached their objective just before dawn. So surprised were the Germans of the Rangers' presence that one captured medical officer exclaimed in disbelief, "You can not be here!" During their movement, they took over 150 prisoners, a development which in itself created a major logistical and security problem as there were not enough Rangers available to guard them.

The Rangers successfully cut off the road between Zerf and the German front lines by integrating rifles, grenade launchers, machine guns, bazookas, mortars and anti-tank mines with observed artillery fire. After an unsuspecting self-propelled gun was ambushed and destroyed in the kill zone, the Germans knew the Rangers' exact location. The Germans realized the consequences should the Zerf road be cut off and immediately set upon the surrounded Rangers. In the first assault, 400 German troops attacked from the northwest while another 200 came in from the northeast. The attack was largely broken up by XX Corps artillery fire. At dawn on February 25, the Germans hit again, this time with a full battalion supported by tanks. Once again, the Germans were driven off with severe losses and with the Rangers capturing another 150 prisoners. By this time, the Rangers were exhausted and critically short of ammunition.

By February 24, the first floating treadway bridges were finally built at the 94th Division's Taben and Stadt bridgeheads. The 10th Armored Division began to move their tanks over these bridges rather than waiting for their own to be constructed in the still contested Ockfen site. The tanks were a welcome sight to the hard-pressed infantrymen of the 94th Division. Forming an ad hoc unit with a Ranger platoon that had been separated from its main force, the tanks from Task Force Riley ran into considerable resistance from German roadblocks and a well-positioned Tiger tank in the town of Irsch. Five Sherman tanks were destroyed before the Rangers and surviving tankers took the village. Moving desperately forward in order to relieve the besieged 5th Ranger Battalion, Task Force Riley pressed on, losing still more tanks and armored personnel carriers before reaching Zerf. Once at Zerf, the task force had to fight through roadblocks protected by German infantry, antitank guns, and tanks. The town was finally taken by midnight of February 25, with 100 more German soldiers being captured.[122]

With the arrival of Task Force Riley at Zerf, the 5th Ranger Battalion was finally relieved. Surrounded and fighting continuously for the past forty-eight hours, the 5th Rangers contributed greatly to the eventual success of the crossing. Equal credit has to go to XX Corps artillery, who enabled the Rangers' ability to cut off the one roadway leading to the enemy defenses. Rather than getting a rest, the Rangers were merely replenished with ammunition and then sent forward to attack the Germans on the high ground west of Zerf on February 28. The tired Rangers took yet another objective, and then held out against German counterattacks for another five days.

The advance toward Trier became something of a race between XX Corps and XII Corps, their Third Army neighbor to the north. Since the start of the offensive, Trier had exclusively been a XX Corps objective, particularly since XII Corps was still busy reducing the last of the enemy salient created during the Battle of the Bulge. On February 23, Patton, frustrated over the lack of progress of the 10th Armored Division's bridgehead, visited the XII Corps' 76th Infantry Division and challenged them to take Trier first. While the 10th Armored Division was slugging north from Zerf, the 76th Infantry would be moving toward Trier from the southwest.

The Germans made one last desperate attempt to defend Trier and regain control of the Saar defenses. Scraping together all available forces, they set up a strong defensive position just north of Zerf. As long as the Zerf-Trier road was blocked, it would be very difficult for American armor to move on Trier, ten miles north. The defensive effort was also designed to buy time. As the fighting swirled around Zerf, elite German Mountain SS Divisions were grouping to the east for a final counterattack designed to regain control of the Saar. It would be Germany's last chance to stem the complete collapse of the West Wall.

The next phase of combat around Zerf was particularly hard fought by both sides. Taking cover in sharply rolling terrain, the Germans covered the approaches with plenty of infantry, machine guns, tanks, 88-mm artillery, and antitank guns. Nathan Prefer recorded the experience of Zerf by one veteran of the Battle of the Bulge: "The opposition was worse than at Bastogne. We lost more vehicles and men. The enemy was sitting on the hills where we couldn't find them or get at them with artillery. They had their artillery zeroed in on the roads. They would hold their fire until we were close and sometimes they would allow the first column to bypass their position and then open up on the second column. The infantry in the half-tracks were vulnerable to the air-burst artillery. There was not enough infantry left at the end to flush out the hills and clear out the gun positions."[123] Leading from the front, officers and NCOs took a heavy toll. Three American battalion commanders, Lieutenant Colonels O'Hara, Clapp, and Miles Standish (the eleventh direct descendent of the famous Pilgrim) were killed in action. Some of the armored infantry companies had all of their half-tracks destroyed. Line company losses were so severe that communications men, tank destroyer troops, and headquarters personnel were pressed into service as infantrymen. Despite the intensive resistance, the American forces from Zerf continued to press north and were able to reach Pellingen, the midway point to Trier, by late evening of February 28.

The final breakout that took Trier came from a drive launched by Task Force Richardson, a mixed armor-infantry combat command. Blowing through the last German roadblock on the evening of March 1, the Task Force suddenly found the main road to Trier undefended. Lieutenant Colonel Richardson pressed forward, and soon was rolling into Trier, catching the German infantry and anti-armor companies posted there completely by surprise. In addition to bagging 800 prisoners, the Task Force was able to capture two Moselle River bridges intact, which allowed an effortless link up with the 76th Infantry Division moving in from the northwest.

While the bridgeheads on the east bank of the Saar were still being contested, most of the 7th FAOB remained on the high ground of the west bank where the established sound and flash OPs were getting good plot results on enemy artillery batteries. Once the armored spearheads broke toward Trier, A Battery observers and command and control elements moved along the Zerf road with the lead American elements.

In his 1945 letter, Lieutenant Slessman summarized the preceding two weeks of the 7th FAOB's A Battery activities and recalled the highlights of the breakthrough of the Switch line and the taking of Trier:

> After a very trying week we made a fair number of locations and the attack jumped off. Once beyond the first crust of dragon's teeth and pill boxes that had to be blasted by TNT, the 10th Armored Division went through us and raced north and east to the Saar River across the river from the city of Saarburg. Again we went to work and had fair luck before a crossing was forced. I was assigned the task of following the armor in its dash to capture the city of Trier, which proved to be an easy mark.

Patton was thrilled at the capture of Trier, but his triumphant personal journey into the conquered city almost ended in disaster when he found himself in the middle of a German mortar barrage. In the midst of the shelling, Patton turned to his chief of staff and said: "In my considered judgment, the thing to do is to get the hell out of here, drive home, and have a drink."

The final capture of Trier came about far quicker than the Americans thought possible. Eisenhower had been worried that taking Trier would bog down the advance of the entire Third Army. Accordingly, he sent Patton a message directing him to bypass the city as he assessed it would take four divisions to capture it. This communiqué reached Patton just as the city fell, and he sent back the immediate reply, "Have taken Trier with two divisions. Do you want me to give it back?"[124] The capture of Trier, and more importantly, the taking of fifteen miles of prime West Wall defenses south of the city, were of immense significance in the final course of the war. Over time, and perhaps overshadowed by the much-publicized Battle of the Bulge, the conventional historical study of World War II has somehow neglected focus on this extremely pivotal campaign. Nathan's Prefer's *Patton's Ghost Corps*, published in 1998, is the only readily available book that sheds significant attention on that dramatic episode of the Second World War.

One person who did appreciate the importance of XX Corps' breakthrough at the Saar was Adolf Hitler. Up to this point, Hitler was secure with the knowledge that although he may have lost occupied France, there was no way that American soldiers had either the fortitude or professional military skills to breach his "impenetrable" West Wall. Even with American and British forces pounding away at the Siegfried Line for the past five months, and despite the advice of his some of his best senior professional commanders, Hitler truly thought his Western Front line would hold. Nathan Prefer presents the reaction of Hitler and Reichsmarschall Hermann Goering to the debacle on the Saar:

> It was non other an authority than Goering, leader of the German Luftwaffe, and second only to Hitler for most of the Second World War in Germany, who pointed out the importance of the Saar-Moselle Triangle campaign. In an interrogation after his capture in 1945 he remarked, "When the first break in the Siegfried Line was made near Ockfen, der Fuhrer was very irritated. After that came the breakthrough near Trier, and that was wholly incomprehensible. We could not believe that these fortifications could be penetrated. The breakthrough near Trier was particularly depressing. That breakthrough and the capture of the Remagen Bridge were two great catastrophes for the German cause.[125]

CHAPTER 12

A Disaster at Lampaden

The final breaching of the West Wall defenses along the Saar and the capture of Trier gave the Allied forces an immensely valuable victory. As a result of these efforts, however, the 94th Infantry and 10th Armored Divisions, the two XX Corps units largely responsible for this success, were both exhausted, short of men and equipment, and out of position for the next phase of operations. In the fighting of February 21 to March 1, XX Corps was focused on moving east across the Saar, and then straight north toward Trier.

When Trier had fallen on March 2, XX Corps fighting units were strung all along a fifteen-mile path between the bridging sites and Trier. Most of the American armor not destroyed in the fighting was now in the vicinity of Trier, and much of the Corps' logistical trail still remained on the wrong side of the Saar.

The next direction that XX Corps would move would be toward the Rhine River, now 120 miles due east. This region, between the Saar/Moselle Rivers and the Rhine, is known as the Palatinate. Moving through the Palatinate would require that XX Corps shift ninety degrees from a south-to-north axis toward Trier, and toward a west-to-east direction from the Saar to the Rhine. It would take XX Corps several days in order to redirect, rebalance, and or replace its worn out front line units to participate in the next all out Third Army push to reach the Rhine.

The German situation was desperate. In addition to the gaping hole that XX Corps sliced through the Siegfried Line, the remainder of the West Wall defenses were being pressed all along the German border. Once the West Wall was overwhelmed, there would be no significant man-made or natural defensive barriers to defend until the invaders reached the Rhine River. Losing this territory would mean that a quarter of Germany, and its most important industrial resources, would be forever eviscerated.

General Hamm, the local German Corps level commander, was convinced that it would be impossible to either hold his current position or even contemplate a counterattack. Accordingly, Hamm recommended that he retreat his remaining forces to more defensible terrain. Berlin, however, overruled Hamm and ordered an immediate counterattack aimed to retake possession of Trier and the lost West Wall bunkers. At his disposal, General Hamm had three divisions, two of which were of exceptionally high quality. On the lower scale of his existing combat power was the 256th Volksgrenadier Infantry Division. This division was a collection of survivors of those shattered elements that had been engaging XX Corps for the past two months. The other two divisions that were recent arrivals to the sector were the 2nd Mountain Division, a crack Austrian Alpine infantry division, and the 6th SS Mountain Division.

Under the control of Heinrich Himmler, the Wafen Schutzstaffeln (SS) divisions were designed to be an elite cadre of highly trained troops with great political devotion to the Nazi cause. On the battlefield, SS Divisions earned a reputation for toughness, fanaticism, and in many cases, sheer brutality. Since August 1944, XX Corps had fought many so-called SS divisions. By in large however, most of the SS units that XX Corps had encountered were SS in name only and were merely reconfigured shadows of the elite divisions that Himmler had once envisioned. The 6th SS Mountain Division was different, and was more of a real "Black Order" unit the true sense of the SS tradition. Formed in 1940 during the occupation of Norway, the 6th SS was a mix of native and ethnic Germans from Tyrol, the Balkans, and Denmark who volunteered to serve in the German Army. As its mountain designation implied, the 6th SS was skilled in mountain warfare when it fought the Soviets in Finland under the most trying of winter combat conditions. Pulled out of Norway in 1944, the division served in the failed Alsace counteroffensive and had been in reserve status until called up to plug the gap in the Saar. The veteran troops of the 6th SS Mountain Division were among the best in one of Germany's last remaining intact SS Divisions.[126]

As they did previously in the Ardennes Offensive, the Germans once again were able to sneak up a sizable strike force right under the noses of the American intelligence efforts. Although news of recently captured prisoners of the 2nd Mountain Division generated some concern within American headquarters, neither Third Army nor XX Corps intelligence analysis produced a warning that a major enemy attack was looming.

While the Germans were preparing to launch a surprise counterattack on March 5, XX Corps continued to regroup its forces to resume the drive eastward. One of the most foremost priorities was to finally relieve the much worn out and depleted 94th Infantry Division in the wake of their two months of unrelentingly brutal winter combat operations. XX Corps intended to pull out the 94th Division and replace it with the 26th Infantry Division, which would come up from the south. In turn, the newly arrived 65th Infantry Division would fill the 26th Division's vacated position. Moving these units in a secure manner would be both a major logistical effort as well as a tactical challenge. XX Corps planned to execute the movements in secrecy during the nights of March 6-8.

Lieutenant Slessman describes the activities and disposition of A Battery, 7th FAOB during this period.

> After the fall of Trier, our corps began to reshuffle its divisions for a new drive to the east and the Rhine. During this period we employed a sound and flash base on the high ground along the east bank of the Saar River. There had been little activity from the enemy since the fall of Trier until the night of March 5, when he leisurely began to shell our command post. Our position at that time was none too secure, as all of the armor was to our north, with a thin [armored] cavalry screen between us and the enemy, and the rest of our battalion had not as yet crossed the river. For all purposes, the cavalry and we had our backs to the river, but according to the latest intelligence, there was only a battered Volksstrum Division in our front.

Lieutenant Slessman had set up A Battery's Command Post at the town of Pellingen, which was midway between the road that connected Zerf to Trier, and about center in the XX Corps' penetration across the Saar. Medic "Doc" Barber remembers treating several casualties that were victims of German artillery that was accurately zeroed in on the road. (One of the men wounded during this time period was Pvt. Charles Jenkins of A Battery, who was hit by shrapnel in the thigh while serving at an OP on March 2.) A Battery had set out a number of sound and flash OPs along the east bank of the Saar. While there were some 94th Infantry Division battalions throughout the area, they were dispersed, leaving wide gaps in the American line. Given the fluid nature of XX Corps' disposition and the perceived lack of threat from a German attack, there was little security available to protect either the OPs or the A Battery CP.

One of A Battery's most forward deployed OPs was Sound Outpost Number One, which was located in the village of Lampaden, three miles southeast of the battery CP at Pellingen. Sound Outpost Number One was manned by Tech 5 Velasquez, PFC Vodila, PFC Biedrzycki, and PFC Ray McGinnis. Other American units located in Lampaden included Company I of the 302nd Infantry Regiment (94th Infantry

Division), and an anti-aircraft section. The first sign of potential trouble came on the night of March 5 when Lampaden's civilians lit lanterns and left the town. When queried of their departure, some of the civilians responded it was at the order of the military government. Later, Private First Class McGinnis would wonder *which* government they meant.

The German attack plan called for three spearheads to hit the unsuspecting American forces. The 256th Volksgrenadier Division would attack to the north, the 2nd Mountain Division to the south, and the 6th SS Mountain Division would attack in the center in an effort to cut the Pellingen-Zerf Road. The very center of the 6th SS Division attack would be directed immediately toward Lampaden, and then advance in the direction of Pellingen. A Battery could not be located more squarely in the path of the SS juggernaut strike. To maximize the element of surprise, the Germans used infiltration tactics to quietly move the 6th SS Mountain Division up to their launch points. In some areas, the Germans had compromised American passwords - countersign codes that were changed nightly to allow friendly troops to approach each other in safety. Using the stolen codes, the attackers were able to silently overwhelm the forward-most outposts. The attack, slated to begin at 2:00 A.M. on March 6, would initially proceed without the artillery support that would have further alerted the Americans to the large scope of the attack.

Attacking Lampaden was the primary objective of the German 2nd Battalion, 11th SS Mountain Regiment, 6th SS Division. A Battery's OP 1 was located in a house on the edge of Lampaden that would be nearest to the direction of the impending attack. In the early morning hours of March 6, the men in OP 1 were startled by the intensive fire of an American anti-aircraft group that was stationed nearby. Rather than firing at aircraft, the guns were depressed low on the horizon, aiming into the waves of the SS infantry that had emerged from the woods just outside the town. Within minutes, the Germans swarmed over Lampaden's outlining buildings, and swept past the house where the A Battery OP was hiding. A large group of SS troopers, still unaware of the presence of the four 7th FAOB forward observers, began to bring their wounded into an adjacent room of the OP building. Whispering into a field telephone landline, the OP attempted to quietly relay their situation to Lieutenant Slessman back in Pellingen. Just as the transmission began the wire was cut. The only information that the A Battery CP gleaned was that some German casualties were being brought into the OP building.

The four observers, expecting that a German hand grenade would be thrown into the room at any second, took whatever cover they could find. The door to their room burst open and a machine gun-wielding German ordered "*Rause!*" Hopelessly outnumbered and completely trapped, they were forced to surrender. A menacing SS major and several guards took Velasquez, Vodila, McGinnis, and Biedrzycki outside the house and lined them up against the wall. For a moment, it seemed like they were about to be executed (a fate that the SS would inflict on other captured and wounded American soldiers that day). At the last second, a German medical officer stepped up and spoke to the SS major at length. After some discussion, the Americans were removed from the wall and were ordered to serve as litter bearers for the growing number of wounded Germans that had been shot in the intensive fighting that now raged in the remainder of town between the 11th SS Regiment and Company I, 302nd. Using poles stuck between the sleeves of coats as stretchers, the prisoners carried wounded Germans to a large brick building that was used as a German aid station. McGinnis carried a German with a gaping wound to his hip, who constantly groaned on the walk to the aid station.

Back at A Battery Headquarters, the CP was completely unaware that the Germans had launched a major counterattack. The Germans had yet to use their artillery, and the sound of the small arms fire did not carry back to Pellingen. Based on the incomplete message received from Lampaden, the A Battery command section was under the impression that OP 1 had taken control of some wounded POWs that needed to be evacuated to the rear. With commo now cut, there was great consternation to send out a relief force as quickly as possible. Lieutenant Slessman writes of his fragmented perception of events that

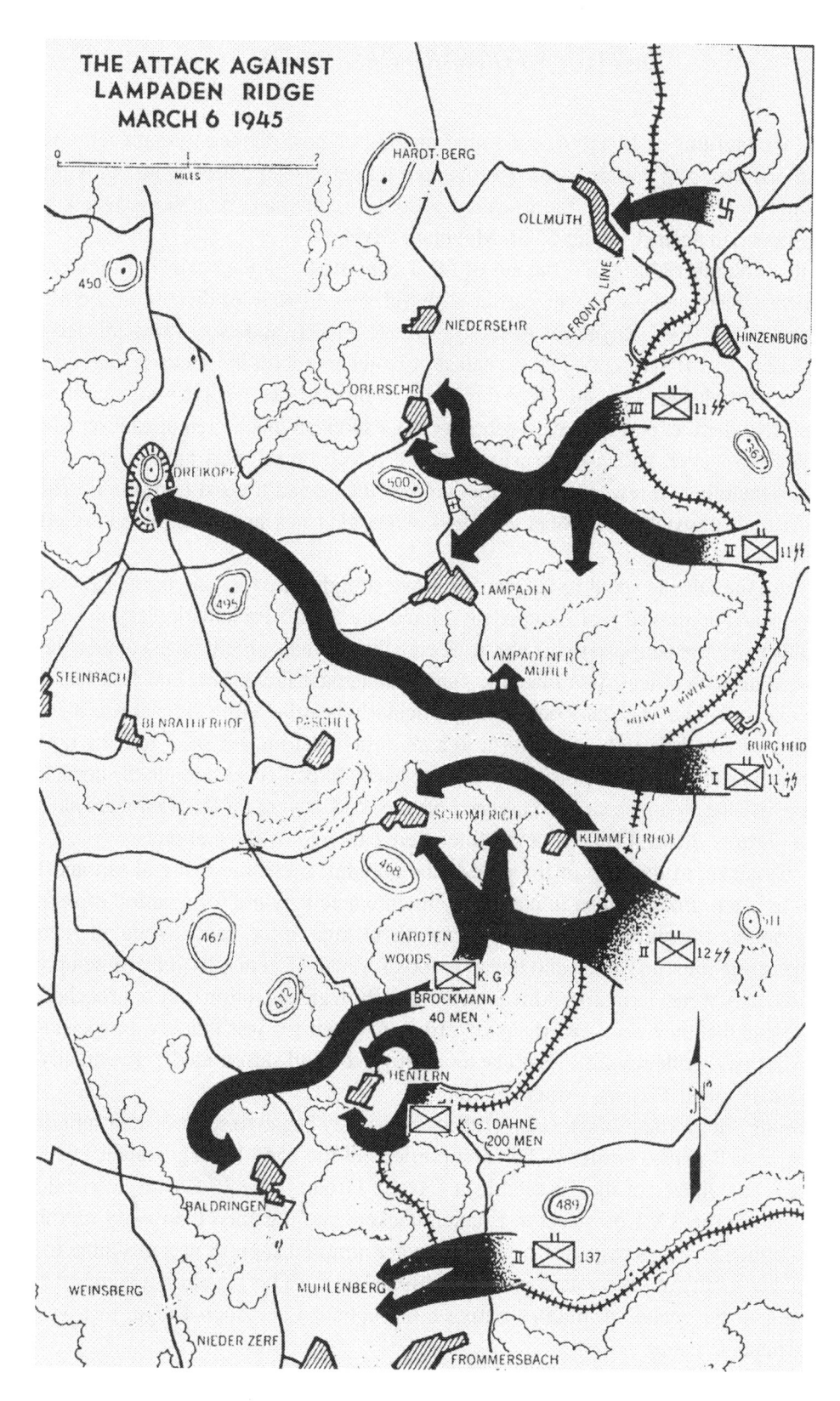

Lampaden

On March 6, 1945, the 6th SS Mountain Division launched a surprise counterattack intended to throw XX Corps back across the Saar River. The center of the attack landed in the village of Lampaden, where a 7th FAOB Battery A Observation Post was overrun. A relief force that was sent out to assist the OP was ambushed. Other American forces in Lampaden held out against fierce assault as the Germans bypassed the town and moved towards Pellingen (4 miles northwest of Lampaden) where they forced the evacuation of the Battery A Command Post. it would take several more days of heavy fighting for XX Corps to fully drive off the German attack.

morning: "Early in the morning of March 6, our sound ranging outpost phoned in that enemy patrols had passed his position and that help was needed. I authorized a twelve-man patrol to go out and escort our outpost to safety, but to my intense regret, the so-called patrol proved to be part of a large attacking force of Germans that had slipped in against us, the 6th SS Mountain Division."

The patrol that volunteered to go to the aid of OP 1 consisted of a jeep carrying Lieutenant Little, driven by T/5 Robert Schaaf, and a weapons carrier with Sgt. Harold Kessler driving Lt. Fern Field, Sgt. Smith, T/5 George Carlton, PFC Raymond Peabody, Private Miller, and two other enlisted men, and followed by a jeep carrying J.B Wright and Al Castanza. Lieutenant Field, the group leader, was the same officer who had been with Master Sergeant Ujczo during his death near Metz, some seven months previous. That event had a profound effect on Field, who subsequently exercised much greater caution when putting his men into danger. However, with the knowledge that a front line OP was now in the need of help, Lieutenant Field and the others threw caution to the wind as they raced toward Lampaden. (Schaaf also had a close brush with death back on October 24, 1944, when his truck hit the mine that killed Sergeant Julius Bagsby.)

Midway toward the OP, the small relief convoy drove straight into the vanguard of the SS advance that had now surrounded and moved past Lampaden. Lieutenant Field's trademark weapon had long been a submachine-gun that he wore strapped to his chest. Seeing the Germans, Field began to raise his weapon. The Germans opened up with at least two machine guns. Lieutenant Field, Sergeant Kessler, and Tech 5 Schaaf were immediately killed. (Schaaf's death was particularly heartbreaking. Schaaf was a very popular young soldier whose wife had recently given birth to a child he would never see. Just the previous day, Schaaf had been proudly showing off a photo of the baby to his buddies.) In addition to the dead, Lieutenant Little was wounded. As the weapons carrier careened off the road, several of the men were able scramble off to safety, while Carlton, Smith, Peabody, and Miller were captured by the Germans.

Wright and Castanza, in the jeep in the rear of the column, heard the firing ahead and had a few additional seconds to react. Both jumped into a nearby ditch where they hid for a period of several hours. The Germans who sprang the ambush moved off and without finding the pair. When all seemed quiet, Wright and Castanza crept into the woods and began to look for help. Eventually they came upon a patrol, but it was uncertain if they were German or American troops. With great caution they approached the group and were ecstatic to find that they were American infantrymen. Their joy was quickly dampened when one of the GIs handed Castanza a rifle saying: "Don't be too happy, we're all surrounded!" Eventually the entire patrol was able to safely make it back to American lines.

By mid-morning, the German attack was in full swing as they began to support their infantry assaults with huge barrages of well-placed artillery. The first portions of the 256th Volksgrenadier Division attack in the north overran the outposts of the 3rd American Cavalry Group. The 3rd Cavalry consolidated their forces from elsewhere in the XX Corps sector, counterattacked, and regained their early morning losses. However, as a consequence of this response, what little other armored support was available to American forces in the center and southern zones was completely stripped away. This situation would leave A Battery in Pellingen, as well as the scattered infantry outposts throughout Lampaden Ridge, in a very tenuous predicament in the hours to come.

The remaining portion of Lampaden that was still in American hands would be a focal point in much of the fighting that followed. Various American outposts that survived the first German attacks pulled back toward the town that became a rallying point for the 3rd Battalion, 302nd Infantry Regiment. Many American soldiers had harrowing adventures getting back to American lines. In a heavy machine gun platoon of the 302nd Infantry, one squad that was set up just outside Lampaden let several infiltrating groups pass by unmolested, and then fired on larger concentrations of unsuspecting SS troops. To conserve ammunition, Wallace M. Gallant, the squad leader, used an M1 carbine and an M1 Garnard to fire at individual soldiers, and saved his machine gun ammo to shoot at groups. While scattering a collection of twenty German officers that had approached his position, he was ordered back into the town. Once in Lampaden, Gallant set up his two remaining machine guns on a manure pile. With most of his squad either killed or wounded, Gallant fired his red-hot machine gun constantly for the rest of the day. Despite the overwhelming pressure, his position held and he commented, "The whole area to my front was covered with German bodies, I was surprised to note the number of different uniforms that they wore." Not every American outpost made it back to Lampaden as successfully as Sergeant. Gallant's squad. One squad from the first platoon of L Company was cut down by German automatic weapons fire. The SS soldiers then came up and machine-gunned the survivors. Two of these wounded played dead and were able to crawl back to Lampaden to report the incident.[127]

One group that was able to make it into Lampaden included three survivors of the ill-fated 7th FAOB convoy, who reported the news of the ambush to Lieutenant Colonel Cloudt, commander of 3/302nd and the senior American commander in Lampaden. This information, along with the repulse of a resupply patrol Cloudt had previously sent out, confirmed to the Americans that Lampaden was now surrounded. The Americans in Lampaden were desperately short of ammunition and overwhelmed with both wounded and prisoners. Cloudt tried to exfiltrate another squad, this one escorting wounded Germans and Americans back toward the town of Dreikopf, two miles to the west. Once the wounded were in safe hands, the squad was to return back to Lampaden with more ammunition. The whole group was captured before they reached American lines.

Quoting the recollections of an American infantry captain, Stephen Ambrose wrote of the ferocious nature of the 6th SS Mountain Division attack in *Citizen Soldiers*: "Although our artillery and mortar fire was poured into the ranks of the fanatical SS men, it was ultimately rifle fire that stopped them. Some of the Germans were dropped in their tracks only a dozen feet from the American positions. Bodies of friend and foe were found literally in the same foxholes, so active was the fighting. The Germans were using with extravagance their only remaining source of defense—the bodies of their soldiers."[128] Throughout the 6th SS Division attack corridor on the greater Lampaden ridge, there were really no actual battle lines per say, rather small pockets of American resistance that tried to hold out against the SS tide. Some villages that became holding positions included Baldringen, Obersher, Schomerich, Hentern, and Ollmuth. XX Corps' response to the surprise attack was initially slow, and it took considerable time for both the 94th Infantry Division and XX Corps Headquarters to figure out what exactly was going on. The 94th Division had originally been intended to be taken out of the line and replaced by the 26th Division the following day. Responding to the attack, XX Corps revised the plans by holding the 94th Division in defense and by ordering the 26th Division to counterattack the Germans.

In the midst of this turmoil, the German attack continued to surge toward the A Battery CP at Pellingen. The Germans had brought their artillery up close and began to hit the area around Pelligen hard. Lieutenant Slessman climbed to the top of a church steeple to get a better view of the situation. In the distance he observed the enemy horse-drawn battery that had set up and was firing on his position. As Slessman called for American artillery support he must have been spotted in return by his German FO counterpart. Shells began exploding around the steeple as Slessman frantically called in a fire mission against the ever-closing in German guns. The battle became a duel between Slessman and the German battery. One enemy shell blew up so close to Slessman that a large piece of shrapnel embedded in the wood between his legs. A salvo of American rounds landed just short and then long of the battery. The target was finally bracketed. With one final adjustment, Slessman ordered the command "Fire for Effect!" The enemy battery virtually exploded and then fell silent.

Although the destruction of the German battery gave a momentary break from the shelling, Lieutenant Slessman remained in a great conundrum. With a quarter of his command unaccounted for and now pressed by German infantry, he had to act quickly. Having now learned that his patrol to Lampaden had been ambushed, Slessman was desperately looking for any possible armor support available so that he, Bill Rogge, and others could go east and try to rescue any survivors. There were simply no tanks to be found, and without them, any additional relief efforts would end in further disaster. Hank Lizak was able to commandeer a kitchen truck and drove out to rescue members from another OP. By doing so, Lizak saved "Broadway Bill" Somers, Nate Westernweig, and Angelo Gallo just in time to save them from being overrun as well. Of this predicament, Slessman wrote:

> Our southernmost flash observation post saw the danger in time and abandoned their position before their hill was overrun. A small diversionary attack to the north had drawn off our screen of cavalry, leaving us in a most delicate situation. Our town was almost untenable, for the Germans began hitting us with barrages of about eighty rounds at a time. I was faced with a difficult decision, trying to decide whether to withdraw at once or attempt to extricate some thirty men and the patrol that then was unaccounted for. Quite frankly I, and many others in the battery, felt that our time on earth was short, as our situation was getting progressively worse. For a time I decided to remain in our present position, a town called Pellingen. It was ideal for defense as it was on high ground with good fields of fire, so we established a defensive line along the outskirts of the town, placing our machine guns and rocket launchers at strategic spots. When it became obvious that the enemy would be on us, I decided to withdraw to the north where I knew the armor was still located. So we sent our trucks out of town to the north, two at a time. I retired from the town after the battery had cleared, with the enemy then about 500 yards to the south. Upon reaching a previously arranged rendezvous to the north, we were greatly relieved to learn that a battalion of our infantry had crossed the river and were now holding the enemy from further advance. It proved to be quite a scrap as it took a regiment three days to clear the enemy from the highway south of Pellingen.

Back in besieged Lampaden, a short truce was arranged when one of the 7th FAOB prisoners, along with a German NCO, approached the American lines bearing a white flag. The German NCO had orders to try to arrange a prisoner exchange with Lieutenant Colonel Cloudt, the American commander. Although he would have been glad to get some of his own men back in addition to being rid of the burden of guarding the German captives, Cloudt was concerned that the released German prisoners would disclose the tenuous status of the weak American defenses. Cloudt stalled the negations as long as he could, but ultimately rejected any terms. The German NCO, along with his 7th FAOB prisoner, returned back to German lines and the battle resumed.

That the Germans were eager to exchange prisoners gave some indication that the Germans were becoming desperate for additional men. This was indeed the case, and while the Germans had greatly disrupted the American lines, it was being accomplished at a frightful cost. By the end of March 6, the 11th SS Mountain Regiment had lost two thirds of their fighting strength. Despite the heavy losses, the Germans would continue to attack the next day to try yet again to drive the Americans back into the Saar. For their part, the American commanders had no intention of retreat, and made plans for an attack of their own.

The Germans, however, would attack first, beginning on March 7. With the support of self-propelled guns, mortars, artillery, and rocket fire, the German infantry lurched forward into the eastern and southern approaches into Lampaden. Prefer depicts the courageous American defense against this attack in *Patton's Ghost Corps*:

> A vicious fight ensued and quickly became very personal. Technical Sergeant James T.

Chapman of the battalion's antitank platoon manned a lone gun against the self propelled guns leading the eastern attack, using every round of ammunition available. He then found a bazooka and began sniping at German armor, destroying four enemy vehicles. Wallace Gallant again manned his machine gun from the manure pile and cut down attacking infantry as he had the day before. Lieutenant Honan and PFC Baxter each fired 60-mm mortars single-handedly to stop the attack coming from their direction. Private First Class Baxter then made an exposed ammunition-resupply run, during which he killed one German and captured three others. He then joined Sergeant Chapman in destroying another enemy armored vehicle. Lt. Douglas Smith, commanding Company M, adjusted 81-mm mortar fire directly on attacking SS troopers with such accuracy that the attack faltered. The Germans did not seize Lampaden.[129]

For their valiant defense of Lampaden, the 3rd Battalion of the 302nd Infantry Regiment received a Presidential Unit Citation. A number of 7th Field Artillery Observation Battalion soldiers were in the midst of this desperate battle, which would turn out to be one of the last such attacks made by the Germans on the Western Front. It would still take several more days of sharp fighting by the 94th and 26th Infantry Divisions to finally repel the German attackers. By nightfall of March 7, however, it was clear that American lines were secure and that the worst of the threat had passed.[130] The carnage left on this battlefield reflected the intensity of fighting. Bodies, shattered vehicles, and equipment were strewn everywhere. Lt. Warren Sockwell recalls seeing a burned-out tank with its charred crewmembers still inside. Lying next to the tank was a dead German soldier being ripped apart by a hog. In a war filled with horrible images, Sockwell remembers this as the most gruesome sight he witnessed.

As for the eight 7th FAOB soldiers who were taken prisoner on March 6, Ray McGinnis provided the following account as his experience as a German prisoner of war:

> The Germans had little food. On a good day I received one piece of bread smeared with lard. Mostly prisoners got potato peal soup or powdered spinach soup. Everyone had diarrhea. We often marched at night and got so cold we would stand next to trees to keep warm. If we traveled by day we carried a panel 75 ft. long with big letters "POW" so Allied planes would not attack. Older German soldiers were ready to surrender but the young soldiers thought Hitler would still save them.
>
> Once I was interviewed by a German who said Axis Sally would broadcast news of my capture so my mother would know. I decided to take a chance and gave the man my mother's name and address. Some radio listener in New Jersey heard Axis Sally and notified my mother before the War Department notified her.
>
> On Easter Sunday I was in Ludwigsburg. I attended a Mass conducted by a chaplain from the British 8th Army who was also a prisoner.
>
> Myself and the other seven men from the 7th FAOB were at Stalag 5A for one week. Then we marched on to Dillingen. On April 27, 1945, we were approaching Munich when the 12th Armored Division of the Third Army liberated us. For us, C-rations and K-rations looked mighty good. Army engineers had to repair runways on a nearby airfield so U.S. C-47 transports could land and take off.
>
> On May 9 planes began flying twenty-five liberated POWs at a time to Rheims, France. Everyone there was celebrating VE Day, but I thought they were cheering for our liberation. From Rheims, we took a train to Le Havre by way of Paris. When we passed through Paris someone awoke me. I said, "I don't care a thing about Paris. Just wake me up when we get

to Memphis."

Other POWs and myself sailed from Le Havre on a Liberty Ship. The third day at sea the engine stopped. I wondered if I would ever reach home. After repairs, we finally reached New York harbor. Then the ferryboat taking us ashore caught fire. I thought, "Will my troubles never end?" But then I reached Camp Kilmer, New Jersey, Fort McPherson, Georgia, and finally Memphis, Tennessee. After a leave of absence I went to Miami Beach and then to Fort Ord, California. There I was offered a promotion to first sergeant if I would sign up for three more years. You guessed it! Raymond "Gene" McGinnis is still a PFC (Proud Friendly Civilian).

CHAPTER 13

To the Rhine

From a historical perspective of March 7, 1945, the massive 6th SS Mountain Division attack on the Lampaden Ridge was overshadowed by the epic American 1st Army seizure of the Remagen Bridge over the Rhine. It is impossible to overstate the value of the Rhine River in the battle for Europe. Rising from the Alps in the south, and 450 miles to Holland in the north, the Rhine was a perfect natural barrier protecting central Germany from any western approach. Wide and fast, steep banks rise on either side. While the Moselle and Saar rivers were difficult enough objectives for the Allied advance, logic deemed that crossing the Rhine would be a far tougher mission. After the West Wall had fallen in the first week of March, it was assumed that any surviving German Army elements would retreat back across the Rhine and then destroy any remaining bridges (there were about twenty bridges in the 200-mile sector between Holland and Frankfurt). Once across, the Germans could hold the eastern bank with seemingly relative ease. As usual, Hitler again interfered with the advice of his professional generals and ordered that the Rhineland, even in the wake of the West Wall collapse, be defended. This mistake would cost the Germans another 400,000 men killed, wounded, or captured, all for a negligible gain in time.[131]

Patton, as could be expected, was frantically trying to get Third Army to be the first across the Rhine. As Ambrose points out in *Citizen Soldiers*, "Third Army had started the February campaign farther from the Rhine than any other army on the Western Front. At last through the Siegfried Line, [Patton] still had so far to go to the Rhine that he feared his would be the last army to cross. 'We are in a horse race with Lieutenant General Hodges. If he beats me, I will be ashamed.' In the past several weeks, Patton was once again at his best. He spent six hours a day in an open jeep, tirelessly inspecting, urging, and demanding his men to always do more, go further, and attack harder. Wherever, whenever, and under every condition, he attacked. His nervous energy, his drive, his sense of history, his concentration on details while never losing sight of the larger picture combined to make him the preeminent American army commander of the war."[132]

In the wake of the Lampaden Ridge battle, the unfortunate and thoroughly exhausted 94th Division, which was by now in even worse shape than it had been when it was due to pull out on March 7, received new orders to stay in line and to participate in the coming dash to the Rhine. Events that occurred in the small Rhine River town of Remagen, seventy-five miles north of Pellingen, would dramatically change the course of Allied plans.

It would be the 1st Army that won the race to the Rhine, with its lead forces closing on the Rhine River cities of Cologne and Bonn on March 6. As was to be expected, almost all of the Rhine bridges were blown sky high by the Germans as the leading tank columns neared the spans. One railroad bridge that remained was at the small town of Remagen, fifteen miles south of Bonn. Waiting to ensure that all possible German forces were safely across the river, the German commander held off blowing up the bridge until an American armored task force was on the west bank of the river. After a mighty explosion that literally lifted the bridge several feet in the air, the smoke cleared to reveal an intact bridge. A small infantry force raced across and soon had control of its eastern approach. Stunned at the unexpected capture of the bridge, the 1st Army was able to push 8,000American combat troops over the bridge in the next twenty-four hours.[133] Within the next week, the bridgehead expanded by an additional 17,000 troops. Although the Germans lashed back with considerable might and were able to contain the bridgehead to a five-mile-wide and ten-mile-long gain, the capture of the bridge had a huge effect on the final Rhine campaign of the other allied armies.

In a rather indirect way, XX Corps contributed to the American victory at Remagen by having thrashed the 11th Panzer Division back in the Saarland in January and February. The once elite 11th Panzer Division never recovered from its battle with XX Corps, and was sent to Bonn to rest following its relief from the Saar-Moselle Triangle. When called into the initial counterattack after the loss of the Remagen Bridge, the 11th Panzer division only had a handful of tanks remaining and was easily repulsed. If the Germans had more armor at Remagen, the final story of the Rhine River crossings may well have had a far more bloody ending for the American troops.

With more and more German territory coming into American control, the invaders began to learn how to deal with the conquered civilian populace. Marinello, posted with XII Corps in Bitburg at the time, recorded his observations of early March 1945:

> Bitburg marked other changes. German civilians started to stay on. Certainly they were in terror. The standard procedure in Germany was for GIs to summon the burgermeister and demand the surrender of enemy soldiers and firearms while setting a curfew. Always the orders were followed to the letter. In the first hours the civilians remained out of sight. But then a few braved coming out, doing things quietly and without interference from the conquerors. What was going through their minds could easily be imagined. Everything was lost. What lay ahead, post-defeat, couldn't be envisioned. Nobody really knew, civilians or GIs, that the props for much greater misery were being put into place. For the moment, destruction and deprivation were everywhere. Yet Germany was to become worse than a nation of beggars. Its people were to survive on what they hoarded and by rummaging through GI garbage cans. Nobody was spared. Not the old, not the women who used their bodies to survive. Germany was in the earliest moments of a physical, moral, and military collapse.
>
> …With a few exceptions, most GIs behaved. The worse they did, condoned by need and military policy, was to commandeer houses, picking the best and doing so in a matter of minutes, tolerating no resistance by the deposed. That, so they could come out of the cold and bed down. The GIs gave the dispossessed the right to move in with somebody else, anybody they chose. Nobody had the right of rejection. Everybody complied meekly. Once the transfer took place, the GIs raided attics for preserved goods and the cellars for wines. Entry into Germany during those first hours brought certain dangers. The GI had to look over his shoulder. Every civilian was seen as a threat. In time, with no incidents, the GIs relaxed.[134]

Just as the Germans had used Trier as a launch point for their Ardennes Offensive, Patton used the Trier to stage the Third Army push for the Rhine, which was designated to launch an all out attack on March 13. It still would take several more days for Patton to bring his three corps (VIII, XII, and XX Corps) on line and be ready to move forward. In the days that followed the German attack on Lampaden Ridge, considerable action kept the 7th FAOB busy. In addition to supporting the reduction of the 6th SS Mountain Division gains, the battalion still had to cover the XX Corps' front and observe inbound fire as well as any other observable enemy activities. During the week of March 9, a flash OP observed a careless German officer conducting an inspection of one of his pillboxes. The report noted in detail that the officer wore polished boots and brass, was smoking a cigar, carrying a cane, and had received a salute from his men. As the battalion history recorded, XX Corps artillery saluted the German officer as well—with twelve cannon. The battalion had further business on March 11, when a heavy-caliber gun was firing into the Third Army sector. The B Battery sound platoon made eight plots between 1:53 and 2:49 A.M. of a large German cannon, which was immediately counterbatteried by XX Corps artillery. Later it was determined that this gun was a 240-mm firing into Luxembourg City, and hitting very close to Patton's CP. The battalion received a commendation from Third Army Headquarters for their work in neutralizing this threat.

Advancing in concert in line with XII Corps, Walker's XX Corps was to move 120 miles to the east to take the city of Ludwigshaven. This would place them on the Rhine River, directly across from the east-bank city of Mannheim. The basic zone of the XX Corps Rhine objective would be Worms to the North, and just below Mannheim, forty miles in the south. XX Corps would lead off the attack, and hoped to bait any undetected German reserve forces that may lay in ambush. If so, VIII Corps would be following XX Corps in order to exploit any German reaction. For this mission, XX Corps received massive reinforcements, and Walker now commanded a virtual army of his own. In addition to the 94th Infantry, 26th Infantry, and 10th Armored Divisions that had previously been with XX Corps, new units included the 80th and 65th Infantries and the 12th Armored Division.

XX Corps' attack planned to have three infantry divisions (the 94th on the left, the 80th in the corps center, and the 26th on the south). Once the infantry cleared the German defenses, the 10th and 12th Armored Divisions, would be unleashed to sweep through and conduct a rapid pursuit. Patton and Walker visited the 94th Division on the eve of the attack and told its commander, "Keep up the good work, you are doing fine." Walker added, "I want you to give them the works right now, night and day keep pushing forward, don't stop, give them everything you have until we get to the [Rhine] river."[135] XX Corps and divisional artillery silently moved forward on March 12. To mask the huge number of cannon that were readied to support the attack, registration was limited to each battery firing only one gun during daylight hours. The relative silence was broken on March 13, when thirty-one artillery battalions let loose to pound all potential targets for a massive fifteen-minute bombardment. At the designated kick off time for the infantry division attacks, the artillery fires shifted to all known German artillery positions, many of which had been identified by the 7th FAOB.

The three XX Corps infantry divisions plunged forward. In many cases in the opening phase of the attack, they met fierce German resistance. In some instances across the line, the Germans responded with eleven sharp counterattacks made by units up to battalion size, and supported by armor. The going was the toughest for the 26th Infantry Division, which had to contend with large segments of the intact West Wall, as well as facing the most difficult terrain in the sector. At first it seemed that the Germans would present an all out strong defensive effort. However, the overwhelming might of the three American infantry divisions supported by XX Corps artillery was too much for them to withstand. After the lead battalions reached their intermediate objectives, many of the German strong points were isolated and cut off from either retreat or reinforcement.

In XII Corps, the 286th FAOB letter batteries reconfigured their sound and flash platoons into smaller, consolidated detachments. They correctly forecasted that traffic jams would be a problem as the advance began, and adjusted accordingly. This reduced the size of the units from 150 down to fifty men. Vehicle support was stripped down to a bare minimum, and the detachment used only one heavy truck and a collection of smaller weapons carriers and jeeps. The men were going to work long hours, in some cases doing double and even triple duty. Speed and maneuverability were the mission's key.

The 286th was headed for the Rhine city of Koblenz, and Marinello writes this of the early stages of the Third Army attack:

Our mission, as usual, was to stay mixed in with the tanks and infantry and just as soon as it was decided that the drive was slowing, hustle out and to set up the necessary mike base and observation points for both sound and flash. For most of the day, the detachment's vehicles lumbered on the roads the Germans were unloading [shellfire] on.

On the other side of the Kyll River, the roads had to be cleared of mines, slowing the advance. Tanks were being knocked out on both sides, this as vehicles were in flames everywhere one looked. The towns leveled during the night were still being hit by the Germans as the Third Army forged on. The earth was rocking, noises shattering. Everything standing was coming down. To at least one man in the many thousands, it almost didn't seem possible that there was a spot anywhere in the world that was tranquil.[136]

On March 15, all of the lead XX Corps infantry divisions reported that opposition was no longer cohesive or coordinated. Walker relayed this information to Patton and obtained permission to launch his two-armor division thrust deep into the enemy's rear. In the early morning hours of March 16, combat commands of both the 10th and 12th Armored Divisions were sent into battle, and by March 18, they were halfway to the Rhine objectives. The Germans didn't have a chance. Those units that tried to resist would be knocked aside by the armor spearheads, and then either rounded up or destroyed by the following infantry divisions. In the period between March 13 and 17, XX Corps was credited with killing 2,300 German troops and capturing another 6,700.

The 12th Armored Division, which had a shorter route to travel, reached the northernmost Rhine objectives at Worms on March 19. The Germans on the west bank of the Rhine finally had permission from Berlin to retreat across the river, and Walker revised the divisional movements in an effort to cut off and trap as many enemy forces as possible. The focus of XX Corps' movement then turned exclusively south, with the 10th Armored Division leading the thrust. The 10th Armored Division was rapidly approaching Kaiserslautern, one of the largest cities in the region and a major German industrial and military supply center. Kaiserslautern was captured on March 21, and with it, the Americans took the largest depot of German military supplies on the west bank of the Rhine.

When possible, the Americans would take advantage and help themselves to what the German Army had left behind. However, not all the spoils of war could be enjoyed. Amos Robinson, Headquarters Battery medic, recalled this experience: "Somewhere with B Battery on our journey through Germany, our troops captured a German meat wagon with some sides of beef. My commander, Captain Clark, was concerned whether or not the beef was fit to eat. Captain Clark asked me to check it and see what I thought. To me the meat did not look or smell too good, and I told him that I would not eat any of it. He said, 'Robinson, that is good enough for me.' He had the meat truck burned to the ground. A lot of the men were disappointed and thought that I was wrong. I was not popular for a while."

Just as in every XX Corps movement throughout the war, 7th FAOB elements were right up in the front in the advance to the Rhine. Lieutenant Slessman described the movement to Kaiserslautern (a little over midway between the Saar River start point and the Rhine).

When our forces had finally regrouped in strength east of the Saar River, the drive to the Rhine was begun. Once in Germany proper, our advance became very rapid due to the excellent road net, particularly the autobahns. We soon captured Kaiserslautern, and then drove east to Mainz and the Rhine River.

As in previous advances, I traveled ahead of my battery with the tanks of the 10th Armored Division, and we sailed down a beautiful four-lane autobahn without a moment's hesitation. Our only delays were caused by detours made necessary by several blown out bridges. We reached the advance of some twenty-five miles. There was no sign of the Wehrmacht when we entered the city, so I decided to look for some comfortable billets for my battery, as our instructions carried us no farther than this city at the time. Part of Kaiserslautern was badly damaged from a visit by our bombers, but the northern section of the city was in pretty fair shape, so I gave that section of the town my full attention. The first place to catch my eye was a large caserne, or military barracks, just off the highway, so I drove to the entrance and proceeded in on foot.

The caserne was a group of large barracks-like buildings made of concrete and painted a camouflage green. In the entrance was a guardroom of the garrison where I found the large garrison flag neatly folded on a shelf. On going into the courtyard we were greeted by a shot that cracked over our heads, fired from one of the surrounding buildings. Realizing that if we left now, we might lose good billets, we decided to root out the boys upstairs, and that proved quite simple, as ten Germans came out with their hands up, and of course they had no weapons and knew nothing about any shooting having occurred. We had just sent them out to the highway to walk to a POW enclosure when two German nurses and another Jerry walked up to surrender. The soldier was a young chap of about sixteen. His emotions got the better of him as he walked up, for he began bawling and the tears really did flow. The two nurses berated him for crying and he would sob back at them in self-defense. He was one of the few Germans in Kaiserslautern that was not happy to have to give up. As it developed, I found the Caserne too filthy and took over some very swanky apartments nearby. There were still civilians in the apartments and when we drove up in front of the buildings, a woman came out, evidently very well to do, and said in perfect English how glad she was that we had come and that the war was over for them. She was very helpful and even offered me a bed, but when I learned that she was a good Nazi and quartered German officers before we came, I moved her and all the other people out of the apartments. The battery lived very luxuriously during our brief stay in that city.

Kurt Rieth penned this letter home on March 20, and gave a sense of the rapid movement and large amount of prisoners that were being taken: "I've finally found a few spare minutes in a busy day to write a letter. You are probably reading all about what is going on in the papers. The amount of prisoners being taken is enormous and things are moving so rapidly it's hard to keep up. I'm speaking more German interpreting over here than I have for a long while. The roads are also crowded with Russians, Poles, etc that have been freed by the American advance. The condition of these people is pitiful."

The March 23 edition of "Seekers News" reported that in one reconnaissance operation, Lieutenant Slessman radioed back to the CP that he was returning with six prisoners, and by the time he arrived, had eighteen POWs in total. The battalion newsletter went on to say that elsewhere in the sector, many of the Germans had a tough time of being captured. Shortly before breakfast one morning, five fully armed "Heinies" and one medic marched up to the A Battery CP. Questioned as to why they were hiking around fully armed behind American lines, they stated that they had walked around all the previous day without anyone paying attention to them so they picked up weapons in order to make someone capture them.

As the 10th Armored Division approached Kaiserslautern, large columns of German vehicles streamed eastward, trying to escape toward the sanctuary of the Rhine. The Germans, desperate to cross the river as quickly as possible, made no effort to camouflage the vehicles or provide for any coordinated air defense. With the improving weather and longer daylight hours, the American warplanes filled the air and descended on the heavily laden vehicle convoys. Dropping bombs and firing rockets, cannons, and machine guns, the planes ripped into the German columns. To complete the destruction, American tanks appeared on either side of the highway and fired into the cauldron. In a scene replicated in 1991 by the American attack on Iraqi columns out of Kuwait City in Desert Storm's "Highway of Death," the destruction savaged on the Germans was extreme. In the road between the towns of Frankenstein and Bad Durkheim, the destruction was particularly noteworthy, as highlighted in both the XX Corps' and 7th FAOB's official histories. The author of *From Bragg to Braunau* noted:

> On the road between Frankenstein and Bad Durkheim, two names faintly suggestive of the conditions on the road, is one of the greatest scenes of destruction we have ever seen. Here on the road, the trains [supply vehicle convoys] and the artillery of what appears to have been a division were caught in a defile and massacred by the air corps. Running down the curving roadway the passerby first notices a few scattered vehicles and dead horses, and then it seems to grow in crescendo until finally he is in the midst of such a twisted mass of death and destruction that single items cannot measure it! The only impression that it made is that this is the acme and ultimate of death, destruction and chaos.

American aircraft were not the only planes to take to the sky. With the Germans having less territory to defend, and with many of their airfields in danger of being overrun, Luftwaffe activity notably increased. As the American tanks neared Ludwigshafen on March 21, they were attacked by a sortie of over 300 Luftwaffe planes. For the first time, XX Corps witnessed Hitler's latest secret weapon—the jet fighter bomber. At seemingly incredible speeds, the jets swept down and strafed the American columns. While a number of conventional propeller-driven aircraft were shot down, all of the jets escaped unscathed.

Despite American air superiority, German aircraft would continue to pose a threat until the very final days of the war. Charlie Wright of the 7th FAOB's B Battery recalled one instance where he was traveling with a convoy of trucks loaded with infantry when a German fighter plane attacked the vehicles. The plane fired upon the convoy in its first run, and then circled back for another strike. This time the Americans were ready, and every machine gun and rifle in the convoy fired at the approaching plane. The plane was hit and skidded to a crash landing in an adjacent field. The infantry leaped out of the trucks and raced for the aircraft. The German pilot, apparently unharmed, crawled out of the cockpit and stood on the wing of plane. Either brave, foolish, or both, the pilot suddenly reached down to grab his pistol. Wright watched on as one of the veteran infantrymen who from a dead run took a perfect kneeling aiming stance. One shot rang out and the pilot fell dead onto the field. Few items were more valued as a war trophy than were German aviator jackets, and an infantryman had this one in his possession before the dead pilot's body was even cold.

In a similar instance that occurred on another day, the men outside B Battery headquarters heard an approaching wave of anti-aircraft gunfire firing at an inbound German plane. The plane was clipped by the fire and crash-landed in a field behind the headquarters tent. Jim Royals was one of the first men on the scene and drew a bead on the cockpit as the German pilot emerged. Royals covered the pilot as he was led up to Battery Headquarters for initial interrogation. The German turned out to be Lieutenant Skinner, who clearly seemed to be relieved to be a prisoner and out of the war. Skinner was still armed at this point, and was emphatic that Royals—as the capturing soldier—be allowed to keep his pistol. Royals did indeed get the pistol and later returned to the plane where he took the pilot's cap insignia as an additional war trophy. The acquisition of the pistol, however, nearly resulted in disaster a short while later. Some of Royals' comrades were examining the piece went it accidentally discharged and sent a bullet into Joseph Gingerelli's upper leg. Fortunately, Gingerelli's wound was not serious and he was eventually able to return to duty.

There always remained the threat that German planes could come out of the sky at any time. Jim

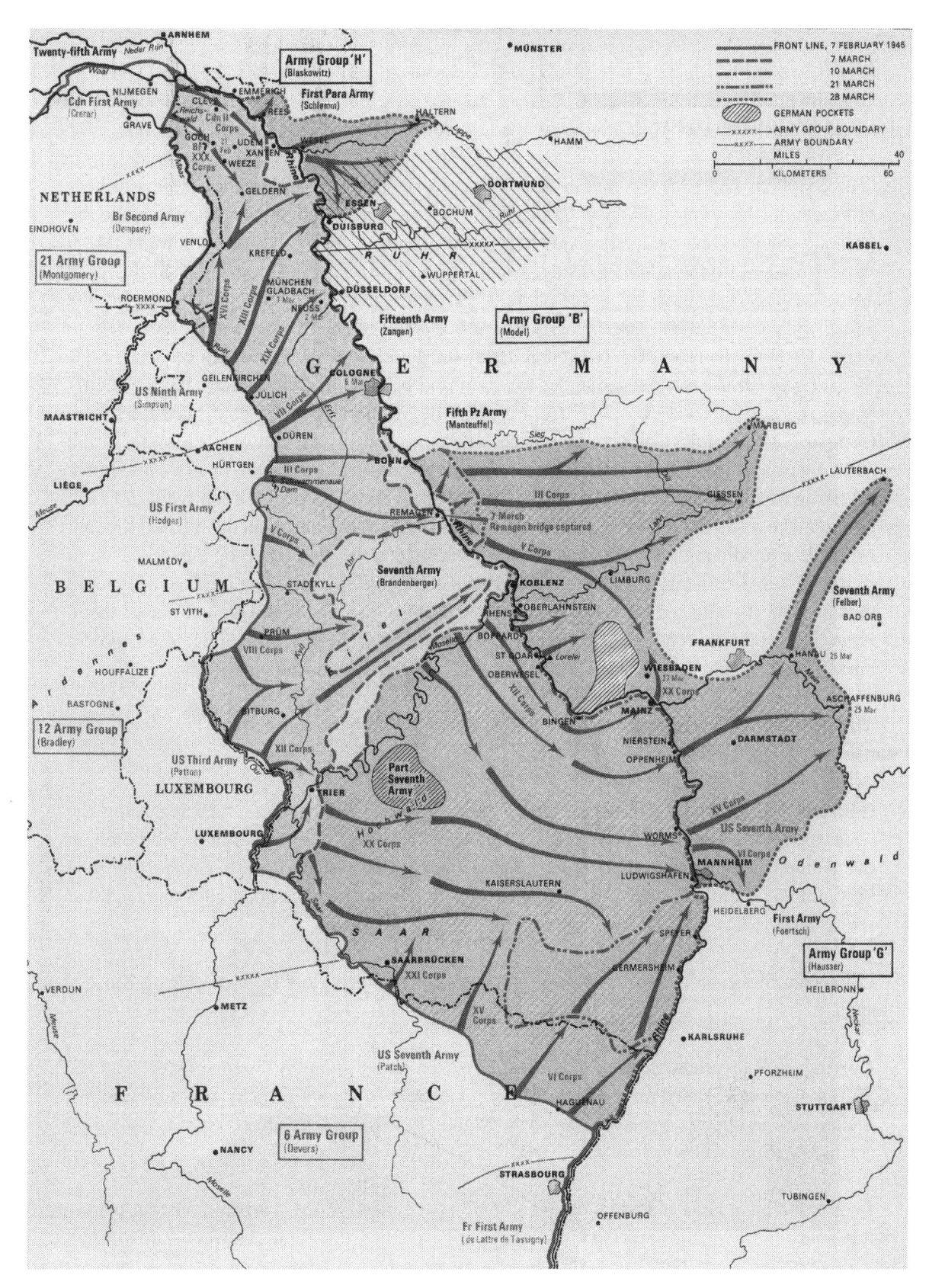

To the Rhine

Following the capture of Trier, XX Corps repulsed a desperate SS attack that tried to replug the German's hole in the Westwall. Third Army then set its sights on breaching the Rhine. Launching on March 13, 1945,

Royals remembers the occasion when B Battery stopped long enough on a Sunday to hold a morning religious ceremony when they were subjected to a Luftwaffe attack:

> The chaplains had picked a nice little hill, tapered to have it easy for the soldiers to hear and see him. The Protestant chaplain picked a rise facing east with the sun shining while the Catholic chaplain had members of his faith facing south. It was a beautiful morning. As a Baptist, I was with the other Protestant worshippers on the eastern sloop. We had, just as a caution, parked our weapons carrier with the .50 cal. machine-gun mounted on a tripod just a few yards down the hill, but we really weren't thinking of enemy planes at the time. There were a lot of men on each side of the hill, ready for the Bible reading and service.
>
> As we all got relaxed and under way, low and behold what appeared to be two enemy planes appeared not very far away from us. As they came nearer, we confirmed they were German. Jace Jarrell, Corporal Lawrence Valentine, and myself ran down the hill to the parked weapons carrier. About the time we reached the truck, one of the planes came in for a strafing run and opened fire. We slid under the truck until it passed. Then we heard both planes make a 180 degree turn. I guess they saw all these guys siting on the hill and thought we made a good target. We climbed on the truck, loaded the ammo belt on the .50 cal., and started to "rat-a-tat bang-bang." A few more machine guns farther down the road opened up then as well. I could see tracers flying all around those two planes and we got one of them. Everybody at the church service ran down and applauded us and were laughing, as no one got hurt. The chaplains then asked for quiet and said a prayer. All ended well.

Marinello writes this after a German air attack on a XII convoy during the Third Army advance to the Rhine:

> Germans had delivered a clear message. The free ride we had until then regarding the wide open skies was over. From then on, the Luftwaffe kept after us, strafing and bombing our columns. Sometimes the Germans stood their ground and dogfights ensued, the men becoming a cheering section. But it wasn't a game. Sometimes the good guys lost, and that wasn't easy to take.[137]

Lieutenant Slessman picked up his story after A Battery's departure from its elegant Kaiserslautern apartments.

> Our stay in Kaiserslautern was very short, however, as we soon hit the road again with the 80th Division and headed for the Rhine River. Outside of a few strafings by the Luftwaffe, we met no serious opposition all the way to the Rhine. In two days our efforts were rewarded by seeing the Rhine valley before us.

Ludwigshafen, a large industrial city and home of the massive I.A. Farben industrial plant, proved a tougher final objective than expected. A bridge still spanned the Rhine between Ludwigshafen and Mannheim, and there were faint hopes that perhaps it could be somehow taken before it was destroyed. Given the strategic importance of the Farben plant, Ludwigshafen was robustly defended by anti-aircraft elements of the 9th Flack Division. The anti-aircraft guns used by the Germans were well suited for dual anti-tank defenses. The 12th Armored Division had the first crack and tried to rush into the city from the north. They were stopped cold by the flack guns and took heavy losses in men, tanks, and armored personnel carriers.

It was now certain that a determined infantry attack would be required to take Ludwigshafen. Heavy artillery was brought forward and the defenders were subjected to a pounding barrage. The trusty 94th Infantry Division, moving past the shattered hulks of armored vehicles destroyed in the first attack, was sent into the fray. The Germans finally destroyed the bridge over the Rhine, which removed the urgency of the attack. The Germans held out for two more days before either rowing over the river or blending into the civilian populace. On March 24, the remaining Germans in Ludwigshafen capitulated and XX Corps was in firm control of all of their assigned territory on the west side of the Rhine River. Their long sought-after goal of virtually every operation since mid September 1944 was finally at hand.[138] The XX Corps' history summarized the achievements of the preceding twelve days of combat operations: "In this crushing defeat of the German forces, vast stores of supplies and equipment had been captured; a 25-mile stretch of the Siegfried Line had been destroyed and overrun; 4,000 square miles of rich coal deposits and vital industrial territory had been captured; 42,888 prisoners had been caged; 4,000 of the enemy had been killed and 7,300 wounded. Also, the enemy forces that were to have been the defenders of the Rhine River line had been obliterated. Future operations for the Allied Forces were greatly eased."[139]

CHAPTER 14

Final Victory: Into the German Heartland

With the capture of Ludwigshafen, there was a dramatic change of the XX Corps' mission and reshuffling of the operational divisions. The 10th and 12th Armored Divisions were transferred to 7th Army control, and the 26th and 94th Divisions were pulled back for a well-deserved rest. Both army and corps-level zones of responsibility were modified, and XX Corps would depart Ludwigshafen and move fifty miles north to the city Mainz, where they would make a Rhine crossing in the direction of Frankfurt. For the next phase of operations, XX Corps would have use of the 4th and 6th Armored Divisions, the 5th, 9th, 65th, and 80th Infantry Divisions, and the 3rd and 16th Cavalry Groups. By March 26, the bulk of XX Corps was concentrated in and around Mainz as they prepared to force a river crossing the night of March 27-28.

Directly across the river from Mainz was the city of Wiesbaden, and just twenty miles to the east lay Frankfurt, one of Germany's largest cities. Due to the Rhine's great width and strong current, crossing it would be the most geographically difficult engineering feat that XX Corps would face in the war. Fortunately for those having to make the attack, recent Allied operations along the Rhine would make this a simpler proposition than other crossing operations XX Corps had faced. In addition to the ever-expanding Remagen bridgehead, a grand front-wide river assault was planned for March 24. For once, Patton was able to steal the show from Montgomery by having XII Corps silently sneak the 5th Infantry Division across the Rhine during the night of March 22-23. This bridgehead met fierce resistance from German officer candidate troops that had been posted in Wiesbaden. The German attack was repulsed and Patton soon had his bridges over at Oppenheim, a town fifteen miles south of where XX Corps later would cross. The next day, Patton crossed over the newly constructed pontoon bridge, and with some ceremony, proceeded to urinate in the Rhine. Montgomery and 1st Army launched their full attack on the night of March 23-24, and the Allies were solidly across Germany's largest natural barrier. Additional Third Army crossings were north of XX Corps at Boppard and St. Goar.

Positioned along the Rhine, the Third Army FAOBs were obtaining great success in picking off those German batteries that were still firing. The 286th FAOB, in support of the XII Corps crossing, identified twenty-two targets in a twenty-four hour period. Marinello: "A major part of our success could be attributed to the improving weather, most notably diminishing winds. Part might have been due to the shrinking enemy artillery that allowed [the enemy's] cannons to better stand out. Regarding our [CP] team, it amazed me how well we functioned together. They never seemed to forget they were in it together and that lives depended on how well everybody performed. The same was true with the OPs, maybe more so, and the survey teams."[140] Lieutenant Slessman wrote of his experiences at Mainz: "We followed hot on the heels of the armor into the outskirts of Mainz, and set up our usual sound and flash bases paralleling the Rhine. Outside of some desultory shelling of the city at nighttime, there was little enemy activity and our engineers soon completed the largest pontoon bridge across the Rhine."

At Mainz, the battalion crossed paths with its first commander, Edward J. McGaw. McGaw was now a brigadier general and commanded the divisional artillery of the 63rd Infantry Division. McGaw, who had never lost interest in the 7th FAOB (he had sent the battalion greetings on its third anniversary when posted in Stourbridge), and mutual regards and good wishes were passed. While waiting for the river crossing, the men of the 7th FAOB had a chance to catch their breath in the wake of the rapid pace of the past several weeks' activities. They also had the chance to organize and ready their equipment for the next phase of operations. Rieth on March 24: "It was interesting to listen to the news these last few days. The radio would say that troops of the Third Army were ten miles from a certain town, and we would already be sitting in it. Today I did a lot of washing and did get all of my equipment straightened out again." On the afternoon before the river assault, some members of the 7th FAOB were even able to take in a Humphrey Bogart-Lauren Bacall movie courtesy of the USO. When recalling his time in Mainz many years later, Victor Salem of A Battery, remembered the more grim experience of finding a dead German soldier floating on the banks of the Rhine River.

While preparing for the Rhine crossing, Tom Delay received a troubling radio message that he quickly disseminated. The message reported that the Germans were believed to have placed barges along the river filled with chemical munitions. Accordingly, all American artillery and air corps units were prohibited from firing at any barge in fear of releasing lethal gasses. As the GIs had long since discarded their gas masks, the notion of possible chemical warfare was quite alarming. (As it turned out, these fears were unfounded, and no such threat actually emerged.)

The XX Corps' assault across the river began with a twenty-minute artillery barrage that began just after midnight on March 27-28. For this river crossing, the infantry was supported by large, motor propelled Navy-operated assault landing craft (instead of the dinky ten-man, oar-powered, assault crafts they had to use during previous river operations.) At first there was some initial small arms and anti-aircraft gunfire from the far side. These defenses were quickly overcome and the 80th Infantry Division began to firmly lodge on the eastern shore. Fourteen hundred German prisoners were taken and there was little evidence that the Germans were able to establish any cohesive type of defense. Linking up with XII Corps elements that had crossed over the Oppenheim bridgehead, XX Corps had established a secure lodgment on the east bank of the Rhine with minimal losses. The engineers immediately went to work, and within twenty-four hours were able to set up an 1,896 foot bridge. This would be the longest tactical bridge built under combat conditions during World War II. The German heartland now lay open to Third Army.[141]

Once across the Rhine, XX Corps was ordered to attack northeast, straight into the center of Germany. Its first intermediate objective would be the city of Kassel, about one hundred miles north of Frankfurt. To keep the advance going as quickly as possible, Walker would have to push his main effort to cut between Wiesbaden and Frankfurt, and not get tied up in either city. Although German resistance was spotty, it still was a dangerous situation for the Americans. While some Germans were surrendering by the thousands, others were ready to fight to the death. The rapid advance made things dicey, as follow-on echelons were as much at risk of enemy fire as were the vanguard troops. Scattered elements of the now-shattered 6th SS Mountain Division were still fighting in XX Corps sectors, making rear area travel almost as dangerous as front line combat. With ultimate victory this close, nobody wanted to be killed in what was obviously the final weeks of the war.

Easter Sunday in 1945 fell on April 1, just short of the one year Easter anniversary when the 7th Field Artillery Observation Battalion departed Camp Shelby for New York. The changes, losses, dangers, hardships, comradeship, and personal growth that each soldier had experienced in the subsequent twelve months were indescribably enormous. In context of what they had gone through, a virtual lifetime of experiences had been packed into that one year. Now, part of the 7th FAOB was located in Ziegenheim on Easter Sunday, a town located by a recently liberated German POW camp. Battalion members visited the camp and found thousands of starving American, British, French, Polish, and Russian former POWs. One thousand of the prisoners were American NCOs (three from the 16th Field Artillery Observation Battalion), and all had been subjected to deplorable conditions. The men of the 7th were impressed with the degree that the POWs had been able to keep body and spirit together. To help make this a memorable Easter, the entire battalion donated their PX rations for one week, plus all the candy, cigarettes, and canned tidbits that could be gathered up to the former prisoners. "Seekers News" described it as probably the most unusual church collection plate effort ever.

The Americans were impressed at the German autobahns; there were no roads like that at the time back in the States. Kurt Rieth on April 2: "We've been covering a lot of territory lately and I only wish that I could give you the details. Some of our traveling was on the autobahn; you can really whiz along when you hit them. Don't worry if the mail doesn't come very frequently for a while, you have to expect that in these fast moving situations." Marinello also commented on the effect of the autobahn and improved weather in supporting Third Army's lightning advance: "The race across Germany was helped almost to a dreamlike degree by its autobahns. A lot of things were now breaking our way. The weather, which from the start had been on [the enemy's] side, became milder, temperatures Spring-like, the skies a crystal blue. It rained only occasionally, the brief, refreshing kind. There were no more deluges, no more rain one day into another and another. Muddy roads were behind us. Nature had become friendly."[142]

Lieutenant Slessman on the XX Corps' drive in the first two days after the Rhine crossing:

We crossed the morning that the bridge was completed, and, following the 6th Armored Division, bypassed Wiesbaden and made a bee line for the city of Frankfurt. We remained just outside of Frankfurt while the infantry went into the city to mop up any resistance, and there was a very bitter battle here with some SS troops. My battery received orders not to remain here [in Frankfurt], but to proceed to the northeast with the 6th Armored to Kassel, our objective. Again it was a rapid road march up an autobahn, and by this time, there were as many Germans behind and beside us as there were in front of us. The Germans would slip out on the highways at night and mine the roads, or ambush supply convoys. The second day we reached the outskirts of Kassel, but here the Germans were not so eager to give up, and a tough firefight was soon in progress between the armor and a flock of Tiger tanks that came roaring out of Kassel to meet us. It was a costly engagement for both sides and the infantry of the 80th Division joined us to help. Unless you actually see one, it would be hard to imagine just how large and formidable a Royal Tiger Tank appears, and actually is. They are really monsters, and their size is accentuated by an extra long gun barrel for the 88-mm gun that protrudes from the main turret. Due to their excessively thick frontal armor, these tanks were very difficult to damage and our Shermans were no match except for the later models with the 90-mm guns.

The fight for Kassel would be a stubborn one. Unlike the individual enemy soldiers from fragmented units that XX Corps had encountered in the past few days, at Kassel they meet intact German units. The biggest threat came from the 166th Infantry Division, which had recently arrived from Denmark and was defending the city along the Fulda and Eder rivers. Although the 6th Armored Division was able to make some small bridgeheads by the evening of March 31, the fast momentum gained over the past two days was halted. XX Corps was further delayed by two large pockets of German forces that remained and threatened the corps' lower left flank. On April 1, the 80th Division continued its attack on Kassel. German infantry, supported by twenty Royal Tiger Tanks that literally came right off a Kassel factory assembly line, made two counterattacks on the left flank. In a pitched battle, the Germans were thrown back, and the 80th Division descended on Kassel. The fight for the city would last several more days, and Kassel would not be

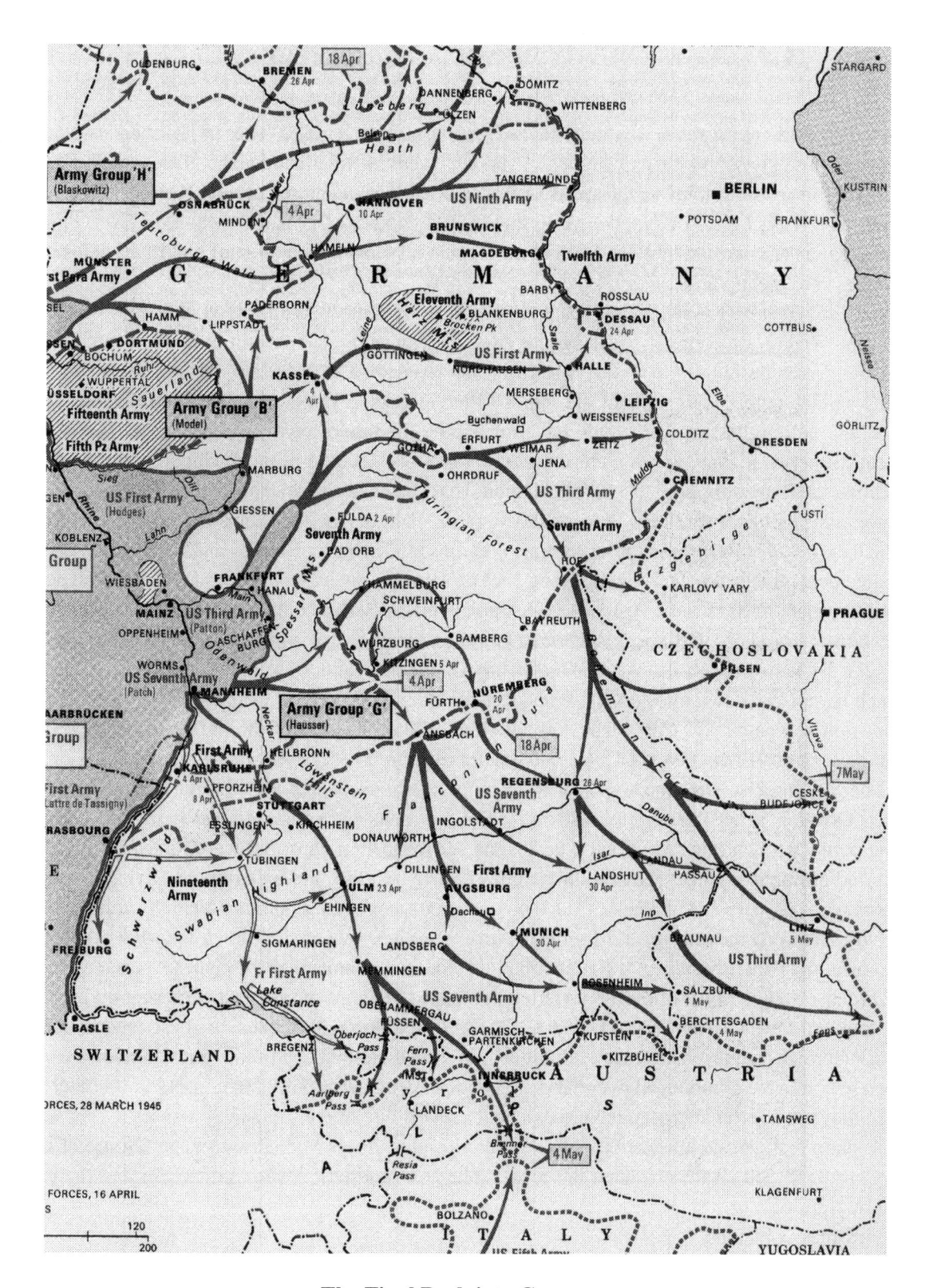

The Final Push into Germany

Once over the Rhine, the autobahns helped the speed of the Third Army drive into central Germany. XX Corps met stiff resistance at Kassel on April 3, 1945. Bypassing the city, the bulk of XX Corps shifted east, quickly reaching Erfurt, Weimar and sitting on the border of Czechoslovakia by Coldiz mid-April. XX Corps had advanced so far ahead of other American units that they had to halt and wait for the other Corps to catch up. The 7th FAOB pulled back and regrouped at Weimar. On April 18, Third Army received new orders that sent them into Bavaria and towards Austria. XX Corps crossed the Danube at Regensburg on April 26. They were on the Inn River across from Braunau, Austria (Hitler's birthplace) when the war ended on May 8, 1945.

considered cleared until April 5. By the time the fighting was over, 5,500 German prisoners, twelve tanks, thirty-five 88-mm guns, and huge quantities of supplies were in American hands. On April 7, Kurt Rieth wrote this about winning some of the spoils of war that had been captured around Kassel; "Everything is fine with me. We got a lot of supplies yesterday from a captured German warehouse. Everything from cigarette lighters to wine and brandy. The Germans are really losing a lot of stuff and [that] helps us when our supplies can't get up fast enough."

Prior to reaching Kassel, XX Corps had been heading almost straight toward Berlin. Once Kassel was reached, Walker was ordered to change his axis of advance directly east in order to eventually link up with Soviet forces pushing in from the Eastern Front. Strategically, there was no longer any question of Germany's quick defeat. For some of the senior Allied leaders, it stood to reason that the more each side captured, the more influence they would have in shaping the fate of post-war Europe. In the weeks that followed, the political dynamics of connecting with the Soviets would be as much consideration as would be defeating the remaining fragments of the demoralized German Wehrmacht. There was disagreement in the senior ranks with how far the Americans should push. Patton, Hodges, Simpson, and Winston Churchill all wanted to press for Berlin and the easternmost regions of Germany. Bradley and Eisenhower disagreed. In an agreement already reached amongst the Allies at Yalta, Germany would be carved into predetermined zones of occupation. It was also calculated that an attack on Berlin could cost as much as 100,000 men. In Eisenhower's opinion, why spend American blood on territory that would only be ceded to the Soviets anyway?[143] By letting the Russians have Berlin, the Americans could move to the southeast, and take up to the Czech border and down into Austria. This decision directly led to XX Corps' next set of orders. From their position at Kassel, XX Corps was now less than 200 miles west of the pre-war Czech border near Chemnitz. That city would be XX Corps' next major objective.

The 80th Infantry Division was sent in to mop up Kassel, which allowed the remainder of the 6th Armored Division to set their sights eastward. The Germans vigorously defended several Fulda River crossing points with entrenched infantry, tanks, and self-propelled guns, but were routed out by close air support and armored assault. Moving thirty miles east by April 4, the 6th Armored Division bypassed a scattered enemy defense at Muhlhausen, and soon reached Langensalza, another ten miles farther. German air activity had been increasing, and fourteen Luftwaffe planes were shot down that day. Approaching Langensalza, the American advance forces found the source of some of these planes when they overran a large German airbase. Some of the aircraft tried to escape at the last minute, but were shot up by the tanks as they took off down the runways. At the 2001 7th FAOB reunion, some of the vets described finding a line of twenty German fighter planes that were hidden on a well-camouflaged road that doubled as a runway. The men remembered climbing all over the planes and pressing every button they could find. Later on they reflected they were fortunate not to have accidentally set off any of the weapon systems!

A sharp battle ensued in the city of Oberdorla (just south of Mulhausen) when a force of German infantry, artillery, and armor defended the town. The 6th Armored Division pitched in and the city was cleared by April 6.

Slessman continues:

Before Kassel was completely taken, the 6th Armored Division was pulled out and given the mission of going east until they met the Russians. My battery was assigned to accompany them, so off we went, covering forty to fifty miles a day. We met only spotty opposition, and soon had passed through Muhlhausen and were about fifteen miles from Halle when we were ordered to stop because we were too far ahead of all the other Allied armies, at least by sixty miles, and therefore had long, unguarded flanks. We received daily visits from the Luftwaffe, particularly from their new jet planes that would bomb and strafe us and be gone before we could even leave our trucks. They were fast as greased lightning, making them a most difficult target for our [anti-aircraft attempts].

I almost got into trouble in one town when I stopped to look at a freshly knocked out German panther tank. I was standing about fifty feet in front of it with my flash officer when the fire in the tank detonated a shell in the tank's gun. The projectile went right between us and hit the wall that we were leaning on. Fortunately for us, it was an armor piercing shell and contained no explosive charge, so we suffered nothing more than having the wits scared out of us.

One of the German jet air strikes hit a 7th FAOB vehicle convoy that Medical Officer Captain Louis del Bello had been traveling in. Like every other soldier in the battalion, del Bello had his share of harrowing experiences in the war. The battalion history reported that some of his experiences included sighting the German sub that almost torpedoed the HMS *Arawa*, being caught out in the open during the battalion's first air raid, and driving into a gigantic shell hole while in blackout drive. His last combat misadventure occurred when being attacked by the fast moving German jet. Although the jet's cannon and machine gun rounds missed his truck, del Bello was wounded when a flying brick that had been kicked up by the fire hit his shin.

Another soldier who was injured in one of these late-war air attacks was Frank de Girolamo, a wireman assigned to Headquarters Battery. In this attack, Tom Delay remembers sitting inside a 4x4 truck getting ready to light a cigarette when he heard the simultaneous drone of a plane engine combined with the barking of its machine gun. Delay dove over the passenger strap and into a ditch, with the cigarette still in his mouth (although he never was able to find his lighter). Following in a GMC truck, de Girolamo likewise jumped out of the back of his vehicle. De Girolamo had been sitting on a wooden crate. In exiting the truck, his rear end got caught on an exposed nail, resulting in a nasty gash to his hindquarters. De Girolamo would later be awarded the Purple Heart Medal for this injury, the nature of which he became the "butt" of many jokes for a long time afterward.

The Third Army FAOBs continued to move right along in the very front of the lightning-paced advance. Ed Marinello writes of the quick pace of the combined sound/flash operations employed by the 286th FAOB:

At some point during each afternoon, never in the morning, a division commander would give us the measure of the day, that is that the drive was winding down and where he expected it to stop for the night. With that, an area map was studied to select the best locations for a mile base, observation posts, and command post. Always the first to start out was the survey team. Meanwhile hills and cellars were scouted. The assignments were carried out in record time. Never did the detachment falter, never did anybody do less than what was expected. The men were never at rest during those drives, working full time so that while the infantry and tankers paused for the night, the sound and flash teams were fully engaged.[144]

Kurt Rieth wrote this letter on April 13, which gives a sense of the speed of the recent operations as well as the reaction of the German populace:

Dear Mother and Dad, First I want to apologize for not writing in such a long time. We've just been too busy advancing and the mail wouldn't have gotten back anyway. It makes you feel good when everything is moving like this although it does wear you out. The dust is thick again, and traveling along the road in a jeep behind a bunch of other trucks puts dust in your eyes, ears, lungs, and clothes. It's interesting to watch the reactions of the civilians when we enter a town. At first when we enter a town they are afraid of us, then, when they see we aren't going to shoot them, they become curious and a few even smile and wave. I picked up a few more souvenirs today and I hope I'll be able to either send or take them home with me. So long for now, Lots of Love, Kurt.

With the 6th Armored Division in the north and the 4th Armored Division leading in the south, XX Corps was an unstoppable force. In those few towns where the German Army tried to resist, the armor would either blast their way through or simply bypass them and let the follow-on infantry battalions destroy the defenders. With the help of XX Corps artillery fire, Weimar and Jena fell on April 13. As the Americans raced to the east, the center median of the autobahn was clogged with thousands of prisoners and displaced citizens moving west. Managing the civil control of newly occupied cities became a major chore for XX Corps, and entire battalions were taken out of line to maintain order and to guard supplies. By April 14, XX Corps had advanced so far forward of other American units they were ordered to halt for several days. In a little over two weeks of operations, XX Corps had moved over 300 miles.

After the Rhine was crossed, XX Corps encountered relatively few instances of coordinated German artillery resistance. XX Corps' heavy artillery battalions, whose primary functions were counterbattery fire, were usually only employed to soften up those German forces that still demonstrated a will to resist.

The speed of operations sometimes made the 7th FAOB's mobility capacity even more important than their counterbattery mission. Upon reaching Weimar, some of the 7th FAOB trucks were ordered stripped of equipment and were used to ferry infantry troops from rear areas to the front. For a period of a few days, Jim Royals and other comrades had nothing to do but guard the piles of equipment that had been off loaded as they waited for the trucks return. Sitting outside in the sidewalk on a pleasant Sunday morning, Royals took notice of an attractive woman passing by and let out a whistle for his buddies' benefit. He was quite surprised when the young lady returned before him, and in perfect English, reprimanded him for his rudeness. After apologizing, Royals came to find out that she was an American girl from Ohio who had married a German college student in Akron. While visiting his relatives in Germany in 1939, the war started and her husband was drafted into the German Army. Along with her young child, she was suddenly stranded with her husband's family in Weimar. Although her husband was unaccounted for at the time, the woman explained that she hoped for his safety and of their eventual return back to Ohio. Immediately striking a friendship, the ever-affable Royals was invited to have dinner with her and her mother-in-law's family that evening. Royals remembers the visit; "I enjoyed the meal and their hospitality. I wrote their names down and her home address in Ohio, but I lost them. I hoped the husband survived and they were able to put the war behind them and have a good life together. I was glad to have the opportunity to meet the people and learned they were very much like us. Their lives were interrupted just as ours."

In the pursuit through Germany, the 7th FAOB was widely dispersed, and at times a squad leader would be the senior-most American soldier in charge of a newly taken town. As was standard operating procedure, all German citizens were required to surrender whatever weapons they owned. The 7th FAOB history described the experience of Corporal Eskinazi (the Moose), wire corporal, A Battery, after his section moved into a German town one night. Being the self-appointed mayor of the town, Eskinazi ordered the townspeople to turn in all firearms, and went to bed expecting to receive a collection of pistols, old Mausers, and shotguns. "The Moose," on arising the next morning, took off the blackout curtain and shouted to his partner, "Look what they brought me, a 155-mm howitzer!" Eskinazi was then informed by his comrades that the big gun had been there unnoticed since they pulled in the previous evening.

One of the challenges in moving through Germany was trying to figure out the different electrical voltages that were in use. If the wrong power source were used, electronic devices would get fried. As described by Supply Sergeant Robert Gieges, Headquarters Battery had a unique voltage meter in the form of Private Leo White. White was a large Midwestern farm boy, who, back at Camp Shelby, could polish off twenty-six pancakes in a single sitting. If an outlet needed checking, someone would get White, who would then wet his finger, stick it in the socket, and then report something like, "Yep, got a pretty tickle from that one, its a 220." He was invariably correct.

In the closing weeks of the war, there were fewer opportunities for the 7th FAOB to perform their counterbattery mission. Still, the batteries continued to support the advance and were ready for whatever missions may come up. A pattern was created where the sound and flash platoons would travel during the day, operate OPs and instruments through twilight and night, and then take off again at the earliest light, day after day, without pause, without rest. Sometimes the men would establish an OP in the afternoon, only to have to leave it an hour later and set up farther on.[145] When fighting did occur, the Germans were often overwhelmed before the batteries could deploy and set up OPs. The tempo of the advance was so quick that often there was no time—or reason for that matter—to conduct survey operations. When the mid April halt occurred, A and B Batteries were ordered back to battalion headquarters in Weimar to await further instructions. Slessman: "Shortly after our battalion was ordered to halt, I received word by messenger to bring the battery to Weimar, and that we had finished our job in the war. We pulled out at once and rejoined the battalion at Weimar. In Weimar, we had no sooner made ourselves comfortable for a long rest in some lovely suburban homes, when I was given the mission of supporting the 4th Armored Division in a drive on Chemnitz and a junction with the Russians. Off we went again going through Jena, home of the Zeiss optics works, Gera, and on to a point just outside Chemnitz. Here again we were stopped by orders from headquarters—we had gone far enough."

For the victors, there was little glory in witnessing the death spiral of Germany. Many of the German industrial centers had been pulverized by Allied bombings and destruction was everywhere. Most pathetic were the thousands of displaced civilians and hungry children. Although the Americans had specific orders against fraternization, almost all the GIs did what they could to share their rations with those most in need. Even Patton, who could hardly be described as a bleeding heart, was affected by the suffering as described by D'este: "[Patton] was particularly moved by a woman with all her worldly goods inside a perambulator, crying on a hillside; by an elderly man with three small children, wringing his hands; and by a woman with five children holding out a tin cup, also crying. Patton recorded in his diary: 'In hundreds of villages there is not a living thing. . . They brought it on themselves but these poor peasants are not responsible. Am I getting soft? I did most of this.'"[146]   By this point, the average German soldier and civilian were more than happy to surrender. After suffering six years of a war that had destroyed all of their major cities and killed millions of their people, all but the most fanatical were thoroughly sick of the war. Most Germans also appreciated being fortunate enough to surrender to the Americans instead of the Russians, and they did their best to be cooperative with the GIs.

It was standard operating procedure (SOP) that the thousands of surrendering German soldiers be rounded up and sent to prisoner of war collection points for further interment. As told by Hank Lizak, there were some exceptions. Lisak was traveling in the A Battery Command Car with Lieutenant Slessman and Tech 5 Rieth (and King, the A Battery German Shepherd mascot) when they came across a solitary, very young German private heading their direction. As was their procedure, Rieth got out of the car to interrogate him and to give him PW control instructions. After a few minutes, Rieth reported to Slessman that this was just a badly shell-shocked boy trying to make his way home and recommended that they just let him go. Slessman considered for a minute and then agreed. They disarmed the private, sent him on his way, and then threw away his rifle at the first opportunity.

Jim Royals tells a similar story about the one prisoner he captured. Toward the closing days of the war Royals was taking a break in a field when he noticed an object near some woods. He went over to it and realized it was a German machine-pistol (commonly referred to as a burp-gun). Unfamiliar with this weapon, he picked it up and checked its action. In doing so, the weapon accidentally discharged, sending a burst of fire into the trees. Royals then heard a distant voice call, "*Kamerad, Kamerad*!" Out from the woods emerged a very scared young German soldier who thought Royals was shooting at him. The prisoner turned out to be a sixteen-year-old boy wearing a uniform jacket and civilian pants. Apparently the boy was a recent draftee who was separated from his unit. As soon as he saw Royals approaching, he had dropped the weapon and then hid in the woods. A brief interrogation quickly determined that this was just a boy trying to get back home. After making an effort to follow official POW procedures in front of the officers, the NCO in charge then directed a jeep driver to take the prisoner back toward the rear and then let him loose after a few miles.

In *Citizen Soldiers*, Ambrose describes that despite themselves, many GIs were surprised to find how much they liked most of the German people they encountered. Clean, hardworking, disciplined, educated, with cute children and middle class in their tastes and lifestyles, the Germans seemed to many American soldiers to be "just like us." One soldier reflected, "The Germans I have seen so far have impressed me as clean, efficient, law-abiding people. In Germany, everybody goes out and works. They are cleaner, more progressive, and more ambitious than either the English or the French."[147] In the invasion through Germany, American troops would usually occupy German homes or businesses, as the tactical situation allowed. By April of 1945, the speed of the advance kept the Americans moving quickly from location to location. Sometimes the German citizens would be ordered out of their homes, at other times they would be allowed to stay. Ed Shock, of the 7th FAOB Headquarters Battery had this experience in an occupied German home:

> Whenever we moved into a town to occupy it, we were allowed to commandeer the houses and sleep in them. Most of the time, the older folks, whose homes they were, were allowed to live in the back part of the house. Such was the situation one day when I received a package from home, which contained a bag of unpopped popcorn. I loved popcorn. I went to the kitchen and asked the woman for a pan. She had a fire going in the old wood stove, so I decided to pop the corn there. When I put the pan on the stove, the woman poured water in it. I said, "NO, NO," and poured the water out. I put the pan back in the fire, and again she poured water in it. Once more I poured the water out, and then prevented her from repeating the process. When the corn started popping she really got excited. They had never seen popcorn before. I shared it with them, and she enjoyed it so much that she wanted some uncooked kernels to plant for the next season. Anyway, I found the older Germans to be good people. They were glad to see the American soldiers and cooperated with us."

In another instance, he recalls:

Once again, we were occupying a town, and had a few days to rest. Donald Dale, the battery comic, found a hen somewhere and decided that he was going to watch that hen until she laid an egg. He was hungry for fresh eggs (as we all were). He followed that hen around all day, waiting for her to lay that egg. When night came and she hadn't produced, we had baked chicken for supper.

Marinello writes of the differences in commandeering homes in the later stages of the invasion of Germany:
As the detachments surged ahead, their living conditions improved in such an extent that they,

it might be said, began to fight the war in a 'stylized' way. Before, in France and Luxembourg, as well as the early towns in Germany west of the Rhine, they had their pick of rubbled houses to protect them, basing selection on which had the best cellar. Deep into Germany the approach to picking out where to stay overnight changed. Choices were made from among an array of fine, well-structured houses on paved streets with wide intersections. [148]

Some of the recently found sympathy for the Germans evaporated when Third Army began to liberate concentration camps and came across thousands of displaced persons that were victims to Nazi invasion. XX Corps and 7th FAOB members were present at Ohrdruf, Buchenwald, Dachau and other labor camps, and saw first hand some of the horror that Hitler had inflicted throughout Europe. Robert Geiges of Headquarters Battery was one who recalled some of the awful sights. The carnage at Ohrdruf, near Gotha, was particularly disturbing, as the Gestapo guards killed many of the foreign worker inmates only hours before the camp was captured. Generals' Eisenhower, Patton, and Walker arrived to inspect the scene. This was Eisenhower's first look at a concentration camp. Appalled, he called it the shock of his life, and then directed that media and politicians visit the camp to make first hand reports of the atrocity to the rest of the world.

Nothing was worse than what was witnessed at Buchenwald. The XX Corps' history describes the scene: "When the infamous concentration camp at Buchenwald was overrun, 21,000 slave laborers and political prisoners were found, all in pitiful condition. There were dirty barracks, bunks four tiers high and no bedding except for an occasional filthy blanket. The incinerators where remains of the starved inmates were cremated were still warm. Bodies piled up like stackwood awaiting disposal, and records in the offices of the camp showed the atrocities that had been committed in the name of medical research. It was a sight to make even battle-hardened veterans leave with set jaws, boding no good for the next enemy units which tried to stop their advances."

Bill Jessel of B Battery was at Buchenwald when Patton ordered the local citizens to march through the camp to observe the horror. It was an understatement to say the GIs had little sympathy for the Nazis at this point. One man in Jessel's squad "raided" the Burgermeister's home while all the townspeople were in the camp. He returned with two socks filled with the Burgermeister's rare coin collection.

Battery A's Stephen Wandzioch was on hand to witness the concentration camp at Dachau, near Munich. He records, "We saw bodies, piled up like cord wood. There were a lot of covered ditches about six feet wide, eight feet deep, and about thirty to forty feet long. Here they dumped bodies, poured lime on top of them, and covered them with dirt. We spoke to a few GIs that were on guard there. They said when they reached the camp they freed hundreds of people that were skin and bones, some who had not eaten anything for days. These scenes there will live in our minds forever."

By April 17, XX Corps was sitting just inside the Czech border awaiting the arrival of the Soviets. New orders arrived for Third Army, which would send them southeast through Barvaria and into Austria. For some time SHAFE had been concerned that the Germans would retreat into some sort of "National Redoubt" in the German and Austrian Alps. At that point, the whereabouts of Hitler were undetermined, and some intelligence analysts speculated that Hitler and SS fanatics would hold out in a final bloody stand in his "Eagles Nest" amidst the rugged Alps Mountain ranges. Worse, it was feared that a surviving Nazi command structure hidden in the mountains could direct a protracted guerrilla war against the Allies. While this scenario never came to pass, Eisenhower was determined not to get the same blind-siding he received in the Battle of the Bulge when he had prematurely written off the German war capability.[149]

The movement toward the Danube River and Austria began on April 18. The XX Corps delay allowed those Germans who were still willing to fight to set up defensive positions. Even though the end was so obviously near, some Germans still fought and more soldiers would die. On April 20 - 21, the 71st and 65th Infantry Divisions battled strong defenses with little gain and lost several tanks in the process. The fighting was especially heavy in Neumarket, which wasn't taken until April 22. Finally on the move again, XX Corps continued south to the next natural obstacle, the Danube River at Regensberg. The 7th FAOB set up its headquarters in a brewery (to the men's great disappointment, devoid of beer) in the town of Wolfskoe. Six combat groups, comprised of light tanks, rangers, and engineers, opened the thirty-five-mile zone to the Danube. The XX Corps' history outlined the tactics these cavalry groups used in the final weeks of the war: "On approaching a defended town, the reconnaissance platoon developed the surrounding terrain; tanks and tank destroyers fired high explosives and smoke shells, causing damage and often fires. Then, following an assault by the tanks and tank destroyers, the Rangers mopped up in dismounted action." The river was reached on April 25. Some light Volksstrum defense was met, but soon Regensberg fell as XX Corps prepared to cross the Danube.

One of the most violent XX Corps artillery strikes of the entire war occurred near Regensberg. On April 26, the 65th Infantry Division was to cross the Danube at the town of Abbach. The attacking infantry wanted the potential enemy strong point in the town neutralized and requested all available artillery support. The XX Corps' 416th Artillery Group, consisting of three battalions of the heaviest field cannon, was on hand to receive the mission. This was the first time in some days that the group had the opportunity to mass fires at one target at the same point in time, and the men were eager to get into action. The bombardment began at 5:25 A.M., with all guns firing at the maximum rate for five minutes. The gunners took to their work with incredible zeal and the noise and pure shock effect of the big guns was incredibly deafening. The XX Corps artillery Headquarters was posted in the center of the group. The force of the guns literally knocked the headquarters men off their feet and into the walls of the command post. By the time the firing ended, the town of Abbach was blown into oblivion.[150] In Abbach and in other scattered villages along the Danube, crossings were forced and the engineers secured pontoon bridges. XX Corps was on the way to the Isar River, which ran to the northeast of Munich.

The depth and speed of the penetration into Germany made it increasingly difficult to keep the unit filled up with replacements. Robert Geiges and Ed Shock found this fact out the hard way when they were ready to cross the Danube and were pulled aside by the first sergeant. New replacements bound for the 7th FAOB were ready to be picked up—all the way in Luxembourg. As the group included an officer, a jeep was required along with a two and a half ton truck. Without the benefit of a map, they set out on the long journey over war torn roads. So as the two friends could keep company with each other in the cab, the jeep was loaded onto the back of the truck at a railhead. They eventually made it to Luxembourg, picked up the new men, but had a hell of time finding the Headquarters Battery, as it had long since moved on by the time they departed. By asking one unit after another, they eventually linked up with the 7th FAOB without major incident. While the greater history of World War II may not focus on such seemingly common tasks, the process of rotating new men into active units was a significant challenge for those soldiers having to make it happen.

By now Third Army was deep in scenic Bavaria. Marinello: "The natural beauty of Bavaria was a revelation. Town after town was idyllic. Streets were paved and wide, houses well and attractively built. Most of all, the landscape was captivating. Advances had been so rapid there was little evidence of destruction. That, of course, was not so with the large urban cities that the air force had already rubbled.[151]" On April 29, three XX Corps divisions were poised along the Isar. For the last time in the war, A Battery set up flash and sound OP installations in support of the 80th Division's crossing operations. German artillery fired from the high ground to the south of the river, which was then silenced by divisional artillery. The river was stormed at several crossing points and secured. This final combat operation of the 7th FAOB was also notable for the introduction of a recently acquired mortar detection capability. Under flash platoon command and control, this was the first time that this radar-based state-of-the-art technology was used on the battlefield. Accurate at relatively short range, the radar systems were able to track the high arch of incoming mortar rounds. Although introduced too late in the war to be considered effective, radar-based shell detection systems would eventually revolutionize counterbattery detection. Today, highly sophisticated radar target acquisition systems can instantly track the exact origin of inbound artillery fire.

On April 30, XX Corps was over the Isar River and headed straight toward the Austrian border. At 3:30 that afternoon, Hitler committed suicide in his Berlin bunker. (Upon learning of Hitler's death, Staff Sergeant Ziobro of A Battery quipped, "I wonder if they will fly their white flags at half mast now.") Even though Hitler was dead, it would be another week before the war was officially over and combat operations continued on. The corps had three infantry divisions in line, oriented south, with an armored division in reserve. Moving beyond the Isar, the 7th FAOB deployed across the entire corps front. In the first days of May, A Battery was on the right flank with its command post at Erding, just outside Munich. B Battery was on the left flank of the corps along the Inns River, just across the border from Austria. The Battalion Headquarters was established a few miles behind B Battery at Pfarrkirchen. XX Corps units consolidated positions, cleared their respective areas, and continued to manage the great flow of prisoners. The men remained on edge even though it was clear the war was all but over. One cool night Jack French was going to sleep under the stars, his sleeping bag zipped up to his neck. Just as he was nodding off, French felt something brush his forehead. Convinced he was about to be bayoneted by a German soldier, French alerted the entire camp with a loud scream. Once fully awake, he discovered that his foe was only a small field mouse. Jack received a scalding from his first sergeant, as there were still real potential enemies about and silence was needed to protect their location.

Kurt Rieth on May 3: "Well, it looks like the war may be over pretty soon, but after waiting for it for such a long time, I don't think I'll even feel excited. We heard the news about Hitler's death last night. It may or may not be true, but in my situation it doesn't make much difference either way. May started off great over here, but it has been raining and snowing for two days and we are certainly fed up with it. I suppose we will move again today. We haven't stayed in the same place for over two days for a long time."

As a climax to this final drive, the last of the 90,000 troops of the German Army Group South surrendered to XX Corps on May 8, 1945. The Second World War finally came to end. For the men of the 7th FAOB's B Battery, it was appropriate that they concluded the war right across the border from Braunau, Austria, Hitler's birthplace. Rieth on May 8:

Well today the war has actually been declared over. It seems strange at night to see lights shining from the windows instead of having everything blacked out. We've already started a baseball league in the battalion. Tonight we had a game between the communication section and the officers and kitchen personnel. Tomorrow I believe we have a stage show scheduled. I spent most of today washing clothes and cleaning up the radio equipment. We went to the local fire station and borrowed the pump to wash our trucks with. We fooled around with it for a few hours but it wouldn't work. The Burgermeister, who is also a mechanic, took it back with him and told us he would fix it and bring it back tomorrow. They are lucky they didn't have a fire around here.

With the fighting over, regular electric power was becoming restored throughout the area. In one instance described by both Tom Delay and the unit history, this development resulted in near catastrophic results for the Headquarters Battery wire section. When possible, the wiremen liked to use the support of existing wire poles as they best protected the lines from being cut by vehicle traffic. While set up along the Inns River, the "wire gang," under Sergeant Daniel Callahan, had laid commo wire over the top of what had been a dead, high tension wire. As had been done a thousand times in the past year, the installation was quickly completed and phone lines had connected various battalion elements. Then, to everyone's surprise, the local hydroelectric plant came on line and the high-tension wire suddenly became live, passing with it the full power charge on the field telephone wire. An enormous 2,300 volts shot though the 110 capacity wire and into the section's telephone switchboard. Tremendous bolts of blue sparks flew in every direction, nearly electrocuting the phone operators. Quick thinking Private Kebbe grabbed an ax and cut the line from the switchboard. As "From Bragg to Braunau" concluded on the event: "Three good Christians, one slightly damaged telephone unit, and the established fact that wire W-110 is not exactly designed as a good conductor for 2,300 volts, but will still bring it in."

On May 9, a column of the Soviet Army linked up with XX Corps units at the Inns River. Vodka flowed and a wild celebration ensued. For others, news of the war's end was anti-climatic. Everyone was exhausted and just wanted to go home as quickly as possible.

Marinello:

At midnight of May 8 it became official. The war ended. The men put down their arms. There was no cheering, no embracing. It was enough that the war was over.[152]

For the first time in what seemed like ages, lights burned freely in the night and the thought of a real homecoming was at hand.

Way back on D-Day, B Battery initiated a betting pool to see who could best predict the end of the war. Most of the men were far too optimistic and guessed that the war would have ended much sooner than it actually did. T/5 Goodwin won the jackpot by coming in closest with his winning entry of April 15, 1945.

In the course of the war, XX Corps and the 7th FAOB had racked up an impressive set of statistical accomplishments. As a corps, they had fought 279 consecutive days in action, traveled 1,300 miles while engaging enemy forces, and captured 431,419 prisoners of war. The 7th Field Artillery Observation Battalion was credited with the following:

Plots of enemy artillery by sound ranging: 2,723
Plots of enemy artillery by flash ranging: 375
Sound registrations and adjustments: 104
Flash registrations and adjustments: 121
Meters of survey performed: 1,280,125
Metro messages delivered: 1,779

The 7th FAOB adjusted many of the 1,707,416 artillery shells fired by XX Corps during the war. The battalion contributed to 5,216 shell reports based on examining 61,634 enemy shells holes. The most important statistic is that the 7th FAOB played a major role in the counterbattery fire of 4,294 fire missions by XX Corps artillery.[153] There is simply no quantifying the amount of American lives that were saved by this capability. Patton had a special place in his heart for XX Corps and General Walker, whom he promoted to lieutenant general on April 27 with the same set of stars that he himself had been promoted with by Eisenhower. On May 21, Patton sent the following commendation to Walker and XX Corps:

John K. Rieth

Subject: Commendation
To: Lieutenant General Walton H. Walker

From the landing of the XX Corps in Europe in England until the termination of hostilities in Europe, you and your corps have been outstanding for dash, drive, and audacity in pursuit and in exploitation.

Your determination and great tactical skill were evidenced in your capture of Metz and subsequent advance to the Saar and capture of Saarlautern.

Your reduction of the Moselle-Saar Triangle and the capture of Trier was a brilliant feat of arms. The operation starting March 13 and terminating May 9, during which you turned the Siegfried Line, destroyed the center of enemy resistance, crossed the Rhine, finally terminating your victorious advance in Austria, were in keeping with your previous exploits and standards.

Of all the corps that I have commanded, yours has always been the most eager to attack and the most reasonable and cooperative.

You and your corps are hereby commended for your outstanding achievements.

Signed,
G.S. PATTON, Jr. General

CHAPTER 15

Occupation Duty and Homeward Bound

Just because the war was over didn't mean that there was no longer a demanding mission for the American forces. Prisoners had to be controlled, civil order established, displaced persons cared for, and a new government installed. To the southeast, there were still German cavalry divisions that had yet to come under allied control, and the threat of a conflict with Yugoslavian forces existed on the southern Austrian border. Some senior officers (including Patton), predicted the cold war that would follow and urged launching a preemptive attack on the Soviets, forcing them out of Eastern Germany, Poland, Czechoslovakia, and back to Russia. While bullets were no longer flying, Germany-Austria remained a volatile place in late spring 1945.

Standing down from a full combat posture, the 7th FAOB continued to hold their place along the German-Austrian border until May 23, when occupation duty assignments were divvied out. For the 7th FAOB, the forward observer mission was put aside and managing the civilian populace would be the first order of business. It didn't take long for the grind of the daily army regime to take the place of fast-paced combat operations. After the experiences of the past year, nobody felt very motivated to return to the garrison army lifestyle they left behind at Camp Shelby long ago. Rieth on May 13: "We are going to start a training schedule next week just like back at basic. Of course, the higher ups figure that they have to keep our simple minds occupied so much we won't think about going home. For my part, I would be happy if they just let me sleep all day. There is also a choice of classes we can take such as French, German, Math, Algebra, etc. I don't suppose anyone will learn much, but it will help pass away the time." As well as maintaining their badly beat up trucks and equipment, the men spent their off duty time at local swimming holes, playing sports, writing home, and listing to the radio. Holding true to his entrepreneurial talents, A Battery's Donald Paschal found an abandoned tailor shop and set up a brisk laundry service.

On May 23, the battalion loaded up, drove by Hitler's childhood home in Braunau, and drove to Andrichfurt, Austria, where they remained for a week. For their next duty assignment, the 7th FAOB lucked out when they were ordered to report for occupation duty to Mondsee, one of Austria's premier summer vacation resorts, located just east of Salzburg. Rieth on May 29:

> I believe that we have finally settled down in our present location and are going to stay awhile. I am now in the town of Mondsee just at the edge of the Austrian Alps. This is the most beautiful scenery that I have ever seen. Mondsee is right at the edge of the lake that bears the same name, and you can imagine how being near a lake makes me happy. This section was quite a well-known tourist spot before the war. On the other side of the lake, the mountains rise almost straight up and are covered with snow on the top. You can probably imagine what a beautiful sight this is. Another fact that I can now reveal is that our battalion is in the

Twentieth Corps. We were attached to this corps ever since we left the States. There has always been a lot of secrecy about it, and it is known over here as the "Ghost Corps." [After ten months, this apparently was the first time that the men could disclose that they were in XX Corps.]

Mondsee was about as good a duty as anyone could have hoped for. There were abundant summertime recreational facilities, horseback riding, a PX, and first rate billeting. Amos Robinson described it as "a wonderful town with snow capped mountains, a large lake, nice cabins to stay in, pretty girls sunbathing on the lake. I was not in a hurry to want to go home."

Shortly after their arrival, the battalion celebrated the fourth anniversary of its activation with a traditional army organizational day celebration. Brigadier General McGaw, the battalion's first commander, flew in to address the battalion. Rieth on June 2:

Today was organization day again for the battalion. Four years ago today the 7th Field Artillery Observation Battalion was activated and on each anniversary we have a celebration. As usual, there were contests between the batteries such as baseball games, races, drill teams, etc. I'm happy to say that A Battery won the cup. There was a beer party down at the lake tonight, but we also have boats and I spend most of my time rowing. There is also a sailboat, but it seems to be reserved mainly for officers and poor enlisted men won't have much of a chance to get it. People [*referring to questions in letters from friends in the States asking if he could visit his German relatives*] don't have the faintest idea of what things are like over here. First of all, you can't fraternize with the civilian population and second, you can't leave the immediate vicinity without signing out in the orderly room. All of our day is occupied and the only time we have off is in the evening. I don't believe I've mentioned that we are billeted in a hotel here in Mondsee. We have a nice big room facing the main street of town and there are only three of us in it. There is running water, lights and a radio. The only trouble is that there are no maids to keep the room clean. It's a lot of work keeping the place sparkling for the inspection each morning.

Life wasn't all fun and games at Mondsee, however. In addition to the myriad of occupation duties, Lieutenant Colonel Schwartz remained as strict as ever and put the battalion on a demanding training schedule. Men still had to post guard duty, and as always, Schwartz insisted on high levels of discipline and strict compliance with regulations. Jess Grisham of Headquarters Battery wrote of his time at Mondsee: "In Mondsee, Austria, I was billeted in the basement of a large Chalet-type building along with several headquarters personnel, including Lt. Col. James Schwartz. One evening, the colonel returned to his quarters. I was one of the guards and did not bother to challenge him with the password (the war was over). The next thing I heard was the unmistakable roar of Schwartz who yelled, 'Who the hell is on guard duty!' It was only thanks to the intervention of Sergeant Major and First Sergeant Skelton that I was not severely punished."

Some members of the battalion were tasked to find former Nazi and SS leaders. Lieutenant Sockwell and a corporal were part of a detail assigned to inspect patients at German hospitals for telltale tattoos that some Nazis supposedly wore on their arms. Sockwell recalls that the corporal was of Jewish faith and took to the mission with a high degree of determination and motivation. (Despite their efforts, this technique rendered no high level Nazi suspects.)

On June 6, in celebration of the one-year anniversary of D-Day, a holiday was declared and the entire battalion was free to take advantage of a day off. Most of the men relaxed by the lake, took in movies, and enjoyed the impromptu break. The stay in Mondsee would last only two weeks, and the battalion again had orders to move back to Germany on June 9. While everyone was reluctant to trade Mondsee for another occupation assignment, good fortune once more smiled on the battalion. The battalion would again be sent to another lakeside resort: Chiemsee.

Located about seventy miles west of Munich, Chiemsee was (and remains) one of Europe's finest vacation spots. Set on a huge and beautiful lake, the centerpiece of Chiemsee is an island that held a spectacular castle built by the "Mad" King Ludwig of Barvaria in the mid 19th Century. Ludwig was obsessed with the French royalty and he virtually bankrupted the Bavarian government building vastly ornamental replicas of French palaces. His palace on Herreninsel, which he only spent nine days in, was among his most elaborate efforts. In addition to guarding the island, some members of the 7th FAOB drew duty as castle guides giving tours to American GIs on rest and relaxation (R&R).

Ed Shock served as a tour guide and recalls his time at Chiemsee: "This was a lovely place, and Chiemsee was a beautiful lake. It beckoned me to go fishing. Somewhere along the way, I had picked up a rod, reel, and tackle box, so I was prepared. I noticed that the natives weren't fishing in the lake—maybe they weren't allowed to, since it had belonged to a 'king.' Whenever I wasn't on tour duty for the castle, I was fishing. I surely enjoyed it and gave my catches to the locals, who were glad to get them." Tom Delay and four other soldiers were posted on guard duty at a resort hotel in the island of Frueninsel, the site of a convent. Tom recalls the plush housing, easy duty, and the opportunity to trade C-rations with the locals in exchange for fresh fish and vegetables.

Most of the battalion was actually housed in the nearby town of Hafling, about seven miles from the resort. Still, this was about as good as an occupation detail could be had. Stables with eight horses were available and many of the men took up horseback riding. On June 19, Kurt Rieth, who was now a full time interpreter, gave this account of a typical day: "I just got back from horseback riding and although I'm a little bit sore, I got a big kick out of it. I've been going riding every evening and each time I enjoy it more. One of the boys here is an excellent rider and he's been showing me how. I'm not too busy lately as I just hang around the orderly room and act as interpreter. Every morning at nine the chief of police reports to me and tells me if anything new has happened and at ten comes the daily interview with the Burgermeister." In addition to the daily tasks of executing occupation duty, the battalion took time out for official photographs to be taken of all three batteries on July 1 - 2.

Not all the men of the 7th FAOB got to enjoy the good life at Mondsee and Chiemsee, as some were reassigned from the battalion for other duties. Bill Jessel of B Battery was detached from the unit to serve as a guard for a newly established German POW camp near Munich.

The army continued to do its best to provide recreational services for the troops, with movies, refreshments, and shows from some of the top performers of the day. Rieth on July 1: "I saw the Jack Benny U.S.O. show last night. He gave a swell performance and it was worth the dusty ride to get there and see him. With him was singer Martha Tilton and Larry Adler, the harmonica virtuoso. Then, about ten minutes before the show was over, Ingrid Bergmann arrived from Munich to joint the cast. She almost stole the show, and it's easy to see why she is a top actress in Hollywood."

At one point or another, almost all the men had the chance to go to Paris for R&R. The editors of *"Seekers News"* gave this review of a trip to Paris in the March 23 edition:

> We stayed in the best hotels, we were treated like visiting firemen, and (you may believe this or not) the MPs had the attitudes of civilian police, desiring only to help you find your way around and make certain you were not "taken in" by the light fingered gentry that infest any big city.
>
> Your reporter suspected that he is getting old, in as much he was the only one of the

seventeen who did not vote the female population of Paris as the most beautiful ever seen. I will have to admit, however, I have never seen a more beautiful bevy of showgirls than those at the Casino de Paris.

…It's my advice for those who get a pass to Paris to get oriented as quickly as possible, obtain a Red Cross map at the club where you are billeted, and go to the booking office at the earliest possible moment after arrival to obtain tickets for the various shows for which you have to pay.

Kurt Rieth on July 5:

I've done quite a bit of traveling since I last wrote you. I was lucky enough to get a three-day pass to Paris, and now am in my room at the Hotel Moderne overlooking the Place de la Republique. It's really some town and it's almost impossible to describe in a letter. Of course, I've been to all the well-known places; the Eiffel Tower, the Cathedral of Notre Dame, Napoleon's Tomb, and about fifty others I can't think of. The trip we had to make to get here was sort of rough, because we had to travel all the way to Luxembourg by truck, and from there we went to Paris by train, which was not too bad. The subways here are free for soldiers and I've been using them quite a bit. It's pretty confusing until you figure out where to get on and off.

While those soldiers in Europe were enjoying liberty passes in Paris, the war in the Pacific continued to rage on. A massive and bloody invasion of the Japanese mainland was a pending probability. In June of 1945, the development of the atomic bomb was a tightly controlled secret. Even those few that were involved in its production could not be certain of its effectiveness in ending the war with Japan, as experience had proven that the Japanese would chose death over surrender. For many of the troops in Europe who had just finished off Hitler, the prospects of going on to fight the Japanese seemed all too likely. Matters were made worse for the men of the 7th when an ugly rumor spread that Lieutenant Colonel Schwartz had volunteered the entire battalion for duty in the Pacific.

Some soldiers fell into certain categories that gave hope for getting out of the Army earlier than most of their comrades. The army had come up with a point system that regulated those soldiers who could leave Europe ahead of their unit's return for a quick discharge. As described by Steven Ambrose: "The point system set up by the army gave a man points for each active-duty service month, points for campaigns, points for medals, and points for being married. The magic number was eighty-five points. The calculating of points became an obsession, as it meant the difference between going straight home, or possibly stay in the army for deployment to the Pacific to fight the Japanese."[154]

By mid July, all nonessential 7th FAOB men with eighty-five points or more were released for transit back home. As it turned out, many of the high point men who left the 7th FAOB for early release actually made it back to the States *after* the battalion's eventual return. Stephen Wandzioch amassed a total of 128 points. In early June he was transferred to XX Corps Headquarters Company in expectation to quickly ship back home. Wandzioch ended up assigned to the XX Corps Headquarters all the way through the summer and did not make it home until mid-September. Once transferred, Wandzioch found that he had no specific duties and could pretty much do freelance-type of work. Assigned a driver and a truck, Wandzioch ended up traveling throughout Germany in search of various supplies. During this time period he established a friendship with three other soldiers of Polish decent. With some time on their hands they made a five-day visit to war-torn Berlin as well as to Poland. In Poland they saw the Auschwitz Concentration Camp. Wandzioch describes the visit:

In Auschwitz they had large furnaces where they burned the bodies. What all four of us could figure was there was a large dressing room where the victims would undress and leave their clothes. They would then enter a shower room with water running from the ceiling. The water would stop running and the gas would be turned on, killing them. The guards would then pick up the bodies and put them on a slide that led to a furnace. They would take the ashes outside for the wind to blow into the sky. We could see piles of ashes that were encrusted by the rain and did not disperse. We only toured this place a short while because the smell made us sick. We could not eat anything the rest of the day. I'm sure that seeing all of this will be in our minds for as long as we live on earth, all four of us.

During the third week of June, the 7th FAOB was removed off of occupational status. As described by Rieth in a June 22 letter, this development was a double-edged sword:

I have some news to give you; it may turn out to be very good or maybe not so hot. The outfit is not classified as occupational troops anymore and this can mean either we are going straight to the Pacific, going to the Pacific via the States, or going to the States and remaining there. There are plenty of rumors going around, but the battery commander told me he thinks we are going to the States. Please don't get excited now, or over optimistic because anything can still happen. At any rate I feel pretty happy about the whole thing. I'm sick of this occupational business. After a while I know it will become so monotonous that I'd be willing to go anywhere. I figure if I get home in the near future it will be within three months.

The battalion began to get ready for the prospect of movement back to the States. Just as they had done the previous year at Camp Shelby, the battalion resumed the same pattern of cleaning and preparing equipment for shipment. Also, the same routine of constant inspection was followed, with Lieutenant Colonel Schwartz personally checking all battalion vehicles on June 29, and personal equipment the following day. By July 11, the battalion was told they would have an August shipping date. Anticipating the voyage home, Rieth wrote this on July 15: "I only wish the trip ahead of us was over, but then it will be a lot more pleasant than the one we had traveling over. It would be a big help if we could get an American ship instead of one of those English tubs."

It had taken years to get the millions of GIs over to the ETO, and it would take another massive logistical effort to get them back home again. As part of the processing, the army would assign shipment orders for the various units that had been lifted from occupation status. To house the soldiers while in transit, the army established huge pre-deployment camps—Camp Lucky Strike and Camp Pall Mall—near shipping ports in France. Units would travel to these locations to await their designated ships for the return back to America.

The 7th FAOB departed Chiemsee on July 18 for the long motor march back to Camp Lucky Strike. The route took them past Ulm, Kaiserslautern, the World War I battlefield of Soissons and finally into the camp. From Kaiserslautern to Soissons, they drove 243 miles, the longest battalion movement in a single day while overseas. Rieth described the trip on July 22:

At last I've found time and opportunity to write a letter again. I'm now at Camp Lucky Strike near Le Havre. We made the whole trip with our trucks covering a distance of 750 miles in four days. Since we have over one hundred trucks in the battalion and were traveling in a convoy, we weren't allowed to travel more than thirty miles an hour. It was monotonous and dusty and I'm glad it's behind us. We shouldn't be here more than ten days, probably less before we hop on the boat. It's just a matter of getting processed, that is turning in equipment and getting new clothes.

In a typical army snafu, there was a mix-up in the shipment orders and no departure date could be assigned. The battalion would have to endure a disappointing long wait at Camp Lucky Strike for an indefinite period. Rieth on July 27: "Well it looks as if we are going to be delayed here at Lucky Strike longer than we anticipated. Our shipping orders have not come through yet and we may have to stay here another ten days. This place is just a wilderness of tents as far as you can see. When the wind blows, which is most of the time, we have miniature dust storms. It seems that wherever they pick a site for an army camp they have to pick a barren wasteland. None of us really mind this however, just as long as we get home in the end." German prisoners worked the kitchen and did kitchen patrol, at least relieving the GIs of that burden. Amos Robinson remembers working side by side with a German medic at sick call.

One problem that A Battery had to deal with was what to do with the battery mascot, King. In the eight-month long journey from Metz to Le Havre, Lieutenant Slessman and others had become quite attached to the young German Shepherd. When in Paris, some of the A Battery men explored options on getting the dog back to the States. Hank Lizak:

While on the French coast in Camp Lucky Strike waiting for a ship to take us back to the US, we had a pass to Paris for some rest and relaxation. During our run through France, B Battery established an acquaintance with the wife of the editor of the Herald Tribune Paris Edition, Jeff Parsons. They were now back in Paris and we were invited for a visit. Lieutenant Slessman wanted to have his dog "King" flown home. As the Parsons were very friendly with Eisenhower's Chief of Staff, General Walter Bedell Smith, we hoped they could somehow swing a favor. We had cocktails with the Parsons and met actress Madeline Carroll who lived in the same building.

Despite the highbrow connections, flying King home would not be an option and King would have to make it back to the States on a troopship.

After almost two weeks, there was still no sign of a departure date. To make matters worse, a rumor circulated that the battalion was slated for eighteen weeks of training back in the States, and then for service in the Pacific Theater. Conditions at dusty Camp Lucky Strike became intolerable, and Lieutenant Colonel Schwartz arranged for the battalion to move to the more desirable Camp Pall Mall at the end of July. While the conditions of Camp Pall Mall were an improvement, Schwartz put the unit back on a traditional training inspection, and it was classic army life all over again. For the combat veterans who wanted nothing more than to be home, this became a frustrating existence.

Kurt Rieth, August 2:

Well, we have changed location again. Since we have to stay over here for a few more weeks, the colonel decided to look for a better camp to move to. This camp is situated very nicely among the trees overlooking the channel. The food is also much better. Those are about the only two advantages we have however. We now must get up at 6:15, stand reveille and spend half the morning getting our equipment in the tents uniform. First, we're told to hang out our musette bags at the head of our beds, then the order comes to hang them at the foot of the bed. Then we are told to hang our mess kits on the outside of the tent. Someone doesn't like this so we lay them on the beds. This stuff is nothing new, only we are not used to it after ¾ of a year in combat. I almost forgot to tell you that after we hit the states this outfit will be classified as strategic reserve, which means we will in all probability remain in the U.S.

No sooner had the 7th FAOB set up operations at Camp Pall Mall to prepare for thirty days of training, when the long awaited shipment orders came through. The battalion packed up as quickly as possible and dashed back to Camp Lucky Strike. Again, it was the classic army bureaucracy of "hurry up and wait," the actual shipment was delayed for more than another week. While the battalion was going through the motions of preparing their equipment for movement one last time, big events occurred in the Pacific. On August 6, 1945, the atomic bomb was dropped on Hiroshima, Japan. A second bomb followed at Nagasaki on August 8. By August 10, it was reported that Japan was ready to surrender. For those still in Europe, there was no longer the worry of having to remain in the army to invade Japan.

Rieth on August 12:

We are back at Camp Lucky Strike again. We were settling down at Camp Pall Mall to a training schedule when alert orders arrived and we were rushed back here to get processed for the voyage. I didn't write any more because we expected to leave any moment, but now things have changed again and we may be here for any time from one to two weeks. Every hour seems like a day sitting around here but at least we have the trip home to look forward to.

Now with the surrender of Japan close at hand you at least don't have to worry about my going to the Pacific anymore. As a matter of fact, you don't have to worry about me at all anymore. All of us feel pretty happy and we can at last look forward to getting out of the army.

All of our equipment is turned in and all the work involved preceding an overseas voyage is done so now we lay around all day and take it easy. I usually take in a movie in the afternoon and go to the Red Cross club for doughnuts and coffee in the evening. The trouble with this life is you become so lazy that doing the least bit of work is an effort. I'd better stop writing now before this heavy pen tires me all out.

As it turned out, the 7th FAOB shipped out of Le Havre on August 14, 1945, on the Liberty Ship S.S. *Leidy*. Along with the 7th FAOB were the 137th Signal Radio Intelligence Company and elements of various quartermaster detachments. In all, the ship held 550 passengers. In the hours before departure, those below the decks heard a tremendous racket of cheering topsides. Official word had just been received of Japan's surrender, which all but ended any lingering rumors of deployment to the Pacific.

The trip started off with some bad weather and many of the men were seasick for the first several days. The *Leidy*'s skipper put the ship into high gear (moving at thirteen knots instead of its standard ten knots) and was able to make the trip back in twelve days, a record time for the ship. Still, the speed of the Liberty Ship was snail-like when matched with the larger cruise ships of the day. At one point in the voyage, the *Queen Mary* appeared over the horizon and passed the *Leidy* as if she was standing still. But compared with the trip over on the HMS *Arawa*, the voyage back to New York seemed like a pleasure cruise. Once the seas calmed, the passengers found the food to be excellent, complete with cocoa hours, fresh milk, eggs, and daily servings of ice cream. The transport commander arranged a wide range of activities to keep the men occupied. Events included bingo games, talent contests, sing-a-longs, religious services, checker tournaments, and access to the troop library. Music and twice-a-day news broadcasts were piped through the ships PA system. A progress chart was posted which showed the route and daily mileage. The final edition of "Seeker News" was published, complete with tips on reacquainting men with life in the States and procedures for filing income tax, mustering out pay, and civil service information.

The voyage was tougher on some of the battalion's mascot dogs. At one point in the trip, tragedy struck when one of the dogs jumped overboard when trying to chase sea gulls (Geiges, who left for the States a few weeks earlier, believes this dog was his beloved "Irish.") Another dog made it all the way to New York, only to fall into the harbor when it became so excited at the sight of land. Someone even went to the trouble of having the Coast Guard search the harbor, but sadly, the dog was never seen again.

The *Leidy* entered New York harbor at long last on August 26. The sense of emotion and jubilation experienced by the men as they rounded the Statue of Liberty (which was blacked out during their last sighting of it) is indescribable.

A band, which reputably had come off of an all-night gig in the city, welcomed the ship as it pulled into the pier. A grainy photograph of the event shows hundreds of joyous GIs, crowding the *Leidy*'s deck under a large unit banner, frantically waving to shore. Don Slessman's dog, King, was one canine that survived the voyage back. Wearing a tiny army jacket with medals attached, it was King who led the battalion off the gangplank.

As the men prepared to disembark, a problem arose for Jim Royals. Waiting anxiously to unload, he was summoned to Lieutenant Colonel Schwartz's cabin. Royals began to panic. The day before they departed France, Royals was driving a jeep at the Le Havre pier when he briefly left it unattended. The regulations at the time required the men to secure the steering wheels with a lock and chain. Royals failed to follow this procedure and sure enough the jeep was stolen. Royals sweated this incident out the entire voyage and was sure he was being called to Schwartz's cabin for some sort of punishment. After formally reporting to the battalion commander, Royals was immensely relieved to learn the summons had nothing to do with the jeep. Schwartz instead asked for Royals' assistance in a problem that arose with the off-loading. The press had somehow picked up the story of Charles Yourkavich's heroic rescue of several wounded men back in the Metz campaign. Reporters were waiting at the end of the gangplank to interview Yourkavich. Yourkavich wanted no part of the special attention and refused to leave the ship without Royals, his close buddy, standing at his side. Royals then got with Yourkavich and the two walked off the ship together. Yourkavich reluctantly spoke with the reporters and the remainder of the off-loading proceeded without incident.

After a quick outprocessing, the vast majority of the men were given furloughs back home. For most of them, the final status of their exact discharge date was uncertain. All that mattered at the time was that they were on the way home. During their furloughs, most of the men received orders to travel to the nearest army installation for outprocessing and discharge; their contributions to winning the Second World War were accomplished.

The return to States almost, but not quite, ended the story of the 7th Field Artillery Observation Battalion. Virtually all the men who went overseas with the battalion were discharged by mid-fall of 1945. For those who were still assigned to the unit, there was much work to do in converting the battalion to a regular army organization. Camp Gruber, Oklahoma, was designated as the first permanent station for the unit. Of all the men and officers that went overseas with the battalion in April 1944, only two, Lts. Frank Johnson and Warren Sockwell, were still with the unit by December 1945. During this period, Lieutenant Sockwell wrote the majority of text for the battalion's history "*From Bragg to Braunau.*" The booklet was published in 1946 and then sent to all battalion veterans at their last home of record address.

After four years service with unit, Lieutenant Colonel Schwartz changed over command to Major Robert E. Panke, who joined from the 285th FAOB. The battalion moved to Camp Hood, Texas in December 1945 and continued its transition to regular army status. When the 617th Field Artillery Observation Battalion deactivated, seventeen officers and 117 men were transferred to the 7th FAOB, bringing the battalion over-strength in officers, and about half strength in enlisted men.

The massive demobilization of the post-war army continued to eliminate most of the army's units, and the 7th FAOB would soon be on the list as well. Despite all of the consolidations of the past several months, the 7th Field Artillery Observation Battalion inactivated on February 10, 1946.

While the 7th FAOB was no longer an active unit, its legacy would live on. On paper, the 7th FAOB would be redesignated as the 525th Field Artillery Observation Battalion on February 5, 1947. The experiences gained by the World War II field artillery observation battalions would carry on even longer. The Second World War was the first time where advanced techniques and equipment were successfully used in counterbattery direction. Each following decade brought further advances to this technology and doctrine. In both Desert Storm in 1991 and Iraqi Freedom in 2003, American forward observers used sophisticated radar-based target acquisition systems that enabled them to direct fire on Iraqi artillery even before the enemy's shells could land. To a large degree, today's U.S. Army Field Artillery still uses lessons learned from its 1940's forefathers.

The 7th Field Artillery Observation Battalion's legacy was built on its combat record in battlefields in France and Germany. Six of its members did not come home, and another twenty-three were wounded. The battalion also earned its share of decorations, with two receiving the Croix de Guerre and ninety-four being awarded the Bronze Star. As an introduction to *From Bragg to Braunau*, the battalion's commander, Lt. Col. James P. Schwartz penned this summary of his unit's wartime accomplishments. It now serves as a fitting conclusion to this history of the 7th Field Artillery Observation Battalion:

TO ALL MEMBERS OF THE 7TH FA OBSERVATION BATTALION

This, the combat history of the 7th Field Artillery Observation Battalion, was written in response to many requests for a record of your achievements in the British Isles, France, Luxembourg, Germany, and Austria during World War II. Each of you has contributed to this incomparable record of achievements, and each member of the Battalion merits the highest praise.

As a vital cog to the XX Corps artillery of General Patton's Third Army, U.S. Army, you gathered glory from Utah Beach in Normandy spearheading across France to Metz, smashing the south flank of the Ardennes counter-offensive, cracking the Siegfried Line, crossing the Rhine at Mainz, pursuing the enemy through Central Germany across the Danube, and finally ending the war on the Austrian frontier. Throughout these five major campaigns you earned the praise of higher commanders for your speed and excellence of communications, survey, target location, adjustment of fires, and general technical superiority. The ever-soldierly conduct of our members and their splendid maintenance of vehicles and equipment in continuous front-line battle positions elicited favorable comment wherever the battalion served.

My greatest honor was to have commanded such a loyal group of American soldiers. To each of you, I extend my personal thanks for your devotion to duty, your great courage, and the splendid spirit that helped our forces gain the final victory.

Signed,
James P. Schwartz
Lieutenant Colonel, Field Artillery

CHAPTER 16

Afterword

In 1998, I took advantage of my own army posting in Germany to follow some of the footsteps of the 7th Field Artillery Observation Battalion. Some observations of that trip and an overview of the XX Corps battlefields today are presented here.

My journey to trace XX Corps' trip would focus on the Metz and Saar river campaigns. Within a two-day window, I tried to cover as much of the ground where hundreds of thousand of men fought seven months of intensive combat. Unlike the U.S. National Parks Civil War Battlefields that many Americans are familiar with, the Metz and Saar campaigns are completely devoid of any markers or battle monuments. Present day tourists are completely on their own to try to figure out what happened on these battlefields. Armed with maps and an assortment of books on the battles, I set out to make the best possible use of my forty-eight hours.

I began my visit with the area south of Metz, where the 5th Infantry Division established their toehold over the Moselle River in mid September 1944. They had expected to take and move beyond the river with the same dash they had done in other similar operations in France throughout August. No Americans at the time had any concept of just how strong and determined the Germans on the other side of the river would be. My first stop was at the bloody Dornot crossing, where a battalion-sized force of the 11th Infantry Regiment valiantly held out for forty-eight hours against an overwhelming attack by German infantry and armor. The Americans occupied a few acres of trees and brush known as Horseshoe Woods, and more than half their number were killed or wounded there. The same woods exist today. With the Moselle flowing alongside a bicycle path, its peacefulness belies the terror of September 8-10, 1944, when 2,000 American and German soldiers became casualties in such a small area of ground.

Continuing on, I went several miles to the east to the towns of Pournoy, Coin, and Sillegny. Here, on September 18-20, 1944, troops of the 5th Infantry and 7th Armored Divisions launched a major assault to punch a breakthrough in the German lines. The Americans crossed over open fields to attack the towns, none of which they were able to wrest full control of. The Germans struck back with tanks, and after two days of brutal combat, the Americans pulled back. It would be another two months before they would finally break through this sector.

Having spent the first part of my army career as an infantry officer, I've developed a pretty good eye for finding the most tactically significant terrain on old battlefields. Matching World War II and modern maps, I quickly found the positions from where the 38th Armored Infantry launched their attack on Sillegny. Two times they charged out of the woods only to be repelled back by withering German fire from the town. On the third try, they were supported by tanks and made it to edge of the town. After a murderous twenty-four hours, they retreated for the last time, losing three battalion commanders and seventy-five percent of their men.

Just inside the wood line, a few hundred yards west of the town, I came across a long line of old American foxholes. The fighting positions have of course eroded over the years, but most were still at a depth of at least three feet. The farther I moved into the woods the more evidence of the battle I could see. Scattered across the ground were old ammunition boxes, cartridges, commo wire, foil from C-ration packages and pieces of shrapnel. Slightly to the rear of the main line, I was drawn to one large rectangular foxhole that seemed to be a mortar position. Sure enough, in the bottom of the hole were half-buried crates of ammunition, and on the rim were three live 88-mm mortar shells. Although rusty and weathered, I had to presume the shells were still explosive and I made sure to keep my distance. I have been to a number of World War II battlefields, but have never seen this much remaining evidence of the fighting as I did in this position near Sillegny.

From Sillegny I headed north to check out some Metz-area forts. Almost all of the forty-three forts that surrounded Metz are still there—most are so expansive I imagine they will be there for centuries to come. While the majority of the forts in Metz are now under French military control and are off limits to the public, I did go to some that are accessible. In the southern outskirts of Metz I visited Fort de Queuleu, one of the larger, pre-1870 forts. During the later stages of the battle, up to 500 German troops defended the fort against attacks of the 5th Infantry Division, until finally surrendering on November 21, 1944. Of all the Metz forts, de Queuleu remains the only one intended to draw tourists. Protected by an expansive moat and thick walls, the perimeter of the fort is so large it took me the better part of hour just to walk around it. In the later stages of the French occupation, the Gestapo used this fort as a mini concentration camp, and today there is a small exhibit on the French Resistance movement.

After my visit to Fort de Queuleu, I drove through the streets of downtown Metz, and passed many of the former German barracks now used for modern day housing, industrial, and government use. Up through the period of World War One, Metz was designed to hold a garrison of 250,000 men, and one can imagine the scope of the facilities required to house such a force. Extremely well built, much of this garrison infrastructure will remain for many decades to come. My next stop brought me to Fort St. Julian, which guarded the northern approach into Metz. Like Fort de Queuleu, St. Julian was one of the older forts that did not have an integrated turret-based artillery system. However, during the month of October 1944, the Germans positioned most of the artillery of the 19th Volk's Grenadier Division in and around the fort in support of the defense of Maizieres. In the final attack on Metz, Task Force Bacon found that Fort St. Julian was one strong point that could not be bypassed, and set out to capture it on November 18, 1944.

Fort St. Julian was designed to resist almost every method of assault imaginable. Protected by a deep moat, forty-foot walls, and a causeway/bridge that led to its huge iron main gate, the fort was big enough to garrison 1,000 defenders. During the battle, the Germans only had 360 men, but still enough to exact a heavy toll should the Americans have attempted a direct infantry assault. After futile tank fire against the main entrance, the Americans wheeled up a big 155-mm cannon. At point blank range, the gun fired ten shells into the iron door—all without result. After shooting twenty more shells into the masonry that held the gate's hinges, the door came down with a resounding crash as Fort St. Julian fell into in American hands. Today, a portion of the fort is now the home to a rather fancy French bistro. One can still see the damage to the main entrance where the 155-mm shells tore off the near impregnable door. The enormous steel door itself is also there as well, lying against one of the fort's walls, slightly dented but otherwise remarkably intact.

Leaving Fort St. Julian, I set out for the west bank of the Moselle to see some of the ground that XX Corps spent the better part of three months fighting over. About twenty miles northwest of Metz is Mercy-le-Haut, where on September 8, 1944, MSG Ujczo was killed when he and Lieutenant Field set up their ill-fated observation post as part of the effort to stem the attack of the 106th Panzerbrigade. Visiting the site, I could see why they set up at this town, as it offered a commanding view over a large area of the German penetration, as well as the location of where their 88s were firing. Like so many of the typical Lorraine villages, Mercy-le-Haut is no larger than eight or so streets, with the dominant building being an ancient chapel in the center of town. The battle scars on many of the walls could have been from either world war. Near the church is a monument to the men of Mercy-le-Haut killed between 1914 and 1918.

That afternoon I drove through those places most prominently listed in the 7th FAOB history, and where the battalion spent some significant time; Jarny and Hatrize, site of battalion headquarters, Mine Ida, where A Battery roughed out the Fall of '44, and Gorze, where B Battery was continuously pounded by Fort Driant. I had to think that most of the battalion veterans would be surprised at how little these villages have changed over the years. The battalion would have selected the sturdiest buildings for their command posts, and I could imagine which ones were occupied by the unit during the campaign. I made a point to stop at the four-building hamlet of Malmaison, near the spot where Harold Lorman was killed by a direct mortar shell hit on September 27, 1944. I planned on visiting the Lorraine Military Cemetery the next day where I knew Lorman was buried, so I wanted to make sure that I had a good sense of this part of the battlefield.

Near Gravelotte, I noticed in the distance a number of monuments not unlike what one would find at a place such as the Gettysburg National Battlefield Park. Intrigued, I drove closer only to find that they were German monuments marking the advance of their disastrously bloody attack there during the 1870 Franco-Prussian War. It is with some irony that the Americans attacked over these fields seventy-four years later, with the Germans defending the same ground held by the French in 1870. No wonder the German commanders made such good use of the terrain at Metz, for since the time they were cadets they studied every aspect of 1870 battle that was fought here.

It was then on to Fort Driant. Not quite knowing what to expect when I got there, I then set out for the location of the most dramatic—and tragic—scene of the Metz campaign. Finding the road that led to Driant was itself a challenge, as the area is completely unmarked. I finally was on a winding narrow road up a steep hill, and figured I was on the right path. It turned out that this was the actual wartime supply road to the back end of the fort. About halfway up to the summit, a large barricade blocked further vehicle traffic. Although some posted signs beckoned otherwise, I continued on toward the fort on foot. It took another thirty minutes of steep climbing before I found myself at a bridge over the moat that marked the main entrance to the expansive fortress. The moat and heavily fortified entrance were about the only readily visible indicators to the strength of this fortification. Once seen first hand, it's difficult to find the adjectives to give a reader the sense of power and scope commanded by Fort Driant.

Spread over 350 acres on the top of a small mountain and built to hold a force of 2,000 defenders, the vast majority of Fort Driant is underground. The whole purpose of the fort was to defend its five batteries of three 100-mm and 150-mm guns each. Once inside, the fort seems to virtually melt into the terrain. However, symbols of the battle are everywhere. Thick fields of barbed wire protected the four main batteries inside the fort. While most of the wire is gone, the thousands of metal posts that held it together still remain upright. I began my exploration of Driant on the southwest corner, where, on October 3, 1944, B Company of the 11th Infantry attacked and penetrated into the center of the fort. From the outside, there is no way the GIs could have had any appreciation to the futility of their mission. Rather than a solid wall, the exterior of the fort was defended by series of strong and well-camouflaged bunkers that interlocked machine gun fire. Standing in the bunkers and observation posts where the Germans met this attack, I was amazed that the company-sized force was even able to make it through the initial defenses.

From here, I followed the path of B Company to Barracks #3. After walking through tall grass and shrubs, I found myself on the roof of the barracks. The exterior side of the barracks is integrated into the landscape. On the interior portion, the length of the barracks is visible as a large four-story building. It is here that a GI dropped some bangalore torpedoes down a ventilation shaft that gained the Americans entry into the maze of tunnels that run under the fort. This began the subterranean nightmare battle that lasted over one week. The histories of World War II contain countless episodes of horrific combat conditions, but I can imagine none worse than was faced by the American and German soldiers battling in the tunnels of Fort Driant in October of 1944. A large segment of the exterior of Barracks #3 lays in ruin, as it was blown apart by American engineers in the last stages of the October battle. While I suppose it may be possible to crawl into an opening and look for some evidence of the tunnels below, I did not give it a second's consideration, realizing the danger of a sudden drop into a dark void. That realization gave me even more appreciation for the courage of the American infantrymen who jumped in there knowing they would be facing a fanatical enemy fighting to the death.

Continuing a few hundred more yards south, I came across the barbed wire posts that protected the four interior gun batteries. Each battery contained three heavily armored, parabolic steel turrets that housed a large caliber cannon. The turrets of each battery are on an enormous rectangle of concrete. All of the twelve cannon in the fort remain in place, still silently pointed in the direction of the XX Corps lines. The barrels of the guns are surprisingly stubby, a feature which allowed the turrets to be retracted when not firing. On close inspection, I could see a series of small nicks on the turrets, evidence of the minuscule damage that direct hits of the strongest American artillery shells and bombs could inflict. All around the turrets I found razor sharp chunks of shrapnel, fragments of the many tons of ordnance fired and dropped on the fort. One item I came across was a blunted armor-piercing solid shell that had been fired from a tank. This must have come from one of the six Sherman tanks that made it to the fort only to be abandoned on retreat.

There was a lot of other debris from the battle still in the fort. Such things as gasoline cans, commo wire and spools, and rusted pieces of assorted equipment remain scattered about. I suddenly noticed dusk was falling and could not believe that several hours had passed as I tried to make sense of this most chaotic of battlesites. I remember it being a powerful and almost eerie moment to stand alone and realize the drama and sacrifice that occurred in this massive fortress. I still had a long walk to make it back to my car and it was completely dark by the time I reached it.

The next day I had another full agenda. I planned on covering the ground of the mid November offensive above Thionville, visiting the Lorraine U.S. Military Cemetery, stopping at key locations of the XX Corps Saar-Moselle Triangle campaign, and then driving home to Bonn. I got an early start and first hit the mid-sized industrial town of Maizieres les Metz. In October 1944, XX Corps artillery blasted Maizieres to pieces as the 90th Infantry Division used the attack on the town as a sort of urban fighting training exercise. I found the location of the city hall that marked the strong point for the German defense. Maizieres was so badly destroyed in the battle that seemingly few pre-war era buildings still exist.

From Maizieres I continued north and crossed over the Moselle at Thionville. Directly across the river from Thionville is the town of Yutz, and immediately on the east bank is a mid 19th Century fort. Although obsolete, it saw heavy fighting on November 11, 1944, and was a significant obstacle for the 95th Infantry Division. Today the fort is something of a monument, and I briefly stopped to examine it. Driving north on the east bank, I found the locations of the XX Corps crossings over the swollen Moselle on November 9, 1944, at Malling and Cattenom. The bunkers of Fort Koeingsmacher, which blocked the advance, are visible from the road but the large fort is inaccessible to the public. I continued a few miles northeast to Kerling, which was the vicinity where the 90th Infantry Division absorbed a German panzer attack. With the bridging behind them finally complete, American armor came up at the last minute to save the day and the bridgehead.

Although it was significantly out of the way for the next part of my trip, I felt compelled to visit the U.S. Military Cemetery of the Lorraine at St. Avold, about thirty miles east of Metz. I'm glad I made the detour, as our military cemeteries in Europe are powerful and poignant reminders of cost of the war. At the end of World War II, families of the deceased had the option of having the remains of their service members either sent home, or interred in the military cemeteries in France or Luxembourg (there are no US soldiers buried on German soil). About twenty percent of the families elected to keep their loved ones in the European cemeteries. I personally think they chose wisely, and I hope most of them had the opportunity to visit these places of honor. The cemeteries are meticulously maintained, and seeing the rows upon rows of markers gives one the impression that these soldiers are resting among comrades. St. Avold is the largest of all American World War II cemeteries and contains the graves of 10,489 soldiers and airmen, most of whom died fighting in the Lorraine. I had previously researched those members of the 7th FAOB who were killed in action, and had determined that Pvt. Harold Lorman was the only one in a European military cemetery. After stopping by the visitor's center, I was directed to the location of his grave, which was about midway in through the massive field. It was quite a long walk. Lorman was Jewish and his Star of David marker stood out distinctly from the predominate sea of simple white crosses. The marker read; HAROLD LORMAN, PVT 7 FA BN, NY, SEPT 27, 1944. I rendered a salute to him and all the other Americans buried there and left St. Avold with a deeper personal understanding to the cost of that war's victory.

From St. Avold I focused my attention away from the Metz and to the Saar-Moselle Triangle campaign, where for four months, XX Corps battled away trying to penetrate the mighty German West Wall defenses. The route to the battlefields took me past the tiny crossroad villages of Filstrof and Colmen, where the 7th FAOB and A Battery Headquarters were located during the campaign. At the time, I did not realize that my father's army photo collection has him posing in front of several buildings in Colman. Had I known that and had those pictures with me that day, I'm sure I could have found the same locations. I made a short side trip a few miles east and crossed over the German border at the Nied River into the town of Hemmersdorf. A Battery had briefly set up there until the Battle of the Bulge forced them to relocate back to France.

Traveling through back roads and farmland, I finally made it to the West Wall fortified area referred to as the Orscholz Switch. Just inside the German border, the area is unremarkable and unless you studied the history, you would never know such major battles had been fought there. I viewed with interest the towns of Tettingen-Butzdorf. Generally speaking, the Germans are meticulously neat and clean, and have long since eliminated most reminders of the Second World War. With a careful eye, you notice that there are no buildings in Tettingen-Butzdorf that seem to predate the war, a sure sign of the havoc that occurred in that bitter winter of 1945. Looking at the woods and hillside that surrounded the towns, I could appreciate first hand the tactical terrain advantage that the defenders held. I imagine that on closer inspection in the field and woods you could probably find evidence of the large concrete bunkers that comprised the West Wall. At that point I really didn't have the time for such detailed exploration and continued to drive the general length of the Switch line to get a feel for the natural strength of the positions.

From Orscholz, I followed the trace of the Saar River to my right and soon was in Saarburg. This area was the center of the XX Corps assault over the Saar River, and viewing the dramatically steep banks on either side helped underscore why this was such a difficult operation. To be honest, by this point in the trip I was starting to get "World War Two overload," and I began to allow my mind to better enjoy the sheer beauty of this spectacular wine country more than trying to imagine what went on in 1945.

There was still one more important destination point on my odyssey to track the 7th FAOB experience, and that was just ahead, the town of Lampaden. On March 6, 1945, the 7th FAOB suffered their most disastrous event of the war when the elite 6th SS Mountain Division overran an A Battery observation post in a surprise attack. The four-man OP was captured and a relief column was ambushed. Three 7th FAOB men were killed, one wounded, and eight taken prisoner. As the German attack continued, the A Battery Command Post in nearby Pellingen was also nearly overrun. Arriving from the south, I found Lampaden to be another nondescript Saar Valley town. Situated on a ridgeline with four roads running through it, I could see why it was selected for an OP and why it would be a priority objective for the German attack. Like many of the other towns I visited that saw heavy fighting in the war, most of the structures in Lampaden (which only consists of a few residential blocks) were relatively modern. On leaving Lampaden to head toward Pellingen, I'm sure I passed the spot where the ambush of the ill-fated patrol occurred. Like so many other small actions of the war, time has swallowed up the history of the specific spot a long time ago as both local people and veterans moved on with their lives.

It was now time for me to move on as well. I passed through Trier as quickly as the evening rush hour would allow, with home still a good three-hour drive away. My forty-eight-hour trip on the trail of the 7th FAOB's history was very rewarding. Due to my recent connection with a number of the battalion's veterans, my interest in the unit had gone beyond simply seeing where my father had served. As well as providing a unique opportunity to visualize the circumstances that I could only imagine, this trip brought forth a renewed appreciation of the distances, hardships, dangers, and dramas that unfolded in those fields and villages all those years ago.

My personal history trip aside, the story of the 7th Field Artillery Observation Battalion is less about the places they fought, but rather more about the sense of comradeship among the men who served. The war experience forged some incredibly strong ties among the battalion's members. In the years that immediately followed the war, many of the men kept in touch with their buddies in a series of 7th FAOB reunions. Gradually, the requirements of building new careers and raising families took the veterans' priority. The gatherings tapered off, and with a few exceptions, most of the men eventually lost contact with each other.

In the late 1980s, some of the men still in touch took the initiative to form a 7th FAOB Association. Starting from scratch, over one hundred veterans were eventually contacted, and annual fall-time reunions were held. The reunions are festive affairs that usually include several days of sightseeing activities ending with a banquet dinner and farewell breakfast. They have also become family events, with wives and other family members now outnumbering the veterans themselves.

A number of the wives told me that many of the vets tended to keep their war experiences quiet until they started to attend the reunions. Whether it was because of the reunions or due to some other compulsion, the men began to open up in a renewed willingness to discuss their wartime service. It seemed for the first several reunions that the men couldn't get enough of sharing army memories. With that cathartic process completed, the members now seem content to simply enjoy each other's company, raise a glass, sing old songs, and catch up on family events. Many of the men who didn't know each other during the war have become the closest of friends through the reunions. The attachment these men have for each other is obvious as they say their annual farewells. As of this writing, the youngest of the vets are now in their late seventies or early eighties. At the conclusion of each reunion, they part knowing that illnesses, travel challenges, and fate itself will likely bring fewer men to next year's roll call. There is a certain urgency to ensure that the legacy of the 7th FAOB lives on; which is in part a precept of this book.

The veterans of the battalion, perhaps partly as a result of what they gained from their experiences with the 7th FAOB, went on to achieve satisfying lives after the war. In writing about the post-war experiences of a company of paratroopers chronicled in *Band of Brothers,* author Stephen Ambrose had the following words to say. It is equally appropriate to summarize the members of the 7th Field Artillery Observation Battalion:

> They had character like a rock, these members of the generation born between 1910 and 1928. They were children of the Depression, fighters in the greatest war in history, builders of and participants in the post-war boom. They accepted a hand-up in the GI Bill, but never took a handout. They made their own way. A few of them became rich, a few became powerful, almost all of them built their houses and did their jobs and raised their families and lived good

lives, taking full advantage of the freedom they helped to preserve.[155]

A brief synopsis of some of the men that made this history come alive is presented in these final pages.

As the Third Army Commander, General George S. Patton Jr. achieved his ultimate lifetime ambition in commanding a victorious army in the world's greatest conflict ever. In his new role as the occupation commander for Barvaria, Patton had a difficult time in the transition to peacetime. Making life politically difficult for Eisenhower, Patton voiced a fierce anti-Soviet rhetoric to the press. He caused further friction by ignoring policy directives to bar former Nazi party members from holding any post-war government offices. In September 1945, the situation came to a head and Eisenhower relieved Patton of command of his beloved Third Army. Instead of commanding thousands of troops, a deeply discouraged Patton was relegated to an administrative position overseeing completion of the army's official history of the war's European operations. Patton was finally due to return back to the United States in mid-December, 1945. Just a few days before his scheduled departure from Germany, Patton sustained severe injuries when his staff car was involved in a vehicle accident in Mannheim. Paralyzed from the neck down, Patton died eleven days after the crash on December 21. He is buried in the U.S. military cemetery in Hamm, Luxembourg, and rests alongside many of the men he commanded.

Lt. General Walton Walker remained in the army and became the commanding general of the 8th Army during the first months of the Korean War. After the desperate and disastrous response to the North Korean invasion, Walker's stoic leadership and tactical finesse were key components in saving the Americans and their allies from a near catastrophic defeat. In an ironic footnote, Walker and Patton would share a common fate in their deaths. In Korea in 1950, Walker was also killed in a vehicle collision when an oncoming truck struck his jeep. He was on his way to decorate soldiers in an awards ceremony.

Lt. Col. James Schwartz was generally remembered by most of the vets as a hard-nosed disciplinarian. Don Slessman, one of his battery commanders, recalls that most of the officers would generally try to avoid him when they could. Perhaps because of his toughness and exacting standards, Lieutenant Colonel Schwartz deserves the ultimate gratitude of his soldiers. While the battalion did suffer combat losses, its casualty rate was surprisingly low, especially considering the ever-present dangerous conditions the men were constantly exposed to. Though part of that good fortune can be attributed to luck, it is also a sign of excellent leadership. Above all else, Schwartz was a stickler for details, a trait he ingrained in his subordinate leaders. From the exasperating inspections at Camp Shelby through his insistence that windshields and canvases be kept down in terrible weather, the men of the 7th FAOB developed a heightened sense of awareness. This characteristic undoubtedly kicked in when the men faced the greatest battlefield dangers, saving lives while still getting the mission accomplished.

One member of the battalion who eventually had the closest relationship with James Schwartz was former Staff Sergeant Stephen Wandzioch. Before being drafted in April 1941, Wandzioch married his high school sweetheart, fathered a baby, and worked for his family's bakery business. The army called on Stephen's baking experience and he served throughout the war as the mess sergeant for A Battery. Upon his discharge, he and his wife had another child and he became the manager for the bakery. Wandzioch kept in touch with James Schwartz after the war. Schwartz had left the active army (although he eventually became a full colonel in the reserves) and became a prosperous businessman. Dividing his time between Albany, New York, and Florida, Schwartz owned a large business enterprise that included large commercial properties in both States. Wandzioch came to work for him in 1961, and wrote of his post-war relationship with Schwartz and of his impressions on the man that few knew as well as he did:

Colonel Schwartz was a fine commanding officer, strict in a way, for he wanted to be proud of his men and for them to be the best unit in the army in all respects. A lot of the men couldn't see eye to eye with him and did not care for him. But I knew him as a very fine man, for I joined him in 1961 to manage his business property in Florida that consisted of a forty-room motel, restaurant, shopping center, liquor store, and a Phillips gas station. He let me run the business as if it were my own, and came up from St. Petersburg once a month or so. I enjoyed working for him for almost twenty years. In a way we became buddies and we would play golf and go bowling when he would come into town. He belonged to the local country club and since he was assessed a monthly fee for the dining room, he would say to me, "Wandzioch, as I have to pay for this, take your wife and have a dinner on me a couple of times each month."

In 1979, James Schwartz developed a brain tumor that led to his death several months later. Stephen Wandzioch continued to work for Schwartz's son for a time, and eventually retired in 1982. Wandzioch currently resides on a twelve-acre estate in Archer, Florida.

Master Sergeant Gerald Ballman came into the army as a college graduate with work experience at the General Motors plant in Dayton, Ohio. While with the 7th FAOB, Ballman became the Headquarters Battery Motor Sergeant. After his discharge from the army, he returned to GM in Dayton, where he became a supervisor in production engineering.

Staff Sergeant Robert"Bob" Geiges sent me his wartime service recollections on audiocassette. A native of Philadelphia, PA, Geiges worked as short order cook, assembler and inspector of fishing rods, and as a bus driver before being drafted in 1941. He was assigned to the 7th's Headquarters Battery where he eventually became the battery's supply sergeant. Geiges was married before his enlistment, and to help bridge their separation, both he and his wife prayed with rosary beads every night throughout the war. He credits this for helping him get through the trials and tribulations of army service and the war itself. Following the war, Geiges returned to Philadelphia, started a family, and resumed employment as a bus driver. When his own son was drafted and sent off to Vietnam, Geiges received a far better appreciation of the hardships that war casts on the parents of those sons serving in combat. Bob came home from work one day to find his wife highly distraught. Fearing the worst about his own son's fate, Bob learned that a close family friend had been killed in action in Southeast Asia. The tragedy brought home to Geiges the terrible worry that his own parents must have had while he was serving in Europe. He didn't find out about the post-war 7th FAOB Association until a decade after its creation and attended his first reunion in 2001. Geiges sums up his experience with the 7th: "In Germany I acquired a small religious plaque that I carried around in my pouch. I recently found it and had it translated, only then did I find its real meaning in 'God Protects You.' I believe it did. The battalion consisted of many fine men and the experience with them changed my life. I saw men at the last reunion that I hadn't seen in fifty-six years, I wish I found out about [the reunions] sooner. There was an excellent sense of teamwork among the battalion and it operated as many individual entities tied together by communications. It was a wonderful experience—as long as you came back."

Tom Delay had one year of college experience at Ohio Western before he entered the Enlisted Reserve Corps in December 1942. Trained as a radio operator, he was midway across the Atlantic when D-Day took place. First assigned to a replacement battalion, Tom joined the 7th FAOB just before the unit shipped out of England for France. During the war he served in the Headquarters Battery commo section where he became Lieutenant Colonel Schwartz's radio operator. When the war ended, Delay returned to college in Ohio, where he eventually completed law school. After working for his father's law practice, Tom served as a Jackson County prosecutor from 1961 to 1981. In December 1981, he was elected as county judge, a position he served until his partial retirement in 1991. At age seventy-nine, Delay still serves as a part-time judge throughout Ohio, where he takes special cases at the request of the state supreme court. Tom also still enjoys playing golf. He and his wife Lee have been married for fifty years and have three children and six grandchildren.

Henry "Hank" G. Lizak entered the army from Astoria, New York, where he had worked as a manager of the shipping and receiving department of Finlay Straus Jewelers in New York City. Rising to the rank of Tech 5, Lisak served in A Battery as a wireman, and later as the driver for the battery commander, Lt. Don Slessman. Lisak returned to New York after the war and spent a career as a sales representative and manager at a Lincoln Mercury and Cadillac dealership. Both his sons played Triple A Baseball. One son, Steven, became the CEO of Mikasa Inc., and his other son, Donald, is the Athletic Director at St. Joseph's College. In preparation for the first edition of this book, Lizak wrote: "The 7th is still alive and we meet each year in various parts of the country. Now our wives, sons, daughters, friends, and relatives come to be part of the strongest bond I have ever known. God Bless all these wonderful men who left their loved ones to serve our country. Combat brings out the best of men, being with honest God-fearing persons makes war bearable. Bill Rogge, Kurt Rieth, Dale Pleak, Lt. Don Slessman, Buzz Bennet and Sidney Wright are some of my best memories of my time in combat. Now in the twilight of my life I treasure the time with the living members of the 7th." The 7th FAOB Association lost a great friend and man when Hank Lisak passed away in February 2003.

One of Lizak's closest friends in the battalion was Tech Sergeant Kurt A. Rieth. Rieth was born in Germany in 1923, and when he was five years old, his family immigrated to America and settled in Cranston, Rhode Island. Growing up in a German-cultured family environment, he retained his German language skills, which he spoke with native-level fluency throughout his life. During the war, Rieth's German came in handy and he was frequently used as a translator for both the Battalion and A Battery commanders. When the war ended, Rieth returned to Rhode Island and back to his job at the Speidel Watchband Company. Working alongside his father, Rieth developed into a master toolmaker and later became a senior engineer in the design shop. He played a key role in the development of Speidel's famous "Twist-o-Flex" watchband and was employed by the company for forty-four years. Rieth married Marian Talley and had two daughters and one son. He died of cancer in 1985 at age sixty-two.

First Lieutenant Donald Slessman came from Fremont, Ohio and graduated from the Virginia Military Institute (Class of 1939). Almost all of the 156 graduates from this class saw service in the war and eleven of them were killed in action. Slessman joined the 7th FAOB in Camp Shelby after being transferred from a conventional field artillery unit. With the 7th Slessman was the B Battery flash officer until fall 1944 when he became the A Battery executive officer. A short while later he took command of the battery. With deep experience as a professional field artillery officer that predated the start of the war, Slessman was well qualified to command A Battery and his troops thought highly of him. The photo of Lieutenant Slessman depicted in this book (of him holding "King," the battery mascot) came from my father's collection. On the back of the photo my father wrote "Lieutenant Slessman, our last battery commander. He was good man." After the war, Slessman continued service in the army reserves back in Ohio. Tasked with organizing a firing battery, the only ordnance Slessman could acquire was one cannon scrounged from the Erie Proving Ground. Despite the lack of firepower, Slessman trained his men well and they excelled when they went to the firing range at Fort Knox. After two years in the reserves with his one-gun battery, Slessman finally had enough of the army. He then worked full time for the family food manufacturing business that his father started in 1905. As of 2003 (and at age eighty-six) Slessman is only just retired from his family business where he held the title of chairman for many years. When asked at the October 2003 reunion if he still plays golf, Don replied; "Not since the day before yesterday!" Slessman spends half the year in Fremont and the remainder in the Florida Keys.

Don Slessman retains fond memories of his dog King. Along with Slessman, King made the transition back to Fremont and became a perfect family pet, while retaining his wartime guard-dog instincts. Every morning King would escort Slessman's father on his daily walk to the factory. The dog would then return home to await the mailman, where he would accompany him on his rounds in order to protect him from other dogs. King's biggest contribution came the day when a vicious neighborhood dog escaped it's leash and charged Slessman's young daughter as she played in the front yard. King watched the scene unfold from inside the house. In a mighty leap, King burst through the screen door and intercepted the attacking dog just before it landed on his daughter. In an instant, King killed the dog with one mighty bite to it's head. Slessman has often pondered what may have happened had King not returned home with him from Europe.

T/5 Amos Robinson was a native of Gastonia, North Carolina, and was one of the original members of the battalion. He served with Headquarters Battery as a driver, and later as a medic. After the war, Robinson got out of the army, married Roy Barber's sister-in-law, Wilma, and went to business school in Memphis. He worked in Charlotte, St. Louis, Kansas City, and Los Angeles. Robinson was employed by the Northrop Aircraft Corporation for twenty-one years, and retired as the chief payroll accountant for over 18,000 employees. As brothers-in-law, Robinson and Corporal Roy Barber maintained probably the closest ties of any 7th FOAB members in the post-war years. From the days back with the Camp Shelby Choir, both were musically inclined, and they went on to jointly compose music that was accepted for the National Country Music Library in Nashville, Tennessee. Robinson writes: "Most, if not all the men and officers, of the 7th were great to get along with. We all became great buddies for the rest of our lives."

Before the war, Roy Barber was working on a Masters Degree in Physiology at the University of Illinois. With the 7th FAOB, medical technician Barber was the NCO medic-in-charge for A Battery. When the war ended, Barber became a psychiatrist and served at Veterans Administration hospitals in Memphis and Gulfport. Barber was a devoted husband to his wife, Oma, and remained by her side through her long battle with Alzheimer's disease. When she died in January of 2002, he composed the following song which chronicled their courtship through the war, and which was featured in the local Memphis newspaper:

I knew right from the moment I saw you, I'd like to change your name to mine.
The night you touched my hand, I was in heaven. The right words were so hard to find.
We said our love would last forever. We'd be faithful sweethearts through all kinds of times.
We took the Frisco train to Memphis, but then the army said, "Get in line."
While I was training hard in Louisiana, among snakes and ivy vines.
You did your part making weapon spark plugs, but our love seemed so out of time.
Thank God before I shipped for England, we arranged that day out in the Ozark hills.
How sweet your lips amid the haystack. So warm your love among the daffodils.
The U-boat stalked our fifty-three ship convoy, our Navy did a noble thing.
One Corvette took the enemy torpedo. Sailors died—for them I'll sing.
Then forming up the great Third Army, we drove Nazis back across the Seine and Rhine.
We freed those still alive at Buchenwald. Surrender terms the Nazis soon signed.
I wondered if our love could last this war through. A guy back home said you'd been true.
So when the war was over and I'm homeward bound, I wrote I'd like to marry you.
Although your welcome home was quite pleasant, our romance has always had a long-time view.
Now fifty-six years or so thereafter, I still am glad of long time love for you.

In remembering his service with the 7th FAOB, Barber states: "I found in the 7th Field Artillery Observation Battalion a warm cooperative association with men from all parts of the USA. Each section highly respected the work of the other and encouraged them. Happily this friendly association has continued years after World War II."

Until he was drafted, PFC John French worked as a printer in Milwaukee, Wisconsin. He served as an observer in B Battery's flash section during the war. When he returned home, French went back into the printing business and for twenty-five years ran a small printing company as president and part owner. Today he resides in Naples, Florida.

Before the war, Jess R. Grisham was a bookkeeper at a food processing plant in Manteca, California. In the 7th FAOB he was assigned as private first class to a survey section with Headquarters Battery. When the war ended, Grisham went to further his education in the agricultural field, and became an inspector of agricultural produce. He was appointed commissioner of agriculture in Siskiyou County, California, where he retired in 1980. Jim and his wife have traveled extensively, and visited the capitals of all continental forty-eight states by car.

Edward Miller (who after the war changed his name from Piatkowski) came from Forest City, PA. Prior to enlisting, Miller worked at a restaurant and bar. With A Battery during the war, Tech 5 Miller served at various times as a cook, flash observer, and battery clerk. Like many other vets following the war, he took advantage of the GI Bill and went to college, graduating from the University of Scranton in 1951 with a degree in business administration. He served as a manager of a Social Security office in upstate New York. He worked with the Social Security Administration for thirty-three years.

Tech-5 Ed Shock entered the army from a farm family in Missouri. As well as being a farmer, Ed also learned something about carpentry, which resulted in his being assigned as the Headquarters Battery carpenter. He spent much of the war in a truck riding alongside Robert Geiges. In speaking of his post-war career, Ed writes: "….When I returned home, there was a great need for housing for all returning soldiers, so I resumed my building career. I owned Shock Construction Company and built homes all around the mid-Missouri area. After forty-five years in the construction business, I was forced to retire due to health." Ed still resides in Missouri.

Like the author, Al Yoder, son of Lt. Marlin Yoder, took a deep interest in his father's World War II experiences after his father had passed on. Yoder provided me with a lot of parallel research on the unit, as well as information on his father. An ROTC graduate from Purdue, Lt. Marlin Yoder was initially assigned to the 286th FAOB. In the Saar campaign, his battery was temporarily assigned to 7th FAOB control. Lieutenant Yoder was transferred to the 7th in the later months of the war, where was assigned to Headquarters Battery. He stayed with the battalion up to the time of its deactivation at Camp Gruber. After the war, Marlin Yoder became a civil engineer and project manager, residing in Auburn, Indiana.

Jim Royals left the army and returned to Georgia to be reunited with his eighteen-year-old wife and two year old son. Unfortunately, he found that the separation caused by the war, as well as their young ages, had caused too much strain and that marriage ended in divorce. Jim latter remarried and went on to have a successful career and family life. Sadly, Jim lost his youngest son in a tragic accident (at age 18), and more recently, his beloved wife Wilma in 2003. " Royals writes: "My oldest son finished high school and served in the army. He now lives a short distance from us. He demonstrates his love for us daily and I thank God neither of us had to give all for his country." I have three grandchildren and one great-grandchild. Jim now lives in Garden City, Georgia. He is a past president of the 7th Field Artillery Observation Battalion Association and remains one of its most active members. Reflecting on military service, Royals sums up some common sentiments that most of his comrades would likely agree on: "I hope my accounts [presented in this book] will portray my true feelings of my love for the country we live in. I pray for peace and harmony and that all wars will cease. Freedom is not free. I am a World War II veteran and am thankful for my country and have many good memories to cherish."

The April 27, 1945, edition of "Seekers News" features Charles "Charlie" Wright as the battalion's "character of the week." Many years later, it would seem that distinction still holds. Wright joined the army from Evansville, Indiana, and transferred into the 7th FAOB from the 87th Infantry Division. Charlie served with B Battery during the war. After his discharge, Charlie did well in the grocery business and as a housing contractor. A service-related medical problem temporally set him off-track, but Wright recovered and went to work as a machinist and shop supervisor with International Harvester, Servel and Bendix Westinghouse. The Wright's had five children, and Charlie's wife of fifty years passed away in 1994. Wright has had a lifelong passion for auto racing where he built and maintained his own equipment that he races in oval tracks and drag strips. In 1963, he built a Hot Rod Roadster that won a bevy of national car awards. He now spends a lot of time with his two late model Corvettes that he still likes to race. Wright is the current serving President of the 7th Field Artillery Observation Battalion Association and has long since been its "poet laureate." He has written two poetry books in the last decade, and regales the association with touching poems during each reunion.

One of Wright's best works, "Boys," aptly captures a veteran's reflection to the days they were young soldiers. It is a fitting tribute to those that served, and especially, those who did not return.

BOYS

For the better part we were just boys
Mixed in with a few young men
Most of us had never been away from home
The shock of Dec 7 changed that
Never will we forget those famous words
Greetings from your friends and neighbors
What the hell they didn't care
We were just so many names
Of course if dad was big time
Some how your name didn't come up
But for the true blue American boys
Some one had to go that was us
We were sent to the four corners of the world
Times were tough but so were we
Better than the rest for we were free
Now many years have passed away
Those of us remaining are old and gray
But in the many far off lands
Are the Boys we lost along the way
Never aging they will always be boys

Chas J. Wright
06-04-02

Awards

Croix de Guerre

Gerrow, Arthur F.

Schwartz, James P.

Bronze Star

Albrinck, Leonard J.
Altman, Norbert W.
Anderson, Clayton O.
Assman, Paul R.
Bahr, Walter G.
Ballman, Gerald J.
Barber, Roy W.
Battistelli, John
Bennett, Caulie, Jr.
Bidwell, Bert A.
Bone, David M.
Bowden, Charles
Callahan, Daniel J.
Carlton, George H.
Carpenter, Raymond A.*
Casadonte, Anthony V.
Castanza, Domenic A.
Chabalowski, Louis C.
Chandler, Keith B.
Clark, Alva J.*
Clark, Richard A.
Clem, Marshall E.
Clements, John T.
Close, Malcolm R.
Cloud, Everett C.
Dressler, Joseph
Ezinga, Claude R.
Fogel, Paul E.
Fouquet, August W.
Fraser, Henry M.
Fuhrman, David E.
Gerrow, Arthur F.
Gingerelli, Joseph
Hartley, Frank J.
Henry, William J.
Hilzinger, Walter R.
Horton, Lyman P.
Jessel, William C.
Knox, Harold E.
Kopp, Raymond S.
Leftheris, Leon N.
Little, Don D.
McGarry, Garry J.
Martin, Charles L.
Meyer, Benjamin C.
Mongiovi, Albert J.
Montemarino, Daniel P.
Murphy, Vincent
O'Brien, Howard E.
O'Laughlin, Michael J.
O'Malley, Francis S.
Ostensen, Koore
Ostrum, Charles R.
Ottersen, Leif
Palmer, Arthur E.
Patterson, Willie
Peterson, Donald B.
Randle, Howard K.
Riccolo, Frank
Roeske, Virgil F.
Rogers, Alton B.
Rogge, William E.
Rutledge, James M.
St. Romain, Layward J.
Salinas, Stephen
Sargood, Burton H.
Schwartz, James P.
Siebels, Robert H. (2)
Skelton, John M.
Slessman, Donald B.
Spielberg, Milton
Sprague, William T.
Story, Harold L.
Strous, Samuel D.
Tatro, Stanley M.
Taylor, Eugene
Taylor, Jack
Tetro, Dominic
Tucker, Malchia, Jr.
Turner, Richard I.
Wandzioch, Stephen F.
Wardell, Samuel*
Weaver, Roy, Jr.
Webb, Vernon H.
West, Jack J.
Whipple, Charles J.
Wright, Jesse B.
Wright, William B.
Yoches, William A.
Yourkavitch, Charles E.
Ziobro, Theodore H.
Zygarowski, Joseph

Purple Heart

Arnaiz, Charles B.
Bone, David M.
Carey, John L.
Carlton, George H.
Del Bello, Louis S.
De Girolamo, Frank A.
Elnick, William
Golden, Raymond H.
Hicks, William B.
Jenkins, Charles T.
Landry, Alfred A.
Little, Don D.*
Miller, William T., Jr.
Moore, Daniel
Mullins, Tennis
Ostrowski, Walter E.
Paulsen, Lester J., Jr.
Schaaf, Robert J.
Snarr, Elbert B.
Souliere, Herve J.
Welch, Wesley
Williams, Joseph W.
Woods, Michael J.

Certificate of Merit

Ballman, Gerald J.
Duffey, John F.
Ruggiero, Antonio F.
White, Leo W.

Commendation

Bowden, Charles
Chandler, Keith B.
Clark, Richard A.
Schwartz, James P.

* Also received Oak Leaf Cluster

Roster of the 7th Field Artillery Observation Battalion

This roster records the post-war hometowns (as of late 1945) for the battalion's members.

Officers

Charles Bowden
    Allston, Massachusetts
Martin C. Beavers
    Washington, D.C.
Walter A. Barlow
    Plainview, Texas
Robert J. Brearton
    Schenectady, New York
Henry M. Burkgart
    Monroe, Louisiana
Keith B. Chandler
    Oak Ridge, Tennessee
Richard A. Clark
    Oklahoma City, Oklahoma
Louis E. Cryder
    Kingston, Ohio
Raymond Carpenter
    Washington, D.C.
Harold A. Delp
    Washington, D.C.
Louis S. Del Bello
    Forrestville, New York
Walter Dmytryk
    Northampton, Massachusetts
Fearn Field
    Rockville, Maryland
Warren S. Frank
    Luray, Virginia
George E. Gladding
    Urbana, Illinois
Basil E. Gravatt
    Washington, D.C.
Archer F. Freund
    Ft. Bragg, North Carolina
Edward S. Goetz

        East Gary, Indiana
John W. Gott
        Whitwell, Tennessee
Robert H. Grady
        Raleigh, North Carolina
Clark S. Evans
        Washington, D.C.
Robert E. Elliott
        Dallas, Texas
William H. Freeman
        Washington, D.C.
Jack B. Harper
        Chicago, Illinois
Maurice Horowitz
        Washington, D.C.
Monroe Heidicorn
        Mt. Vernon, New York
Louis C. Hengst
        Woodlawn, Texas
William J. Henry
        Arlington, New Jersey
Benjamin Hecht
        Washington, D.C.
Robert C. Johnson
        Westfield, New York
Stuart G. Jillson
        Washington, D.C.
Frank L. Johnson
        Hammond, Louisiana
Richard L. Hull
        Tulsa, Oklahoma
George J. Hawkins
        Decatur, Illinois
Howard Hoffmeister
        Wauwatosa, Wisconsin
Floyd B. Kelsey
        Roanoke, Indiana
Robert C. Kurt
        Washington, D.C.
Kenneth R. Koboldt
        St. Louis, Missouri
Thomas F. LaVanway
        Villa Park, Illinois
Joseph A. Malloy
        Chicago, Illinois
Harold E. Meyer
        Elgin, Illinois
James R. Maddox
        Memphis, Tennessee
Reed Huff
        Salt Lake City, Utah
John J. McDonald
        Washington, D.C.
Theodore K. Morse
        New York, New York
Edward J. McGaw
        New York, New York
Don. Dale Little
        College Station, Texas
Hugh P. Osborne
        Washington, D.C.
Koore Ostenson
        Brooklyn, New York
Charles E. Ofenstein
        Fort Smith, Arkansas

Robert E. Panke
        La Crosse, Wisconsin
Donald B. Peterson
        Woodbine, Iowa
Vivian F. Powell
        Washington, D.C.
Robert M. Rohrberg
        Hempstead, New York
Virgil F. Roeske
        Deer Creek, Minnesota
Douglas H. Smith
        Washington, D.C.
Kenneth F. Schenkle
        Washington, D.C.
Nicholas G. Stadtherr
        Washington, D.C.
James P. Schwartz
        Ithaca, New York
Harold R. Story
        Brooklyn, New York
Leon T. Scarbrough
        Bryson City, N.C.
William T. Sprague
        Hagerstown, Maryland
Donald B. Slessman
        Fremont, Ohio
Robert J. Smith
        Fostoria, Ohio
Hugh A. Skinner
        Yates City, Illinois
Warren S. Sockwell
        Huntsville, Alabama
George E. Tucker, Jr.
        Rome, Georgia
William M. Trible
        Washington, D.C.
Lloyd A. Van Duesen
        Waukegan, Illinois
Frank B. Wolcott
        Washington, D.C.
Bowman T. Whited
        Washington, D.C.
John Wilson, Jr.
        Washington, D.C.
Frank C. Whittelsey
        Washington, D.C.
Charles J. Whipple
        Chicago, Illinois
William A. Wackernagel
        Millville, N.J.
Cecil Y. Wright
        Hattiesburg, Mississippi
Marlin D. Yoder
        Auburn, Indiana
William A. Yoches
        Peoria, Illinois
John G. Zur Schmiede
        New Albany, Indiana
Elmer J. Kaehler
        Washington, D.C.
James B. Zahner
        Kansas City, Missouri

Enlisted Personnel

Abelio, Donald S.
        Chicago, Illinois
Agneta, Antonio N.
        New York, New York
Ainsworth, Winford L.
        (No address given)
Albrinck, Leonard J.
        Cincinnati, Ohio
Almerico, Leo L.
        Tampa, Florida
Altman, Norbert W.
        New Bavaria, Ohio
Alter, Albert D.
        Manchester, New Hampshire
Alarcon, Alfrcd
        New York, New York
Ames, Richard E.
        Auburn, Indiana
Anfuso, Nunzio
        Long Branch, New York
Anthony, Harry R.
        Maplewood, Ohio
Aschan, Reino E.
        New York, New York
Assman, Paul R.
        Cincinnati, Ohio
Allred, Paul C.
        Oak Ridge, North Carolina
Almieda, Manuel
        Plymouth, Massachusetts
Alpers, Kenneth E.
        Maplewood, New Jersey
Anderson, Clayton O.
        Cape Elizabeth, Maine
Anderson, William E.
        Baltimore, Maryland
Anderson, James W.
        Westwood, Massachusetts
Andreini, Aldo A.
        Newark, New Jersey
Andrews, James P.
        Brooklyn, New York
Arany, Alex
        Youngstown, Ohio
Arim, Maurice J.
        Detroit, Michigan
Arnaiz, Charles B.
        Graniteville, Vermont
Arnold, Guy W.
        (No address given)
August, Lawrence
        Rockaway, New Jersey
Bagsby, Julius R.
        Old Hickory, Tennessee
Balli, Walter T.
        Bellevue, Ohio
Ballman, Gerald J.
        Dayton, Ohio
Banton, Ernest J.
        Baltimore, Maryland
Barnes, David T.
        Little Rock, Arkansas

John K. Rieth

Barrett, John J.
    Dover, New York
Battistelli, John
    New Bedford, Massachusetts
Bauler, Franklin N.
    Chicago, Illinois
Beavers, Vernon E.
    Durham, North Carolina
Belcher, Alexander D.
    Havaco, West Virginia
Bella, Andrew J.
    Dayton, Ohio
Bennett, Caulie, Jr.
    Ridgeland, South Carolina
Bennett, Ernest H.
    Nashville, Tennessee
Bethea, Alton
    Dillon, South Carolina
Biedrzycki, Edward H.
    Scranton, Pennsylvania
Birney, Clarence H.
    Powell, Wyoming
Bishop, Elmer D.
    Johnson City, Tennessee
Bitticks, William A.
    Walnut Hill, Illinois
Blackwelder, Daniel A.
    Cincinnati, Ohio
Boisky, Lloyd
    Athens, Georgia
Bone, David N.
    Decatur, Illinois
Bostwick, Calvin H.
    Cortland, New York
Brady, Jay E.
    Ada, Oklahoma
Braunstein, Rubin
    Bronx, New York
Brennan, Clarence E.
    St. Louis, Missouri
Brown, Claude F.
    Three Rivers, Michigan
Brown, James K.
    Lonaconing, Maryland
Bullock, George A.
    Reading, Ohio
Burgamy, Lawrence
    Lamesa, Texas
Burris, Basil E.
    Elden, Missouri
Butler, Howard C.
    Mason City, Iowa
Byrd, John H.
    Erie, Pennsylvania
Babb, Earnest
    Campbello, South Carolina
Bahr, Walter G.
    Bluffton, Missouri
Baier, Charles, Jr.
    Howard Beach, New York
Baker, Carl
    Ignacio, Colorado
Bannister, Geoffrey H.
    New Brunswick, New Jersey

Barber, Roy M.
    Cape Girardeau, Missouri
Barlow, Carson E.
    Dayton, Ohio
Barnard, Floyd B.
    Albany, Ohio
Barrall, Robert J.
    Nanticoke, Pennsylvania
Bartos, Henry D.
    East Barnard, Texas
Bastian, Richard J.
    Burbank, California
Battistelli, John
    New Bedford, Massachusetts
Beasley, Hal J.
    Sylva, North Carolina
Begley, Justus E.
    (No address given)
Bella, Andrew J.
    (No address given)
Bennett, Henry R.
    Tupelo, Mississippi
Benson, Russell E.
    Hartford, Connecticut
Bereswill, Wilfred F.
    St. Louis, Missouri
Bermes, Donald M.
    Streator, Illinois
Berzonsky, Norman J.
    Bakerton, Pennsylvania
Bethune, Clyde E.
    Pittsburgh, Pennsylvania
Brutler, Howard A.
    Milwaukee, Wisconsin
Bitticks, William A.
    (No address given)
Blake, Anerson C., Jr.
    Pocahontas, Mississippi
Blankenship, J. J., Jr.
    Birmingham, Alabama
Blascak, George W.
    Springfield, Massachusetts
Blessing, William W.
    Harrisburg, Pennsylvania
Boesch, Robert C.
    Forrest Hills, New York
Bolem, Donald W.
    Albany, Ohio
Bosi, Bruno E.
    Brooklyn, New York
Bottomley, Jack H.
    Greystone, Rhode Island
Boucher, Gerrard M.
    Manchester, New Hampshire
Boulware, Barrett
    Allendale, South Carolina
Bradley, Frank L.
    Philadelphia, Pennsylvania
Brannock, James R.
    Essex, Missouri
Bratcher, Paul L.
    Smithville, Tennessee
Brandier, Henry L.
    Newark, New Jersey

Brown, Edward P.
    Miami, Florida
Byram, Samuel T., Jr.
    Washington, D.C.
Burke, James A.
    Baltimore, Maryland
Burrell, Paul R.
    Bronx, New York
Carbal, Manuel
    Providence, Rhode Island
Callahan, Daniel J.
    Woodside, New York
Capp, Edward
    New York, New York
Carey, John L.
    Waterbury, Connecticut
Carlton, George H.
    Wauchula, Florida
Carpenter, Raymond A.
    Sprakers, New York
Casadonte, Anthony V.
    Philadelphia, Pennsylvania
Castanza, Domenic A.
    Garfield, New York
Castriotta, Ralph
    Brooklyn, New York
Caswell, Harold A.
    Haverhill, Massachusetts
Caouette, Alfred F.
    Greenville, New Hampshire
Chase, Dennis J.
    Vassalboro, Maine
Clarkson, James F.
    Clifton Heights, Pennsylvania
Clem, Marshall E.
    Wellington, Illinois
Clements, John T.
    Narberth, Pennsylvania
Chrisop, Marle A.
    Geneseo, Illinois
Cohen, Frank
    Philadelphia, Pennsylvania
Colarossi, Ralph
    Corona, New York
Cole, Ben W.
    Lake City, South Carolina
Cooper, Donald F.
    Short Hills, New York
Cooksey, Lynn E.
    Kansas City, Missouri
Condron, Joseph G.
    New Hartford, Connecticut
Cosko, William C.
    Donora, Pennsylvania
Cox, Joe B.
    Gary, Indiana
Currier, Roland L.
    Douglas, Wyoming
Cali, Frank A., Jr.
    New Orleans, Louisiana
Campanella, Parry R.
    Rumson, New Jersey
Card, George A.
    Gladwin, Michigan

Carney, James A.
    Terre Haute, Indiana
Carter, Roscoe F.
    Lyme, New Hampshire
Cecilli, Guy
    Lynn, Massachusetts
Centura, Joseph J.
    Chicopee, Massachusetts
Chabalowski, Louis C.
    Chicago, Illinois
Chaffer, Donald M.
    Brooklyn, New York
Chin, James P., Jr.
    New York, New York
Chism, Andrew R.
    Springfield, Illinois
Ciolek, Alex
    Detroit, Michigan
Cirincione, Samuel L.
    Buffalo, New York
Clark, Alva J.
    Bronson, Michigan
Clemmensen, Alan A.
    Chicago, Illinois
Close, Malcolm R.
    Murraysville, Pennsylvania
Cloud, Everett C.
    Columbus, Ohio
Clover, Clarence W.
    Steelville, Missouri
Cockrell, Virl E.
    Danville, Illinois
Coco, Charles J.
    Brooklyn, New York
Cohen, Nathaniel L.
    Rockaway Beach, New York
Compton, Floyd M.
    Trumansburg, New York
Cook, Albert J.
    Montrose, Georgia
Corsi, Louis J., Jr.
    Cleveland, Ohio
Crawford, John D.
    Anawalt, West Virginia
Creekpaum, Norwood S.
    Omaha, Nebraska
Crouch, Ben T., Jr.
    Columbia, South Carolina
Culley, Robert J.
    Cresson, Pennsylvania
Cusano, Angelo A.
    New Haven, Connecticut
Cushma, Edward L.
    Passaic, New Jersey
Czarnecki, Roy F.
    Chicago, Illinois
Damiano, Walter F.
    New York, New York
Daniels, Joseph H.
    Memphis, Tennessee
Day, Doyle R.
    Grove, Oklahoma
Deatherage, W.
    Artesia, New Hampshire

De Michele, Joseph
    Darby, Connecticut
Demott, Michael J.
    Newark, New York
Dilette, Anthony F.
    New York, New York
Dombrowski, Edward J.
    Brooklyn, New York
Downey, Patrick
    Brownstown, Indiana
Doyle, Sylvester
    Jacksonville, Florida
Ducote, Florien T.
    Bunkie, Louisiana
Duffey, John F.
    Scituate, Massachusetts
Duke, Robert G.
    Nashville, Tennessee
Daidone, James T.
    Passaic, New Jersey
Dale, Donald A.
    Chicago, Illinois
Dallman, Robert A.
    Milwaukee, Wisconsin
Daniell, Jeff W.
    Cadwell, Georgia
Daniel, Ralph R.
    Concord, North Carolina
Daniels, George L.
    Springdale, Pennsylvania
Davis, Archie Y.
    Colorado Springs, Colorado
Dawson, Jerome
    Wellsboro, Pennsylvania
Day, Doyle R.
    Grove, Oklahoma
De Forest, Charles A.
    Warren, Pennsylvania
De Girolamo, Frank A.
    Brockton, Massachusetts
De Lay, Thomas S.
    Jackson, Ohio
De Michele, Joseph
    (No address given)
Deeg, Frank H., Jr.
    Glendale, New York
Devore, William R.
    Hollidays Cove, West Virginia
Dickinson, Langdon T.
    Detroit, Michigan
Diorio, John
    Glenside, Pennsylvania
Dokulil, Milton J.
    Omaha, Nebraska
Donat, Joseph
    Boston, Massachusetts
Dougherty, Deo W.
    Hawley, Pennsylvania
Dougherty, James J.
    Newark, New Jersey
Dowden, Ralph L.
    Baltimore, Maryland
Drane, Robert R.
    Harrisburg, Missouri

Dressler, Joseph
    Brooklyn, New York
Duffy, Thomas M.
    Richmond, Virginia
Edwards, John J.
    Allentown, Pennsylvania
Elgersma, Sam
    Primghar, Iowa
Erickson, John B.
    Portland, Oregon
Eskinazi, Joseph B.
    New York, New York
Essary, John R.
    Tazewell, Tennessee
Estes, Charles F.
    Greenville, South Carolina
Ezinga, Claude R.
    Grand Rapids, Michigan
Eggleston, Kenneth P.
    Wilmerding, Pennsylvania
Eldredge, Robert H.
    Niagara Falls, New York
Elijah, George G.
    Seattle, Washington
Elliott, Graydon W.
    Coldwater, Michigan
Elnick, William
    Bronx, New York
Elsperman, William H.
    Sikeston, Missouri
Elsrode, Eugene E.
    Kansas City, Missouri
Evans, Thomas J.
    Camden, New Jersey
Evans, Robert R.
    Chester, Pennsylvania
Everson, Harold A.
    Keyport, New Jersey
Fagan, Thomas J.
    Bronx, New York
Fancher, Edward L.
    St. Louis, Illinois
Fancher, Howard L.
    St. Louis, Illinois
Fehr, Albert L.
    Freeport, Illinois
Ferdna, Walter
    Lakeview, New York
Floyd, Homer H.
    Almont, Michigan
Filan, Thomas F.
    Orange, New Jersey
Finnegan, Edward J.
    Middletown, New York
Forte, Michael F.
    Brooklyn, New York
Fouquet, August W.
    Rochester, New York
Fowler, William E.
    Brooklyn, New York
Fox, Andrew L.
    Statesville, North Carolina
Fraser, Henry M.
    Nyack, New York

John K. Rieth

Freedman, David
　Bronx, New York
Friedman, Meyer
　New York, New York
Fulco, Salvatore N.
　Hartford, Connecticut
Fuller, Harold E.
　Hardwick, Vermont
Fuller, William B.
　Anderson, South Carolina
Fura, John W.
　Lockport, New York
Fallon, Joseph R., Jr.
　Boston, Massachusetts
Fancher, Edward L.
　(No address given)
Feibel, Harry W.
　Bronx, New York
Feichtel, John S.
　Stiles, Pennsylvania
Felts, Clarence M.
　Nashville, Tennessee
Finnell, John M.
　Corning, Tennessee
Fisher, William L.
　Richmond Hill, New York
Flaherty, Harry F.
　Boston, Massachusetts
Fleischman, Joel S.
　Forrest Hills, New York
Fogel, Paul E.
　Freeport, Illinois
Foulkes, Emery R.
　(No address given)
Franklin, William D.
　Great Falls, South Carolina
Freed, John A.
　Providence, Rhode Island
Freedman, Chester J.
　Millinocket, Maine
French, John G.
　Milwaukee, Wisconsin
Friedman, Ralph
　New York, New York
Fuhrman, David E.
　York, Pennsylvania
Gamble, Leslie G.
　Elsmere, Delaware
Gaudet, Joseph R.
　Andover, Massachusetts
Gamrin, Abraham
　Roxbury, Massachusetts
Gelfman, Milton
　Brooklyn, New York
Gentile, Pasqual W.
　Brooklyn, New York
Gerrow, Arthur F.
　Upper Darby, Pennsylvania
Giesh, Flavian X.
　Seneca Falls, New York
Gillilland, Earl T.
　Mound City, Missouri
Gingerelli, Joseph
　Nutley, New York

Glennon, Lawrence T.
　Kansas City, Missouri
Godsey, Dennis W.
　Nickelsville, Virginia
Goens, Elwood
　Waynesburg, Kentucky
Golden, Raymond H.
　Friendsville, Pennsylvania
Goldstein, Samuel H.
　Peabody, Massachusetts
Gordon, Paul H.
　Davis City, Iowa
Gorecki, Frand
　Hudson, New York
Goodman, Abraham
　New York, New York
Goodman, Joseph
　Philadelphia, Pennsylvania
Grabowski, Michael S.
　Cleveland, Ohio
Griffin, Delbert N.
　Winston-Salem, North Carolina
Groman, Walter
　Camillus, New York
Guerrero, Robert B.
　Needle, California
Gunter, John A.
　Fayetteville, North Carolina
Galbreath, Albert W.
　Seneca, Georgia
Gallo, Angelo C.
　New York, New York
Gamble, James E.
　Sparta, Tennessee
Gehenio, Francis H.
　(No address given)
Geiges, Robert H.
　(No address given)
Gengler, Gordon C.
　Delphos, Ohio
Gentile, Pasquale W.
　(No address given)
Gessner, Wyman E.
　(No address given)
Gies, Walter A.
　Detroit, Michigan
Gigliotti, Thomas, Jr.
　(No address given)
Gilbert, Andrew E.
　Seattle, Washington
Goodwin, George E.
　Norwood, Connecticut
Gos, Robert C.
　Fulton, New York
Gour, William A.
　Butler, Pennsylvania
Grady, William P.
　(No address given)
Graham, William F.
　Pomaria, South Carolina
Grande, Carmen J.
　Hastings-on-Hudson, New York
Green, Stanley M.
　New York, New York

Grisham, Jess R.
　Manteca, California
Hagan, Edward A.
　New York, New York
Hagen, Howard E.
　St. James, Minnesota
Haines, Marion D.
　Louisville, Kentucky
Haines, Clyde L.
　Tacoma, Washington
Hall, Charles H.
　Brooklyn, New York
Hall, John C., Jr.
　Houston, Texas
Hampton, Anton E.
　Elsie, Nebraska
Hampton, Harold D.
　Jacksonville, Florida
Hansen, Walter M.
　Haddonfield, New Jersey
Hannum, Fred J.
　McKeesport, Pennsylvania
Hard, Aven A., Jr.
　Denver, Colorado
Harding, Thomas J.
　Syracuse, New York
Harris, Bradford E.
　Hartford, Connecticut
Hartley, Frank J.
　New Orleans, Louisiana
Hasenjager, William C.
　Chicopee Falls, Massachusetts
Hasselbach, Donald E.
　Euclid, Ohio
Hatley, John H. M.
　Ryegate, Vermont
Haust, Merle L.
　Romulus, New York
Hawkins, Robert J.
　Milwaukee, Wisconsin
Heard, Joseph E.
　Itta Bena, Mississippi
Helton, John W.
　(No address given)
Herman, Edwin
　Ness City, Kansas
Herman, Henry G.
　Sloan, New York
Herod, Clarence J.
　San Antonio, Texas
Hershkowitz, Morris
　Bronx, New York
Hicks, Dorsey F.
　Preston, Maryland
Hicks, Everett C.
　Madison, New Jersey
Hicks, William R.
　Caldwell, Georgia
Hildenbrand, Christian
　Coatesville, Pennsylvania
Hillery, Henry L.
　(No address given)
Hitchens, George W.
　(No address given)

PATTON'S FORWARD OBSERVERS

Hilzinger, Walter R.
    Brooklyn, New York
Hinman, Fred S.
    Horton, New York
Hoag, Wilbur E.
    Albany, New York
Hockaday, Frank J.
    Butte, Montana
Hogue, Elmer F.
    Kansas City, Missouri
Hukill, Martin R.
    Wilmington, Delaware
Holm, William D.
    Minneapolis, Minnesota
Holmes, Horace F.
    Birmingham, Alabama
Horton, Lyman P.
    Greenwich, Connecticut
House, Walter W.
    Hornell, New York
Howard, Clinton S.
    Rupert, Idaho
Howard, John H.
    Syracuse, New York
Hoyt, Dana R.
    Jamestown, New York
Humphreys, Teddy
    Meriden, West Virginia
Huntley, Frank E.
    Waterville, Maine
Hynson, James R.
    Wilmington, Delaware
Holloway, Russell O.
    Rothville, Missouri
Holt, Arthur H.
    Chicago, Illinois
Hopson, Fred S.
    Dolores, Texas
Hoskins, Louis
    MacArthur, Ohio
Houldin, Robert F.
    Spring Valley, New York
Hudson, James H.
    Greenwood, South Carolina
Huebert, Robert E.
    Buffalo, New York
Huffaker, Edward W.
    Knoxville, Tennessee
Huffman, Walter V.
    Alamosa, Colorado
Hughes, James R.
    Spartanburg, South Carolina
Hyatt, Albert T., Jr.
    Wilmington, Delaware
Ingber, Solomon
    Far Rockaway, New York
Inman, Jack C.
    Spartanburg, South Carolina
Itjen, Fred W., Jr.
    Astoria, New York
Iwanski, Jerome P.
    Cheektowaga, New York
Ingram, James C.
    Cleveland, Mississippi
Jarratt, Jack
    Marshfield, Missouri

Javor, Peter J.
    Chicago, Illinois
Jessel, William C.
    Buffalo, New York
Joeris, Fred B.
    Abilene, Texas
Jones, Frank C.
    Danville, Illinois
Jones, Horace, Jr.
    Niagara Falls, New York
Jones, John C.
    South Bend, Indiana
Jones, William T., Jr.
    Detroit, Michigan
Josephson, Joseph
    Bronx, New York
Joyeusaz, Armand J.
    Atlantic City, New Jersey
Jachetta, Joseph J.
    San Francisco, California
Jackson, Verner H.
    San Francisco, California
Jarrell, Jack
    Logan, West Virginia
Jenkins, Charles T.
    (No address given)
Johnson, Ernest A.
    (No address given)
Johnson, Robert M.
    Portland, Oregon
Johnson, Harold S.
    Woodhull, Illinois
Joyce, Lawrence B.
    (No address given)
Joyner, Marvin J.
    Mannsville, New York
Jurgens, James J.
    Mansfield, Ohio
Kanar, Arthur C.
    Syracuse, New York
Katz, George I.
    Tenafly, New Jersey
Karpman, Irvine I.
    Bronx, New York
Kelley, Robert E.
    Toledo, Ohio
Kessler, Harold
    Brooklyn, New York
Kutniewski, Stanley J.
    Central Falls, Rhode Island
Kinsella, Hugh J.
    Troy, New York
Kneipp, Frederick J.
    New Orleans, Louisiana
Koerschner, Walter E.
    Peninsula, Ohio
Koon, W. W.
    Pomaria, South Carolina
Kopp, Raymond G.
    Syracuse, New York
Kougasian, Peter
    Yonkers, New York
Kozak, Jred J.
    New York Mills, New York
Kramer, Julius
    Brooklyn, New York

Kreutz, Charles L.
    Norwood, Ohio
Kruger, Arnold A.
    Coronado, California
Kuntz, Ellsworth P.
    Philadelphia, Pennsylvania
Kuznicki, Thaddeus T.
    Dunkirk, New York
Karcher, Edward A.
    Roseburg, Oregon
Kawalec, Zygmunt A.
    Chicopee, Massachusetts
Kebbe, Dean R.
    Detroit, Michigan
Kedenburg, Richard H.
    Brooklyn, New York
Keefe, William R.
    Cincinnati, Ohio
Kelley, Carmon T.
    Sharon, Tennessee
Kelly, Gerald J.
    Brooklyn, New York
Kenderdine, William H.
    Perkasie, Pennsylvania
Kenderick, Merril C.
    Covina, California
Kernaghan, Jeremiah J.
    Philadelphia, Pennsylvania
Kidd, Fred W.
    Bluefield, West Virginia
Kierce, James T.
    Brooklyn, New York
Kliebert, Mark F.
    Vacherie, Louisiana
Knauf, Robert E.
    Chilton, Wisconsin
Knox, Harold E.
    Medicine Lodge, Kansas
Koerschner, Walter E.
    Peninsula, Ohio
Kolodzik, Emil W.
    Middletown, Ohio
Koon, W. W.
    Johnson, South Carolina
Kozminski, Benedict A.
    Grand Rapids, Michigan
Kossuth, Gary J.
    Basking Ridge, New Jersey
Kozma, Kenneth J.
    Bronx, New York
Kramer, Julius
    Brooklyn, New York
Kreishrimer, C. R.
    Cleveland, Ohio
Kruger, Arnold A.
    Coronado, California
Kusterman, William
    New York, New York
Kutch, Basil
    Passaic, New Jersey
Lang, Leo G.
    Olean, New York
Langston, Jerome B.
    Spartanburg, South Carolina
Landry, Alfred A.
    Manchester, New Hampshire

John K. Rieth

Lappin, James B., Jr.
　　Cleveland, Ohio
Lefstein, Harold
　　Bronx, New York
Leroy, Abram A.
　　Seneca, South Carolina
Leshinsky, Nathan
　　Brooklyn, New York
Lewis, Franklin B.
　　Orange, Connecticut
Lisanti, Donato D.
　　Bronx, New York
Link, Cecil E.
　　Charlotte, North Carolina
Lindwall, Lars E.
　　Brooklyn, New York
Lindsey, William E.
　　Baton Rouge, Louisiana
Lorman, Harold
　　Rockaway Beach, New York
Lockwood, Paul M.
　　Elkland, Pennsylvania
Love, John W.
　　Chicago, Illinois
Lungo, Angelo J.
　　Montclair, New Jersey
Lyon, Fred
　　Chicago, Illinois
Lyons, Charles J.
　　Cheektowaga, New York
La Frenz, John P.
　　Jamaica, New York
La Marca, Carl J.
　　Bronx, New York
Lane, Robert G.
　　Mt. Juliet, Tennessee
Larkin, Michael J.
　　Kingston, New York
Lauffer, Paul F.
　　(No address given)
Lawson, Edward J.
　　Medford, Massachusetts
Le Vance, Alonzo M.
　　Toms River, New Jersey
Leftheris, Leon N.
　　Farrell, Pennsylvania
Legg, Lawrence D.
　　Lafayette, Indiana
Lescow, Ernest J.
　　Jersey City, New Jersey
Leswing, Phillip R.
　　Willow Grove, Pennsylvania
Letendre, Fernand J.
　　Manchester, New Hampshire
Lewis, Thomas A.
　　Union City, New Jersey
Libby, Lester K.
　　Kidonville, Maine
Lizak, Henry G.
　　Astoria, New York
Lococo, Thomas
　　Pittsburgh, Pennsylvania
Logan, William A.
　　Seneca, South Carolina

Lokken, Robert M.
　　Appleton, Wisconsin
Loste, Robert D.
　　Ogden, Utah
Lubay, Charles J., Jr.
　　North Braddock, Pennsylvania
Lunsford, Dave N.
　　Timberlake, North Carolina
Maher, Walter J.
　　New Haven, Connecticut
Malinowski, Boleslaw
　　Frackville, Pennsylvania
Maney, Linwood C.
　　Burnsville, North Carolina
Martin, Charles L.
　　Livingston, Tennessee
Martin, William J.
　　Galeton, Pennsylvania
Marinucci, Albert A.
　　Cleveland, Ohio
Masone, Peter J., Jr.
　　Waterbury, Connecticut
May, Leon S.
　　Charleston, West Virginia
Mays, Harold H.
　　New Castle, Delaware
Maturo, John J.
　　New Haven, Connecticut
Mathus, John
　　Jersey City, New Jersey
Matteoli, Italo F.
　　Stockton, California
McCann, Donald M.
　　Charleroi, Pennsylvania
McCox, Howard V.
　　Brooklyn, New York
McCutcheon, Louis W.
　　Charleston, South Carolina
McDonald, John A.
　　St. Louis, Missouri
McGahee, Robert F.
　　Chickasaw, Alabama
McGauhey, Hugh A.
　　New York, New York
McGinnis, Raymond E.
　　Memphis, Tennessee
McIntire, Richard J.
　　Akron, Ohio
Maull, William T.
　　Charleston, South Carolina
MacDonald, Hayden G.
　　Chicago, Illinois
Meeks, Milner B.
　　Limona, Florida
Mercer, Gerald A.
　　Bolivia, North Carolina
Metzger, Robert C.
　　Cleveland, Ohio
Meyer, Albert A.
　　Ashland, Pennsylvania
Miller, Donald O.
　　Portland, Maine
Miller, Kenneth E.
　　Wheeling, West Virginia

Miller, William T., Jr.
　　Pittsburgh, Pennsylvania
Minton, David L.
　　Macon, Georgia
Mistretta, Joseph J.
　　Peabody, Massachusetts
Mitchell, Raymond R.
　　Kingston, New York
Mucha, Joseph M.
　　Chicago, Illinois
Murphy, Vincent R.
　　Wilmington, Delaware
Murphy, William A. P.
　　Bronx, New York
Muzyczka, George M.
　　Plainfield, New Jersey
Moore, Daniel F.
　　Westminster, South Carolina
Mongiove, Albert J.
　　Cheektowaga, New York
Montemarano, Daniel F.
　　Olyphant, Pennsylvania
Morris, Howard T.
　　Georgetown, Delaware
Montgomery, Barton L.
　　Monmouth, Illinois
Moses, Robert
　　Newton, North Carolina
Moul, Marcus D.
　　Erie, Pennsylvania
Mroz, George E.
　　Cleveland, Ohio
Macaluso, Alfred E.
　　Lodi, New Jersey
Maki, Benhart T.
　　Franklin Mine, Michigan
Makosky, Charles A., Jr.
　　(No address given)
Manalili, Vincent J.
　　Brooklyn, New York
Martin, Charles L.
　　Livingston, Tennessee
Mason, John F.
　　Cleveland, Ohio
Massias, Gustav T.
　　Chicago, Illinois
Matteoli, Italo F.
　　Stockton, California
Mattern, Clarence A.
　　(No address given)
Mature, John J.
　　New Haven, Massachusetts
McAvoy, Bernard F., Jr.
　　Joplin, Missouri
McCaffrey, Daniel J.
　　Philadelphia, Pennsylvania
McCaffrey, Walter C.
　　Long Beach, New Jersey
McCombs, Nelson
　　Dixiana, Alabama
McGarry, Garry J.
　　New York, New York
McGrath, Joseph W.
　　Cincinnati, Ohio

McIntire, Richard J.
    Akron, Ohio
McKean, Richard E.
    Muscatine, Iowa
Menefee, David T.
    Washington, D.C.
Meyer, Benjamin C.
    Belleville, Illinois
Meyer, Henry E., Jr.
    Pond Eddy, New York
Michael, Sidney
    New York, New York
Montgomery, Robert W.
    Willow Grove, Pennsylvania
Moschiano, Samuel L.
    Rochester, New York
Mulford, Paul H.
    Wellsboro, Pennsylvania
Mullins, Tennis
    Harts, West Virginia
Munson, Glendy J., Jr.
    New Orleans, Louisiana
Murray, Joseph
    Pepin, Wisconsin
Murray, George N.
    Port Huron, Michigan
Musen, Harold L.
    (No address given)
Muzzall, Warren C.
    Memphis, Tennessee
Nadler, Milton
    Cleveland, Ohio
Nastri, Frank
    Brooklyn, New York
Nessler, Jacob A.
    Bronx, New York
Napier, Carl
    Whitesburg, Kentucky
Neal, James F.
    Woodville, Texas
Newell, Harry V., Jr.
    Cameron, Missouri
Nicastri, Vito
    New York, New York
Noble, Richard S.
    Inglewood, California
North, Carl O.
    Pocatello, Idaho
Nutter, Belmont E.
    Monessen, Pennsylvania
O'Laughlin, Michael J.
    Worcester, Massachusetts
Olson, Lawrence R.
    Far Hills, New Jersey
O'Neal, Kenneth P.
    Pine Prairie, Louisiana
O'Neal, John J.
    Buffalo, New York
Orbach, Martin A.
    Astoria, New York
Osgood, Clair W.
    Olean, New York
Ostensen, Koore
    Brooklyn, New York

Ostrow, Harry
    New York, New York
Ostrowski, Walter E.
    Lowville, New York
Otwell, Quinton
    Winnsboro, Louisiana
Over, James D.
    Roaring Spring, Pennsylvania
O'Brien, Howard E.
    Easton, Maryland
O'Connor, Timothy P.
    Buffalo, New York
O'Malley, Francis S.
    Port Austin, Michigan
O'Shaughnessy, John J.
    Seaford, New York
Ostrum, Charles R.
    Nunda, New York
Ottersen, Leif
    Duluth, Minnesota
Pace, Frank J.
    New York, New York
Palm, Gustav B.
    Brooklyn, New York
Pappadopoulos, Constantinous
    New York, New York
Paschal, Donald I.
    Fayetteville, North Carolina
Patterson, Willie
    London, Kentucky
Paulsen, Lester D., Jr.
    Mason City, Iowa
Paragallo, Frank J.
    Brooklyn, New York
Payne, Lewis E.
    Skyland, Ohio
Peabody, Raymond A., Jr.
    Waterford, Connecticut
Peck, Jackson S.
    Wilmington, Delaware
Peck, James H.
    New Rochelle, New York
Peters, Walter J.
    Yonkers, New Jersey
Peterson, John
    (No address given)
Petrovits, John P.
    Torrington, Connecticut
Phelps, Sydney G.
    Swanton, Vermont
Piatkowski, Edward J.
    Forrest City, Pennsylvania
Pilon, Romeo A.
    Hartford, Connecticut
Pistilli, Michael P.
    Syracuse, New York
Pobieglo, Mattthew P.
    Chicopee Falls, Massachusetts
Pollock, Howard M.
    Peoria, Illinois
Pollack, Harold G.
    Brooklyn, New York
Pope, Angelo M.
    Chicago, Illinois

Poeter, Albert E.
    Syracuse, New York
Posadni, Matthew S.
    Rochester, New York
Powell, John D.
    Hickory, North Carolina
Powers, Herbert
    Patterson, New Jersey
Powers, Joseph E.
    Middle Village, New York
Primgeola, Antonio
    New York, New York
Purfuerst, Erich F.
    Garfield, New York
Pyritz, Harold F.
    Rochester, New York
Pacheco, Joseph
    Tiverton, Rhode Island
Palmer, Arthur E.
    Irvington, New Jersey
Patterson, Willie
    London, Kentucky
Pattison, Robert G.
    Staples, Minnesota
Pellicoiaro, Vito J.
    Brooklyn, New York
Percey, Fred T., Jr.
    Rutland, Vermont
Perrino, Raymond P.
    Bronx, New York
Perrino, Joseph J.
    Bronx, New York
Peterson, Jerome O.
    (No address given)
Peters, Howard A.
    (No address given)
Pickett, Herbert I.
    Chattanooga, Tennessee
Pillar, Walter W.
    Brooklyn, New York
Platt, Gary S.
    Los Angeles, California
Pleak, Dale E., Jr.
    Indianapolis, Indiana
Pooley, Douglass W.
    Jackson Heights, New York
Prescott, Paul L.
    Harrisburg, Pennsylvania
Pfretzloff, Glen F.
    Cleveland, Ohio
Prewitt, James H.
    Burkesville, Kentucky
Puczylowski, Joseph P.
    Milwaukee, Wisconsin
Puhr, John J.
    Independence, Missouri
Purdy, Bernard J.
    Brooklyn, New York
Quinn, William G.
    Salem, Massachusetts
Raico, Joseph F.
    New York, New York
Randle, Howard K.
    Rensselaer, Indiana

John K. Rieth

Rapp, Frederick
    Troy, New York
Raymond, Chester A.
    Teaneck, New Jersey
Redmond, Clayton A.
    Bangor, Maine
Reed, Claude
    Alma, West Virginia
Reid, Carl
    Easley, South Carolina
Rentachler, Mames R.
    Louisville, Kentucky
Rick, George J.
    Buffalo, New York
Ritchie, Dewey A.
    Thomasville, North Carolina
Robinson, Amos Q.
    Gastonia, North Carolina
Rubbiero, Antonio R.
    Brooklyn, New York
Rutledge, James M.
    Fairfield, Alabama
Rabinouitz, Leo
    Dorchester, Massachusetts
Radosky, Michael S.
    Chicago, Illinois
Rainey, Henry
    Big Clifty, Kentucky
Ramsay, Robert L.
    Berlin, New Hampshire
Randle, Howard K.
    Rensselaer, Indiana
Rank, Donald A.
    Antigo, Wisconsin
Rankin, Leonard E.
    Estesburg, South Carolina
Rathyen, Raymond
    Bayonne, New Jersey
Rau, Theodore S.
    Louisville, Kentucky
Ray, Daniel D.
    Peabody, Massachusetts
Ray, Ezra A.
    Decatursville, Tennessee
Reina, Joseph A.
    Buffalo, New York
Riccolo, Frank
    Dwight, Illinois
Richardson, Alvin C.
    Lawrence, Kansas
Rieth, Kurt A.
    Cranston, Rhode Island
Rivers, Glenn E.
    Maplewood, Missouri
Roach, Leo E.
    Cleveland, Ohio
Rogers, Alton B.
    Hendersonville, Tennessee
Rogge, William E.
    Wabash, Indiana
Roll, Richard A.
    West Allis, Wisconsin
Rollins, Howard E., Jr.
    Springfield, Massachusetts
Romanowski, Felix E.
    Detroit, Michigan
Rose, Robert H.
    Birmingham, Alabama
Rosner, Max
    Bronx, New York
Royals, James W. E.
    Brunswick, Georgia
Rudy, Edward
    Patton, Pennsylvania
Russo, Cataldo M.
    Waynesburg, Pennsylvania
Ryan, John J.
    Cleveland, Ohio
Rydbeck, Edwin H.
    Chicago, Illinois
Salinas, Stephen
    Ft. Worth, Texas
Salamy, Victor J.
    Brooklyn, New York
Sarafinski, Edward J.
    Palo Alto, California
Sargood, Burton H.
    Hanover, Massachusetts
Santoro, Joseph
    Bronx, New York
Scarbrough, James P.
    Fristoe, Missouri
Schaaf, Robert J.
    Kent, Ohio
Schaeper, Joseph G.
    Cincinnati, Ohio
Schereck, Charles
    Chicago, Illinois
Scheiterle, Edward M.
    Olean, New York
Schmicker, John F.
    Philadelphia, Pennsylvania
Schroeder, Edward H.
    Shrub Oak, New York
Schultz, Robert L., Jr.
    Syracuse, New York
Schwoeppe, Noble E.
    St. Matthews, Kentucky
Serritella, Victor W.
    Chicago, Illinois
Setzer, Marcus
    Hickory, North Carolina
Sfreddo, Alfred R.
    Stafford Springs, Connecticut
Shand, Charles F.
    Richmond, New York
Sheinkopf, Joseph
    Bronx, New York
Sherrin, Marvin R.
    Pageland, South Carolina
Shibler, Earl L., Jr.
    Lake Lynn, Pennsylvania
Siebels, Robert H.
    Peoria, Illinois
Simonse, Alphense P.
    Newark, New York
Simonelli, Edward
    Brooklyn, New York
Skelton, John M.
    Oakland City, Indiana
Smith, Curtis E.
    Fort Smith, Arkansas
Smith, Donald E.
    Corning, Ohio
Smith, John D.
    Brookford, North Carolina
Smith, Robert D.
    Fayetteville, North Carolina
Smith, Victor V.
    Battle Creek, Michigan
Snarr, Elbert B., Jr.
    Strasburg, Virginia
Snyder, Charles L.
    Baltimore, Maryland
Soch, Robert A.
    Fredonia, New York
Solomon, Jerome
    Detroit, Michigan
Somers, Norman
    Bronx, New York
Souliere, Herve J.
    Fall River, Massachusetts
Spicer, John H.
    Montgomery, Alabama
Spielberg, Hilton
    Long Island City, New York
Starkel, Adolph G.
    West Hartford, Connecticut
Strausbaugh, Eugene R.
    Chillicothe, Ohio
Stone, Henry
    Brighton, Massachusetts
Stewart, Lonnie C.
    Dickson, Tennessee
Strous, Samuel D.
    Chillicothe, Ohio
Stonebrook, Elmer V.
    Cleveland, Ohio
St. Romain, Layward J.
    Plaucheville, Louisiana
Sutera, Joachim T.
    New Orleans, Louisiana
Sutliff, Arthur R.
    Caldwell, New Jersey
Swasey, Joseph J., Jr.
    Albany, New York
Szymonik, Max J.
    Holyoke, Massachusetts
Sabre, Paul W.
    Billerica, Massachusetts
Saczawa, Henry J.
    Chicopee, Massachusetts
Sanford, Dorsey D.
    Greensboro, North Carolina
Sargood, Burton H.
    Hanover, Massachusetts
Scallon, Edmund T.
    St. Albans, New York
Schereck, Charles
    Chicago, Illinois
Schum, John J., Jr.
    Clinton, Connecticut

PATTON'S FORWARD OBSERVERS

Scott, George B.
    Anderson, Indiana
Semon, George
    Jacobs Creek, Pennsylvania
Sennett, Francis J.
    Madison, Wisconsin
Setter, Urban F.
    Pueblo, Colorado
Severns, Claudie L.
    Santa Rosa, California
Shafran, Sidney
    Morristown, New Jersey
Shagam, Solomon
    Chicago, Illinois
Shand, William J.
    Bala Cynwyd, Pennsylvania
Shaver, Arthur J.
    St. Louis, Missouri
Shinkle, David A.
    Painesville, Ohio
Shock, Edward M.
    Columbia, Missouri
Skinner, Vincent B.
    Bristol, Connecticut
Small, Walter H.
    Portland, Maine
Smith, Victor V.
    Battle Creek, Michigan
Smith, Grady D.
    Trumann, Arkansas
Smith, Franklin H.
    Bay City, Michigan
Smith, Curtis E.
    Ft. Smith, Arkansas
Snyder, Frederick E.
    York, Pennsylvania
Solomon, Jerome
    Detroit, Michigan
Solomon, Herschel
    New York, New York
Stamm, William
    Ozone Park, New York
Starrett, George A.
    Detroit, Michigan
Stasiowski, Fred A.
    Chicopee, Massachusetts
Stegeman, Thomas C.
    Lima, Ohio
Steinman, Benjamin
    Philadelphia, Pennsylvania
Stephens, Richard N.
    Clarksburg, Ohio
Stewart, Lonnie C.
    Dickson, Tennessee
Storms, Russell W.
    Hawthorne, New Jersey
Sullivan, Samuel
    Washington, North Carolina
Surges, Carroll J.
    Milwaukee, Wisconsin
Sweenie, Robert C.
    Lincoln, Nebraska
Swisher, Ernest, Jr.
    Gladstone, New Jersey

Szczygielski, John S.
    Cleveland, Ohio
Tabor, Stanley W.
    Burlington, Vermont
Talbott, Wilson O.
    Mt. Vernon, Ohio
Talley, Joe E.
    Greensboro, North Carolina
Tallman, Simon E.
    Marion, Ohio
Tansey, Francis M.
    Albany, New York
Tash, Harold
    Washington, D.C.
Trucer, Carl J.
    Kirkwood, Missouri
Taylor, Eugene C.
    Akron, Ohio
Taylor, Jack
    Chapel Hill, North Carolina
Tennison, Robert G.
    Pruitt, Arkansas
Tench, Leonard F.
    Alloy, West Virginia
Teska, Bernard E.
    Milwaukee, Wisconsin
Tetro, Dominic
    Mt. Vernon, New York
Thomas, Harry B.
    Milford Center, Ohio
Tigner, Armon R.
    Asheville, Ohio
Tkachuk, John
    Peabody, Massachusetts
Tobin, Richard F.
    Cleveland, Ohio
Tolliver, William F.
    Maynardville, Tennessee
Tomlin, Edward W.
    West Lake, Ohio
Trabulsi, Louis E.
    Fairview, New Jersey
Trammell, Hogan D.
    Lexington, Kentucky
Tricarico, Joseph J.
    Brooklyn, New York
Tucci, Mark J.
    Cleveland, Ohio
Tucker, Malchia, Jr.
    Columbus, Georgia
Tuckey, Richard C.
    Newcastle, Maine
Turnbull, Frederick A., Jr.
    Brooklyn, New York
Turner, Richard I.
    Columbia, South Carolina
Turturro, Andimo
    Watertown, New York
Tansky, Arthur R.
    Mamoroneck, New York
Tatro, Stanley M.
    Albany, New York
Taylor, Lewis G.
    Adolphus, Kentucky

Taylor, Robert J.
    Poughkeepsie, New York
Thompson, Elwood M.
    Chicago, Illinois
Tice, Frank E.
    Toms River, New Jersey
Tkachuk, John
    Dedham, Massachusetts
Trepkus, Benedict
    Barre Plains, Massachusetts
Trickey, Stanley W.
    Toledo, Ohio
Truex, George R., Jr.
    Red Bank, New Jersey
Tupac, George J.
    Chisolm, Minnesota
Ujczo, Emeric F.
    Cleveland, Ohio
Ulis, Max
    Chicago, Illinois
Urschalitz, Charles A.
    Findlay, Ohio
Ursem, William A.
    Cleveland Hts., Ohio
Untied, James E.
    Frazeysburg, Ohio
Unger, William E.
    Smithsburg, Maryland
Uniacke, John F.
    Mamoroneck, New York
Urban, Andrew J.
    Bronx, New York
Van Auker, Arthur W.
    Mansfield, Ohio
Valentine, Lawrence D.
    Belleville, Ohio
Van Reen, Frank
    Hawthorne, New Jersey
Van Voorhis, Charles A.
    Yonkers, New York
Vedder, Howard B.
    Hunter, New York
Veeck, Andrew H.
    Malverne, New York
Valasquez, Vincent F.
    Kansas City, Kansas
Venturi, Peter
    Newark, New Jersey
Vlahakis, Costas
    Stamford, Connecticut
Vodila, Edward
    Passaic, New Jersey
Vogelsang, Arthur A.
    New York, New York
Vander Heyden, D. P.
    Belle Plaine, Iowa
Vinceslio, Nicholas P.
    Astoria, New York
Vought, Robert L.
    Aurora, West Virginia
Waldman, Leo
    Long Island City, New York
Walsh, William J.
    Bronx, New York

Walkerm, James D.
    North Caldwell, New Jersey
Wandzioch, Stephen F.
    Buffalo, New York
Wangel, Martin
    Brooklyn, New York
Ward, George W.
    Campaign, Tennessee
Wardwell, Samuel
    Rochester, New York
Warren, Wiley E.
    Murfreesboro, North Carolina
Was, Geza
    Columbia, Ohio
Wass, Harland W.
    West Buxton, Maine
Werver, Roy, Jr.
    Cranesville, New York
Weaver, Willfred
    Marion, Ohio
Webb, Vernon H.
    Pinetops, North Carolina
Weizer, Andrew J.
    Cleveland, Ohio
Weissman, Joseph S.
    New York, New York
Weisswange, Albert H.
    New York, New York
Welch, Wesley E.
    Ballston Spa, New York
Wells, Charles H., Jr.
    Shelby, North Carolina
West, Jack J.
    Columbus, Ohio
Wheeler, Tom I.
    Chester, South Carolina
White, Leo J.
    Fall River, Massachusetts
Williamson, William C.
    Holbrook, Massachusetts
Wilson, Nolan W.
    Kingston, Ohio
Wilson, Ralph I.
    Cuyahoga Falls, Ohio
Winfrey, Calvin
    Brumley, Missouri
Wisniewski, Edward
    Cleveland, Ohio
Wright, Jesse B.
    Knoxville, Tennessee
Wright, William H.
    Fort Worth, Texas
Wollenberg, Merlin J.
    Lexington, Ohio
Woods, Matthew F., Jr.
    St. Louis, Missouri
Woods, Michael J.
    New York, New York
Woolum, James M.
    Akron, Ohio
Waddell, Rufus C.
    Durant, Mississippi
Waddington, Stanley A.
    Patterson, New Jersey

Ward, George W.
    Champaign, Tennessee
Warthen, Sylvester R.
    Hazel Park, Michigan
Webb, Orley
    Sparta, Tennessee
Webb, William D.
    Guin, Alabama
Weidler, Homer C.
    St. Louis, Missouri
Weigel, Harry A.
    Johnstown, Pennsylvania
Wesler, Paul L.
    West Hartford, Connecticut
Westenzweig, Nathan
    Brooklyn, New York
Weyer, Hugo W.
    (No address given)
White, Leo W.
    Worthington, Iowa
Williams, Joseph, Jr.
    Fall River, Massachusetts
Williamson, William C.
    Holbrook, Massachusetts
Williams, Clarence B.
    (No address given)
Williams, Henry J.
    Chelsea, Alabama
Winsper, Roy T.
    Cleveland, Ohio
Woods, Ernest A., Jr.
    St. Joe, Arkansas
Wright, Sidney
    Monks Corner, South Carolina
Wright, Charles J., Jr.
    Evansville, Indiana
Young, Daniel E.
    Buffalo, New York
Youngs, John A.
    Asheville, North Carolina
Yates, Howard R.
    Worcester, Massachusetts
Yourkavitch, C. E.
    Fleetwood, Pennsylvania
Zaic, Albin
    Ridgewood, New York
Zaino, Ralph
    Brooklyn, New York
Ziebro, Theodore H.
    Cheektowaga, New York
Zlotkowski, Marion
    Brooklyn, New York
Zot, Frank C.
    Austin, Pennsylvania
Zuccarelli, Frank F.
    Trenton, New Jersey
Zehring, William R.
    Kokomo, Indiana
Zettle, Frank S.
    Berwick, Pennsylvania
Zimmerschied, Elmer J.
    Cole Camp, Missouri
Zmitrovich, Joseph I.
    Hazleton, Pennsylvania

Zummo, Anthony L.
    Brooklyn, New York
Zuniga, Joe
    Chicago, Illinois
Zygarowski, Joseph
    Holyoke, Massachusetts

ENDNOTES

[1] D'este, Patton, a Genius for War, 605.

[2] Matloff, American Military History, 419.

[3] American Heritage, World War Two, 397.

[4] Sawicki, Field Artillery Battalions of the U.S. Army, Volume 1, p. 15.

[5] D'este, Patton, a Genius for War, 398.

[6] The U.S. Army General Board, Field Artillery Observation Battalions in Combat, 7.

[7] American Heritage, World War Two, 397

[8] Marinello, On the Way: Patton's Eyes and Ears on the Enemy, 11.

[9] Blair, Clay, Hitler's U-Boat War, the Hunters, 1942-1945, Modern Library, NY, 2000 edition. All of Blair's references to the U-Boat attack are from pages 510-512. Additional information on the USS Donnell and U-473 were obtained from various internet sources.

[10] Kemp, The Unknown Battle: Metz, 1944, 13.

[11] Schmidt, XX Corps Operations. 13-14..

[12] Kemp, The Unknown Battle: Metz, 1944, 13.

[13] Schmidt, XX Corps Operations. 16.

[14] Ambrose, Citizen Soldiers, 84

[15] Marinello, On the Way: Patton's Eyes and Ears on the Enemy, 17.

[16] Kemp, The Unknown Battle: Metz, 13.

[17] D'este, Patton, a Genius for War, 3-4.

[18] Ibid, 627.

[19] Ibid, 636.

[20] Schmidt, XX Corps Operations. 50.

[21] Ibid, 60.

[22] Ambrose, Citizen Soldiers, (a number of references from page 92-106 on the closing actions of the Normandy campaign are consolidated in this footnote.)

[23] The U.S. Army General Board, Field Artillery Observation Battalions in Combat, 1.

[24] Marinello, On the Way: Patton's Eyes and Ears on the Enemy, 39.

[25] Gabel, The Lorraine Campaign

[26] Marinello, On the Way: Patton's Eyes and Ears on the Enemy, 27.

[27] The U.S. Army General Board, Field Artillery Observation Battalions in Combat, 6.

[28] Marinello, On the Way: Patton's Eyes and Ears on the Enemy, 221.

[29] Ibid, 103.

[30] Marinello, On the Way: Patton's Eyes and Ears on the Enemy, 40, 147.

[31] The U.S. Army General Board, Field Artillery Observation Battalions in Combat, 10.

[32] Marinello, On the Way: Patton's Eyes and Ears on the Enemy, 115.

[33] Ibid, 23.

[34] Ibid, 79.

[35] The U.S. Army General Board, Field Artillery Observation Battalions in Combat, 3.

[36] Schmidt, XX Corps Operations. 74.

[37] Ibid, 75.

[38] Eastman, XX Corps Artillery, p. 15.

[39] Schmidt, XX Corps Operations. 79.

[40] Marinello, On the Way: Patton's Eyes and Ears on the Enemy, 128.

[41] Ambrose, Citizen Soldiers, 114.

[42] Weigley, Eisenhower's Lieutenants, 329.

[43] Schmidt, XX Corps Operations, 122.

[44] Kemp, The Unknown Battle, Metz, 39.

[45] Ambrose, Citizen Soldiers, 63.

[46] Kemp, The Unknown Battle, Metz, 72-74.

[47] MacDonald and Mathews, Three Battles-Arnaville, Altuzzo and Schmidt, 9.

[48] Kemp, The Unknown Battle, Metz, 46-53.

[49] Schmidt, XX Corps Operations, 168

[50] Kemp, The Unknown Battle, Metz 54-65.

[51] Ibid, 79.

[52] Ibid, 96-97.

[53] Ibid, 99-101.

[54] Greenbert, Rolling Advance Stymied, p.29.

[55] Vannoy, Everything is Committed; Patton's Costly Obsession, p.38.

[56] Ambrose, Citizen Soldiers, 137-140.

[57] Vannoy, Everything is Committed; Patton's Costly Obsession, p.42.

[58] Kemp, The Unknown Battle, Metz, 115-116.

[59] Ambrose, Citizen Soldiers, 140.

[60] Kemp, The Unknown Battle, Metz, 120.

[61] Ibid, 139.

62 Ambrose, Citizen Soldiers, 136.

63 Marinello, On the Way: Patton's Eyes and Ears on the Enemy; 19-21, 35-36, 39.

64 Ibid, references to the 286th FAOB's response to the rail gun come from pages 54-67.

65 Ibid, 75-87.

66 Kemp, The Unknown Battle: Metz, 128

67 Gable, The Lorraine Campaign

68 Ibid.

69 Kemp, The Unknown Battle: Metz 136.

70 Eastman, XX Corps Artillery, p. 24.

71 Kemp, The Unknown Battle: Metz 133-134.

72 Schmidt, XX Corps Operations, 181.

73 Gable, The Lorraine Campaign.

74 Kemp, The Unknown Battle: Metz, 138.

75 Gable, The Lorraine Campaign.

76 Eastman, XX Corps Artillery, p. 27.

77 Schmidt, XX Corps Operations, 187.

78 Eastman, XX Corps Artillery, p. 28.

79 Kemp, The Unknown Battle: Metz, 163.

80 Eastman, XX Corps Artillery, p. 28.

81 Ambrose, Citizen Soldiers, 164-165.

82 Schmidt, XX Corps Operations, 207.

83 Gable, The Lorraine Campaign

84 Ibid.

85 Ambrose, Citizen Soldiers, 165.

86 Kemp, The Unknown Battle: Metz, introduction.

87 Eastman, XX Corps Artillery, p. 29.

88 Marinello, On the Way: Patton's Eyes and Ears on the Enemy; 71.

89 Gable, The Lorraine Campaign

90 Ibid

91 Prefer, Patton's Ghost Corps, 24-25.

92 Ibid, 34.

93 Eastman, XX Corps Artillery, p. 30.

94 Marinello, On the Way: Patton's Eyes and Ears on the Enemy, 26.

[95] Ambrose, Band of Brothers, 173-174.

[96] Gable, The Lorraine Campaign

[97] Ambrose, Band of Brothers, 174.

[98] Dupuy, Hitler's Last Gamble, 65.

[99] Ambrose, Band of Brothers, 174.

[100] Dear, The Oxford Companion to World War II, 52.

[101] D'este, Patton, A Genius for War, 695.

[102] Marinello, On the Way: Patton's Eyes and Ears on the Enemy; 146-150.

[103] Eastman, XX Corps Artillery, p. 36.

[104] Prefer, Patton's Ghost Corps, 50-55.

[105] Ibid, 69-78.

[106] Ibid, 79-89.

[107] D'este, Patton, A Genius for War, 706.

[108] Prefer, Patton's Ghost Corps, 90-94.

[109] Gable, The Lorraine Campaign

[110] Marinello, On the Way: Patton's Eyes and Ears on the Enemy; 29.

[111] Ibid, 161.

[112] Prefer, Patton's Ghost Corps, 110-111.

[113] Ibid, 119.

[114] Ibid 121-122.

[115] Eastman, XX Corps Artillery, p. 66.

[116] D'este, Patton, A Genius for War, 708.

[117] Prefer, Patton's Ghost Corps, 142.

[118] Ibid, 147-148

[119] Ibid, 143.

[120] Ibid, 152.

[121] Ibid, 154.

[122] Ibid, 156-173.

[123] Ibid, 180

[124] D'este, Patton, A Genius for War, 708.

[125] Prefer, Patton's Ghost Corps, 6

[126] Ibid, 191.

[127] Ibid, 196-197.

[128] Ambrose, Citizen Soldiers, 411.

[129] Prefer, Patton's Ghost Corps, 197.

[130] Other than 7th FAOB sources, most other information provided on the Lampaden Battle is cited to Prefer, Chapter 22, Lampaden and Beyond.

[131] Ambrose, Citizen Soldiers, 416.

[132] Ibid, 411-413.

[133] Hechler, The Bridge at Remagen, 139-142.

[134] Marinello, On the Way: Patton's Eyes and Ears on the Enemy; 178.

[135] Prefer, Patton's Ghost Corps, 200.

[136] Marinello, On the Way: Patton's Eyes and Ears on the Enemy; 183.

[137] Ibid 185.

[138] Prefer, Patton's Ghost Corps, assorted notes on the final dash to the Rhine taken from pages 200-204.

[139] The XX Corps, It's History and Service in World War II.

[140] Marinello, On the Way: Patton's Eyes and Ears on the Enemy; 198.

[141] Prefer, Patton's Ghost Corps, 207.

[142] Marinello, On the Way: Patton's Eyes and Ears on the Enemy; 213.

[143] Ambrose, Citizen Soldiers, 453

[144] Marinello, On the Way: Patton's Eyes and Ears on the Enemy; 187.

[145] Ibid, 199, 212.

[146] D'este, Patton, A Genius for War, 726.

[147] Ambrose, Citizen Soldiers, 449.

[148] Marinello, On the Way: Patton's Eyes and Ears on the Enemy; 209.

[149] Ambrose, Band of Brothers, 258-259.

[150] Eastman, XX Corps Artillery, p. 76.

[151] Marinello, On the Way: Patton's Eyes and Ears on the Enemy; 210.

[152] Ibid, 218

[153] Eastman, XX Corps Artillery, p. 79.

[154] Ambrose, Band of Brothers, 281.

[155] Ibid, 293.

BIBLIOGRAPHY

Books that specifically cover the more prominent XX Corps operations that the 7th FAOB participated in are not that easily found. However, there are several excellent sources that were invaluable in preparing this history of the 7th FAOB. For those interested in further reading, the following works are recommended.

Much of the 7th FAOB's extensive combat service occurred at Metz from September through November, 1944, and at the Saar Moselle Triangle from January 1945-March 1945. Two excellent books that cover this period in detail are Anthony Kemp's *The Unknown Battle: Metz, 1944*, and Nathan Prefer's *Patton's Ghost Corps: Cracking the Siegfried Line*. Both of these books give graphic accounts about the desperate nature of these major battles that conventional study of World War II history often overlooks. Kemp's book is out of print but can be obtained from internet sources, while Prefer's is more recent and more easily found.

For overall XX Corps operations, the *XX Corps; History and Service in World War II* is the most extensive source that has been written. First published in 1950 and later reprinted in 1984, this is considered one of the better official unit histories of the war. This book can also be obtained from internet book-finding services and can run between $50 - $150 per copy.

To gain the perspective from a soldier serving in a Third Army FAOB, Edwin Marinello's *On the Way: General Patton's Eyes and Ears on the Enemy* is superb. Marinello's accounts as a forward observer were used extensively in this book. *On the Way* is also out of print and is best obtained through book-finding sources.

Perhaps the most compelling author to emerge in the study of World War II is Stephen Ambrose. Ambrose has written an excellent series of books that largely focus on the experience of the common soldier. I found his *Citizen Soldiers* to be immensely invaluable in understanding how the war was fought on the Western Front from July 1944 through May 1945.

BOOKS

Anonymous. *The XX Corps: Its History and Service in World War II*. Osaka, Japan, 1951.
Anonymous. *From Bragg to Braunau, The Seventh Field Artillery Observation Battalion*. 1946.
Ambrose, Stephen E. *Band of Brothers*. New York: Simon & Schuster, 1992.
Ambrose, Stephen E. *Citizen Soldiers*. New York: Simon & Schuster, 1997.
Atkinson, Rick. *An Army at Dawn: The War in Africa, 1942-1943, Volume One of the Liberation Trilogy*. New York: Henry Holt and Company, 2002.
Bookman, John & Powers, Stephen T. *The March to Victory*. Niwot, Colorado: University Press of Colorado, 1994.
Blair, Clay. *Hitler's U-Boat War: The Hunted, 1942-1945*. New York: Modern Library, 2000.
Dear, I.C.B & Foot, M.R.D. *The Oxford Companion to World War II*. Oxford: Oxford University Press, 1995.
D'Este, Carlo. *Patton: A Genius for War*. New York: Harper Perennial, 1996.
Dupuy, Trevor. *Hitler's Last Gamble*. New York: Harper Perennial, 1994.
Eastman, Russell V. *The History of the XX Corps Artillery*. Mayer, Miesbach, Germany, 1945.

Hechler, Ken. *The Bridge at Remagen*. Missoula, Missouri: Pictorial Histories Publishing Company, Inc, 1957.
Kemp, Anthony. *The Unknown War Battle: Metz, 1944*. New York: Stein and Day Publishers, 1980.
Natkiel, Richard. *Atlas of World War II*. Greenwich, Connecticut: The Military Press, 1985.
Marinello, Edward A. *On the Way: General Patton's Eyes and Ears on the Enemy*. New York: Kroshka Books, 1998.
MacDonald, C. and Mathews, S. *Three Battles-Arnaville, Altuzzo and Schmidt*. Washington, D.C.: Government Printing Office, 1952.
Prefer, Nathan N. *Patton's Ghost Corps*. Novato, California: Presidio Press, 1998.
Sawicki, James A. *Field Artillery Battalions of the U.S. Army, Volume 1*. Dumfries, Virginia: Centaur, 1977-78.
Sulzberger, C.L. *The American Heritage History of World War II*. New York: American Heritage Publishing Co, 1966.
Time-Life Editors. *The Time-Life History of WW II*. New York: Barnes & Noble, Inc, 1995.
Weigley, Russell, F. *Eisenhower's Lieutenants*. Bloomington, Indiana: Indiana University Press, 1981.

ARTICLES AND OFFICIAL REPORTS

Anonymous, *Seekers News*, Issues 1-23 (December 1944 – August 1945), Official 7th Field Artillery Observation Battalion Newsletter published by 7th FAOB Headquarters.
Anonymous, "The Reduction of Fortress Metz," 1 September – 6 December 1944, An Operational Report, XX Corps, United States Army.
Brigadier General J.D. Balmer; Colonel L.J. Compton, Lt. Col. J.G. Harding, "Report on the Study of the Field Artillery Observation Battalion," The General Board, United States Forces, European Theater, 1945.
Gabel, "The Lorraine Campaign," United States Army Command and General College Study Series.
Greenberg, Lawrence M., "Rolling Advance Stymied," *World War II Magazine*, July 1991.
Hymel, Kevin M. "War as He Saw It: Patton's Unpublished Photos." *WW II History*, Sovereign Media, Reston, VA., September 2002.
Murray, Williamson, 1944, "A World in the Balance," Leesburg, VA, *MHQ: The Quarterly Journal*, Autumn 2000.
Ramsey, Winston, G. "Clearing the Rhine, London," *After the Battle Magazine*, Issue 73, 1991.
Reynolds, Michael, "Massacre at Malmedy," *World War II Magazine*, Leesburg, VA, February 2003.
Schmidt, Robert, L., XX Corps Operations, "1 August – 22 November 1944: A Study in Combat Power: United States Army Command and General Staff Thesis," Fort Leavenworth, KS, 1985.
Vannoy, Allyn R. "Everything is Committed; Patton's Costly Obsession," *World War II Magazine*, Leesburg, VA, May 2002.

ORAL HISTORY INTERVIEWS, WRITTEN ACCOUNTS, LETTERS, PAPERS, ETC.

Original source information came from the following 7th Field Artillery Observation Battalion members/ family members via oral histories, letters, written records, and photographs:

Paul Asman, Roy Barber, Gerald Bailman, Thomas DeLay, Walter Damiano, John French, Robert Geiges, Jess Grisham, William Jessel, Hank Lizak, Edward Miller, Don Pascale, Arnold Price, Kurt Rieth, Amos Robinson, William Rogge, James Royals, Victor Salem, James Schwartz, Edward Shock, Donald Slessman, Warren Sockwell, Sid Shafran, Bill Williamson, Charles Wright, Marlin Yoder, and Stephen Wandzioch.

MAPS

Maps came from Anthony Kemp's *The Unknown War Battle: Metz, 1944*, Richard Natkiel's *Atlas of World War II*, Nathan Prefer's *Patton's Ghost Corps*, and *The XX Corps: Its History and Service in World War II*.

PHOTOGRAPHS

Photographs came from the collection of the author, William Jessel, Amos Robinson, Ed Miller, Bill Williamson, Al Yoder, Warren Sockwell, and *From Bragg to Braunau, The XX Corps: Its History and Service in World War II*, and internet sources (photo of USS Donnell).

Lightning Source UK Ltd.
Milton Keynes UK
UKHW05f0003210518
322914UK00001B/5/P